Questions About This Publication

For assistance with shipments, billing or other customer service matters, please call our Customer Services Department at: 1-631-350-2100.

To obtain a copy of this book, call our Sales Department at: 1-631-351-5430 Fax: 1-631-673-9117

Toll Free Order Line: 1-800-887-4064 (United States and Canada)

See our web page about this book:
www.arbitrationlaw.com

Printed in the United States of America
ISBN 978-1-937518-72-1

This is the eighth edition of the *Baker & McKenzie International Arbitration Yearbook,* an annual series established by the Firm in 2007. This collection of articles comprises reports in key jurisdictions around the globe on arbitration. Leading lawyers of the Firm's International Arbitration Practice Group, a division of the Firm's Global Dispute Resolution Practice Group, report on recent developments in national laws relating to arbitration and address current arbitral trends and tendencies in the jurisdictions in which they practice.

For this 2014-2015 edition, the topic of Section C of each chapter is local arbitration institutions. Each jurisdiction sets out key features of its local institutions.

The aim of this *Yearbook* is to highlight the more important recent developments in international arbitration, without aspiring to be an exhaustive case reporter or a text-book to arbitration in the broad sense. It is hoped that this volume will prove a useful tool for those contemplating and using arbitration to resolve international business disputes.

JurisNet, LLC
71 New Street
Huntington, New York 11743 USA
www.arbitrationlaw.com

The Baker & McKenzie International Arbitration Yearbook 2014-2015

JURIS

TABLE OF CONTENTS

Table of Contents

Table of Contents

Table of Contents

Table of Contents

Table of Contents

Table of Contents

Table of Contents

Table of Contents

Table of Contents

Table of Contents

Table of Contents

Table of Contents

FOREWORD

On behalf of Baker & McKenzie's International Arbitration Practice Group, it is a great pleasure to present to you the eighth annual edition of our *International Arbitration Yearbook*. Initially published by our European offices in 2007, the *Yearbook* has expanded to include developments in jurisdictions in Asia, Latin America and North America and has become a valuable resource for clients and colleagues in the international business community.

Our 2014-2015 *Yearbook* covers 45 jurisdictions and is organized by country. As in past years, the first section (Part A) describes important recent developments and trends in national legislation and practice affecting the conduct of international arbitration. The second section (Part B) refers to noteworthy case law in each country, and in a feature that first appeared in the second edition of the book, a third section (Part C) focuses on an important current topic in international arbitration.

This year's topic is local arbitration institutions. Each jurisdiction was invited to describe the history and background of its local institutions, the types of disputes handled, and the most recent available statistics for numbers of disputes handled. Each jurisdiction was also asked to set out the key features of arbitration in each institution, such as its position on the confidentiality of arbitration, the availability of expedited procedures and consolidation of disputes, and any time limits for rendering of the award. Jurisdictions were also invited to describe how costs and fees are typically dealt with by the institution and to mention any special or unusual features of its procedure.

Foreword

The diversity and breadth of Baker & McKenzie is clearly displayed in these chapters. Overall, this *Yearbook* provides critical commentary about world-wide developments in this fascinating field of law that directly affects the risks and challenges of doing business locally and internationally and managing the disputes that follow.

As with past editions, this *Yearbook* does not aspire to be a guide to arbitration in a general sense, nor is it intended as a comprehensive case reporter. Instead, it is a selection of the most noteworthy developments in the countries on which we comment. We trust that these materials will be helpful to those who contemplate arbitration as a process for resolving disputes in international business transactions, especially with respect to choice of venue. As demonstrated by the *Yearbook*, national courts play a critical role in enforcing arbitration agreements and awards, and supervising the arbitral process generally.

We welcome any comments you may have on the content of this edition and any suggestions about topics you would like to see included in future editions.

This publication would not be possible without the effort and diligence of our colleagues from around the world who drafted the chapters and our regional editors who reviewed their submissions. We are grateful to them for their contributions. We take this opportunity to also thank Jennifer Bartlett, Tessa Gromia, Pilar Segretin, Nadine Sequeira, Mary Umsted, and Anya Wilson-Fish for their assistance in preparing this year's book.

Liz Williams
Executive Editor

2014-2015 Baker & McKenzie Yearbook Editors

Executive Editor

Liz Williams is a Senior Professional Support Lawyer in Baker & McKenzie's London office with responsibility for knowledge management and training for the Firm's Global Dispute Resolution Practice Group. She has eight years' experience as a PSL and 10 years' fee-earning experience in insurance litigation and arbitration and general commercial dispute resolution. Ms. Williams serves as chair of the Refugee Law Practice Group in Baker & McKenzie's London office and is a Fellow of the Higher Education Academy in the UK as well as co-author of Strong & Williams, *Complete Tort Law: Text and Materials* (Oxford University Press, 2d ed., 2011.)

Editorial Committee: Baker & McKenzie International Arbitration Group

Co-Chairs:

Grant Hanessian is a Principal in the New York office and serves as co-chair of the Firm's International Arbitration Group. He has more than 25 years of experience as counsel and arbitrator in disputes concerning energy, construction, commodities, financial services, insurance, intellectual property and other matters. Mr. Hanessian is Vice Chairman of the Arbitration & ADR Committee of the United States Council for International Business, the US national committee of the International Chamber of Commerce (ICC); a member of the ICC Commission on Arbitration, the ICC Task Force on International Arbitration and Financial Institutions (co-leader on subcommittee on Investment Disputes) and the ICC Task Force on International Arbitration with States and State Entities, the AAA-ICDR International Advisory Committee, the New York State Bar Association Task Force on International Arbitration, the International Arbitration Club of New York, the Arbitration Committee of the International Institute for Conflict Prevention and Resolution, the Club Español del Arbitraje, North American Advisory Council, the London Court of International Arbitration, and the New York City Bar Association International Law Committee. Mr. Hanessian is editor of ICDR Awards and Commentaries (Juris 2012), the first collection of ICDR awards, and co-editor of the Gulf War Claims Reporter (ILI/Kluwer 1998), International Arbitration Checklists (Juris 2d ed., 2008), and Baker & McKenzie's North American International Litigation & Arbitration Newsletter. He is recommended by Chambers Global and Chambers USA, PLC Which Lawyer, Legal 500 and International Who's Who of Commercial Arbitration in the field of international arbitration.

Guenter Pickrahn is a Principal in the Frankfurt office of Baker & McKenzie, editor in chief of the German Arbitration Journal (SchiedsVZ) and member of the advisory board of the German Arbitration Institution (DIS), as well as a member of the LCIA. He is co-chair of the Firm's International Arbitration Group and serves on the steering committee of the Firm's Europe, Middle East and Africa Dispute Resolution Practice Group. Dr. Pickrahn's arbitration practice includes all aspects of commercial, domestic and international disputes, both as a party representative and as an arbitrator. He has particular expertise in post-acquisition disputes and disputes involving complex technical issues.

Steering Committee:

José María Alonso is Managing Partner and head of the Litigation & Arbitration Department at Baker & McKenzie's Madrid office and member of the Steering Committee of the International European Disputes Practice Group.

Jonas Benedictsson is a Partner in Baker & McKenzie's Stockholm office. His practice includes various aspects of arbitration, litigation, alternative dispute resolution and insolvency. Mr. Benedictsson leads Baker & McKenzie's Dispute Resolution Practice in Stockholm.

Claudia Benavides is a Partner in Baker & McKenzie's Bogotá office. She heads the Dispute Resolution practice group of the Bogotá office and represents a variety of clients in domestic and international arbitrations.

Leng Sun Chan SC is a Principal in Baker & McKenzie Wong & Leow, Singapore, where he serves as head of the Disputes Group. He is Baker & McKenzie's Asia-Pacific Head of International Arbitration.

Vladimir Khvalei is a Partner in Baker & McKenzie's Moscow office and heads its CIS Dispute Resolution Practice Group. Mr. Khvalei serves as a Vice President of the ICC International Court of Arbitration and is included in the list of arbitrators of the arbitration institutions in Austria, Russia, Belarus, Kazakhstan and Dubai, and as Chairman of the Board of the Russian Arbitration Association.

James Kwan is a Partner in the Dispute Resolution Group of Baker & McKenzie in Hong Kong, where he leads the arbitration practice. He specializes in international commercial arbitration, with a focus on M&A, technology, sale of goods, infrastructure, and energy disputes; and has a range of international experience, having represented clients in arbitrations in Hong Kong, Asia, the Middle East, U.S. and Europe under the major institutional rules.

Michael L. Morkin is the Managing Partner of Baker & McKenzie's Chicago office. He advises US and non-US companies on a broad range of international dispute resolution issues. Mr. Morkin has handled arbitrations in Asia, Latin America, Europe, the Caribbean and throughout the United States under the rules of institutions including the ICC, ICDR, UNCITRAL, AAA, London Maritime Arbitrators Association and numerous ad hoc arbitrations. He has arbitrated disputes in the areas of power, fuel supply, reinsurance, shipping, post-acquisition, intellectual property, construction, sports, distribution and supply agreements and other commercial arrangements. He is a frequent lecturer and author on a wide variety of international disputes topics, having published articles and chapters of texts in the US, Europe and Asia.

Joaquim T. de Paiva Muniz is a Partner in Baker & McKenzie's Rio de Janeiro office and a professor of Business Law and Arbitration, teaching graduate courses at Fundação Getúlio Vargas (FGV). Mr. Muniz is Chairman of the Arbitration Commission of the Rio de Janeiro Bar (OAB/RJ) and coordinator for the arbitration courses of the Rio de Janeiro Bar, including a lato sensu graduate course. He is also Chairman of the Rio de Janeiro section of the Brazilian Institute of Corporate Law (IBRADEMP) and author of many articles on international arbitration and Brazilian corporate law, including co-author of Arbitration Law of Brazil: Practice and Procedure (Juris Publishing 2006) and Arbitragem Internacional e Doméstica (Forense 2009).

Edward Poulton is a Partner in the London office of Baker & McKenzie and a member of the Firm's Global Dispute Resolution Practice Group. He focuses his practice on international arbitration, complex litigation, commercial and investment treaty arbitration and public international law. Mr. Poulton's experience ranges from contract and M&A disputes to more specialist claims in the banking sector and investment treaty claims. He has acted as advisor and advocate in many international arbitrations under the rules of the major arbitral institutions and serves as an arbitrator under both the ICC and LCIA rules. Mr. Poulton's client base covers a wide range of sectors, including financial services, electronics, aviation and telecommunications. He is a member of the Law Society of England & Wales, ICC, LCIA, Young International Arbitration Group, and Investment Protection Forum of the British Institute of International and Comparative Law.

Regional Editors

Asia-Pacific:

Angela Ang is a Professional Support Lawyer in Baker & McKenzie's Hong Kong office and a Senior Associate in the Hong Kong Dispute Resolution Group. She has represented clients in a broad range of contentious matters in the areas of commercial litigation, corporate insolvency and cross-border investigations. Ms. Ang is qualified as a solicitor in Hong Kong, Victoria (Australia) and England & Wales.

Sarah Burton is an Associate from the Sydney office of Baker & McKenzie and is a member of the firm's Global Dispute Resolution Practice Group. Ms. Burton trained at the London office of Baker & McKenzie before moving to Sydney on qualification. She has experience of working on international arbitration and litigation in both London and Sydney as well as on a number of cross-border transactions. She is currently a member of the Asia-Pacific Life Sciences Group and regularly advises international life science clients on regulatory compliance and product liability issues.

Jo Delaney is a Special Counsel in the Sydney office of Baker & McKenzie and member of the Firm's Global Dispute Resolution

Group. She has 15 years' experience in commercial, construction and investment arbitrations under the ICC, LCIA, SIAC, AAA, UNCITRAL and ICSID arbitration rules covering a diverse range of industries, including energy, resources and infrastructure, general construction and telecommunications and information technology. Ms. Delaney is a Council member of the Australian branch of the Chartered Institute of Arbitrators, Vice Chair of the IPBA Arbitration and Dispute Resolution Committee and member of the ILA Management Committee, AFIA General Committee, ACICA, Arbitral Women, Young ICCA, and Young ICSID.

Carinne Kamdar is an Associate from the London office of Baker & McKenzie and a member of the Firm's Global Dispute Resolution Practice Group, and is currently on secondment in Baker & McKenzie's Singapore office. Her experience covers a broad spectrum of contentious and non-contentious work, including international arbitration in both London and Singapore, commercial litigation, and public law. Ms. Kamdar is a member of the Law Society of England & Wales the LCIA Young International Arbitration Group and is a founding member of the Young Public Law Lawyers Group.

Europe, Middle East and Africa:

Richard Allen is an Associate and Solicitor Advocate in the London office of Baker & McKenzie and a member of the Firm's Global Dispute Resolution Practice Group. His experience covers a broad spectrum of contentious and non-contentious work, including commercial and competition litigation, international arbitration, public law and regulatory advice. The current focus of his practice is in the fields of aviation law and public international law. He is a member of the Law Society of England & Wales, the LCIA Young International

Arbitration Group, the Royal Institute of International Affairs (Chatham House), the International Law Association, and the International Legal Network of Avocats Sans Frontières.

Yindi Gesinde is an Associate and Solicitor Advocate in the London office of Baker & McKenzie and a member of the Firm's Global Dispute Resolution Practice Group. Her experience covers a broad spectrum of contention and non-contentious work, including commercial litigation, anti-bribery and corruption investigations, trust litigation, public law, international arbitration and regulatory advice. She is a member of the Law Society of England & Wales, the Association of Contentious Trust and Probate Specialists, the Young Fraud Lawyers Association, the LCIA Young International Arbitration Group, and the Young Public Lawyers Group.

Ben Ko is an Associate and Solicitor Advocate in the London office of Baker & McKenzie and a member of the Firm's Global Dispute Resolution Practice Group. His practice consists of a variety of contentious work, including commercial litigation, international arbitration, and white collar crime. Mr. Ko is a member of the Law Society of England & Wales, the LCIA Young International Arbitration Group, and the Young Fraud Lawyers Association.

Fiona Lockhart is an Associate in the London office of Baker & McKenzie and a member of the Firm's Global Dispute Resolution Practice Group. Her experience covers a broad spectrum of contentious and non-contentious work, including commercial litigation, international arbitration, public law and regulatory advice. Ms. Lockhart is a member of the Law Society of England & Wales, the LCIA Young International Arbitration Group and Young Public Law Lawyers Group.

Louise Oakley is an Associate in the Dispute Resolution Department of the London office of Baker & McKenzie. Her experience covers a broad spectrum of contentious and non-contentious work, including commercial litigation, international arbitration, and product liability matters. She is a member of the Law Society of England & Wales and the LCIA Young International Arbitration Group.

Anjuli Patel is an Associate in the London office of Baker & McKenzie and a member of the Firm's Global Dispute Resolution Practice Group. She has experience of international arbitration in London and Hong Kong, as well as experience in a wide range of contentious and non-contentious work, including commercial litigation, business crime and fraud, banking litigation, construction litigation and product liability. Ms. Patel is a member of the Law Society of England & Wales and the LCIA Young International Arbitration Group.

Luke Richardson is an Associate and Solicitor Advocate in the London office of Baker & McKenzie and a member of the Firm's Global Dispute Resolution Practice Group. His experience covers a broad range of contentious and non-contentious work, including commercial litigation, contentious trusts work, public-law and regulatory advice and international arbitration. He is a member of the Law Society of England & Wales and the Young Public Lawyers Group.

Amy Smith is a trainee in the Dispute Resolution Department of Baker & McKenzie's London office, where she assists with a broad range of matters, including commercial litigation, international arbitration and public law work. She graduated in 2012 with an LLB in English law from the University of Bristol.

Emily Tilden-Smith is an Associate in Baker & McKenzie's London Dispute Resolution Group and has had broad contentious and advisory experience in general Commercial Litigation, Arbitration, Public Law, Trusts Disputes and Business Crime. Ms Tilden-Smith is a member of the LCIA Young International Arbitration Group and the Young Public Lawyers Group.

William Jones is a trainee in the Dispute Resolution Department of Baker & McKenzie's London office. He assists on matters in the areas of international arbitration, enforcement of arbitration awards, and commercial, public law and product liability litigation.

Latin and North America:

Laura Zimmerman is an Associate in the Litigation Practice Group of Baker & McKenzie's New York office. Her practice focuses mainly on international arbitration and commercial litigation matters for foreign and domestic clients, including work on arbitration matters administered by the ICC, ICDR, and ICSID.

William H. Richardson, CIArb is a Partner based in the Toronto office of Baker & McKenzie. He is a member of the Firm's International Arbitration Practice Group. With more than 30 years' experience in all manner of civil litigation, Mr. Richardson now focuses on international commercial arbitrations, including intellectual property disputes for which he is a recognized expert internationally. Mr. Richardson is a Fellow of the Chartered Institute of Arbitrators (UK), the world's leading professional body for promoting the settlement of disputes by arbitration, mediation and other alternative dispute resolution methods.

David Zaslowsky has practiced in the area of international commercial litigation and arbitration for more than 27 years. He has appeared in various federal and state courts (trial and appellate) throughout the United States and has participated in arbitrations, both inside and outside the United States, before the AAA, ICC, ICDR, Iran-United States Claims Tribunal, HKIAC and NASD, as well as in *ad hoc* arbitrations. Mr. Zaslowsky currently serves on the ICC Task Force on Decisions as to Costs. He is included in the *Chambers USA Guide* for his expertise in International Arbitration. He is also on the roster of arbitrators for the ICDR and the AAA.

THE BAKER & MCKENZIE INTERNATIONAL ARBITRATION YEARBOOK TOPICS

YEAR	NO. OF JURISDICTIONS	TOPICS EXAMINED
2008	28	Independence and Impartiality of Arbitrators
2009	27	Parallel Proceedings Before State Courts and Arbitral Tribunals
2010-2011	35	Insolvency Issues in Arbitration
2011-2012	37	Public Policy in International Arbitration
2012-2013	40	Grant and Enforcement of Interim Measures in International Arbitration
2013-2014	43	Regulation of Counsel Conduct in International Arbitration
2014-2015	45	Local Arbitration Institutions

LIST OF ABBREVIATIONS AND ACRONYMS

AAA	American Arbitration Association
ACICA	Australian Centre for International Commercial Arbitration
ADR	Alternative Dispute Resolution
BIT	Bilateral Investment Treaty
Buenos Aires Convention	Mercosur Accord on International Commercial Arbitration, 1998
CIETAC	China International Economic and Trade Arbitration Commission
ECT	Energy Charter Treaty
Geneva Convention	European Convention on International Commercial Arbitration, Geneva, dated April 21, 1961
HKIAC	Hong Kong International Arbitration Centre
JCAA	Japan Commercial Arbitration Association
IBA Rules	International Bar Association Rules on the Taking of Evidence in International Commercial Arbitration
ICC	International Chamber of Commerce
ICC Arbitration Rules or ICC Rules	Rules of Arbitration of the International Chamber of Commerce
ICDR	International Centre for Dispute Resolution (part of the AAA)

ICDR Rules	International Arbitration Rules of the International Centre for Dispute Resolution, 2003
ICSID	International Centre for the Settlement of Investment Disputes
ICSID Convention	Convention on the Settlement of Investment Disputes between States and Nationals of Other States
LCIA	London Court of International Arbitration
LCIA Arbitration Rules or LCIA Rules	Arbitration Rules of the London Court of International Arbitration, 2014
NAFTA	North American Free Trade Agreement
New York Convention	United Nations Convention on the Recognition and Enforcement of Foreign Arbitral Awards, 1958
Panama Convention International	Inter-American Convention on Commercial Arbitration, 1975
SCC	Arbitration Institute of the Stockholm Chamber of Commerce
SIAC	Singapore International Arbitration Centre
UNCITRAL	United Nations Commission on International Trade Law
UNCITRAL Model Law	United Nations Commission on International Trade Law Model Law on International Commercial Arbitration, 1985, amended in 2006

UNCITRAL Rules	United Nations Commission on International Trade Law Arbitration Rules, 1976, as revised in 2010 and 2013
WIPO	World Intellectual Property Organization
WIPO Rules	World Intellectual Property Organization Arbitration Rules, 1994
ZPO	Zivilprozessordnung [German Code of Civil Procedure]

ARGENTINA

Santiago L. Capparelli[1] and Julian Bordacahar[2]

A. LEGISLATION, TRENDS AND TENDENCIES

A.1 Legislation

There is as yet no federal legislation in force in Argentina specifically dealing with arbitration. Instead, the country's civil procedure codes contain arbitration regulations. Because Argentina is a federal country, each province has its own civil procedure code. The National Code of Civil and Commercial Procedure ("CPCCN") applies to the Autonomous City of Buenos Aires, and in federal courts.[3] Because the provincial codes tend to be consistent with the CPCCN as to arbitration, this report covers only the CPCCN.

A.2 Trends and Tendencies

In recent years, there have been several failed attempts to enact specific arbitration legislation, typically sponsoring the adoption

---

[1] Santiago Capparelli is a Partner in Baker & McKenzie's Buenos Aires office. He practices litigation, alternative dispute resolution and international and domestic arbitration and has represented parties in ad hoc arbitral proceedings, as well as in proceedings administered by the ICC and local arbitral institutions, such as the Buenos Aires Stock Exchange Market Arbitral Tribunal, the Buenos Aires Grain Market Arbitral Tribunal and the Private Center for Mediation and Arbitration.

[2] Julian Bordacahar is an Associate in Baker & McKenzie's Buenos Aires office. He practices litigation and international and domestic arbitration. He has been involved in proceedings administered by the ICC and local arbitral institutions, such as the Buenos Aires Stock Exchange Market Arbitral Tribunal. He teaches both International Commercial and Investment Arbitration, at the School of Law of the University of Buenos Aires.

[3] Código Procesal Civil y Comercial de la Nación, [National Code of Civil and Commercial Procedure], Law No. 17.454, Sept. 20, 1967, as restated in Decree 1042/1981, Aug. 18, 1981, et seq.

of the UNCITRAL model law or portions thereof. However, Argentina has very recently enacted a joint Civil and Commercial Code to replace the existing Civil Code and Commercial Code, set to take effect in 2016. The new Code includes a specific chapter regulating arbitration agreements (Sections 1649 to 1665). Although arbitration will therefore be regulated as a specific type of contract, without taking into account its jurisdictional characteristics, the new Code will at last provide some substantive federal legislation on arbitration.

The new Code incorporates several well-known and useful arbitration principles favorable to the development of arbitration in Argentina. The most relevant provisions include: (i) the principle of *kompetenz-komptenz*; (ii) severability of arbitration agreements; (iii) the tribunal's power to render interim measures; (iv) exclusion of court jurisdiction when an arbitration agreement exists; (v) presumption in favor of arbitrability; and (vi) the obligation of arbitrators to be available and to disclose any matter that might affect their impartiality. Several of these principles are already applied by Argentine courts, but their express inclusion into the domestic legal system is a very positive development.

However, the new Code also includes other potentially problematic provisions. Particularly, the vague and ambiguous wording of the provisions providing (i) for the non-arbitrability of disputes where public policy is compromised (Article 1649), and (ii) that parties cannot waive their right to challenge an award in court (*impugnación judicial*) (Article 1656), provide cause for concern.

As to the former, in our view the provision should be interpreted to uphold the arbitrability of private disputes featuring issues of public policy, as otherwise a party may too easily challenge the tribunal's jurisdiction by contending that the dispute is not arbitrable because it touches upon public policy. This view is supported by the legislative explanation for the new Code, which indicates that this provision aims to prevent the State or any State entity from arbitrating disputes.

As to the latter provision, precluding parties from waiving their right to "appeal" awards would run counter to (i) the CPCCN, which does not allow parties to waive the right to request annulment of the award, but does allow parties to waive their right to appeal it; and (ii) the international principle of finality of arbitral awards. Since this statement is included in Article 1656, which deals expressly with a court's power to revise awards when called upon to decide their validity, it should be interpreted as referring only to parties' rights to challenge the validity of or request clarification concerning awards, rather than a right to appeal the merits of the award.

B. CASES

B.1 Stipulation to Court with Jurisdiction to Annul an Award

In the case of *YPF S.A. v. AES Uruguaina Emprendimientos S.A. et al.*,[4] the Court of Appeals found that, based on the principle of party autonomy, parties are entitled to stipulate which court has jurisdiction to decide an annulment request. The dispute arose out of a contract, governed by Argentine law, for the supply of gas from Argentina to Brazil. The parties' arbitration agreement provided for ICC arbitration in Montevideo, Uruguay. The parties had stipulated that they could use the annulment procedures pertaining to the validity or clarification of awards provided by Art. 760 of the CPCCN, and that the Argentine

---

[4]   *Cámara Contencioso Administrativo Federal Nacional de Apelaciones de la Capital Federal* (Federal Administrative Court of Appeals), Section IV, *YPF S.A. v. AES Uruguaina Emprendimientos S.A.et al.*

courts would have exclusive jurisdiction over any recourse filed against the award.

YPF sought to annul the tribunal's partial award on liability in the commercial courts of Argentina. The other parties challenged the Argentine court's jurisdiction, arguing that under international law (such as the New York, Panama, and Buenos Aires Conventions) and mandatory public policy, only the courts of the seat have jurisdiction to annul an award, so the parties could not choose an alternate court.

The court found that while the New York and Panama Conventions provide that courts at the seat will have jurisdiction to annul awards, they do not bar the parties from adopting a different solution. Likewise, while the Buenos Aires Convention provides that an award can only be challenged at the courts of the seat (Art. 22.1), it also allows the parties to deviate from any of the Convention's provisions (Art. 3(c)). Thus, the Court found that parties are free to choose the court which will have jurisdiction to decide on the annulment of awards.

B.2 Annulment of Partial Awards

In *Pluris Energy Group Inc. et al. v. San Enrique Petrolera S.A. et al.*,[5] the National Court of Appeals on Commercial Matters held that reserving the right to challenge the validity of a partial award had no legal value, and thus did not preserve the right to seek annulment of the partial award. Furthermore, the court held that a challenge to the validity of the final award could not include a revision of the partial award.

---

[5] *Cámara Nacional de Apelaciones de la Capital Federal* (National Court of Appeals on Commercial Matters), Section B, 21/04/2014, *Pluris Energy Group Inc. et al. v. San Enrique Petrolera S.A.et al.*

Under the CPCCN, a motion to set aside an award must be filed within five days after service upon the party. However, after the Respondents were served with a partial award on liability, they merely reserved the right to challenge the validity of the partial award once the final award was rendered. After the tribunal issued its final award deciding on the quantum of damages and the allocation of costs, the Respondents filed an annulment request against both the final and the partial award. They argued that the partial award constituted part of the final award and that this, coupled with their earlier reservation of rights, allowed them to challenge the validity of both awards simultaneously.

The court found that while the partial award did not resolve all of the issues which the Tribunal was called to decide upon in the arbitration, it did resolve in a final fashion the issues that were the subject of the partial award. Hence, the respondents should have filed an annulment request within the time period provided by the CPCCN. The court reasoned that rights are meant to be exercised, not to be reserved; thus the respondents' reservation of rights had no legal value whatsoever.

C. LOCAL ARBITRATION INSTITUTIONS

C.1 Buenos Aires Stock Exchange Arbitral Tribunal

Background

The procedures for arbitrations administered by the General Arbitration Tribunal of the Buenos Aires Stock Exchange were institutionalized in 1963, appointing permanent arbitrators to act exclusively as amiable compositeurs. Its arbitration rules (the "BASEAT Rules") have since undergone several modifications, including a significant reform in 1993.

Types of Disputes Handled

The Tribunal may handle any disputes related to monetary rights regarding production, commerce, or services that are subject to settlement.

Numbers of Disputes Handled

No statistics are publicly available.

Provisions on Confidentiality of Arbitration

Section 24 of the BASEAT Rules provides that arbitration proceedings are deemed confidential.

Availability of Expedited Procedures

Section 49 of the BASEAT Rules provides for the Tribunal to issue an award based solely on the documents submitted, if the parties only offered documentary evidence and there is no dispute between the parties about the existence and content of such documentary evidence.

Consolidation of Disputes between the Same Parties and Joinder of Third Parties

This is not specifically addressed. However, Section 24 of the BASEAT Rules provides that in all matters not specifically regulated, the parties can refer to the provisions set forth in the CPCCN. Thus, the CPCCN provisions on consolidation and joinder of third parties may be available by reference.

Time Limits for Rendering of the Award

Time limits for rendering the award are to be agreed by the parties or otherwise determined by the Director of Proceedings in the preliminary hearing held immediately after the parties file their full claims and counterclaims. The typical period set is 60 days on which the stock market is open, starting from the date on which the docket is ready for the issuance of the award.

Fee Structure

The claimant must pay a filing fee upon initiating the arbitration, based on a scale set forth in the rules as a percentage of the amount in dispute. The more substantial the amount in dispute, the lesser the percentage to be paid as a filing fee. Currently, the highest filing fee would be ARS240,000. A party filing a counterclaim must pay a fee on the same scale. These fees include both the fees of the arbitrators and the Director of Proceedings, as well as administrative costs (hearing facilities, etc).

Treatment of Costs of the Arbitration

The general principle of "loser pays all" will apply by reference to the CPCCN. The Tribunal can, however, depart from this general principle and allocate costs differently in exceptional circumstances.

Special or Unusual Features (If Any)

Unless expressly agreed otherwise, the Tribunal will resolve the disputes in the arbitration acting as amiable compositeur (and not acting as a "de iure" Tribunal). If a "de iure" arbitration is selected, the parties maintain the right to appeal the award unless expressly waived in the arbitration clause or a subsequent document.

Recent Developments (If Any)

Not applicable.

C.2 Managerial Mediation and Arbitration Centre

Background

The Managerial Mediation and Arbitration Centre was formed in 1997 by several law firms and accounting firms from the city of Buenos Aires. It offers and administers both mediation services (applying its own set of rules) and arbitration (adopting the UNCITRAL Rules).

Types of Disputes Handled

Although there is no express reference in the rules to the types of disputes, the Centre usually handles commercial cases pertaining mainly to energy, construction, infrastructure and post-M&A disputes.

Numbers of Disputes Handled

No statistics are publicly available.

Provisions on Confidentiality of Arbitration

None.

Availability of Expedited Procedures

Not applicable.

Consolidation of Disputes between the Same Parties and Joinder of Third Parties

Section 17(5) of the UNCITRAL Rules authorizes the tribunal to allow third parties to intervene as parties to the proceedings, if such third parties are signatories to the arbitration agreement.

Time Limits for Rendering of the Award

None.

C. Local Arbitration Institutions

Fee Structure

The claimant must pay a fixed filing fee of 1% of the amount in dispute, but not less than USD250 nor exceeding USD2,500. Upon filing the complaint, the claimant need only pay a USD250 provisional advance of this fee. The party or parties complete payment of the remaining portion of the fee according to the proportion of costs assigned to them in the award. A party filing a counterclaim must meet the same obligation. These fixed filing fees do not include the fees of the arbitrators, which are fixed on a scale provided by the Centre and borne as decided in the award.

Treatment of costs of the arbitration

Section 40 of the UNCITRAL Rules provides that the tribunal may allocate costs as it sees fit.

Special or Unusual Features (If Any)

Unless expressly preserved, it is understood that by agreeing to arbitrate under the UNCITRAL Rules, the parties are waiving the right to appeal the award.

Recent Developments (If Any)

Not applicable.

C.3   Centre of Mediation and Arbitration ("CEMARC")

Background

CEMARC was formed and functions within the Argentine Chamber of Commerce, and administers mediation and arbitration proceedings under its own rules (the "CEMARC Rules".

Types of Disputes Handled

Although there is no express limitation in the rules to the types of disputes, the Centre usually handles commercial cases pertaining mainly to energy, construction, infrastructure and post-M&A disputes.

Numbers of Disputes Handled

No statistics are publicly available.

Provisions on Confidentiality of Arbitration

Under Section 16 of the CEMARC Rules, CEMARC and the arbitrators are bound by a duty of confidentiality, and absent the parties' agreement cannot disclose the existence of the dispute, the names of the parties, the information received during the course of the arbitration, nor the final award. The rules do not prescribe any duty of confidentiality for the parties, presumably because confidentiality can be specified in the arbitration clause if the parties so desire.

Availability of Expedited Procedures

Section 31 of the CEMARC Rules permits the tribunal to issue an award based solely on the documents submitted by the parties, if the parties offer only documentary evidence. CEMARC also has an appendix for pre-arbitral precautionary measures, providing specific procedures for parties seeking protective actions before the initiation of the arbitration. Parties submitting disputes to CEMARC inherently agree to be bound by this appendix, unless expressly excluded in the arbitration agreement or subsequent document.

Consolidation of Disputes between the Same Parties and Joinder of Third Parties

The CEMARC Rules provide for both the possibility of consolidation of proceedings (Section 28) and the joinder of third parties (Section 18). Section 18 expressly contemplates the possibility of the tribunal joining a party on its own initiative or by application of the parties, if it is convinced that such third party is subject to the arbitration agreement. Further, the rules contemplate the possibility that a third party may voluntarily request to be joined as a party in the proceedings, and allow for this if the existing parties agree and the joinder does not oblige the tribunal to return to an earlier procedural stage.

Time Limits for Rendering of the Award

The award must be issued no later than 6 months from the date on which the Director of Proceedings passes the docket to the tribunal. The tribunal may request extensions to the aforesaid term, which are to be granted if appropriate circumstances exist (Section 41 of the CEMARC Rules).

Fee Structure

The Claimant must pay a fixed filing fee upon initiating the arbitration. The administrative fees, as well as the arbitrators' and Director of Proceedings' fees, are calculated based on the amount in dispute, on a scale set forth by CEMARC. The more substantial the amount in dispute, the lesser the applicable percentage to be paid. Once the complaints and responses to any potential counterclaim are filed, CEMARC requests that the parties share the estimated cost to cover all the above fees. After the arbitration is completed but before the issuance of the award, CEMARC notifies the parties of the final amount to be covered by each of the parties.

Treatment of Costs of the Arbitration

Section 43 of the CEMARC Rules provides that absent agreement of the parties, the tribunal has discretion to allocate the costs of the arbitration in the award.

Special or Unusual Features (If Any)

Section 48 of the CEMARC Rules provides that unless expressly agreed otherwise, the parties waive their right to appeal the award by agreeing to arbitrate under CEMARC.

Recent Developments (If Any)

Not applicable.

C.4 Arbitral Chamber of the Buenos Aires Grain Exchange

Background

Formed by Decree No. 931/98, this institution functions within the Buenos Aires Grain Exchange. It administers both mediations and arbitrations, in the latter acting only as an amiable compositeur.

Types of Disputes Handled

The Board of the Grain Exchange will act as an arbitral tribunal in all disputes related to the commerce and functioning of the grain market.

Numbers of Disputes Handled

No statistics are publicly available.

Provisions on Confidentiality of Arbitration

Section 6 of the Board's rules provides that the institution is authorized to publicize the arbitral awards that it believes are relevant to the general interest of the grain commerce. Section 13 provides that mediation proceedings will be deemed confidential, but there is no express provision regarding the confidentiality of arbitration proceedings.

C. Local Arbitration Institutions

Availability of Expedited Procedures

The tribunal will attempt to issue the award solely based on the documentary evidence submitted, the general usages of the grain trade, and the parties' behavior regarding the issues in dispute. Additional evidence can be produced if the tribunal is convinced of its manifest relevance and necessity.

Consolidation of Disputes between the Same Parties and Joinder of Third Parties

No reference in the rules.

Time Limits for Rendering of the Award

The award must be issued no later than 40 days from the date on which the docket is sent to the tribunal for resolution, but the tribunal may extend this term if it deems it advisable. Section 48 of the Board's rules provides that awards issued after the allotted timeframe will not be inherently challengeable, unless the parties expressly object before the issuance of the award.

Fee Structure

No express scale is provided to determine costs. Section 50 of the Board's rules provides that the costs of the arbitration will be fixed based on the expenses related to the proceedings (tribunal's expenses, fees and costs of any expert appointed by the tribunal, and the expenses that the parties might have incurred for their claims and defenses).

Treatment of Costs of the Arbitration

Section 50 of the Board's rules provides that the tribunal will allocate the costs of the arbitration as it sees fit in the award.

Special or Unusual Features (If Any)

Unless expressly agreed otherwise, by agreeing to arbitrate the parties are waiving their right to appeal the award (Sections 53 and 58 of the Board's rules).

Recent Developments (If Any)

Not applicable.

AUSTRALIA

Leigh Duthie,[1] Jo Delaney[2] and Erika Williams[3]

A. LEGISLATION, TRENDS AND TENDENCIES

A.1 Legislation

International arbitration in Australia continues to be governed by the *International Arbitration Act 1974* (Cth) ("IAA"), to which no legislative amendments were made in 2014.

A.2 Trends and Tendencies

Investor-state dispute settlement ("ISDS") in investment treaties and free trade agreements ("FTAs") is a topical issue. The Australian government continues to consider ISDS on a case-by-case basis, as reported in last year's Yearbook. ISDS has been or is to be included in the FTAs with Korea and China, but not Japan. Notably, the Senate Committee has rejected a Bill to exclude ISDS provisions in new trade and investment agreements. Australia continues to negotiate bilateral FTAs with Asian countries, such as India and Indonesia, as well as regional agreements such as the Trans-Pacific Partnership Agreement.

---

[1]   Leigh Duthie is a Partner in Baker & McKenzie's Melbourne office with extensive experience acting for major Australian and international corporations and government agencies in complex claims in the construction, infrastructure, resources and energy industries in international and domestic arbitration, expert determination and court proceedings in all major Australian courts.

[2]   Jo Delaney is Special Counsel in Baker & McKenzie's Sydney office with 15 years experience resolving complex cross border disputes through international arbitration based in London and Sydney.

[3]   Erika Williams is an Associate in Baker & McKenzie's Sydney office with experience in arbitration and litigation. The authors would like to thank Jahan Navidi in the Sydney office for his assistance with this chapter.

The inclusion of ISDS in bilateral and regional FTAs may have a dramatic impact on the arbitral landscape in Australia and the Asia-Pacific region.

B. CASES

B.1 Third Parties in International Arbitration

Section 7 of the IAA provides that reference to a "party" to an arbitration agreement includes "a person claiming through or under a party". The courts have stayed court proceedings where a related third party who is not a party to the arbitration agreement acts "through or under a party" who is party to it. In *Flint Ink NZ Ltd v Huhtamaki Australia Pty Ltd*,[4] Huhtamaki Australia ("Huhtamaki Aus") commenced third party proceedings against Flint Ink New Zealand Ltd ("Flint Ink") in relation to a claim brought by a customer for faulty packaging of yoghurt. Huhtamaki Aus claimed the fault arose from the ink supplied by Flint Ink pursuant to a supply agreement ("Supply Agreement") between Flint Ink and Huhtamaki New Zealand ("Huhtamaki NZ"). Flint Ink requested a stay of the court proceedings on the basis of the arbitration clause in the Supply Agreement, arguing that Huhtamaki Aus was claiming "through or under" Huhtamaki NZ. That argument was accepted, and the third party proceedings were stayed pending the outcome of an arbitration under the Supply Agreement.[5]

---

[4] [2014] VSCA 166.

[5] A similar argument was raised in *KNM Process System Sdn Bhd v Mission NewEnergy Ltd* [2014] WASC 437 but not accepted on the facts of the case. A stay was granted on different grounds.

B.2 Public Policy and the Scope of Natural Justice

A breach of natural justice may be contrary to public policy under s. 19 of the IAA and thus a ground for challenging enforcement of an award. In *TCL Air Conditioner (Zhongshan) Co Ltd v Castel Electronics Pty Ltd*,[6] the full court of the Federal Court of Australia ("FCA") confirmed that for an award to be set aside on the ground of natural justice, there must be a "real practical injustice or real unfairness". Natural justice in the context of international commercial arbitration is different to the concept of natural justice in administrative law and does not encompass the bias rule, no evidence rule or no hearing rule. The court is not entitled to review or revisit the factual findings under the guise of assessing procedural fairness. A real practical injustice or real unfairness should be demonstrated without a detailed re-examination of the facts. On this basis, the court rejected the arguments of TCL Air Conditioner (Zhongshan) Co Ltd that the award should not be enforced as requested by Castel Electronics Pty Ltd due to the denial of procedural fairness.[7]

B.3 Execution of Awards against Assets in Australia

The Australian courts have taken measures necessary to freeze or secure assets for the purpose of enforcing an award or to appoint receivers to sell assets to satisfy an award.[8] In *Traxys Europe SA v Balaji Coke Industry PVT Ltd (No 5)*,[9] the FCA appointed receivers to sell shares in an Australian company after finding

---

[6] [2014] FCAFC 83.

[7] A similar approach had been adopted in *Emerald Grain Australia Pty Ltd v Agrocorp International Pte Ltd* [2014] FCA 414 and was subsequently followed by the Supreme Court of NSW in *William Hare UAE LLC v Aircraft Support Industries Pty Ltd* [2014] NSWSC 1403.

[8] See, for example, *Gujarat NRE Coke Limited Jagatramka v Coeclerici Asia (Pte) Ltd* [2013] FCAFC 19 reported in last year's Yearbook.

[9] [2014] FCA 976.

that a purported sale of those shares to a third party was as "sham" transaction entered into to avoid enforcement of the award. An award had been issued in London in favor of Traxys Europe SA ("Traxys"), a Luxembourg company that provided services to the mining industry, in an arbitration with Balaji Coke Industry Pvt Ltd ("Balaji"), an Indian company importing, manufacturing and supplying coal and coke. Balaji held shares in an Australian company and purported to sell those shares to another Indian company. However, the court found that the transaction was a "sham". There was no attempt to formalize the share sale transaction by, among other things, preparing, executing and registering a share transfer. Receivers were appointed so that the shares could be sold and the proceeds distributed to Traxys.

C.   LOCAL ARBITRATION INSTITUTIONS

C.1   Australian Centre for International Commercial Arbitration ("ACICA")

Background

Established in 1985, ACICA is one of Australia's international dispute resolution bodies. Its objective is to promote and facilitate the efficient resolution of commercial disputes in Australia and internationally, with the aim of delivering expediency and neutrality of process, enforceability of outcome and commercial privacy to parties in dispute. ACICA has its own arbitration rules ("ACICA Rules"). It has published an exposure draft of the ACICA Arbitration Rules 2015 ("Exposure Draft"). ACICA is the sole default appointing authority competent to perform the arbitrator appointment functions under the IAA.[10]

---

[10]   IAA, ss. 18(1) and 18(2); *International Arbitration Regulations 2011* (Cth), s. 4.

C. Local Arbitration Institutions

Types of Disputes Handled

ACICA facilitates the resolution of commercial disputes through international and domestic arbitration and mediation.

Numbers of Disputes Handled

No statistics are available.

Provisions on Confidentiality of Arbitration

The ACICA Rules provide for confidentiality. All matters relating to the arbitration (including the existence of the arbitration), the award, materials created for the purpose of the arbitration and documents produced by another party which are not in the public domain must not be disclosed to a third party without prior written consent from the parties. Exceptions include disclosure required for a court application or as required by law.[11] Hearings are held in private unless the parties agree in writing otherwise.[12] Parties must ensure that witnesses who have access to confidential information comply with these confidentiality obligations.[13]

Availability of Expedited Procedures

The ACICA Rules include the ACICA Expedited Arbitration Rules ("Expedited Rules"), which apply if agreed to by the parties.[14] The Exposure Draft proposes that the Expedited Rules apply where the amount in dispute is less than AUD5,000,000, unless the parties agree otherwise. The Expedited Rules provide

---

[11]   ACICA Rules, r. 18.2.

[12]   ACICA Rules, r. 18.1.

[13]   ACICA Rules, r. 18.4.

[14]   ACICA Expedited Arbitration Rules, r. 2.1.

for ACICA to appoint a sole arbitrator within 14 days of commencement of the arbitration.[15] There is no hearing unless there are exceptional circumstances or the arbitrator or the parties require a hearing.[16] The statement of defense is required within 28 days of ACICA communicating the notice of arbitration (which contains the statement of claim) to the respondent.[17] The arbitrator is required to make the final award within four to five months of his or her appointment.[18]

Consolidation of Disputes between the Same Parties and Joinder of Third Parties

The current ACICA Rules do not provide for consolidation or joinder, but they are proposed in the Exposure Draft.[19] Arbitrations between the same parties may be consolidated upon request by a party.[20] When deciding whether to consolidate two or more arbitrations, ACICA will consider, among other things, whether the parties have agreed to consolidation, if the claims are made under the same arbitration agreement or if claims are made under separate arbitration agreements, whether the claims relate to the same subject matter.[21] The Exposure Draft proposes that an additional party may be joined if it is bound by the same arbitration agreement.[22] A Request for Joinder must be submitted

---

[15] ACICA Expedited Arbitration Rules, rr. 8.1 and 8.2.

[16] ACICA Expedited Arbitration Rules, r. 13.2.

[17] ACICA Expedited Arbitration Rules, r. 18.1

[18] ACICA Expedited Arbitration Rules, r. 27.

[19] Exposure Draft of the ACICA Arbitration Rules, r. 11A and r. 11B.

[20] Exposure Draft of the ACICA Arbitration Rules, r. 11A.1.

[21] Exposure Draft of the ACICA Arbitration Rules, r. 11A.1.

[22] Exposure Draft of the ACICA Arbitration Rules, r. 11B.1.

to ACICA by an existing party[23] or an additional party wishing to be joined. [24] A response must be submitted within 15 days.[25]

Time Limits for Rendering of the Award

The ACICA Rules and the Exposure Draft do not provide a time limit for rendering of the award. Under the Expedited Rules, the final award must be made within four months of the Arbitrator's appointment, or five months if there is a counterclaim.[26]

Fee Structure

The claimant must pay a non-refundable registration fee of AUD2,500 to ACICA when it submits a notice of arbitration.[27] The parties must share equally ACICA's administrative fees, which depend on the amount in dispute.[28]

Treatment of Costs of the Arbitration

The ACICA Rules prescribe that the costs of arbitration shall in principle be borne by the unsuccessful party. However, the tribunal may apportion the costs between the parties if it finds that apportionment is reasonable, taking into account the circumstances of the case.[29]

---

[23] Exposure Draft of the ACICA Arbitration Rules, r. 11B.3.

[24] Exposure Draft of the ACICA Arbitration Rules, r. 11B.6.

[25] Exposure Draft of the ACICA Arbitration Rules, r. 11B.5 and r. 11B.7.

[26] ACICA Expedited Arbitration Rules, r. 27.

[27] ACICA Rules, Appendix A. The Exposure Draft proposes this amount be revised to AUD2,750.

[28] All amounts are exclusive of GST unless stated otherwise.

[29] ACICA Rules, r. 41.1.

Special or Unusual Features (If Any)

The ACICA Rules are up to date in that they include provisions on confidentiality, emergency arbitrator provisions, interim measures of protection and expedited rules.

Recent Developments (If Any)

ACICA published the Exposure Draft to update the ACICA Rules. The Exposure Draft includes articles providing for consolidation and joinder of parties;[30] that the law of the seat shall be the governing law of the arbitration agreement unless the parties have agreed otherwise;[31] and for tribunal-appointed experts.[32]

C.2 Australian Maritime and Transport Arbitration Commission ("AMTAC")

Background

AMTAC is an ACICA commission that promotes and provides services for maritime and transport dispute resolution in Australia and the Asia Pacific region. It has its own arbitration rules ("AMTAC Rules").

Types of Disputes Handled

AMTAC facilitates the resolution of maritime and transport disputes through arbitration.

Numbers of Disputes Handled

No statistics are available.

---

[30]   Exposure Draft of the ACICA Arbitration Rules, rr. 11A and 11B.

[31]   Exposure Draft of the ACICA Arbitration Rules, r. 19.5.

[32]   Exposure Draft of the ACICA Arbitration Rules, r. 28.

C. Local Arbitration Institutions

Provisions on Confidentiality of Arbitration

The AMTAC Rules have the same confidentiality provisions as the ACICA Rules.[33]

Availability of Expedited Procedures

AMTAC provides a Rocket Docket procedure for disputes involving claims less than AUD100,000 if the parties agree to its application. It involves one arbitrator dealing with the case on documents only (i.e. no hearing) for an arbitrator's fee of AUD4,000 and registration fee of AUD1,000.[34] A final award must be issued within three months of the commencement of the arbitration.

Consolidation of Disputes between the Same Parties and Joinder of Third Parties

The AMTAC Rules do not provide for consolidation or joinder of third parties.

Time Limits for Rendering of the Award

Under the AMTAC Rules, the arbitrator must make the final award within four months of the notice of appointment or five months if there is a counterclaim.[35] The final award must be within three months of the arbitration's commencement under the Rocket Docket procedure.

---

[33] AMTAC Arbitration Rules, r. 14.

[34] Both amounts are exclusive of GST.

[35] AMTAC Arbitration Rules, r. 27.

Fee Structure

The claimant must pay a non-refundable registration fee of AUD2,000 to AMTAC.[36] This registration fee includes 10 hours of administrative assistance from AMTAC. Any further assistance is charged at a rate of AUD300 (inclusive of GST) per hour.[37]

Treatment of Costs of the Arbitration

The AMTAC Rules prescribe that the costs of arbitration shall in principle be borne by the unsuccessful party. However, the tribunal may apportion costs between the parties if it finds that apportionment is reasonable, taking into account the circumstances of the case.[38]

Special or Unusual Features (If Any)

The AMTAC Rules are up to date as they include provisions on confidentiality, emergency arbitrators, interim measures of protection and expedited rules.

Recent Developments (If Any)

Not applicable.

C.3 The Institute of Arbitrators and Mediators Australia ("IAMA")

Background

Founded in 1975, IAMA provides services and training in all areas of dispute resolution. Its new arbitration rules came into effect from 2 May 2014 ("IAMA Rules").

---

[36] AMTAC Arbitration Rules, Appendix A, r. 1.2.

[37] AMTAC Arbitration Rules, Appendix A, r. 2.1.

[38] AMTAC Arbitration Rules, r. 36.1.

C. Local Arbitration Institutions

Types of Disputes Handled

IAMA facilitates the resolution of disputes using all types of alternative dispute resolution methods, including arbitration, mediation, conciliation, adjudication and expert determination.

Numbers of Disputes Handled

No statistics are available.

Provisions on Confidentiality of Arbitration

The IAMA Rules provide that hearings shall be held in camera unless the parties agree otherwise.[39] No confidentiality provisions are included.

Availability of Expedited Procedures

The IAMA Rules do not include separate expedited procedures.

Consolidation of Disputes between the Same Parties and Joinder of Third Parties

The IAMA Rules do not provide for consolidation, but do provide for joinder of a third party if the person is a party to the arbitration agreement.[40]

Time Limits for Rendering of the Award

Under the IAMA Rules, the tribunal must use its best endeavors to issue its award within 365 days of its appointment. If it is unable to do so, the tribunal must notify IAMA and the parties of the reasons for the delays.[41]

---

[39] IAMA Arbitration Rules, art. 28, para. 3.

[40] IAMA Arbitration Rules, art. 17, para. 5.

[41] IAMA Arbitration Rules, art. 16.

Fee Structure

When submitting a notice of arbitration, the claimant must pay a non-refundable registration fee of AUD500 to IAMA.[42] IAMA charges a nominee fee, which is prescribed in relation to the amount in dispute.[43] Schedule 1 of the IAMA Rules also caps the arbitrator's total remuneration and the amount of legal costs depending on the amount in dispute.[44]

Treatment of Costs of the Arbitration

The IAMA Rules prescribe that the costs of arbitration shall in principle be borne by the unsuccessful party. However, the tribunal may apportion the costs between the parties if it finds that apportionment is reasonable, taking into account the circumstances of the case.[45]

Special or Unusual Features (If Any)

The IAMA Rules include provisions on interim measures of protection.

Recent Developments (If Any)

As mentioned above, the new IAMA Arbitration Rules came into effect on May 2, 2014.

---

[42]   IAMA Arbitration Rules, Schedule 1.

[43]   IAMA Arbitration Rules, Schedule 1.

[44]   IAMA Arbitration Rules, Schedule 1.

[45]   IAMA Arbitration Rules, art 42, para 2.

AUSTRIA

Stefan Riegler[1] and Alexander Zollner[2]

A.   LEGISLATION, TRENDS AND TENDENCIES

A.1   Legislation

On January 1, 2014, the long-awaited revision to the procedure for setting aside arbitral awards came into force. The previous legal framework required parties seeking to set aside an arbitral award in Austria to go through three levels of courts in order to receive a final and binding decision. This was considered as a burden in terms of both time and costs, and therefore made Austria arguably a less attractive place of arbitration. In addition, having to go through a lengthy court process might have discouraged some parties from challenging awards.

To address these issues, the Austrian legislator shortened the procedure. As of January 1, 2014 the Austrian Supreme Court ("OGH") is the only court having jurisdiction over disputes on the setting aside of an arbitral award (in this context the OGH was also vested with the competence on additional issues related to arbitral proceedings). The OGH determines at its own discretion whether and by which means evidence is collected and whether an evidentiary hearing should be held.

In August 2014, the OGH rendered its first decisions under this new procedure; two of these judgments are discussed below.

---

[1]   Stefan Riegler is a Partner in Baker & McKenzie's Vienna office. He has significant experience in representing clients before state courts and arbitral tribunals and currently primarily focuses his practice on international arbitration. In addition, Mr. Riegler is increasingly working as an arbitrator.

[2]   Alexander Zollner is a Junior Associate in Baker & McKenzie's Vienna office. He focuses his practice on international arbitration and commercial litigation.

B. CASES

B.1 The Notion of Consumer in the Context of Austrian Arbitration

In its decision of December 16, 2013,[3] the OGH clarified open questions regarding the application of s.617 of the Austrian Code of Civil Procedure ("ACCP"), a consumer protection provision setting out several conditions under which consumers may enter into arbitration agreements. The OGH held that the provision does apply to arbitrations in the context of corporate law disputes between shareholders and hence also to joint venture agreements. In addition, the OGH clarified that s.617 of the ACCP applies to arbitral proceedings with the seat of the arbitral tribunal within Austria (irrespective of whether the dispute is national or international).

The parties to the agreement were a Bulgarian individual, a Liechtenstein establishment, an English private equity fund and a Cypriot company. The English private equity fund commenced arbitral proceedings against the individual and the Liechtenstein establishment, who objected to the jurisdiction of the arbitral tribunal by arguing that the arbitration agreement did not comply with s.617 of the ACCP. The arbitral tribunal rejected the Respondents' objection in an arbitral award, which in turn was challenged. The OGH held that the provision does apply in this context.

The OGH further determined that the consumer status pursuant to s.617 of the ACCP has to be assessed on a case-by-case basis and according to Austrian law. Whether a shareholder is deemed to be a consumer or a businessperson has to be assessed from a commercial perspective in the context of the relevant factual

---

3   OGH, 12 December 2013, 6 Ob 43/13m.

matrix. In the present case, neither the Bulgarian individual nor the Liechtenstein establishment was considered to be a consumer, and therefore the action to set aside the arbitral award failed.

B.2 Challenged Arbitrator Entitled to Aliquot Fees

In its decision of February 17, 2014,[4] the OGH held that an arbitrator who was successfully challenged due to reasons which arose only during the course of an arbitration may be entitled to aliquot fees for work already conducted by him or her.

The chairman of the arbitral tribunal was successfully challenged and replaced after the oral hearing had taken place. The remaining arbitrators and a new chairman rendered an award based on the previous hearing and evidence and did not repeat any procedural steps.

The arbitrator's contract only provided for fees on the basis of the entire procedure, which depended on whether a final and legally valid award was rendered or not. The contract did not contain provisions dealing with the question of whether there was any entitlement to fees or a proportion of fees for work done in the event of his removal.

The OGH based its decision on a supplementary interpretation[5] of the arbitrator's contract. It stated that reasonable parties who agreed on fees only for the entire arbitration would not have agreed that the entitlement to fees should cease in circumstances where the arbitrator's mandate is terminated early. Rather, reasonable parties would have agreed that the arbitrator's fees should be reduced proportionately to the share of the work done.

---

[4]   OGH, 17 February 2014, 4 Ob 197/13v.

[5]   By means of supplementary interpretation a gap in a contract is filled by a provision which reasonable parties would have agreed on in case they had foreseen the gap in the contract.

The question of whether this would also apply if the work had to be repeated was left open by the OGH.

B.3 Relevance of Failure to Disclose

In two (almost identical) decisions of August 5, 2014,[6] the OGH determined whether the failure to disclose facts possibly giving rise to a challenge to an arbitrator might itself constitute a ground for challenge. Notably, these decisions were the first to be handed down by the OGH under the new procedural framework described above.

Both decisions of the OGH dealt with materially the same facts. The parties to the disputes were on the one side a former shareholder of a company and on the other side the remaining shareholders of that company (and in one case the company itself). In both arbitrations, the same arbitrator was appointed and in turn challenged by the former shareholder for the same reasons. The former shareholder asserted that the arbitrator did not disclose the fact that he was a member of the advisory board of a fund established by him and that a prominent member of the law firm that represented the remaining shareholders and the company in the arbitration was also a member of this advisory board. The former shareholder argued that the failure to disclose this fact in itself constituted a ground to challenge the arbitrator.

The OGH held that the connection between the weight of the failure to disclose and the likelihood of the relevant circumstances constituting a ground for challenge needs to be assessed on a case-by-case basis. It is important to establish whether the arbitrator deliberately concealed the information in order to avoid a possible challenge. Further, the OGH considered that it is not always clear which facts and details have to be

---

6   OGH, 5 August 2014, 18 ONc 1/14p; OHG, 5 August 2014, 18 ONc 2/14k.

disclosed; not every detail which has not been disclosed leads to the reasonable assumption that the arbitrator is not impartial and independent. In the present case, the OGH held that despite the fact that the arbitrator violated the duty of disclosure by not revealing his membership to the advisory board, it could not be assumed that he concealed this fact to avoid a challenge. Thus, the challenge was dismissed.

C. LOCAL ARBITRATION INSTITUTIONS

C.1 Vienna International Arbitral Centre

Background

The Vienna International Arbitral Centre ("VIAC") was founded in 1974 and began its work on January 1, 1975. Prior to the formation of VIAC, nine Regional Economic Chambers were entitled to establish a permanent arbitral institution for the settlement of commercial disputes. These regional arbitral centers were responsible for handling both national and international cases. In 1974 the Austrian Federal Economic Chamber ("AFEC") was empowered to establish a permanent arbitral center for settling disputes in which at least one party has its place of business outside of Austria.

Types of Disputes Handled

According to Article 1 of the VIAC Rules of Arbitration (the "Vienna Rules"), VIAC is competent to settle disputes in which at least one party has its place of business outside of Austria. The deciding factor for this requirement is the date on which the arbitration agreement was concluded.[7] However, VIAC may also have jurisdiction if agreed upon by parties whose place of

---

[7] *Horvath/Trittmann* in Handbook Vienna Rules [2014] Art. 1 mn 6.

business or usual residence is in Austria, as long as the dispute is "international in character".[8] The term "international" is similar to "cross-border" and has historically been interpreted very broadly. For example, an arbitral tribunal determined that it had jurisdiction in a case between two Austrian companies where both companies had foreign shareholders, where the articles of association had been drawn up in English and the arbitration agreement contained a clause that the proceedings must be conducted in English. However, VIAC does not have jurisdiction to determine purely domestic disputes.

Numbers of Disputes Handled

In 2013, VIAC received 56 new cases (2012: 70, 2011: 75) and as at December 31, 2013 had 76 pending cases. The aggregated amount in dispute was EUR1.36 billion. The statistics for 2013 show that mostly European parties arbitrate before VIAC: 94 European parties, 11 Asian parties, one African party and one American party were involved in a VIAC arbitration. In 2013, 50 arbitrators came from Europe and only one arbitrator from Asia. The nature of disputes in 2013 was widely spread and comprised general trade (21%), machinery (17%), finance (16%), construction and engineering (14%), business services (10%), distribution (10%), energy (8%), share purchase agreements (2%) and real estate (2%).[9]

Provisions on Confidentiality of Arbitration

Article 30(2) of the Vienna Rules contains the principle that arbitral proceedings are private, and therefore the public is not entitled to be present at procedural meetings, oral hearings or the taking of evidence. Privacy of arbitral proceedings has to be

---

[8]   Article 1(1) of the Vienna Rules.

[9]   The statistics are available at http://www.viac.eu/en/service/statistics.

distinguished from a duty of confidentiality. The Vienna Rules do not contain an explicit provision stating that the parties are obliged to keep information confidential. An obligation of confidentiality is only incumbent on the Board of VIAC,[10] the Secretary General and his or her deputy,[11] and the arbitrators.[12] It is argued by some commentators that these provisions imply a general obligation of confidentiality on parties arbitrating under the Vienna Rules.[13]

Availability of Expedited Procedures

Article 45 of the Vienna Rules provides for an expedited procedure. Those rules apply if the parties have agreed on them either in their arbitration agreement or subsequently, until the submission of the Answer to the Statement of Claim. The regulations for expedited procedures alter the "normal" rules, which will still be applicable wherever Article 45 of the Vienna Rules does not state differently. In an expedited procedure, the dispute will automatically be decided by a sole arbitrator; however, the parties may agree otherwise. The time limits for the payment of the advance on costs and for the joint nomination of the arbitrator will be 15 days only. In case of default, the Board will nominate the arbitrator. The arbitral tribunal must render its award within six months of transmission of the file to the arbitral tribunal. However, if it does not comply with this time limit, the arbitration agreement will not be invalid, nor will the arbitral tribunal lose its jurisdiction over the case. Further, Article 45(9) of the Vienna Rules sets out a number of other restrictions designed to streamline and shorten the proceedings.

---

[10]   Article 2(2) of the Vienna Rules.

[11]   Article 4(4) of the Vienna Rules.

[12]   Article 16(2) of the Vienna Rules.

[13]   *Schwarz/Konrad*, The Vienna Rules [2009] para. 20-167.

Consolidation of Disputes between the Same Parties and Joinder of Third Parties

The Vienna Rules include provisions on both the consolidation of disputes and the joinder of third parties. According to Article 14 of the Vienna Rules, the joinder of a third party to arbitration proceedings requires the consent of the arbitral tribunal upon the request of a party or the third party. After considering "all relevant circumstances"[14] and hearing the parties and the third party, the arbitral tribunal determines in which form or for which part of the proceedings the joinder is to take place. On the other hand, Article 15 of the Vienna Rules regulates the consolidation of two or more pending cases. Upon the request of a party to the arbitration, the consolidation of disputes is permissible only if the place of arbitration is the same in all of the arbitration agreements upon which the claims are based and either the same arbitrator(s) has/have been appointed or all the parties agree to the consolidation.[15]

Time Limits for Rendering of the Award

The Vienna Rules do not provide a specific time limit for rendering an award (unless the parties have agreed upon the rules for the expedited procedure). However, upon the declaration of the closure of the proceedings, the arbitral tribunal must inform the parties of the anticipated date by which the final award will be rendered.

Fee Structure

Pursuant to Article 44 of the Vienna Rules the procedural costs can be divided into three main categories: (1) the costs related to

---

[14]   Article 14(1) of the Vienna Rules.

[15]   Article 15(1) of the Vienna Rules.

the arbitral institution (including the arbitrators' fees),[16] (2) the costs incurred by the parties,[17] and (3) all other costs resulting from the procedural steps ordered by the arbitrators in accordance with Article 43(1) of the Vienna Rules and those which do not fall into either of the other two cost categories.[18]

Treatment of Costs of the Arbitration

Whilst the Secretary General has the power to fix the costs related to the arbitral institution (including the arbitrators' fees),[19] the arbitral tribunal determines the costs incurred by the parties and all other costs and determines the allocation of costs in general either by way of a separate award on costs or in the award on the merits. The arbitral tribunal allocates costs in the manner it deems appropriate, unless the parties have agreed otherwise.[20]

Special or Unusual Features (If Any)

The Vienna Rules do not contain any unusual features.

Recent Developments (If Any)

There have been no recent developments.

---

[16]   Article 44(1) 1.1 of the Vienna Rules.

[17]   Article 44 (1) 1.2 of the Vienna Rules.

[18]   Article 44 (1) 1.3 of the Vienna Rules; *Heider/Fremuth-Wolf* in Handbook Vienna Rules [2014] Art. 44 mn 2.

[19]   Article 44 (2) of the Vienna Rules.

[20]   Article 37 of the Vienna Rules.

BELARUS

Alexander Korobeinikov[1]

A. LEGISLATION, TRENDS AND TENDENCIES

A.1 Legislation

International arbitration in Belarus continues to be governed by the Law on the International Arbitration Court[2] (the "International Arbitration Law"), which was enacted on July 9, 1999. The law is based on the UNCITRAL Model Law, and since its enactment, no significant amendments have been made to it. In addition, the Economic Procedural Code adopted on December 15, 1998 contains provisions relating to challenging and enforcing local and foreign arbitral awards.

A.2 Trends and Tendencies

In addition to court-appointed mediation, in July 2013 the Belarusian Parliament adopted the Law On Mediation,[3] which sets forth rules for out-of-court mediation. Among other things, this law sets out: (i) requirements which need to be met for being appointed as a mediator; (ii) mandatory terms of agreements to commence mediation proceedings; (iii) rules of registration for mediation institutions; and (iv) rules for enforcement of agreements concluded as a result of mediation. It also states that these agreements can be enforced in state courts. This law came into force in January 2014, and the application of its provisions

---

[1] Alexander Korobeinikov is a Senior Associate at Baker & McKenzie's Almaty office and a member of the Firm's International Arbitration Practice Group.

[2] The Law of the Republic of Belarus *On the International Arbitration Court* No. 279-Z dated 9 July 1999 (as amended).

[3] The Law of the Republic of Belarus *On Mediation N 58-Z* dated 12.07.2013.

will need to be clarified by subordinate legislation and relevant court practice.

As a result of the reform of the Belarusian judicial system which began in November 2013, two separate court systems were consolidated: the economic courts, which previously reviewed commercial cases, and the courts of general jurisdiction, which previously reviewed other civil cases, as well as criminal and administrative cases. Pursuant to amendments adopted in July 2014, cases involving challenges to local arbitral awards should be reviewed by regional economic courts and the court decisions on these cases can be appealed to the Court of Appeal. Previously, these cases were reviewed only by the Supreme Economic Court (which was liquidated as a result of the consolidation of two court systems), whose decisions came into force immediately and could only be appealed to the cassation panel of the Supreme Economic Court.

B. CASES

Belarusian court decisions are not publicly disclosed. Therefore, we are not aware of any significant court decisions in Belarus in relation to arbitration in the last year. However, Belarusian courts usually take an arbitration-friendly approach, though they have comparatively limited experience in dealing with arbitration-related cases.

C. LOCAL ARBITRATION INSTITUTIONS

After the adoption of the Law on Domestic Arbitration Courts[4] in July 2011 and relevant sub-laws regulating the procedure of

---

[4] The Law of the Republic of Belarus *On Domestic Arbitration Courts N 301-Z* dated 18.07.2011.

establishment and registration of arbitration institutions, the number of arbitration institutions registered in Belarus significantly increased, and currently there are 25 arbitration institutions.

The oldest and most popular of them is the International Arbitration Court at the Belarusian Chamber of Commerce and Industry (the "IAC"), which was established in 1994.

C.1 The IAC

Background

The IAC was established in 1994 shortly after the collapse of the Soviet Union and the declaration of the independence of the Republic of Belarus. In the absence of any relevant local laws, the IAC's activity was based on the provisions of the Geneva Convention, which was ratified by the Republic of Belarus in 1964.

Types of Disputes Handled

The IAC handles all types of commercial disputes between local and foreign companies, except disputes which are non-arbitrable under Belarusian law (e.g., disputes relating to rights over immovable property located in Belarus, privatization contracts, IP rights, etc.). The IAC also reviews commercial disputes between local companies.

Numbers of Disputes Handled

No statistics are available.

Provisions on Confidentiality of Arbitration

Confidentiality of arbitration is one of the cornerstone principles of arbitration proceedings in Belarus, and it is set forth in the International Arbitration Law. Under the International

Arbitration Law and the IAC Rules of Arbitration,[5] confidentiality applies to all documents and information disclosed by parties during the arbitration proceedings and to the arbitral award.

Availability of Expedited Procedures

Under the IAC Rules of Arbitration, the expedited procedure is available only for disputes between local companies where the disputed amount does not exceed approximately USD120,000.

Consolidation of Disputes between the Same Parties and Joinder of Third Parties

The IAC Rules of Arbitration do not contain any special rules relating to the consolidation of disputes and joinders of third parties.

Time Limits for Rendering of the Award

Under the IAC Rules of Arbitration, the general term for rendering an award is six months from the date of the constitution of the tribunal (three months for disputes between local companies). However, this term may be extended by the Chairman of the IAC.

Fee Structure

The arbitration fees for disputes where one of parties is a foreign company consist of: (a) the registration fee, amounting to EUR150; and (b) the arbitration duty, amounting to up to EUR22,825 plus 0.4% of the amount of the claim greater than EUR2,000,000 (plus VAT). The registration fee is included in the amount of the arbitration duty.

---

[5]   The most recent version of these Rules was adopted on 17 March 2011.

C. Local Arbitration Institutions

For disputes between local companies, the rates of arbitration fees are much lower and amount to up to approximately USD3,840, plus 0.1% of the amount of the claim greater than approximately USD120,000 (plus VAT).

The above arbitration fees can be reduced if the dispute is reviewed by a sole arbitrator or under the expedited procedure rules.

Treatment of Costs of the Arbitration

Under the IAC Rules of Arbitration, the Tribunal orders the costs of the arbitration to be borne by the claimant in the arbitration proceedings in proportion to the amount of its claim granted by the tribunal. For example, if the claimant is awarded 60% of the amount claimed, it is responsible for 40% of the costs. If a claimant is wholly successful, the respondent is responsible for the entirety of the parties' costs.

Special or Unusual Features (If Any)

There are no special or unusual features.

Recent Developments (If Any)

There are no recent developments.

BELGIUM

Koen De Winter[1] and Michaël De Vroey[2]

A. LEGISLATION, TRENDS AND TENDENCIES

International arbitrations commenced in Belgium since September 1, 2013 continue to be governed by the Belgian Arbitration Act of June 24, 2013, to which no legislative amendment was made in 2014.

B. CASES

B.1 Provisional or Protective Measures Before or During Arbitration Proceedings

Pursuant to Article 1683 (previously Article 1679, §2) of the Judicial Code, "it is not incompatible with an arbitration agreement for a request to be made to a court for an interim or conservatory measure before or during arbitral proceedings and for a court to grant such measure, nor shall any such request imply a waiver of the arbitration agreement."

In a judgment of May 15, 2014, the Commercial Court of Brussels held (in line with established case law) that, notwithstanding an arbitration clause contained in an agreement

---

[1]   Koen De Winter is a Partner in Baker & McKenzie's Antwerp office and heads the office's Dispute Resolution Practice Group. During his 30-year professional career, he has gained extensive experience in domestic and international litigation and arbitration on a large variety of commercial matters.

[2]   Michaël De Vroey is an Associate in Baker & McKenzie's Antwerp office and a member of the Firm's Global Dispute Resolution Practice Group, as well as a member of the Intellectual Property Practice Group.

between the parties, the court had jurisdiction to hear an application for a court-appointed expert, as the appointment of an expert is a provisional and protective measure.[3]

Note that Article 1683 of the Judicial Code now explicitly allows a request to be made to a State Court not only during arbitral proceedings, but also before.

C. LOCAL ARBITRATION INSTITUTIONS

C.1 CEPANI

Background

CEPANI is the Belgian Centre for Arbitration and Mediation, and is currently the main centre for dispute resolution in Belgium. It was founded in 1969, under the auspices of the Belgian National Committee of the ICC and the Federation of Belgian Enterprises (VBO/FEB).

Types of Disputes Handled

CEPANI distinguishes between two types of disputes, each of which are governed by a different set of rules: disputes of limited financial importance, where the principal claim and the counterclaim (if any) together do not exceed the amount of EUR25,000; and all other disputes, where the principal claim and the counterclaim (if any) together exceed the amount of EUR25,000.

CEPANI also handles ".be" domain name disputes.

---

[3] Commercial Court of Brussels, 15 May 2014, JT 2014, vol. 6579, 684.

C. Local Arbitration Institutions

Numbers of Disputes Handled

No statistics are available.

Provisions on Confidentiality of Arbitration

Arbitration proceedings are confidential, unless agreed otherwise by the parties or where there is a legal obligation to disclose. The arbitrator is, in each case, bound by a strict obligation of confidentiality.

Domain name disputes are, in principle, not confidential, and previous decisions can be found at http://www.cepani.be/en/domain-names-be/decisions-past-cases.

Availability of Expedited Procedures

There is no expedited procedure, but a party may request interim or conservatory measures that cannot await the constitution of the arbitral tribunal. If such a request is made, the CEPANI appointments committee or the president of CEPANI then appoints an arbitrator who provisionally decides on the measures urgently requested. The appointment takes place within two working days of receipt of the request by the secretariat of CEPANI. In principle, the arbitrator deciding on the interim and conservatory measures renders his or her decision within 15 days of receipt of the file, at the latest. The arbitrator deciding on the interim and conservatory measures may not be appointed as an arbitrator in an arbitration that is related to the dispute at the time of the request.

Consolidation of Disputes between the Same Parties and Joinder of Third Parties

When one or more contract, each of which contains an arbitration agreement providing for the application of the

CEPANI Rules of Arbitration (the "CEPANI Rules"), gives rise to disputes that are closely related or indivisible, the CEPANI appointments committee or the president of CEPANI may order their consolidation.

The CEPANI Rules provide that the application for consolidation shall be granted when it is presented by all the parties and they have agreed on the manner in which the consolidation shall occur. If the parties do not agree, the CEPANI appointments committee or the president of CEPANI may grant the application for consolidation once they have considered the following factors:

a) whether the parties have excluded consolidation in the arbitration agreement;

b) whether the claims made in the separate arbitrations have been made pursuant to the same arbitration agreement and, if the claims have been made pursuant to more than one arbitration agreement, whether they are compatible and whether the proceedings involve the same parties and concern disputes arising from the same legal relationship;

c) the progress made in each of the arbitrations;

d) whether arbitrators have been appointed in any of the arbitrations and, if so, whether any of the arbitrators are the same; and

e) the place of arbitration provided for in the arbitration agreements.

Except as otherwise agreed by the parties, the appointments committee or the president may not order consolidation of arbitrations in which a decision has already been rendered with regard to preliminary measures, admissibility or as to the merits of a claim.

A party may also call upon a third party to join the proceedings. The admissibility of such joinder requires an arbitration agreement between the third party and the parties to the arbitration, and is subject to the unanimous consent of the arbitral tribunal.

Time Limits for Rendering the Award

The arbitral tribunal shall render the award within six months of the date of the terms of reference. The terms of reference must be signed by the parties and the members of the arbitral tribunal and contain the following information:

a) the name, first name, corporate name, function, address, telephone and fax numbers, e-mail address and VAT number of each of the parties and their respective representatives;

b) the address of each of the parties to which all notifications or communications arising in the course of the arbitration should be sent;

c) a succinct recital of the circumstances of the case;

d) a statement of the parties' claims with an indication, to the extent possible, of the amounts claimed or counterclaimed;

e) a determination of the issues that are in dispute (unless the arbitral tribunal deems it to be inappropriate);

f) the full names, first names, descriptions, and addresses of each member of the arbitral tribunal;

g) the place of the arbitration; and

h) any other particulars that the arbitral tribunal may deem to be useful.

The six-month time limit may be extended pursuant to a reasoned request from the arbitral tribunal or, upon its own motion, by the secretariat.

Fee Structure

The fees and costs of the arbitrators are determined by the secretariat in accordance with the amount in dispute and within a fee scale prescribing a minimum and maximum limit. For proceedings commenced since January 1, 2013 with a single arbitrator, fees range from a minimum of EUR1,500 for disputes up to EUR25,000 to a maximum of EUR140,000 plus 0.012% of the amount exceeding EUR50 million. The administrative expenses of CEPANI are fixed at 10% of the fees and are subject to VAT.

Each request for arbitration made pursuant to the rules must be accompanied by an advance payment of EUR500 for administrative expenses. This payment is non-refundable and is credited to the Claimant's portion of the advance on costs for arbitration. For arbitrations of limited financial importance, advance payment is EUR250.

If a tribunal of three arbitrators has been appointed, the above rates of costs and fees are multiplied by three.

Any party who requests interim or conservatory measures must pay an amount of EUR15,000, including EUR3,000 for CEPANI's administrative expenses.

Treatment of Costs of the Arbitration

The arbitration costs include the fees and expenses of the arbitrator, as well as the administrative expenses of the secretariat. They are fixed by the secretariat on the basis of the amount of the principal claim (and any counterclaim), according to the scale of costs for arbitration in effect on the date of the commencement of the arbitral proceedings.

In exceptional circumstances, the secretariat may fix the arbitration costs at a higher or lower figure than that prescribed by the scale of costs for arbitration.

C. Local Arbitration Institutions

Should the total amount in dispute exceed EUR25,000, the secretariat may increase the amount of the arbitration costs in accordance with the scale of costs for arbitration.

Special or Unusual Features (If Any)

Not applicable.

Recent Developments (If Any)

Not applicable.

C.2 Others

Other arbitration institutions in Belgium include the Association for International Arbitration (Brussels); the Council for Arbitration (*Raad voor Arbitrage*); Mediar (*De Belgische Arbitrage Instelling/L'institution Belge d'Arbitrage*); the Reconciliation Commissions for Construction (*Verzoeningscommissie Bouw/Commission de conciliation construction*) and for Second-hand Vehicles (*Verzoeningscommissie Tweedehandsvoertuigen/ Commission de conciliation véhicules d'occasion*); the Real Estate Conciliation, Arbitration and Mediation Board (*Kamer van verzoening, arbitrage en bemiddeling inzake onroerend goed/Chambre de Conciliation, d'Arbitrage et de Médiation en matière Immobilière*); the Furniture Disputes Commission (*Geschillencommissie Meubelen/Commission de Litiges Meubles*); the Arbitration Commission for Consumers and Textile Carers (*Commissie voor Arbitrage Consumenten en Textielverzorgers / Commission d'Arbitrage Consommateurs - Secteur de l'entretien du textile*); the Travel Disputes Commission (*Geschillencommissie Reizen/Commission de Litiges Voyages*); and the Belgian Arbitration Commission for Sports (*Belgische Arbitragehof voor de Sport / Cour Belge d'Arbitrage pour le Sport*).

BRAZIL

Joaquim de Paiva Muniz,[1] João Marçal R. Martins da Silva,[2] Luis Alberto Salton Peretti,[3] and Giovanny Ferreira Russo[4]

A. LEGISLATION, TRENDS AND TENDENCIES

A.1 New Civil Procedure Code to Favor Arbitration in Brazil

On December 16, 2014, the Brazilian Senate approved the text of the New Civil Procedure Code ("NCPC"), a federal statute regulating judicial proceedings before federal and state courts nationwide, which will come into force by early 2016.

---

[1] Joaquim T. de Paiva Muniz is a Partner in Baker & McKenzie's Rio de Janeiro office and a professor of Business Law and Arbitration, teaching graduate courses at Fundação Getúlio Vargas (FGV). Mr. Muniz is Chairman of the Arbitration Commission of the Rio de Janeiro Bar and coordinator to the arbitration courses of the Rio de Janeiro Bar, including a *lato sensu* graduate course, Chairman of the Rio de Janeiro section of the Brazilian Institute of Corporate Law (IBRADEMP), and author of many articles on international arbitration and Brazilian corporate law, including co-author of *Arbitration Law of Brazil: Practice and Procedure* (Juris Publishing 2006) and Arbitragem Internacional e Doméstica (Forense 2009).

[2] João Marçal Martins da Silva is an Associate in the arbitration practice of Trench, Rossi e Watanabe Advogados, Rio de Janeiro. He holds a Master's degree in Public Law from the Fundação Getúlio Vargas (FGV). He is a Lecturer of Arbitration Law at the Superior School of Law of the Brazilian Bar Association (Rio de Janeiro Section), and the founder and director of the Brazilian Association of Students of Arbitration.

[3] Luis Alberto Salton Peretti is a Senior Associate in the arbitration practice of Trench, Rossi e Watanabe Advogados, São Paulo. He holds Master's degrees in Economic Law from the Paris Institute of Political Studies (SciencesPo), in Law and Economic Globalization from the University Paris I Panthéon Sorbonne, and in Comparative Law from the University of Paris II Panthéon Assas.

[4] Giovanny Ferreira Russo is an Associate in the São Paulo office of Trench, Rossi e Watanabe Advogados, with a practice focused on commercial arbitration and litigation. He has a degree in Law from the Mackenzie Presbyterian University.

The NCPC responds to widespread clamor for swifter administration of justice in Brazilian courts and provides for increased institutional reliance on and support of ADR mechanisms. Judges will be required to foster amicable conciliation of lawsuits, and appellate courts will provide conciliation and mediation facilities and make available a roster of conciliators and mediators. For instance, the NCPC provides for a conciliation hearing to be held after service of process and before the defendant is required to submit its answer. This conciliation hearing can also be converted into a mediation under the NCPC.

The NCPC also includes regulations on the cooperation between arbitral tribunals and state courts. It provides for the use of an arbitral letter (*carta arbitral*), through which arbitrators may request and obtain court support in favor of arbitration. In addition, the NCPC provides for confidentiality of the judicial proceeding related to an arbitration that is subject to confidentiality. The NCPC also regulates the recognition and enforcement of foreign arbitral awards, consolidating the favorable treatment granted by current case law and under the terms of the New York Convention.

A.2 Reform Bill for the Brazilian Arbitration Act Pending

As we reported in last year's *Yearbook*, in early 2013 a special commission chaired by Justice Luis Felipe Salomão of the Superior Court of Justice (the highest court for non-constitutional matters) began evaluating the need to change the Brazilian Arbitration Act. In October 2013, the commission submitted a bill of law reforming the Brazilian Arbitration Act to the Federal Senate, which approved the bill in December 2013. Currently, the House of Representatives is analyzing two amendments to the bill, the most controversial of which concerns the possibility of the Executive Power issuing decrees to regulate the procedure for arbitration involving State-owned companies.

The Federal Senate will then consider confirmation of any amendments, and, after approval, the bill will be sent to the president for approval. The reform of the Brazilian Arbitration Act is expected to be passed in 2015.

A.3 CISG Officially In Force in Brazil

The United Nations Convention on Contracts for the International Sale of Goods ("CISG") has now officially entered into force in Brazil, upon the enactment of Presidential Decree N. 8.327. While this legislation was released in October 2014, the decree itself clarifies that it applies retroactively from April 1, 2014.

A.4 Special ADR Courts to Be Created in Brazil

In November 2014, the National Council of Justice, which is the public entity supervising the judiciary branch in Brazil, announced that beginning in 2015, all major cities in Brazil will have specialized courts dedicated to arbitration and mediation. These courts will be competent to decide issues such as enforcement of arbitration agreements, motions to set aside arbitral awards, and request for enforcement of arbitral decisions. This decision follows the successful example set by Rio de Janeiro, where in response to a request from the Rio de Janeiro Bar, the business courts are competent to judge cases involving arbitration.

B. CASES

B.1 Recognition of an Arbitration Award Not Enforced at the Seat

In *CIMC Raffles Offshore Limited et al. v. Schahin Holding S.A. et al*,[5] a special chamber of the Brazilian Superior Court of Justice

---

[5] STJ, Special Court. Request for Foreign Arbitral Award Recognition No. 9.880/EX, judged on May 21, 2014.

("STJ") considered the recognition and enforcement of a foreign arbitration award rendered in New York under the rules of the International Centre for Dispute Resolution. The losing party ("Schahin") objected to enforcement in Brazil on the ground that the award had not yet become enforceable in New York, the seat of the arbitration. Schahin alleged that (i) the award had to be ratified by a New York court, and (ii) the award was invalid because Schahin was not properly served.

The STJ unanimously found that the fact that an arbitration award was not enforced at the seat did not prevent recognition in Brazil and granted the *exequatur*. This is a clear example of the pro-arbitration position of the Brazilian court responsible for recognizing arbitral awards.

B.2   Recognition of Unreasoned Arbitration Awards

In *Newedge USA LLC v. Manoel Fernando Garcia*,[6] the STJ considered whether to recognize an arbitral award that did not specify the reasons for the decision. The arbitration was seated in New York and conducted under the rules of ICE Futures US Inc.

Claimant Newedge USA LLC, an entity based in Chicago, prevailed in arbitration against respondents Fluxo-Cane Overseas Limited, a legal entity incorporated in the British Virgin Islands, and Manoel Fernando Garcia, a Brazilian citizen. The arbitral award required respondents to pay compensation for defaulting under a brokerage contract.

The respondents objected to recognition because the arbitral award did not spell out the reasons for the decision. The STJ rejected this argument, ruling that "the reasoning adopted by the arbitration awards follows the standards in force in the country of the seat. The fact that it is concise cannot prevent recognition."

---

[6]   STJ, Special Court. Request for Foreign Arbitral Award Recognition No. 5.692/US, judged on August 20, 2014.

The decision is particularly notable since unreasoned awards have historically been the subject of heated debate in Brazil. Section 26, II of the Brazilian Arbitration Act provides that a statement of the grounds for the decision is a mandatory requirement for domestic arbitration awards, and precedents exist against recognition of unreasoned foreign judgments.[7]

C. LOCAL ARBITRATION INSTITUTIONS

The reenactment of the Brazilian Arbitration Act in 1996 paved the way for the development of arbitration law and institutions. Local institutions have sprouted up to such an extent that a 2011 survey registered over 100 legitimate arbitration institutions across the country. Although users are still advised to exercise caution before resorting to unknown local arbitration institutions, there are many reliable and a few world-class arbitration institutions in Brazil.

This section showcases those Brazilian institutions equipped to handle international cases, which should by no means be interpreted as a derogation of the services of other local arbitration institutions. Specifically, the sections below report on the activities of institutions located in the states of São Paulo (C.1), Rio de Janeiro (C.2), Minas Gerais (C.3), and some other noticeable arbitration centers located across the country (C.4).

[7] Brazilian Supreme Federal Court ("STF"), Request for Foreign Arbitral Award Recognition No. SE 2.424, Reporting Justice Antônio Neder, judged on December 14, 1979. Request for Foreign Arbitral Award Recognition No. SE 2.476, Reporting Justice Antônio Neder, judged on December 19, 1979.

C.1 São Paulo

AMCHAM

The Center for Arbitration and Mediation of the American Chamber of Commerce for Brazil (Amcham)[8] was founded in 2000 and renewed its mediation and arbitration rules in 2014. It currently manages more than 80 arbitration proceedings and has a considerable infrastructure, including rooms for hearings and meetings in São Paulo and in more than 14 other major cities across the country. The Advisory Board of Arbitration and Mediation Center of Amcham gather the most prominent practitioners of arbitration and law firms of the country.

CAM/CCBC

The Center for Arbitration and Mediation of the Chamber of Commerce Brazil-Canada (CAM/CCBC)[9] began its activities in 1973, before the enactment of the Brazilian Arbitration Act, which makes it the most experienced arbitration institution in Brazil. It is the largest of the major arbitration centers in Brazil and has grown significantly over the last years. CAM/CCBC has several exchange agreements weaving a web of cooperation with arbitration centers located in Europe, Latin America, and Asia. Its arbitration roster lists prominent local and international practitioners and its hearing facilities are slick and up to date. The CAM/CCBC secretariat is responsive and capable of managing disputes seated across Brazil and elsewhere with a level of efficiency that earned it the ISO 9001 certification.

In 2012, CAM/CCBC revamped its arbitration rules in line with international standards and predominant practices. As an accolade for the institution's rising international importance, the

---

[8]   http://www.amcham.com.br/

[9]   http://ccbc.org.br/

C. Local Arbitration Institutions

CAM/CCBC arbitration rules will be adopted during the 23rd edition of the Willem C. Vis International Commercial Arbitration Moot in 2015-2016.

CIESP/FIESP

The Chamber of Conciliation, Mediation and Arbitration of São Paulo[10] is the second largest Brazilian arbitration institution, established in 1995 under the patronage of two industries' unions comprising a large stake of Brazilian GDP: the Center of Industries of the State of São Paulo ("CIESP") and the Federation of Industries of the State of São Paulo ("FIESP"). It is steered by two retired Chief Justices of the Brazilian Supreme Court, Sydney Sanches and Ellen Gracie Northfleet, affording substantial prestige and ensuring independence and prudence in handling procedural questions prior to the commencement of arbitration. The secretariat is composed of staff well-versed in arbitration matters and competent in case management, and the center has its own state-of-the-art hearing facility.

CMA/BOVESPA

The Market Arbitration Chamber ("CAM") was instituted under the auspices of the São Paulo Stock, Commodities and Futures Exchange ("BM & F Bovespa").[11] With a new set of rules revised in 2011, this arbitration center offers a specialized forum for settling issues related to business law, with a specific focus on stock market and corporate law. The CAM administers arbitrations arising from disputes between companies whose shares are listed at BM & F Bovespa, as well as disputes between other legal entities and individuals. In order to enter into the

---

10   http://www.camaradearbitragemsp.com.br

11   http://www.bmfbovespa.com.br/pt-br/regulacao/camara-de-arbitragem-do-mercado/ camara-de- arbitragem-do-mercado.aspx?idioma=pt-br

highest listing segment of BM &F Bovespa, *Novo Mercado* (New Market), companies are required to include a commitment to CAM arbitration in their bylaws.

Other Relevant Centers

There are other arbitration institutions providing good arbitration services in São Paulo, especially to Brazilian parties, such as the Arbitration and Mediation Center of the Portuguese Chamber of Commerce in Brazil,[12] the Arbitration and Mediation Chamber of Eurocâmaras,[13] the Arbitration Council of the State of São Paulo - CAESP,[14] and the Mediation and Arbitration Center of the Institute of Engineering.[15]

C.2 Rio de Janeiro

CBMA

Established in 2002 by three trade associations, namely the Commercial Association of Rio de Janeiro ("ACRJ"), the Federation of Industries of Rio de Janeiro ("FIRJAN"), and the National Confederation of Private Insurance and Capitalization Companies ("CNSEG"), the Brazilian Center of Mediation and Arbitration ("CBMA")[16] is the most renowned arbitration chamber of Rio de Janeiro. It has hearing facilities and an efficient secretariat. The arbitrators and mediation rosters include competent and well-reputed practitioners.

---

[12] http://www.camaraportuguesa.com.br/arbitragem/default.asp?idioma=1

[13] http://www.euroarbitragem.com.br/pt/index.php

[14] http://www.caesp.org.br/site/

[15] http://ie.org.br/camara/

[16] http://www.cbma.com.br/. Author Joaquim de Paiva Muniz is one of the arbitration directors of CBMA.

C. Local Arbitration Institutions

FGV

The Fundação Getúlio Vargas Chamber for Conciliation and Arbitration[17] is the mandatory venue for disputes relating to power purchase agreements under the MAE (free energy market).

C.3 Minas Gerais

CAMARB

The Business Arbitration Chamber - Brazil ("CAMARB")[18] was created in 1998, initially linked to the Federation of Industries of the state of Minas Gerais. After a few years, with the association of other entities, it became functionally independent. CAMARB is headquartered in Belo Horizonte, the capital of the industry and natural resources-laden state of Minas Gerais, but it also has facilities in Rio de Janeiro and São Paulo, administering procedures of various natures, such as engineering, construction, and mining disputes. CAMARB also holds an important competition for graduate students with an interest in arbitration, following the same values has the *Vis Moot*.

C.4 Other States

ARBITAC

The Center for Mediation and Arbitration of the Chamber of Commerce of Paraná ("ARBITAC")[19] began as an institute for mediation that later committed to arbitration, with a focus on the areas of industry, national and international commerce, and services. ARBITAC has a reliable steering committee, competent secretariat, and an experienced arbitrators' roster. It is also

---

[17] http://camara.fgv.br/

[18] http://camarb.com.br/

[19] http://www.arbitac.com.br/

committed to promoting debate and events and encouraging the study of mediation and arbitration as effective methods for conflict resolution.

CAMFIEP

The Center for Arbitration and Mediation of the Federation of Industries of Paraná ("CAMFIEP")[20] was established in 2005 in Curitiba with the mission of administering arbitration and mediation proceedings in an efficient, ethical, and confidential manner. It is sponsored by reputable local practitioners and includes respectable practitioners in its roster of arbitrators.

CAMERS

The Chamber of Arbitration, Mediation and Conciliation of the Center of Industries of Rio Grande do Sul ("CAMERS")[21] aims to boost investment in that state by improving the business environment. This institution intends to strengthen the use of alternative dispute resolution mechanisms, but also to streamline and facilitate domestic and international business transactions.

CBMAE

The Brazilian Chamber of Business Arbitration and Mediation ("CBMAE") is an entity of the Confederation of Trade and Business Associations of Brazil ("CACB"), which was established in 2000 via a partnership between the Inter-American Development Bank and a Brazilian public entity, the Brazilian Micro and Small Business Support Service ("Sebrae"), which aims to raise awareness of alternative dispute resolution methods. Focusing mainly on the domestic demand for alternatives to the

---

[20]   http://www.fiepr.org.br/para-empresas/camara-de-arbitragem/

[21]   http://www.camers.org.br/

C. Local Arbitration Institutions

Brazilian courts, CBMAE comprises a network of arbitration and mediation chambers and outposts across Brazil dedicated to extrajudicial conciliation. It cooperates with public policy makers on proposing measures to encourage the use of alternative dispute resolution mechanisms and develops products and services to increase the availability of information technology to local ADR centers.

CANADA

Matthew J. Latella[1] and Matt Saunders[2]

A. LEGISLATION, TRENDS AND TENDENCIES

A.1 Legislation

International arbitration in Canada is, for the most part, a matter of provincial jurisdiction. Each province and territory has enacted legislation adopting the UNCITRAL Model Law, occasionally with slight variations, as the foundational law for international arbitration. Canada's federal parliament has also adopted a commercial arbitration code based on the UNCITRAL Model Law, which is applicable when the federal government or one of its agencies is a party to an arbitration agreement or where a matter involves an area of exclusive federal jurisdiction under Canada's constitution. In addition, each of the provinces and the federal government has, either directly or indirectly, adopted the New York Convention.

In 2011, the Uniform Law Conference of Canada (the "Conference") appointed a working group to formulate recommendations to update Canada's laws relating to international commercial arbitration in accordance with the 2006 UNCITRAL Model Law amendments. The report was released on August 18, 2012, and was followed by a discussion paper in January, 2013, which set forth recommendations concerning the

---

[1]   Matthew Latella is a Partner in Baker & McKenzie's Toronto Office, and the head of the Office's International Arbitration Practice Group.

[2]   Matt Saunders is an Associate in Baker & McKenzie's Toronto Office, and a member of the Firm's Global Dispute Resolution Practice Group. His practice focuses on commercial litigation in the areas of fraud, white collar crime, class actions, and arbitration.

preparation and implementation of a new Uniform International Commercial Arbitration Act (the "Uniform Act"). At the Conference's August 2013 meeting, the working group presented and received comments on drafts of the proposed Uniform Act. The working group subsequently released a final report and commentary in March, 2014. The Conference is expected to adopt the amended Uniform Act. Thereafter, the Uniform Act will be open for adoption into federal and provincial legislation.

A.2 Trends and Tendencies

Canada remains a jurisdiction that strongly supports international arbitration. The past few years have been marked by increased awareness of international arbitration, the promotion and utilization of arbitration for international commercial matters, and the promotion of Canada as an ideal place to arbitrate international commercial disputes.

In general, Canadian courts are increasingly applying the UNCITRAL Model Law and the general principles of arbitration to hold parties to the bargains they have made through enforceable arbitration agreements. Where an arbitration agreement exists between parties, and it is arguable that the arbitration agreement is valid and covers the subject-matter of the dispute, Canadian courts have shown a willingness to stay judicial proceedings in favor of arbitration.

Courts are now also being called upon to address the narrow issue of interim relief. Although arbitrators are given broad powers to grant interim relief, courts have demonstrated an inclination to make interim orders for injunctions, and for the detention, preservation and inspection of property, which are consistent with the UNCITRAL Model Law.

Unlike domestic arbitration awards in Canada (which generally may be appealed, with leave, on a question of law), international arbitral awards are final and cannot be appealed. Consistent with the New York Convention, the powers of Canadian courts are limited to a judicial review of whether the tribunal lacked or exceeded its jurisdiction in making an award, or where there was a lack of proper conduct and procedure during the proceeding.

B. CASES

B.1 Limits on Review of Arbitral Decisions Involving Contractual Interpretation

On August 1, 2014, the Supreme Court of Canada ("SCC") released its decision in *Sattva Capital Corp. v. Creston Moly Corp.,*[3] which limited the circumstances where a court may review arbitral decisions involving contractual interpretation. While *Sattva* was a case involving the review of a domestic arbitral award under different legislation than applies to international arbitral awards, it remains significant, as Canada's top court provided a strong endorsement of deference generally to findings of commercial arbitrators, as the original triers of fact.

The case involved a dispute over the date that should be used to determine the price of certain shares, and thus the number of shares to which Sattva was entitled. During the nearly two-month span between the proposed dates, the price of the shares had increased from 15 to 70 cents, resulting in a disparity of nine million shares owing, depending upon which of the parties' competing contractual interpretations was adopted. After the arbitrator found in favour of Sattva, the respondent, Creston, sought leave to appeal the arbitrator's decision pursuant to s.31(2) of British Columbia's Arbitration Act[4] (the "BC

---

[3] 2014 SCC 43.

[4] RSBC 1996, c. 55.

Arbitration Act"), but was initially denied leave by the court of first instance, the BC Supreme Court. However, Creston was successful in appealing this decision before the BC Court of Appeal. The BC Supreme Court then heard the merits of the appeal and upheld the arbitrator's award in favor of Sattva. Creston appealed again and was successful before the BC Court of Appeal in having the decision overturned.

After granting Sattva leave to appeal the decision of the BC Court of Appeal, the SCC restored the decision of the BC Supreme Court in favor of Sattva, noting that appeals from commercial arbitration decisions are narrowly circumscribed under the BC Arbitration Act. For leave to be granted from a commercial arbitral award under s.31(2), the appeal must be on a question of law alone and cannot involve questions of mixed fact and law. The court held that contractual interpretation was a determination of mixed fact and law. Generally, courts use a practical, common-sense approach that considers the contract's factual matrix in order to determine the rights of the parties to the contract. Contractual interpretation was therefore distinguished from questions of law, which have the ability to determine rights among parties beyond those immediately before the court.

The SCC held that the standard of reasonableness, which affords a higher level of deference to the original trier of fact, will almost always apply to commercial arbitrations conducted pursuant to the BC Arbitration Act. Exceptions to this approach would include rare circumstances involving constitutional questions or question of law of central importance to the Canadian legal system as a whole, which may be outside of the adjudicator's expertise. Given that the statutory test for granting judicial review of domestic arbitral awards is easier to satisfy than the test for judicial review of international awards, this deferential decision of Canada's highest court to an arbitrator in a domestic arbitration reinforces Canada's status as an arbitration-friendly jurisdiction.

B.2 Use of Mareva Injunction to Secure an International Arbitration Award

In *Sociedade-de-Fomento Industrial Private Ltd. v. Pakistan Steel Mills (Private) Ltd.*,[5] the British Columbia Court of Appeal considered, for the first time, whether a *Mareva* injunction could be used to secure an international arbitration award, in circumstances where the parties had little connection to the enforcing jurisdiction and where the arbitration award could have been enforced elsewhere.

Sociedade-de-Fomento Industrial Private Limited ("SFI"), an iron ore mining and exporting company based in India, obtained an ICC award against Pakistan Steel Mills Corporation (Private) Limited ("PSM") for almost USD9 million (the "ICC Award"), but faced challenges in its enforcement. After learning that PSM was making arrangements to import coal from Canada, SFI obtained an *ex parte Mareva* injunction preventing PSM from removing the coal from the jurisdiction without first paying security for the award into the BC court.

Following a 30-day detention of the coal vessel with PSM posting the security, during which time SFI obtained orders appointing a receiver to market the coal for sale and increasing the amount of security PSM was to post, PSM eventually posted the requisite security, and the vessel departed for Pakistan. SFI then obtained judgment against PSM for the full amount of the award, plus post-award interest. PSM subsequently applied for an order that the *Mareva* had been wrongly granted and seeking a declaration that SFI should be liable for damages stemming

---

[5]   2014 BCCA 205.

from the detention of the coal. The chambers judge held that SFI was liable for damages in an amount to be determined, based on her conclusion that SFI had not made full and frank disclosure to the *ex parte* judge of its ability to enforce its award in Pakistan. This conclusion was based, in part, on the chambers judge's conclusion that the limited association of either party with BC made the ability of SFI to enforce its award elsewhere and, in particular, in Pakistan, a material fact that should have been disclosed to the *ex parte* judge who originally granted the *Mareva*.

SFI appealed this ruling to the BC Court of Appeal, which unanimously concluded that the chambers judge had erred in failing to properly apply BC's international arbitration legislation, which incorporates the New York Convention and the UNCITRAL Model Law.[6] These laws require BC courts to recognize and enforce international arbitration awards in the same manner as domestic awards. The BC Court of Appeal held that the chambers judge erred in making an implicit assumption that there was an onus on SFI to turn first to Pakistan's courts because of the parties' limited association with British Columbia. Further, the court held that the chambers judge failed to properly address the fact that a real and substantial connection is legislatively presumed to exist in a proceeding to enforce an international arbitral award, and that her *de facto forum non conveniens* analysis applied to the *Mareva* stage of the proceeding was "illogical". Moreover, since the New York Convention expressly contemplates an action by a petitioner to enforce a foreign arbitral award, the court held that it would not be logical to recognize the presumed jurisdictional connection for the final judgment, but disregard it for interlocutory

---

[6]   *International Commercial Arbitration Act*, RSBC. 1996, c. 233; *Foreign Arbitral Awards Act* RSBC 1996, c 154.

purposes. The BC Court of Appeal further held that the availability of enforcement proceedings in a foreign jurisdiction did not imply an onus on the party to first look to that foreign jurisdiction. In addition, the court concluded there had been no material non-disclosure, noting that SFI had not said it was not possible to enforce its award in Pakistan, but that it would be challenging, which implies it could have been enforced, but with some difficulty. On December 18, 2014, PSM's application for leave to appeal the BC Court of Appeal's decision to the SCC was dismissed, with costs.

B.3 Enforceability of an Award Subject to Review by the SEC

In *New York Stock Exchange LLC v. Orbixa Technologies Inc.,*[7] the Ontario Court of Appeal unanimously upheld the reasons, conclusions and disposition of the Ontario Superior Court of Justice when it allowed an application by the New York Stock Exchange ("NYSE") to enforce a judgment recognizing a New York arbitration award.

Orbixa Technologies, Inc. ("Orbixa"), a company headquartered in Toronto, entered into a contract with the NYSE to distribute its information to third-party users. The contract also included an arbitration clause that provided for any claim under it to be resolved through arbitration in New York. Following a dispute between the parties over Orbixa's designation of third-party users and NYSE's fees, the NYSE gave notice to terminate the contract and issued Orbixa an invoice for unpaid fees. Orbixa submitted the matter to arbitration and sought an injunction to prevent the NYSE from terminating the contract and for relief from NYSE's fees. Following a hearing, the arbitrator dismissed all of Orbixa's claims and declared that the NYSE could

---

[7]   2014 ONCA 219.

terminate its contract. Orbixa was ordered to pay NYSE in excess of USD3.5 million within 30 days (the "Award").

After failing to pay the Award within 30 days, Orbixa sought a review of the arbitrator's decision by the U.S. Securities and Exchange Commission (the "SEC"). Prior to the SEC's issuing a decision, the NYSE brought a motion before the Ontario Superior Court of Justice to enforce the Award in Ontario.

The NYSE submitted that, pursuant to the contract, the International Commercial Arbitration Act[8] ("ICAA") and the UNCITRAL Model Law, the NYSE was entitled to have the Award recognized as binding and enforceable in Ontario. Orbixa argued that, with an application pending before the SEC, the court should dismiss the matter as premature or alternatively refuse to enforce the Award as a matter of public policy.

One of the grounds provided by the UNCITRAL Model Law upon which a court may refuse to recognize or enforce an arbitral award is if it is not binding. Article 34(3) of the Model Law imposes a three-month limitation period on a party making such a challenge (i.e. an application for setting aside the award cannot be made after three months have passed from the date on which the applicant receives the award). The court reviewed the wording of the Model Law and determined that the relevant date to consider whether the application for enforcement is premature is not when the submission for recognition or enforcement is made, but, rather, when the matter comes before the court.

Accordingly, the court held that, as the date of the hearing was beyond the three-month period where Orbixa could seek a review, the award was binding. The court also found that its

---

[8]   RSO 1990, c I.9.

enforcement would not violate public policy, since Orbixa was not denied the principles of justice and fairness in a fundamental way when it was given a full hearing in New York. The court allowed the application and issued a judgment recognizing the award. Orbixa was required to pay the Canadian dollar equivalent of the Award, along with interest and costs. Orbixa's appeal to the Court of Appeal for Ontario was dismissed with costs.

C. LOCAL ARBITRATION INSTITUTIONS

C.1 International Centre for Dispute Resolution ("ICDR")

Background

Established in 1996 as the global component of the AAA, the ICDR provides conflict management services in more than 80 countries, including Canada.

Types of Disputes Handled

The ICDR offers a variety of services to handle any dispute, including mediation, early neutral evaluation, fact-finding, dispute review boards, and arbitration.

Numbers of Disputes Handled

No statistics are available.

Provisions on Confidentiality of Arbitration

Subject to applicable law, all information divulged during the arbitration will remain confidential.

Availability of Expedited Procedures

Expedited procedures apply to arbitrations where no claims exceed CAD250,000.00 exclusive of interest and the costs of arbitration. The parties may agree to the application of the expedited procedures on matters of any claim size.

Consolidation of Disputes between the Same Parties and Joinder of Third Parties

Parties who wish to join an additional party can submit to the administrator a notice against the additional party. No additional parties can be joined after the appointment of an arbitrator unless all the parties, including the additional party, agree. At the request of a party, the administrator may appoint a consolidation arbitrator who will have the power to consolidate two or more arbitrations.

Time Limits for Rendering of the Award

Parties who elect to pursue the expedited procedure will receive an award within 30 calendar days of the close of the hearing or the date established for the receipt of the parties' final statements and proofs. Unless specified by law, determined by the administrator, or otherwise agreed to by the parties, the final award will be made no later than 30 days from the date of the closing of the hearing.

Fee Structure

Fee structure information is available at https://www.icdr.org/icdr/ShowPDF?doc=ADRSTAGE2025294.

Treatment of Costs of the Arbitration

The arbitral tribunal may fix costs in the award and allocate them among the parties in a manner it deems reasonable.

Special or Unusual Features (If Any)

Not applicable.

C. Local Arbitration Institutions

Recent Developments (If Any)

As of January 2015, the ICDR provides dispute resolution services across Canada.

C.2 Canadian Commercial Arbitration Centre ("CCAC")

Background

Based in Quebec, the CCAC is a nonprofit organization that has provided alternative dispute resolution services for over 25 years.

Types of Disputes Handled

The CCAC provides the following arbitration and alternative dispute resolution services: international arbitration; general commercial arbitration; commercial conciliation and mediation; conciliation and mediation in franchise matters; specialized arbitration for disputes arising between members of the Investment Industry Regulatory Organization of Canada and their clients; arbitration for new residential buildings; and motor vehicle arbitration.

Numbers of Disputes Handled

No statistics are available.

Provisions on Confidentiality of Arbitration

Not applicable.

Availability of Expedited Procedures

Expedited proceedings are available for international arbitration. The applicable expedited rules of procedure are available at http://www.ccac-adr.org/en/arbitrage-international.php#procedure _acceleree.

Consolidation of Disputes between the Same Parties and Joinder of Third Parties

Not applicable.

Time Limits for Rendering of the Award

Not applicable.

Fee Structure

Fee structure information is available at http://www.ccac-adr.org/en/tarifs.php.

Treatment of Costs of the Arbitration

The treatment of costs will differ depending on the type of arbitration sought. In an international arbitration, the tribunal will fix the costs and decide which of the parties will bear them or in what proportion will they be shared.

Special or Unusual Features (If Any)

Not applicable.

Recent Developments (If Any)

Not applicable.

C.3 British Columbia International Commercial Arbitration Centre ("BCICAC")

Background

The BCICAC was established in 1986, and is a nonprofit organization located in Vancouver, British Columbia. It provides a wide range of alternative dispute resolution services and maintains panels of both international and domestic experts.

C. Local Arbitration Institutions

Types of Disputes Handled

The BCICAC provides the following services: general domestic and international commercial arbitration; mediation; resolution of domain name disputes; and resolution of underinsured motorists' disputes.

Numbers of Disputes Handled

No statistics are available.

Provisions on Confidentiality of Arbitration

Under the BCICAC's Domestic Commercial Arbitration Rules of Procedure, all hearings, meetings and communications between the parties, the arbitration tribunal and the center are private and confidential, unless otherwise agreed to. Similarly, under the BCICAC's International Commercial Arbitration Rules of Procedure, all matters related to the arbitration or award are confidential and cannot be disclosed except as required by law.

Availability of Expedited Procedures

Domestic Commercial Arbitration Shorter Rules of Procedure are available for expedited proceedings. A copy of these rules can be found at http://bcicac.com/arbitration/rules-of-procedure/domestic-commercial-arbitration-shorter-rules-of-procedure/.

Consolidation of Disputes between the Same Parties and Joinder of Third Parties

Not applicable.

Time Limits for Rendering of the Award

Not applicable.

Fee Structure

Fee structure information is available at http://bcicac.com/resources/fee-schedule/.

Treatment of Costs of the Arbitration

Under the Domestic Rules, the arbitration tribunal will determine liability for costs and may apportion them as they see appropriate. The International Rules allow the arbitrator to fix the costs to a reasonable amount in the final arbitral award.

Special or Unusual Features (If Any)

Not applicable.

Recent Developments (If Any)

Not applicable.

CHILE

Antonio Ortúzar[1] and Rodrigo Díaz de Valdés[2]

A. LEGISLATION, TRENDS AND TENDENCIES

A.1. Legislative Framework

Arbitration in Chile remains governed primarily by the Organic Code of Courts ("OCC"), the Code of Civil Procedure ("CCP") and Law 19.971 on International Commercial Arbitration (the "ICA Law").[3] Chile is also a signatory to the New York Convention, the Panama Convention and the ICSID Convention. Additionally, most of the free trade agreements as well as the BITs that Chile has entered into provide for specific arbitration mechanisms to settle disputes arising from their application. There was no significant legislative change in arbitration law in Chile during 2014.

Likewise, there have been no major changes with respect to enforcing awards. For a foreign arbitral award to be recognized and enforced in Chile, it must be subject to an *exequatur* procedure as set forth in article 246 of the CCP. This procedure

---

[1] Antonio Ortúzar is Of Counsel in the Santiago office of Baker & McKenzie and a member of the Dispute Resolution and Antitrust Practice Groups. He is widely experienced in civil, commercial and constitutional litigation as well as in arbitration. He also serves as arbitrator at the Center of Arbitration and the Chamber Commerce of Santiago.

[2] Rodrigo Díaz de Valdés is a Principal in the Santiago office of Baker & McKenzie and a member of the Dispute Resolution and Antitrust Practice Groups. He is widely experienced in civil, commercial and constitutional litigation as well as in arbitration. He also serves as arbitrator at the Center of Arbitration and the Chamber Commerce of Santiago.

[3] The ICA Law is based entirely on the UNCITRAL Model Law.

is heard by the Supreme Court which, without re-examining the merits of the case, will generally grant the *exequatur,* provided that the arbitral award is "authentic" and "effective" and complies with the requirements set forth in Articles 35 and 36 of the ICA Law, as well as the requirements set forth in the New York Convention (and, when applicable, the Panama Convention).

A.2. Trends and Tendencies

There were no significant trends to report in arbitration in Chile in 2014.

B. CASES

This year, there are three cases relating to the application of the ICA Law that are worthy of discussion. One case concerns an *exequatur* for the enforcement of a foreign arbitral award, the second concerns a motion of nullity of an international business arbitral award, and the third concerns a complaint appeal (*recurso de queja*) to challenge an arbitral award in the context of an international arbitration.

B.1 Enforcement of Award Issued in Barcelona, Spain[4]

This case concerns the enforcement of an arbitration award issued by an arbitrator in an arbitration constituted in Barcelona. The Provincial Assembly of Barcelona issued a judgment rejecting a request to nullify the award. The losing party opposed enforcement of the award in Chile, arguing that it violated the Chilean public order because the composition of the arbitral tribunal was not in conformity with the agreement of the parties. The contract established that the differences in interpretation should be resolved by an arbitrator appointed by the "Chamber

---

[4]   *Laboratorios Kian S.A.* (Supreme Court, 2014, docket No. 1270-2014).

of Commerce of Barcelona". In the event, the award was rendered by an arbitrator appointed by the "Consulate of the Sea of the Chamber of Commerce, Industry and Navigation of Barcelona". The losing party also complained that the arbitrator determined that his jurisdiction extended to resolving discrepancies in the interpretation of the contract, but not those related to its implementation. The losing party also argued that because the proceeding concerned a judgment from a Spanish court, *exequatur* under the Law of International Arbitration and the New York Convention was not the appropriate procedure because these applied exclusively to arbitration awards.

The Supreme Court dismissed all of the challenges and granted the *exequatur*. Regarding the allegation that *exequatur* of the judgment of the Provincial Assembly of Barcelona was not appropriate, the Supreme Court stated that although the judgment was issued by a civil court, it formed an indivisible unit with the award of the Arbitrator.

Regarding the other allegations, the Supreme Court reiterated the principle that the purpose of the *exequatur* procedure is to verify compliance with certain minimum requirements and not to reconsider the merits of the case. The challenge was seen as an effort to ask the court to re-examine the arbitrator's interpretation of his jurisdiction under the arbitration clause. It was, therefore, rejected.

B.2 Expert Reports within Tribunal Discretion; Foreign Lawyers Permitted[5]

In this case the appellant sought to nullify an international commercial arbitration award for violation of the public law of

---

[5] *Constructora EMEX limitada v. Organización Europea para la Investigación Astronómica en el Hemisferio Sur* (Court of Appeals of Santiago, 2014, docket No. 9211-2012).

Chile. More specifically, the appellant alleged that there was a due process violation because the arbitrator refused to permit an expert report that the appellant considered was crucial evidence. The appellant also complained that the tribunal allowed one of the parties to use foreign lawyers to conduct the arbitration in Chile.

The Court of Appeals rejected the nullity motion. It explained that both the CCP and the ICA Law establish an expert report as one method of evidence which may be requested by the parties, but it was only mandatory when expressly mandated by law; otherwise, use of an expert report was within the discretion of the tribunal.

The court also rejected the argument that lawyers were not allowed to conduct an arbitration in Chile, noting that the ICA Law does not require that an arbitration may be conducted only by Chilean lawyers. Furthermore, the appellant accepted the actions of such agents throughout the arbitration without making any objection, so the court considered it inappropriate to then seek annulment on that ground.

B.3 Nullity Motion Is the Only Procedure for Challenging an Award[6]

In this case, the Court of Appeals of Santiago dismissed motion to nullify the award under Article 34 of the ICA Law. The losing party then brought a "complaint appeal" before the Supreme Court. The Supreme Court explained that Article 34 of the ICA Law establishes the nullity motion as the only procedure for challenging an award and, therefore, dismissed the appeal as inadmissible. The Supreme Court also noted that under Article 63 of the Organic Code of Courts, which regulates the complaint appeal, only the Court of Appeals—not the Supreme Court—may resolve a complaint appeal.

---

[6] *Constructora EMEX limitada v. Ministros de la Corte de Apelaciones de Santiago* (Supreme Court, 2014, docket No. 8699-2014).

C. LOCAL ARBITRATION INSTITUTIONS[7]

C.1 Arbitration and Mediation Center of the Santiago Chamber of Commerce ("AMC")

Background

The AMC is a nonprofit institution founded in 1992 by the Chamber of Commerce of Santiago with the support of the Bar Association of Chile and various branches of the Confederation of Production and Trade in Chile.

Types of Disputes Handled

The AMC handles arbitration and mediation for resolving domestic and international disputes.

Numbers of Disputes Handled

Since its creation in 1992, the AMC has handled more than 2,000 cases.

Provisions on Confidentiality of Arbitration

The process is confidential. Only the parties, the arbitrator and the AMC have access to it, unless both parties agree otherwise.

Availability of Expedited Procedures

The AMC regulations do not establish special expedited procedures. Because, however, the will of the parties prevails, they can set their own rules of procedure.

---

[7] There are other regional arbitration institutions such as Valparaiso Arbitration and Mediation Center and Bio Arbitration and Mediation Center.

Consolidation of Disputes between the Same Parties and Joinder of Third Parties.

The AMC regulations do not have specific provisions regarding consolidation. However, the Tribunal is allowed to accept the joinder of third parties or the consolidation of cases between the same parties according to the general rules of the Code of Civil Procedure.

Time Limits for Rendering of the Award

The arbitral tribunal must issue a final decision within the six months from the notification of the lawsuit for a domestic arbitration, or within six months from the answer of the lawsuit (or expiry of the deadline to do) for an international arbitration. This period may be extended for up to six months by the arbitral tribunal if deemed necessary.

Fee Structure

The fees depend on three factors: the amount in dispute, the nature of the arbitration, and the number of arbitrators. The minimum arbitrator fee in domestic arbitration is 50 tax units. An administration fee of 10% of the arbitrator fee is also charged, subject to a minimum of 50 tax units. The administration fee must be paid by the parties in equal proportion, notwithstanding the eventual award regarding costs. In international arbitration, the minimum arbitrator fee is USD2,500, and the minimum administration fee is also USD2,500.

For mediations, the mediator fee is 7 tax units per hour of mediation, with a minimum of 14 tax units, and the administration fee is 10% of the mediator fee, also with a minimum of 14 tax units.

C. Local Arbitration Institutions

Treatment of Costs of the Arbitration

The costs of the arbitration shall be borne by the losing party unless the tribunal decides to prorate them between the parties considering the circumstances. However, the parties may establish at the beginning of the arbitration that costs will be shared equally.

Special or Unusual Features (If Any)

The administration of arbitration proceedings is done through a online system called E-CAM. This software enables the creation, maintenance and monitoring of national and international arbitration proceedings online with interaction of arbitrators, parties and the AMC.

Recent Developments (If Any)

In September 2014, the AMC signed a cooperation agreement with the Chilean Chamber of Construction in order to develop the implementation of Dispute Boards. The Dispute Board is an alternative system for early resolution of disputes, under which a panel of independent experts helps the parties to resolve their disputes through informal assistance and issuing recommendations or decisions, according to the model adopted. It usually operates in contracts with certain technical content, where the timely resolution of any dispute is a particularly attractive advantage for the parties.

C.2 National Center of Arbitration of Chile ("NCA")

Background

The NCA was created in 2007 by independent professionals to constitute an alternative to institutional arbitration in Chile.

Types of Disputes Handled

The NCA handles arbitration and mediation for resolving domestic disputes.

Numbers of Disputes Handled

Since its creation in 2007, the NCA has handled 102 cases.

Provisions on Confidentiality of Arbitration

The process is confidential; thus, only the parties, the arbitrator and the NCA have access to it. The Code of Ethics of the NCA states that the arbitrator shall keep confidential all matters relating to arbitration. Violation can lead to expulsion from the list of arbitrators.

Availability of Expedited Procedures

The NCA regulations establish three procedures: regular, abbreviated and a special abbreviated procedure for arbitration which does not exceed 700 tax units. In the latter two procedures, certain phases are omitted, and there are tighter deadlines and limited possibilities for appeal.

Consolidation of Disputes between the Same Parties and Joinder of Third Parties

The NCA regulations do not have specific provisions regarding consolidation. However, the Tribunal is allowed to accept the inclusion of third parties or the consolidation of cases between the same parties according to the general rules of the Code of Civil Procedure.

Time Limits for Rendering of the Award

In the regular procedure, the arbitrator should render the award within six months from the beginning of the arbitration; in the abbreviated procedure, within 60 days from the beginning of the arbitration; and, in the special abbreviated procedure, within five days from the answer of the lawsuit or from the evidence hearing if there was such a hearing.

Fee Structure

The fee structure depends on the monetary value of the claim. The maximum arbitrator fee is 28,250 tax units. The NCA charges an administrative fee equal to 10% of the arbitral fees, with a minimum of 10 tax units.

Treatment of Costs of the Arbitration

In the final award, the arbitrator must determine the party responsible for the costs. A party who has been fully defeated without having a plausible reason for litigating must always be ordered to pay the costs.

Special or Unusual Features (If Any)

The NCA has established a pro bono arbitration system to assist people in need in cases that Chilean law considers to be subject to binding arbitration.

Recent Developments (If Any)

Not applicable.

CHINA

James Kwan,[1] Peng Shen[2] and Ying Wu[3]

A. LEGISLATION, TRENDS AND TENDENCIES

A.1 Legislation

International arbitration in mainland China continues to be governed by the PRC Arbitration Law effective on September 1, 1995 and amended on August 27, 2009; the Interpretation of the Supreme People's Court concerning Some Issues on Application of the Arbitration Law of the People's Republic of China effective on December 31, 2008; the PRC Civil Procedure Law amended on August 31, 2012; and the corresponding judicial interpretations. No legislative amendments were made in 2014 with respect to international arbitration.

A.2 Trends and Tendencies

The Shanghai International Arbitration Center (SHIAC) has established the China (Shanghai) Pilot Free Trade Zone Court of Arbitration in China (Shanghai) Pilot Free Trade Zone (the

---

[1] James Kwan is a Partner in the Dispute Resolution Group of Baker & McKenzie in Hong Kong, where he leads the arbitration practice. He specialises in international commercial arbitration, with a focus on M&A, technology, sale of goods, infrastructure, and energy disputes; and has a range of international experience, having represented clients in arbitrations in Hong Kong, Asia, the Middle East, U.S. and Europe under the major institutional rules.

[2] Shen Peng is a Consultant in the Dispute Resolution Group of Baker & McKenzie in Beijing. He represents international and domestic clients in domestic and international disputes in China. Prior to working in private practice, Shen Peng was a judge of the Beijing People's Court.

[3] Ying Wu is an International Associate in the Dispute Resolution Group of Baker & McKenzie in Beijing. She represents international and domestic clients in domestic and international disputes in China.

"FTZ") to perform arbitration services. Correspondingly, SHIAC has also formulated the China (Shanghai) Pilot Free Trade Zone Arbitration Rules for the purpose of resolving disputes in connection with the FTZ, which became effective on May 1, 2014. Specifically, the FTZ's arbitration mechanism introduces the following reforms which are different from the SHIAC Arbitration Rules: (1) the FTZ Arbitration Rules introduce an emergency arbitrator system; (2) parties can enter into a hybrid dispute resolution arrangement, in which arbitration is first preceded by a mediation process for identifying the parties' respective demands and possible solutions. If mediation fails to resolve the dispute, a tribunal is then empowered to render a decision and issue an award; (3) the FTZ Rules allow consolidation of related arbitrations or arbitrations involving the same or similar subject matter into a single arbitration if all relevant parties agree; and (4) parties to disputes concerning sums of money greater than RMB100,000 but less than RMB1,000,000 can apply for a summary procedure that is both faster than conventional arbitration and entails lower service fees.

In addition, SHIAC established the Shanghai International Aviation Arbitration Court in August 2014. It has recently updated its arbitration rules to reflect this development.

B. CASES

B.1. CIETAC/UNCITRAL Hybrid Arbitration Clause Valid

In 2014, a PRC court for the first time confirmed the validity of a hybrid arbitration clause, i.e. an arbitration administered by CIETAC using the UNCITRAL Arbitration Rules.[4]

---

[4] Case No.: (2012) Zheyongzhongquezi No.4 by Zhejiang Ningbo Intermediate People's Court.

B. Cases

INVISTA Technologies Sàrl (the "Licensor"), an affiliate of INVISTA Sàrl, entered into two technology licensing agreements with Zhejiang Yisheng Petrochemical Co. Ltd., a Chinese petroleum company (the "Licensee"). The agreements provided for disputes to be resolved by arbitration, which "shall take place at CIETAC" using the UNCITRAL Arbitration Rules.

In July 2012, the Licensor commenced arbitration against the Licensee. The Licensee applied to the Ningbo Intermediate People's Court arguing that the arbitration clauses were invalid because they referred to ad hoc arbitration, as the UNCITRAL Arbitration Rules are commonly used for ad hoc arbitration. Ad hoc arbitration is not recognized under PRC law. The Licensee also argued that the phrase "shall take place at CIETAC" should not be interpreted as arbitration administered by CIETAC.

The Ningbo Intermediate People's Court reported this case to the Zhejiang Higher People's Court. After consulting the Supreme People's Court (the "SPC"), Zhejiang Higher People's Court confirmed that the arbitration clauses were valid. The Ningbo Intermediate People's Court finally held that given CIETAC's involvement, the arbitration agreement in dispute does not amount to ad hoc arbitration.

In practice, CIETAC has administered several arbitrations under the UNCITRAL Arbitration Rules. However, this is the first time the PRC courts have decided on the validity of such a hybrid arbitration agreement.

B.2. KCAB Arbitration Clause Invalid

The Beijing No. 2 Intermediate People's Court has confirmed that an arbitration clause referring to a foreign arbitration institution is invalid if the contract contains no foreign-related factor.[5]

---

[5] Case No. (2013) Erzhongmintezi 10670 by Beijing No. 2 Intermediate People's Court.

A domestic company signed a cooperation agreement with a wholly foreign invested company ("WFOE") in 2007. Such companies are considered to be domestic under PRC law; investment or ownership by a foreign company does not make it foreign. The agreement was signed and performed in Beijing. The agreement referred to arbitration by the Korean Commercial Arbitration Board ("KCAB").

Disputes arose between the parties. The WFOE commenced arbitration before the KCAB. The domestic company filed a counterclaim. In 2013, KCAB rendered its award in favor of the domestic company. The domestic company sought enforcement of the award before the Beijing No. 2 Intermediate People's Court.

On January 20, 2014, Beijing No. 2 Intermediate People's Court rejected the domestic company's application. The court held that PRC law does not permit parties to submit a contractual dispute without a foreign-related factor to a foreign arbitration institution or foreign ad hoc arbitration, and therefore the arbitration clause in the cooperation agreement was found to be in violation of PRC law and thus invalid.

B.3. SHIAC Has Jurisdiction Where "CIETAC Shanghai Sub-Commission" Chosen

The Shanghai No. 2 Intermediate People's Court rendered a ruling on December 31, 2014, confirming that the Shanghai International Arbitration Center (SHIAC), as an independent arbitral institution, has jurisdiction over arbitrations where parties have agreed in their arbitration clause to arbitrate before the "China International Economic and Trade Arbitration Commission Shanghai Sub-Commission".[6] As indicated in SHIAC's post dated December 31, 2014, the Shanghai No. 2

---

[6] Case No.: (2012) Hu Er Zhong Min Ren (Zhong Xie) Zi Di 5 Hao.

Intermediate People's Court's decision has been approved by the SPC according to the SPC's Notice dated September 4, 2013.[7]

The share purchase agreement in dispute provided for disputes to be submitted to the "China International Economic and Trade Arbitration Commission Shanghai Sub-Commission for arbitration". Due to the conflict between CIETAC and the former CIETAC Shanghai Sub-Commission (now SHIAC), one party commenced arbitration before CIETAC on November 21, 2012. Both parties subsequently applied to Shanghai No. 2 Intermediate People's Court to determine the validity of the arbitration agreement.

The Shanghai No. 2 Intermediate People's Court considered that CIETAC Shanghai Sub-Commission was established through a formal procedure and legitimately registered in the Bureau of Justice of Shanghai Municipality and that it had been officially renamed "Shanghai International Economic and Trade Arbitration Commission"/"Shanghai International Arbitration Center". Therefore, SHIAC, as the agreed arbitral institution, had the power to arbitrate and render arbitral awards based upon the arbitration clause in dispute.

C. LOCAL ARBITRATION INSTITUTIONS

Before the adoption of the PRC Arbitration Law in 1995, CIETAC and the China Maritime Arbitration Center ("CMAC") were the only arbitral institutions in the PRC that were qualified to administer foreign-related cases. Following the entry into force of the PRC Arbitration Law, more than 200 domestic arbitral institutions have been established in the PRC. Domestic arbitral institutions are now able to hear international cases,

---

[7]   http://www.shiac.org/NewsDetails.aspx?tid=7&nid=844.

considerably diminishing the traditional distinction between these two forms of arbitral institutions.

C.1 China International Economic and Trade Arbitration Commission ("CIETAC")

Background

CIETAC, established in April 1956, is the largest arbitration institution in China. With headquarters in Beijing, CIETAC has a South China Office (in Shenzhen), Shanghai Office, Tianjin International Economic and Financial Arbitration Center (Tianjin Sub-Commission) and Southwest Sub-Commission in Chongqing, as well as a branch office in Hong Kong.

CIETAC awards have been enforced in more than 140 countries. Nearly 20,000 arbitrations have been concluded involving parties from more than 70 countries and regions outside mainland China.

CIETAC's new arbitration rules (the "2015 Rules") come into effect on January 1, 2015. The 2015 Rules amend CIETAC's current rules implemented on May 1, 2012 (the "2012 Rules") and bring China's arbitration regime closer to international practices.

Types of Disputes Handled

CIETAC can accept a wide range of cases, including international, foreign-related and domestic disputes.

Numbers of Disputes Handled

CIETAC has not published its case statistics for 2014. The number of disputes handled by CIETAC was 1043 in 2013, 720 in 2012, 1282 in 2011, 1382 in 2010 and 1329 in 2009.

C. Local Arbitration Institutions

Provisions on Confidentiality of Arbitration

CIETAC arbitration proceedings are confidential. The parties and their representatives, the arbitrators, the witnesses, the interpreters, the experts, the appraisers appointed by the arbitral tribunal and other relevant persons must not disclose any substantive or procedural matters relating to the case. The arbitration hearings must be conducted in private, but the existence of the arbitration, the award, the materials created and documents produced in the arbitration are not covered by the Rules.

Availability of Expedited Procedures

Under the 2012 Rules, the summary procedure applies to cases in which the amount in dispute does not exceed RMB2 million or as agreed by the parties regardless of the amount in dispute. This amount is increased to RMB5 million in the 2015 Rules.

Consolidation of Disputes between the Same Parties and Joinder of Third Parties

The 2012 Rules generally provide that CIETAC can decide to consolidate two or more arbitration cases after obtaining all parties' agreement, but are silent on the joinder of third parties. The 2015 Rules provide for the joinder of parties upon filing a request to CIETAC on the basis that the arbitration agreement on its face binds the party. The CIETAC Arbitration Court determines the application if the tribunal has not been constituted. The 2015 Rules provide for consolidation of arbitrations if (1) all claims in the arbitration are made under the same arbitration agreement; or (2) the claims in the arbitration are made under multiple arbitration agreements that are identical or compatible and the arbitrations involve the same parties as well as legal relationships "of the same nature" or multiple contracts consisting of a principal contract and its ancillary contracts; or (3) all the parties to the arbitration have agreed to consolidation.

The 2015 Rules also provide that a party may commence a single arbitration concerning multiple contracts if: (1) the contracts consist of a principal contract and ancillary contracts or such contracts involve the same parties as well as legal relationships of the same nature; (2) the disputes arise out of the same transaction or the same series of transactions; and (3) the arbitration agreements in the contracts are identical or compatible.

Time Limits for Rendering of the Award

The time limits for rendering of the award differ in foreign-related cases (including Hong Kong, Macau and Taiwan) and domestic cases. In foreign-related cases, the tribunal must render the award within six months from the date on which it was formed. In domestic cases, the time limit is four months. In cases applying summary procedures, the time limit is three months. These time limits can be extended if the tribunal so requests.

Fee Structure

CIETAC adopts different fee standards for domestic cases and foreign-related cases (including Hong Kong, Macau and Taiwan). For domestic cases, CIETAC charges a case acceptance fee and handling fee, both of which are calculated based on the amount in dispute. For foreign-related cases, CIETAC charges a fixed case registration fee of RMB10,000 and an arbitration fee calculated based on the amount in dispute.

For financial disputes, the same fee standard applies to domestic cases and foreign-related cases. CIETAC charges a fixed case registration fee of RMB10,000 and an arbitration fee calculated based upon the amount in dispute.

C. Local Arbitration Institutions

The CIETAC Hong Kong Arbitration Center has its own fee schedule. It charges a fixed registration fee of HKD8,000 and an administration fee based on the amount in dispute.[8]

Treatment of Costs of the Arbitration

The arbitration fees and expenses shall in principle be borne by the losing party. However, the arbitral tribunal may apportion such fees and expenses between the parties in appropriate proportion, taking into account the relevant circumstances of the case.

Special or Unusual Features (If Any)

None.

New Developments (If Any)

From January 1, 2015, CIETAC will concurrently use the new name "Arbitration Institute of the China Chamber of International Commerce".

The changes in the 2015 Rules are substantial, some of which have been identified above. The 2015 Rules introduce a new body called the Arbitration Court. The 2012 Rules provided that the arbitration was administered by the Secretariat. The Arbitration Court will take over this function and will designate a case manager to each case to assist with the procedural administration of the case.

With respect to arbitrations by the former Shanghai and Shenzhen sub-commissions, the 2015 Rules provide that:

> Where the sub-commission/arbitration center agreed upon by the parties does not exist or its authorization has been terminated, or where the agreement is ambiguous,

---

8   http://cn.cietac.org/help/index.asp?hangye=6.

the Arbitration Court shall accept the arbitration application and administer the case. In the event of any dispute, a decision shall be made by CIETAC.

As the 2012 Rules came into effect before CIETAC Hong Kong was set up, a new chapter (Chapter VI) has been introduced in the 2015 Rules for arbitrations administered by CIETAC Hong Kong. They provide that unless otherwise agreed by the parties, the seat of an arbitration administered by CIETAC Hong Kong shall be Hong Kong and the arbitral award shall be a Hong Kong award. They also provide that CIETAC Hong Kong arbitral tribunals are empowered to grant interim relief.

Further, the 2015 Rules provide for emergency arbitrators. Parties can apply for an emergency arbitrator to grant urgent interim relief before the constitution of the tribunal.

Dispute between CIETAC and Its Shanghai and South China Sub-Commissions

CIETAC previously established sub-commissions in Shanghai and Shenzhen, which could accept and administer arbitration cases with CIETAC's authorization. However, the former CIETAC South China Sub-Commission (in Shenzhen) and the former CIETAC Shanghai Sub-Commission refused to adopt the 2012 Rules, which provided for the administration of arbitration proceedings by a CIETAC sub-commission only if the arbitration clause stipulated that the sub-commission would be the administrating institution and the sub-commission was explicitly named in the arbitration clause. Otherwise, the arbitration proceedings would be administered by the CIETAC headquarters in Beijing, even if the arbitration clause provided for the seat of arbitration or the hearing to take place in Shanghai. This led to the split. The CIETAC Shanghai Sub-Commission announced that it was an independent arbitration commission named "CIETAC Shanghai Commission", subsequently changing its name to "Shanghai International Economic and Trade Arbitration Commission"/"Shanghai International Arbitration Center". It published its own arbitration rules based on the old CIETAC 2005 rules. The former CIETAC South China Sub-Commission also changed its name to South China International Economic and Trade Arbitration Commission and is concurrently using the name of "Shenzhen Court of International Arbitration" ("SCIA"). SCIA adopted its own rules effective from December 1, 2012.

In response, CIETAC announced the termination of the authority of the CIETAC Shanghai Sub-Commission and the CIETAC South China Sub-Commission to accept and administer arbitration cases. The announcement also prohibited the two former sub-commissions from using the CIETAC name.

On December 31, 2014 CIETAC announced its plan to reorganize its sub-commissions in Shanghai and Shenzhen as branches of CIETAC.[9] According to the 2015 Rules, the reorganized CIETAC South China Sub-Commission is to administer arbitration cases that the parties have agreed to arbitrate before CIETAC South China Sub-commission (CIETAC Shenzhen Sub-commission), and the reorganized CIETAC Shanghai Sub-commission is to administer arbitration cases that the parties have agreed to arbitrate before CIETAC Shanghai Sub-Commission. Without CIETAC's authorization, no other institutions have the right to accept or administer such arbitration cases.

---

[9]   http://www.cietac.org/index.cms.

COLOMBIA

Claudia Benavides,[1] Cristina Mejia and Catalina Brando[2]

A. LEGISLATION, TRENDS AND TENDENCIES

A.1 Legislation

Domestic and international arbitration in Colombia continue to be governed by Law 1563 of 2012 ("Law 1563"), to which no legislative amendment was made in 2014. Law 1563 entered into force in October, 2012 and the law in this area is yet to be consolidated.

A.2 Trends and Tendencies

As a consequence of Law 1563, the Center of Arbitration and Conciliation of the Chamber of Commerce of Bogota (the most important arbitration center in Colombia) produced new sets of rules for domestic and international arbitration. The rules entered into force on July 1, 2014 and apply to all requests for arbitration filed after that date.

---

[1]   Claudia Benavides is a Partner in Baker & McKenzie's Bogotá office. She heads the Dispute Resolution practice group of the Bogotá office and represents a variety of clients in domestic and international arbitrations.

[2]   Cristina Mejia is an Associate in Baker & McKenzie's Bogotá office, admitted to the bar in Colombia and New York. Catalina Brando is a Junior Associate within the Dispute Resolution practice group admitted to the bar in Colombia.

Colombia

B. CASES

B.1 The Constitutional Court Elucidates the Congruence Principle[3]

A party to a trademark license (the "Agreement") filed an arbitration lawsuit claiming breaches by the other party to the Agreement. The claimant subsequently (and within the prescribed timeframe) amended the arbitration suit to also seek a declaration that the Agreement was a commercial agency contract. The defendant denied both the breaches and that the Agreement was a commercial agency contract. The arbitrator found in favor of the claimant.

The defendant filed a motion to set aside the award before the Higher Court of Bogotá based on subsection 8 of section 163 of Decree 1818 of 1998 (the applicable law at the time that the annulment petition was filed—the "Law"). Subsection 8 allows the court to annul an award where the award has been decided by matters that were not subject to arbitration or the award has conceded more than was requested in the arbitration. The Higher Court found that in declaring the existence of a commercial agency contract, the arbitrator had conceded more than was requested in the lawsuit because the facts narrated in it never stated that the agreement subscribed by the parties was, in fact, a commercial agency contract.

The claimant in the arbitral proceeding then filed a constitutional action ("acción de tutela") against the ruling of the Higher Court. It claimed that the annulment decision violated both the legal regulation and the jurisprudence of the Supreme Court of Justice and the Constitutional Court in relation to the action to set aside an award.

---

[3]   Constitutional Court. Ruling T-714 of 2013. Justice Jorge Ignacio Pretelt Chaljub.

B. Cases

In considering the claim, the Constitutional Court determined the following:

i.   A constitutional action can be filed against a judicial decision that violates fundamental rights (i.e. due process, equality, etc.).

ii. The arbitration award must obey the constitution and the Law. The award must only decide upon the matters claimed and argued by the parties in the lawsuit and its reply (the congruence principle). The congruence principle is defined by the Law and by jurisprudence as the necessary coherence between the request of the claimant, what was proven in the course of the judicial/arbitration process and what is acknowledged in the ruling or award.

iii. When the congruence principle is not obeyed by the arbitration tribunal, due process is violated because the defendant does not have the opportunity to oppose what is granted by the final decision.

iv. The action to set aside an award has been defined by the Law and by jurisprudence as a remedy that only analyzes the award on formal aspects and never on the merits.

v.   If a decision to set aside an award is taken on the merits of the case, the court would be infringing the Law and the jurisprudence. This infringement constitutes a valid ground to file a constitutional action against the judicial decision.

Applying the above rules, the Constitutional Court confirmed the first and second instance decisions on the constitutional action. It found that the award complied with the congruence principle and, accordingly, revoked the decision of the Higher Court.

B.2. Only Claimant and Defendant Must Expressly Consent to Arbitration[4]

A constitutional action was filed requesting that a particular subsection of Law 1563 be declared unconstitutional. The subsection states that when a third party guarantees compliance with obligations derived from a contract containing an arbitration agreement, the effects of any final domestic arbitration award made in relation to the agreement will also bind the third party.

The claimant claimed that the subsection is unconstitutional because the Colombian Constitution provides that the parties (including impleaders) must give their consent to enable an arbitrator to rule. The Constitutional Court found that the subsection does not violate the Constitution. It highlighted the fact that the legislator has wide faculties to determine the procedural law provided that regulation does not violate constitutional rights and principles, and there was no such violation in this case. The Court reiterated the importance of the parties' consent to the arbitration procedure, but found that the concept of a "party" is limited to the procedural scenario and, in that sense, impleaders cannot be technically considered as parties. Only the claimant and defendant can be considered a party in the procedural sense and, accordingly, it is only the claimant and defendant that must give their express consent to arbitrate.

The Court further observed that, when the third party guarantees compliance with a contract containing an arbitration agreement, it knows that future disputes will be subject to arbitration. It is, therefore, able to foresee and participate in any future arbitration process.

Finally, the Court confirmed that the this particular subsection of Law 1563 only applies to contracts that were subscribed after

---

4   Constitutional Court. Ruling C-170 of 2014. Justice Alberto Rojas Ríos.

B. Cases

Law 1563 came into force, and only to domestic arbitration. Impleaders in international arbitration must provide their express consent to arbitrate for an award to be binding on them.

B.3 Sanction for Frivolous Claim[5]

In late 2011, Proyectar Soluciones en Arquitectura e Ingenieria Ltda. ("Proyectar") and Corporación para el Desarrollo de los Parques y la Recreación de Santa Fé de Bogotá ("Corparques") (together, the "Parties") entered into a civil works agreement for the architectural and structural design, construction and theming of a restaurant for the total sum of COP852,610,779 (the "Agreement").

Proyectar brought a claim against Corparques for breach of the Agreement and estimated under oath that the total value of the damages suffered was COP95million, consisting of a principal amount of COP82,607,773 plus interest.

The tribunal rejected the claims filed by Proyectar in the arbitration and found that although Corparques did not properly challenge Proyectar's estimation of damages, Proyectar was not able to substantiate the amount claimed. The tribunal sanctioned Proyectar by ordering it to pay Corparques a sum equivalent to 5% of the estimated claims. The tribunal explained that the provision of the General Procedural Code that enabled it to impose this penalty (article 206) is there to discourage the filing of frivolous claims and procedures guided by threat rather than by justice.

Article 206 has, however, subsequently been recently amended.[6] Going forward, a sanction will only be applied where the

---

[5] Arbitration Award of February 28, 2014. Proyectar Soluciones en Arquitectura e Ingeniería Ltda. v. Corporación para el Desarrollo de los Parques y la Recreación de Santafé de Bogotá. Arbitrator Ana Zenobia Giacomette Ferrer.

[6] By Law 1743 of December 26, 2014.

tribunal finds that the estimation of the amount claimed results from gross negligence or reckless action on behalf of the claimant. In addition, rather than being paid to the other party, the sanction will be paid to a special fund of the Superior Council of the Judicial Branch.

C. LOCAL ARBITRATION INSTITUTIONS

Colombia has various local arbitration institutions. The most recognized and used arbitral institution is the Arbitration and Conciliation Center of the Chamber of Commerce of Bogotá

The chambers of commerce of other main cities have also created arbitration centers. There are arbitration centers within the chambers of commerce of Medellin, Cali, Barranquilla, Cartagena, Bucaramanga, and Pereira.

Other arbitration centers functioning in Bogotá are the Arbitration Center of Fenalco (which is a center within an association of merchants) and the recently created Arbitration Center of the Superintendence of Corporations.

C.1 Arbitration and Conciliation Center of the Chamber of Commerce of Bogotá

Background

The Arbitration and Conciliation Center of the Chamber of Commerce of Bogotá (the "Arbitration Center") was founded in 1983. Since its foundation, the Arbitration Center has created various initiatives to promote arbitration, including: the enactment of rules for domestic and international arbitration in keeping with global trends in international arbitration; the use of virtual "secretaries"; and the implementation of special gratuitous programs to arbitrate disputes involving small businesses.

C. Local Arbitration Institutions

Types of Disputes Handled

The Arbitration Center handles disputes in both domestic and international commercial arbitration.

Numbers of Disputes Handled

No statistics are available.

Provisions on Confidentiality of Arbitration

According to the rules of the Arbitration Center, both international and domestic arbitration is confidential unless the parties agree otherwise.

Availability of Expedited Procedures

The rules of the Arbitration Center do not provide for expedited procedures.

Consolidation of Disputes between the Same Parties and Joinder of Third Parties

In domestic arbitration, the rules of the Arbitration Center allow the consolidation of disputes if (i) the parties agree on the consolidation and (ii) the arbitral lawsuits are filed under the same arbitral agreement. If the lawsuits are filed based on different arbitral agreements, the consolidation of disputes is allowed if the disputes are between the same parties and arise from the same contractual relation and the arbitral agreements are compatible. Joinder is allowed and often used. Third parties may join the arbitral procedure as necessary joinders, permissive joinders or impleaders.

The rules for international commercial arbitration do not provide specific requirements for the consolidation of disputes or joinder of third parties. The consolidation of disputes and the joinder of third parties are allowed if the circumstances justify the consolidation or the joinder of third parties and if the arbitrators consider it appropriate to do so.

Time Limits for Rendering of the Award

For domestic arbitration, the rules of the Arbitration Center provide that the time limit for rendering the award is the one provided by the parties in the arbitral agreement. If the parties do not provide for a time limit, the time limit is six months from the termination of the hearing called "the first hearing of the arbitral procedure" (Law 1563 of 2014). The first hearing of the arbitral procedure is the hearing in which the tribunal declares its jurisdiction to hear the case and decrees the evidence that is going to be heard by the tribunal. Such hearing usually takes place between two to three months after the arbitration lawsuit has been filed. This six-month time limit for domestic arbitration can be extended by the parties for another six months.

In international arbitration, the arbitrators have six months from the date the counterclaim is filed to render an award.

Fee Structure

The rules of the Arbitration Center contain fee rates for both domestic and international arbitration. The administrative fees for international commercial arbitration range from USD2,750 for an amount in controversy of up to USD50,000, to USD0.01% of the amount in controversy for amounts over USD128million. Similarly, arbitrators' fees range from USD2,750 to 0.05% of the amount in controversy.

Treatment of Costs of the Arbitration

In international arbitration, the costs of the arbitration generally must be assumed by the defeated party. However, in some cases, the tribunal may assign a share of the costs to each of the parties, depending on the circumstances.

The costs include: (ii) the fees of the arbitrators; (ii) travel and other reasonable expenses incurred by the arbitrators; (iii) the reasonable costs of expert's advice required by the tribunal; (iv) when approved by the tribunal, reasonable travel expenses sustained by the witnesses heard within the proceeding; (v) legal and other kinds of costs caused to the parties when the amount is considered reasonable by the tribunal; and (vi) fees and reasonable expenses of the Arbitration Center.

Special or Unusual Features (If Any)

None.

Recent Developments (If Any)

The rules of the Arbitration Center referred to above entered into force on July 1, 2014.

CZECH REPUBLIC

Martin Hrodek[1] and Kristína Bartošková[2]

A. LEGISLATION, TRENDS AND TENDENCIES

A.1 Legislation

On January 1, 2014 Act No. 216/1994 Coll., on Arbitration Proceedings and Enforcement of Arbitration Awards was amended to expand its scope to regulate proceedings before arbitration commissions of industry associations. Arbitration commissions are bodies which settle disputes that arise internally within an industry association. Several Czech industry associations, particularly in the domain of sports, such as the Czech Olympic Committee, have established such arbitration bodies. These arbitration bodies have heard a number of cases since the amendment was passed.

A.2 Trends and Tendencies

Arbitration continues to be a popular method of dispute resolution for Czech clients. This is true for both domestic and international disputes. For smaller domestic disputes, clients tend to use the Arbitration Court of the Czech Economic Chamber and the Czech Agrarian Chamber (the "Arbitration Court"), which handles more than 3,000 disputes annually. For larger domestic and international disputes, clients tend to resolve disputes using the ICC Rules,

---

[1] Martin Hrodek heads the Dispute Resolution Practice Group in Baker & McKenzie's Prague office. He specializes in litigation and arbitration matters, particularly those relating to mergers and acquisitions. He also advises on a wide range of commercial matters, including private equity, divestitures and private competition claims.

[2] Kristína Bartošková is an Associate with the Dispute Resolution Practice Group in Baker & McKenzie's Prague office.

VIAC[3] Rules or the LCIA Rules, even if disputes are purely domestic. One reason for this is that the Czech Supreme Court will tend to favor whichever is perceived to be the weaker party in the dispute. Czech clients will often agree an arbitration clause providing for a dispute to be decided by international arbitration as a way of avoiding this potential bias.

In the sphere of investment arbitration, over the last year the Czech Republic has witnessed an exceptionally high number of cases initiated against the state.[4] The majority of these cases were brought by investors in solar energy installation,[5] who contested significant amendments to Czech laws that placed a levy on electricity generated from solar power plants. The state refused the claimants' request to hear the claims together in a single proceeding, which is partly why so many claims have been brought.[6]

B. CASES

B.1. Arbitration Agreements for Domain Disputes Found Invalid

On December 17, 2013, the Czech Supreme Court issued a decision[7] that arbitration agreements concluded for settlement of

---

[3] Vienna International Arbitral Center.

[4] *UNCTAD's annual review of investor-State dispute settlement (ISDS) cases.* April 2014. available at: http://unctad.org/en/PublicationsLibrary/webdiaepcb2014d3_en.pdf.

[5] The regulatory actions affecting the renewable energy sector gave rise to seven separate claims against the Czech Republic.

[6] Luke Peterson: *Following PCA decision, Czech Republic thwarts move by solar investors to sue in single arbitral proceeding; meanwhile Spain sees new solar claim at ICSID.* IA Reporter. January 1 2014. available at: http://www.iareporter.com/articles/20140102.

[7] Decision of the Supreme Court of the Czech Republic file No. 23 Cdo 3895/2011 dated 17 December 2013.

disputes concerning domain names registered by CZ.NIC,[8] a top level domain registrar, were deemed invalid.

The case centered on a dispute resolution mechanism established by CZ.NIC. The claimant argued that the arbitration award issued by the Arbitration Court should be set aside for want of jurisdiction due to the alleged absence of an arbitration agreement between the claimant and the respondent.

Under the dispute settlement mechanism in question, an entity registering a domain name would automatically accede to the "Rules on Alternative Settlement of Disputes" to govern any dispute arising between the claimant, as the owner of the domain name, and a third party. Pursuant to these rules, a third party that believed its rights were affected by registration of a specific domain name could refer the dispute either to the Czech courts or to the Arbitration Court. In such cases, the owner of the domain name would be obliged to submit to the jurisdiction of the Arbitration Court under the Rules on Alternative Settlement of Disputes, if the third party so elected.

According to the Supreme Court's decision, the agreement between the domain name owner and CZ.NIC to settle disputes involving third parties by arbitration pursuant to the rules of the Arbitration Court did not amount to a sufficiently clear intention to bind the domain name owner. The agreement was found to be invalid as under Czech law, an agreement, including an arbitration agreement, may be formed only when one party makes a clear and unequivocal offer that is duly accepted by the other party.

In light of the state of the law at the time, the above decision of the Supreme Court was not surprising. However, on January 1, 2014 the Act No. 89/2012 Coll., Civil Code introduced a new

---

[8] CZ.NIC is a Czech association that *inter alia* administers .cz domain names.

approach to contract creation. It is not yet entirely clear what impact this change will have on the Supreme Court's decision, and it remains to be seen whether such dispute resolution clauses will be enforceable.

B.2. Failed Enforcement of *Diag Human* Arbitral Award

In August 2008 an *ad hoc* arbitral tribunal rendered its final decision in the *Diag Human* case, ordering the Czech Republic to pay a blood plasma supplier damages of USD485 million. Nevertheless, the decision did not bring this long-running dispute to an end, as the arbitration agreement provided for a revision mechanism under which each party had the right to have the award reviewed by a new arbitral panel before it became final. Indeed, following the 2008 award both parties applied for review of the award. The formation of the review panel became the subject of a further dispute, which was only resolved in August 2014.

Between 2008 and 2014 *Diag Human* attempted several times to enforce the arbitration award issued in August 2008 in various jurisdictions on the basis of the New York Convention. The Austrian Supreme Court, as well as the French Supreme Court, refused to enforce the award due to the ongoing review proceedings. Further, on the basis that the findings of the Austrian and French Supreme Courts could not be re-litigated before the English courts,[9] in May 2014 the English High Court also refused to enforce the award.[10]

On July 23, 2014 the review panel finally discontinued the arbitral proceedings.[11] Nonetheless, this did not allow Diag

---

[9]   An application of the doctrine of issue estoppel.

[10]   [2014] EWHC 1639 (Comm).

[11]   Surprisingly, the findings of these decisions are interpreted by each of the

Human to enforce the award. On August 14, 2014 the US District Court for the District of Columbia held that it had no jurisdiction to consider Diag Human's application for enforcement, stating that the dispute between Diag Human and the Czech Republic did not arise out of a commercial relationship between the parties.[12] The judge adopted a very narrow interpretation of the "commercial nature" of the dispute for the purposes of applying the New York Convention, stating that: "[...] there were no commercial dealings between plaintiff and the Czech Republic itself. Although this alleged interference had commercial consequences for the company, and the arbitration panel ultimately awarded damages to address commercial losses, there was no pre-existing legal relationship of commercial subject matter between Diag Human and the Czech Republic."[13]

Despite the failed attempts to enforce the award in various jurisdictions, Diag Human has stated that it intends to continue to pursue its claim.

B.3. Award Unenforceable Due to Invalidity of Arbitration Clause

The Czech Supreme Court has tackled the question of whether an award rendered by a legal entity that is not a permanent arbitration court established by law is valid.[14]

---

parties to the dispute in an entirely different way, although the only apparent conclusion was that the review process has been formally discontinued.

[12] United States District Court (District of Columbia), Memorandum Opinion of Judge Amy Berman Jackson, Diag Human S.E. v. Czech Republic – Ministry of Health, Civil Action No. 13-0355 (ABJ) dated 14 August 2014.

[13] *Ibid*, p.8.

[14] Decision of the Grand Chamber of the Supreme Court of the Czech Republic file No. 31 Cdo 958/2012 dated 10 July 2013.

Until 2009, an arbitration clause pursuant to which a dispute is to be decided by an *ad hoc* arbitrator, the identity of the arbitrator being determined with reference to a list of arbitrators employed by a legal entity other than a permanent arbitration court, was repeatedly deemed to be valid. Further, any award handed down by such an entity would itself be valid and enforceable.[15]

However, from 2009 onwards a number of court decisions have called this into question. The Supreme Court recently decided that such an arbitration agreement is void and, therefore, any arbitrator appointed under it lacks the power to issue an award, and that such an award is unenforceable.

The case will have serious ramifications, particularly as the Supreme Court stated that any ongoing enforcement proceedings based on such an arbitration award must be discontinued, and that any court in charge of such proceedings should find that the arbitrator/tribunal lacked the requisite power to issue any award.

Although there is a clear rationale behind not affording these "self-proclaimed arbitration courts" the same position as permanent arbitration courts established by law, this decision is likely to pose a number of practical problems. In particular, creditors seeking to enforce arbitration awards arising from such clauses might face discontinuation of enforcement proceedings after a long-running arbitration. This could be particularly problematic if the original claim had since become time-barred. Further, it is possible that such creditors might bring claims for damages against the Czech Republic based on the *volte face* of the courts.

Consequently, in order to avoid such drastic consequences, we strongly recommend that *ad hoc* arbitrators are not determined

---

[15] For reference see e.g. decision of the Supreme Court of the Czech Republic file No. 32 Cdo 2282/2008 dated 31 July 2008.

with reference to a list of arbitrators of a legal entity other than a permanent arbitration court established by law, as such an arbitration clause is likely to be found to be unenforceable by the Czech courts.

C. LOCAL ARBITRATION INSTITUTIONS

As noted above, the most used arbitration institutions within the Czech Republic are the Arbitration Court of the Czech Economic Chamber and the Czech Agrarian Chamber.

FRANCE

Jean-Dominique Touraille,[1] Eric Borysewicz[2] and Karim Boulmelh[3]

A. LEGISLATION, TRENDS AND TENDENCIES

International arbitration in France is governed by the Decree of January 13, 2011 that came into force on May 1, 2011 ("the Decree"), which introduced Articles 1504 to 1524 into the French Code of Civil Procedure. No legislative changes were made to these provisions in 2014. The courts are applying these provisions with a view to increasing the effectiveness of international arbitration as regards both awards rendered in France and international awards rendered abroad.

---

[1] Jean-Dominique Touraille is a Partner in Baker & McKenzie's Paris office and leads the office's Litigation & Arbitration Practice Group. He regularly delivers presentations on various subjects related to his area of practice, which includes distribution, product liability and post-acquisition disputes. He is actively involved in cases relating to ICC arbitration and in enforcement measures in the French legal system.

[2] Eric Borysewicz is a Partner in Baker & McKenzie's Paris office and a member of the Litigation and Arbitration Practice Group in Paris. He represents clients in international arbitrations under ICC Rules and other arbitration institutions. He focuses his practice on risk management issues, advising clients on major litigations involving industrial and infrastructure project. He also assists clients in drafting and negotiating complex industrial and infrastructure project agreements, as well as in renegotiating existing agreements following an unforeseen change in circumstances.

[3] Karim Boulmelh is a Senior Associate in Baker & McKenzie's Paris office and a member of the Litigation and Arbitration Practice Group in Paris. He intervenes in lawsuits related to commercial law and industrial risks before judicial courts and arbitral panels, whether under major arbitration institutions and rules (ICC, UNCITRAL, AAA, ICSID,OHADA) or under ad hoc arbitral tribunals. He handles litigation matters related to telecommunication services, energy and industrial gases, engineering and construction, aircraft and satellite industries.

France is thus generally considered as one of the most arbitration-friendly forums in the world. Arbitration is widely recognized in France as the standard dispute resolution mechanism in international trade and commerce.

B. CASES

B.1 Award May Be Set Aside for Non-Disclosure by an Arbitrator

Two recent rulings by the Paris Court of Appeal and the French Supreme Court, *Cour de Cassation,* have clarified the extent of the arbitrators' and parties' duties when they become aware of circumstances likely to raise a reasonable doubt as to the arbitrator's independence and impartiality.

In a ruling of October 14, 2014, the Paris Court of Appeal specified that an arbitrator must disclose circumstances having occurred after constitution of the arbitral tribunal and likely to raise a reasonable doubt as to an arbitrator's independence and impartiality notwithstanding that these circumstances may be public knowledge.[4]

Two French companies, AFG and Columbus, and a company incorporated under the laws of Delaware, CFH, entered into an agreement to assign the entire share capital of CFH to Columbus. Columbus initiated arbitration proceedings against AFG after the latter cancelled the transaction. CFH joined the arbitration proceedings.

After the arbitral award was rendered by the arbitrator, AFG lodged an appeal before the Paris Court of Appeal against the

---

[4] Paris Court of Appeal, October 14, 2014, Auto Guadeloupe Investissements (AGI) v/Columbus Acquisitions Inc.

decision to enforce the arbitral award rendered on the ground that the arbitral tribunal had been wrongfully constituted. It was alleged that the arbitrator had failed to disclose that one of the partners of his firm was representing the sole shareholder of CFH while the proceedings were pending.

The defense of Columbus and CFH was twofold. Firstly, they argued that this information was public knowledge as it had been published on the firm's website and in *Lexpert*, a legal journal for lawyers. In other words, they tried to show that the arbitrator had no obligation to disclose the information because it was public knowledge and easily accessible to the parties. Secondly, they put forward the fact that the law firm's fees for the deal in question had been insignificant, and therefore this information was not likely to raise a reasonable doubt as to the arbitrator's independence and impartiality.

The Paris Court of Appeal dismissed both of these arguments. The Court ruled that it is not reasonable to require the parties to undertake continuous research and regular analysis of the publicly available information regarding the arbitrator. In the case at hand, the information regarding the deal was not publicly available before the constitution of the arbitral tribunal.

The Court of Appeal also specified that notwithstanding the alleged insignificance of the law firm's fees for the deal in question, it was clear from the deal's size and the number of lawyers involved, as well as the publicity given, that the deal was important for the firm. Therefore the information was likely to raise a reasonable doubt as to the arbitrator's independence and impartiality, and it should have been disclosed by the arbitrator. The Court of Appeal thus set aside the award because of the arbitrator's failure to inform the parties of the existence of the deal and the involvement of the law firm.

According to Article 1456 of the French Civil Procedure Code, to avoid the award being set aside, the arbitrator should have disclosed the circumstance likely to create a reasonable doubt as to his independence and impartiality without delay following the occurrence of such circumstance.

The ruling would have probably been different had the party in question been informed of these circumstances during the course of the arbitral proceedings and had it failed to raise the issue until the action before the Court of Appeal to set aside the award. This is the conclusion which can be reached from a decision of the *Cour de Cassation* rendered on June 25, 2014.[5]

In that case, the arbitration proceedings were governed by the 1998 ICC Arbitration Rules. Article 11.2 states: "[f]or a challenge [of an arbitrator] to be admissible, it must be sent by a party either within 30 days from receipt by that party of the notification of the appointment or confirmation of the arbitrator, or within 30 days from the date when the party making the challenge was informed of the facts and circumstances on which the challenge is based if such date is subsequent to the receipt of such notification."

While it had been informed of the facts on which a challenge could have been based, a party failed to comply with the time frame specified by Article 11.2 of the ICC Arbitration Rules. The request for challenge of the arbitrator's appointment was therefore dismissed by the ICC Arbitration Court. The party in question later brought an action to set aside the award before the Paris Court of Appeal on the ground that the arbitral tribunal had been wrongly constituted.

The Paris Court of Appeal set aside the arbitral award, noting that the period of admissibility of the request for the challenge of an arbitrator under the ICC Rules was not binding on the state

---

[5]   Cour de cassation, n° 11-26529, Technimont v/ Avax.

courts as regards the admissibility of an action to set aside the award and that failure to comply with this time period provided in the arbitration rules of the relevant institution did not constitute a waiver of the right to invoke the arbitrator's lack of independence and impartiality.

This decision was quashed by the *Cour de Cassation* on the grounds that a party that knowingly refrains from making a request to challenge an arbitrator within the timeframe stipulated by the applicable rules of the arbitration institute is deemed to have waived its entitlement to argue that an arbitrator is not independent or impartial.

The *Cour de Cassation* thus confirmed that the rules of an arbitral institution are binding not only on the parties who have consented to them, but also on the state courts. The state courts will be precluded from setting aside an award on the grounds of lack of impartiality and independence of an arbitrator where the applicant failed to raise the issue with the institution in due time.

B.2 Contrasting Approaches to Consistency of Awards with International Public Policy

Since the *Thalès*[6] and *Cytec*[7] cases, it is a well-established principle in France that an arbitral award may be set aside for violation of the international public policy only if such violation is "*blatant, actual and concrete*". This minimalist approach has been confirmed by the *Cour de Cassation* in its decision of February 12, 2014.[8] However, the judgment of the Paris Court of Appeal dated March 4, 2014[9] shows that there may still be a

---

[6] CA Paris, November 18, 2004, n° 2002/19606.

[7] Cass. Civ. 1, June 4, 2008, n° 06-15.320.

[8] Cour de cassation, n° 10-17076, Schnieder v/ CPL.

[9] Paris Court of Appeal, March 4, 2014, Gulf Leaders for Managemet and Services Holding Company v/ Crédit Foncier de France.

degree of uncertainty regarding the scope of the Court's review regarding this issue.

In the case before the *Cour de Cassation*, Schneider, an Austrian company, brought an action before the Paris Court of Appeal claiming that the arbitral award was inconsistent with international public policy as: (i) the arbitrator had determined that there was a fraud but failed to draw conclusions arising from this finding and (ii) the arbitrator enforced contracts which had been concluded in violation of the Nigerian anti-bribery statute.

The Court of Appeal dismissed the claims. Regarding the alleged fraud, the court reaffirmed the well-known principle according to which the judge reviewing the legality of the arbitral award is not entitled to revise the award. Indeed, before the arbitral tribunal, Schneider had refrained from seeking cancellation of the contract on the grounds of fraud, and the court thus could not decide this matter on the merits as the arbitral tribunal would have done had Schneider raised the argument in the course of arbitral proceedings. Regarding the claim of bribery, the court ruled that the argument had been raised before the arbitral tribunal and it was apparent from the award that the arbitral tribunal considered the issue and ruled that bribery had not been established. Thus, once again the Court of Appeal repeated that it was not entitled to revise the arbitral award. The *Cour de Cassation* upheld the analysis of the Court of Appeal, considering that Schneider was actually claiming for revision of the arbitral award.

The *Cour de Cassation* implicitly confirmed its case law according to which (i) bribery may be considered as inconsistent with international public policy[10] and (ii) most importantly, such

---

[10]   Paris Court of Appeal, September 30, 1993 European Gas Turbines SA v/ Westman International Ltd.

inconsistency of the award with international public policy will be considered restrictively. Indeed, in the case at hand, the Court of Appeal merely checked that the arbitral award stated that the bribery argument had been raised before the tribunal and dismissed, without any additional review.

However, on March 4, 2014, the Paris Court of Appeal[11] adopted a different approach as to the extent of the review of the arbitral award's compliance with international public policy. As in the previous case, Gulf Leaders, a Saudi Arabian company, was alleging that the arbitral tribunal had enforced a contract concluded pursuant to bribery and that notwithstanding the fact that evidence of bribery had been found during the arbitration proceedings, the arbitral tribunal dismissed the claim, considering that the bribery had not been proved.

This time, however, the Paris Court of Appeal considered that when a party alleges that a contract has been obtained further to bribery, the judge must analyze all the elements in order to determine whether the enforcement of the award is actually inconsistent with international public policy. The court dismissed the claim to set aside the award, but only after having addressed the arguments of the claimant and having considered that no bribery was established. The Paris Court of Appeal thus adopted a less restrictive approach to checking whether an arbitral award complies with international public policy. On June 4, 2014, an appeal was lodged against this decision before the *Cour de Cassation*. The decision is thus awaited to clarify this point.

---

[11] Paris Court of Appeal, March 4, 2014, Gulf Leaders for Management and Services Holding Company v/ Crédit Foncier de France.

C. LOCAL ARBITRATION INSTITUTIONS

C.1 The ICC International Court of Arbitration

Background

The International Court of Arbitration of the ICC is the most recognized arbitration institution worldwide. It was created in 1923 as an institution for the administration of arbitration proceedings commenced under the aegis of the ICC, which itself is a business organization founded in Paris a few years earlier in 1919 in order to promote international trade and business. The ICC has developed a very sophisticated and trusted set of rules for arbitration.

Types of Disputes Handled

A very large variety of disputes covering a broad spectrum of economic activity worldwide is brought before arbitral tribunals acting under the ICC Arbitration Rules. According to ICC statistics, parties to arbitration proceedings come from 139 different countries, and approximately 10% of the cases involve states or state-owned entities.

Numbers of Disputes Handled

Over the decades, ICC arbitration has become one of the most trusted alternative dispute resolution tools and the most commonly used in the world by the international business community. The ICC International Court of Arbitration handles over 1,500 cases, and each year approximately 700 new cases are filed with the ICC.

Provisions on Confidentiality of Arbitration

Arbitration under the ICC Rules is commonly considered to be—and is generally treated as being—strictly confidential. However, there is no provision that clearly sets forth an obligation of confidentiality. The main reason for that is that most of the time, the issue of confidentiality will depend on the procedural rules applicable to the arbitral proceedings, i.e. on the law of the seat of the arbitration. Therefore, and unless the law clearly states that arbitration is confidential by nature, it is advisable that the parties provide for confidentiality in their arbitration clause. This being said, the International Court of Arbitration is nevertheless bound by a strict duty of confidentiality. Article 6 of Appendix 1 of the Arbitration Rules related to the statutes of the International Court of Arbitration provides that the work of the court is of a confidential nature, which constitutes a guarantee that arbitration proceedings handled under the aegis of the ICC will be treated with the required confidentiality by the court.

Availability of Expedited Procedures

With new ICC Rules that entered into force on January 1, 2012, the ICC introduced long-awaited provisions that allow a party seeking emergency measures to have recourse to an emergency arbitrator. The emergency arbitrator rules are applicable to all ICC arbitration agreements entered into after January 1, 2012, unless the parties have opted out of this provision in their arbitration agreement or they have agreed to another pre-arbitral procedure. In 1990, the ICC developed a specific set of rules for the so-called pre-arbitral referee procedure, which allows parties to apply to a single arbitrator for urgent provisional measures. However, unlike the emergency arbitrator provided for in the 2012 Rules, the pre-arbitral referee requires the parties' prior mutual consent.

Provisions on Consolidation of Disputes between the Same Parties and Joinder of Third Parties

As regards consolidation and joinder of third parties, the ICC has significantly developed its Rules as modified in 2012. The new

Rules codify the previous practice of the International Arbitration Court in such matters. The ICC Court of Arbitration may, at the request of a party, "consolidate two or more arbitrations pending under the Rules into a single arbitration, where: [...] all of the claims in the arbitrations are made under the same arbitration agreement".[12] The same provision further states that "the Court may take into account any circumstances it considers to be relevant, including whether one or more arbitrators have been confirmed or appointed in more than one of the arbitrations and, if so, whether the same or different persons have been confirmed or appointed". The new Rules do not include two of the conditions required under the 1998 version of the Rules, i.e. (i) that the terms of reference have not been signed yet or approved by the court, and (ii) that the arbitrations are in connection with the same legal relationship. Therefore, the conditions for consolidation are less stringent under the new Rules. However, and as regards joinder of third parties, Article 6 of the ICC Rules prevents the joinder of any additional party after the arbitral tribunal has been constituted, unless the parties agree otherwise.

Time Limits for Rendering of the Award

The time limit for rendering the award of the tribunal under the ICC Rules is six months from the day on which the terms of reference are established. However, this time limit is in practice very often extended either upon request of the arbitral tribunal or on the courts own initiative.

Fee Structure

The ICC fees are composed of a non refundable USD5,000 administrative fee payable at the filing of the Request for

---

[12] Article 10 of the ICC Rules.

arbitration, plus administrative expenses calculated on a percentage-based scale proportionate to the amounts in dispute. Similarly, the arbitrators' fees are calculated on the basis of a portion of the amount in dispute and fixed according to a calculated range between a minimum fee and a maximum fee. The ICC International Arbitration Court sets the appropriate fee within this range depending on the nature of the dispute, the reputation of the arbitrators and the required amount of work.

Treatment of Costs of the Arbitration

Under the ICC Rules, while the administrative costs and the arbitrators' fees are fixed by the court, it is for the arbitral tribunal exclusively to decide which of the parties shall bear the arbitration costs, including the ICC administrative and the arbitrators' fees, and in what proportion.

Special or Unusual Features (If Any)

Finally, one of the unusual features of ICC arbitration compared to many other arbitral institutions in the world is the scrutiny of the award. Article 33 of the ICC Rules provides that before any signing of the arbitral award by the tribunal, the court shall review the draft award and may lay down modifications to the form of the award. The court may also draw the arbitral tribunal to points of substance. Such scrutiny of arbitral awards and such prior approval as to the form of the arbitral award prior its rendering is a way for the ICC International Court of Arbitration to ensure the enforceability of the arbitral award rendered under its auspices.

Recent Developments

Not applicable.

C.2 Other Local Arbitration Institutions

There are many other arbitration institutions in France. Some of them attempt to attract both domestic and international arbitrations, such as the Centre for Mediation and Arbitration of Paris, founded in 1995 by the Paris Chamber of Commerce, or the International Chamber of Arbitration of Paris founded in 1926 and affiliated with the Paris Trade Exchange. Others are very much specialized, such as the *Chambre Arbitrale Maritime de Paris*, which has a great reputation for maritime law disputes. Others are regional, such as the *Chambre d'arbitrage of Grenoble*, or clearly affiliated to a specific sector of activity, such as the *Chambre arbitrale des cafés et poivres du Havre*, which is the main arbitral body for international professionals in the coffee market.

GERMANY

Ragnar Harbst,[1] Heiko Plassmeier[2] and Jürgen Mark[3]

A. LEGISLATION, TRENDS AND TENDENCIES

A.1 Legislation

International arbitration in Germany continues to be governed by the German Arbitration Act of 1998 as set forth in the ZPO. There have been no relevant changes in the past year.

A.2 Trends and Tendencies

This year, international arbitration has become the subject of a heated public debate in Germany (and other parts of Europe). This debate has been triggered by the critics of the envisaged Transatlantic Trade and Investment Partnership Agreement ("the TTIP") which is supposed to include an Investor to State Dispute Settlement ("the ISDS") provision. The European Commission, EU Member States and the European Parliament consider the

---

[1] Ragnar Harbst is a Partner in Baker & McKenzie's Frankfurt office. He has acted in numerous international arbitration proceedings, both as party representative and as arbitrator. His practice focus is on construction and infrastructure related disputes. Mr. Harbst is also qualified as a Solicitor in England and Wales.

[2] Heiko Plassmeier is a Counsel in Baker & McKenzie's Düsseldorf office. He advises and represents clients from various industries, including the energy and automotive sectors, in domestic and international litigation and arbitration cases and has acted as an arbitrator. Besides his dispute resolution practice, he also handles insolvency matters.

[3] Jürgen Mark is a Partner in Baker & McKenzie's Düsseldorf office. He practices in the areas of litigation and domestic and international arbitration. Mr. Mark has also acted as arbitrator in ad-hoc, ICC and DIS arbitration proceedings relating to corporate and post-M&A disputes, major construction projects, product distribution and product liability.

ISDS to be an important tool for protecting EU investors abroad.[4]

The main criticism of the TTIP negotiations seems to be that the intended investment protection provisions of the TTIP will undermine European standards of consumer and environmental protection. There is also a concern that it will prevent European legislators and governments from passing laws (or will at least limit their ability to do so), as such legislative measures could negatively affect US investments in Europe and thus potentially create an obligation to compensate investors. This debate has put the ISDS increasingly at center stage, along with the perceived ability of arbitration to satisfactorily deal with investment disputes. During the course of this debate, arbitral tribunals have been denounced as "secret courts" and arbitration proceedings as "shadow justice in luxury hotels"[5] conducted by lawyers from major international law firms who are biased and influenced by their own economic interests. It has also been claimed that the proceedings lack transparency, are nonappealable and provide unjustified privileges to business enterprises to the detriment of the community in which they operate.[6]

Apparently influenced by the public debate, the German Federal Minister of Justice, Heiko Maas, suggested in October 2014 that disputes between investors and states should be decided by state courts and not by international arbitral tribunals.[7] His position

---

[4]   European Commission – Trade Policy in Focus: Transatlantic Trade and Investment Partnership (TTIP): Questions and answers.

[5]   "Schattenjustiz - Im Namen des Geldes" ("Shadow Justice - In the Name of Money"), Die Zeit of February 27, 2014, p.15.

[6]   Von Frankenberg, "Rechtsstaaten vor privaten Schiedsgerichten ("Rule-of-law States Before Private Arbitral Tribunals"), Deutsche Richterzeitung 2014, p. 238.

[7]   "Justizminister warnt vor Schiedsgerichten" ("Justice Minister Warns Against Arbitral Tribunals"), Frankfurter Rundschau of October 1, 2014.

was supported by the president of the German Federal Supreme Court, who expressed the opinion that by introducing the ISDS, European states would transfer areas which are core functions of good government to a "private system of parallel justice".[8]

As Germany is traditionally an arbitration-friendly country, this rhetoric came as a surprise. Although the criticism so far has focused on investment arbitration, it is possible that the debate could ultimately also affect international commercial arbitration. It is hoped that the discussion in Germany and elsewhere in Europe will be rationalized and brought to an objective level[9] and that proper information about international arbitration and its advantages will be promulgated to avoid any further political debate.

B. CASES

B.1 Challenge to Arbitrator Admissible Even if Award is Rendered in the Meantime

In a decision of January 3, 2014,[10] the Court of Appeal Munich addressed the question of whether a party who challenged an arbitrator before the competent court for an alleged lack of impartiality could still pursue the challenge after the arbitral tribunal had rendered its award, which was also challenged.

A party to the arbitration challenged the chairwoman of the tribunal because of an alleged improper *ex parte* contact between

---

[8]   "BGH-Präsidentin Limperg kritisiert private Schlichtungsstellen" ("President of the Federal Supreme Court Criticizes Private Arbitration Bodies"), Die Welt of October 2, 2014.

[9]   Risse, ("Wehrt Euch endlich! Wider das Arbitration Bashing" ("Defend Yourselves! Against Arbitration Bashing"), SchiedsVZ 2014, 265.

[10]   File no. 34 SchH 7/13.

her and the other party's attorney. The applicant submitted that the chairwoman had shared sensitive information concerning the proceedings with the opponent. The chairwoman rejected the application and declined to step down. Accordingly, the applicant filed a challenge with the Court of Appeal Munich (the "Challenge"). A few months after the application was filed, the arbitral tribunal rendered its final award. The applicant also filed proceedings to vacate the award.

As a prerequisite to its decision on the Challenge, the court had to decide whether the Challenge had become procedurally inadmissible, given proceedings to vacate the award had been commenced in the interim. The court held that there was still a justified interest in pursuing the Challenge, as the reasons for which the arbitrator had been challenged would not necessarily be dealt with in the application to vacate the award. Were the award to be set aside on grounds other than the challenged arbitrator's lack of impartiality, the arbitrators—including the chairwoman—would, as a matter of principle, remain in office and be tasked with determining the matter afresh. The Court of Appeal Munich subsequently granted the Challenge.

B.2 Waiver of Right to Challenge an Allegedly Biased Arbitrator

By a decision of June 16, 2014, [11] the Court of Appeal Munich tackled the issue of how to treat objections against an arbitrator that were only raised during proceedings for the recognition and enforcement of the arbitral award.

The decision concerned an arbitration about the dissolution of a partnership between two tax consultants. In the course of the arbitral proceedings, the tribunal tasked an independent expert with evaluating the net value of the partnership. The respondent disagreed with the result and presented two party-expert

---

[11] File no. 34 Sch 15/13, SchiedsVZ 2014, 257.

opinions, which reached different results. The arbitral tribunal rendered a decision against the respondent, following the results of the opinion of the independent expert.

During the proceedings for recognition and enforcement of the award, the respondent argued that the composition of the arbitral tribunal had been defective.[12] The respondent argued that a close personal friendship and economic ties existed between the chairman and the tribunal-appointed expert, rendering the chairman biased.

The court did not deal with the allegation of bias for procedural reasons. It was of the opinion that a challenge to an arbitrator, as a rule, becomes inadmissible once an arbitral award has been rendered. The court held that reasons for challenging an arbitrator that become known only after the award has been rendered could only be raised in proceedings to set aside an award or, exceptionally, in enforcement proceedings, in a particularly blatant and grave case of bias. As a rule, however, a party is precluded from raising a bias argument if this argument could and ought to have been raised in the arbitral proceedings. Indeed, the ZPO requires a party that seeks to challenge an arbitrator to raise the issue in writing with the tribunal within two weeks of becoming aware of the facts that give rise to the challenge.[13]

The respondent further argued during the enforcement proceedings that the tribunal: (a) did not grant him an opportunity to be heard, as it did not sufficiently deal with arguments raised in his party expert's opinions; and (b) ought to have instructed a new expert in accordance with the ZPO. The court held that the relevant ZPO provision was only applicable in

---

[12]   Within the meaning of Sec. 1059, para. 2 no. 1 lit. d of the ZPO.

[13]   Sec. 1037 para. 2 ZPO.

state court, not arbitral, proceedings, it being the arbitral tribunal's prerogative to decide whether it was in a position to reach a decision based on the available evidence. If the tribunal decided that it was, the decision not to request another expert opinion would not be a violation of the right to be heard. Holding otherwise would have led to the tribunal's decision-making process being subjected to state court review.

B.3 Sports Arbitration Based on Unconscionable Agreement? —The Pechstein Case

The 2010/2011 edition of this Yearbook reported on two decisions of the Swiss Federal Tribunal rejecting a challenge brought by the famous German speed skater Claudia Pechstein against an arbitral award banning her from any competition for two years because of blood doping.[14] Ms. Pechstein did not accept this result and pursued her case in the German courts.

On 26 February 2014, the District Court Munich I issued a decision[15] that casts doubt on the future of sports arbitration in Germany. German speed skater, Claudia Pechstein, claimed damages against the German Skating Association (*Deutsche Eisschnelllauf-Gemeinschaft e.V*, "the DESG") and the International Skating Union ("the ISU") in respect of a two-year suspension the ISU imposed on her in 2009 for alleged violations of the ISU Anti-Doping Rules. The DESG (a member of the ISU) supported the ISU in enforcing the suspension in Germany.

Before entering the Skating World Championship in Hamar, Norway in 2009, Ms. Pechstein signed an entry form that provided that she accepted the ISU Constitution, which

---

[14]   The Baker & McKenzie International Arbitration Yearbook 2010-2011, Switzerland, 410-423.

[15]   File No. 37 O 28331/12, SchiedsVZ 2014, 100.

established an ISU Disciplinary Commission and recognized the Court of Arbitration for Sport in Lausanne, Switzerland ("CAS"), as the arbitration tribunal authorized to issue final and binding awards (the "ISU Arbitration Agreement"). Several arbitration agreements (the "DESG Arbitration Agreements") were also in place between Ms. Pechstein and the DESG, which provided for exclusive submission of all disputes relating to breaches of anti-doping regulations that may result in a suspension to arbitration under the German Institution of Arbitration Sports Arbitration Rules.

After the ISU Disciplinary Commission's decision to ban Ms. Pechstein from competitions and practice for two years, both she and the DESG filed appeals against this decision with CAS. CAS confirmed the Disciplinary Commission's decision, and Ms. Pechstein's two further appeals to the Swiss Federal Tribunal also failed.

Ms. Pechstein applied to District Court Munich I for a declaration of the suspension's illegality and for damages to recover losses suffered during her suspension period. To overcome the ISU's objection that the District Court lacked jurisdiction because of the ISU Arbitration Agreement, Ms. Pechstein claimed nullity of the ISU Arbitration Agreement for unconscionability, arguing that she had been coerced into concluding it and the DESG Arbitration Agreements against her will.

The District Court Munich I accepted that Ms. Pechstein had been coerced and declared the DESG and ISU Arbitration Agreements void because Ms. Pechstein had no choice but to sign them; for example, signature of the ISU Arbitration Agreement was a condition of access to skating competitions. The court found that there was a "structural inferiority" on Ms. Pechstein's part, as the ISU could force her to agree to arbitration or otherwise face a ban from her profession. The ISU

Arbitration Agreement was held to have had "unusually burdensome consequences" for Ms. Pechstein, as it deprived her of access to state courts, instead forcing her into proceedings without public hearings and without a right to legal aid.[16] The court had a number of criticisms of CAS, including that CAS arbitrators can only be chosen from a closed list, which is compiled without "authoritative influence" from the athletes.

However, the District Court Munich I ruled that Ms Pechstein's application for a declaration of the suspension's illegality was inadmissible, as this issue was the subject matter of the CAS proceedings and could thus not be re-opened for *res judicata* reasons. Despite the assumed unconscionability of the ISU Arbitration Agreement, the court held that it had to recognize the CAS award. The New York Convention was held not to be an obstacle to recognition, since Ms Pechstein had not relied on the alleged invalidity of the ISU Arbitration Agreement or challenged the jurisdiction of CAS at any point during the CAS arbitration proceedings, thus precluding that objection.

Ms Pechstein filed an appeal against this judgment with the Court of Appeal Munich, which issued an interim judgment confirming that the ISU Arbitration Agreement was invalid on competition grounds. It held that the CAS decision was not enforceable in Germany and that the German courts had jurisdiction to decide on Ms. Pechstein's claim for damages. The ISU filed an appeal against this judgment to the German Federal Supreme Court, which is yet to be heard. Should Ms. Pechstein be successful, it could mean that all such arbitration agreements (and decisions of sports arbitral tribunals) could be invalid in Germany on the basis of "structural inferiority" between the governing body and the athlete.

---

[16] Although given that the amount claimed was EUR3,584,126, it is difficult to see why this was material.

B.4 ***"Ne Ultra Petita"* in Arbitration**

It is unclear whether the principle that a court or tribunal may not, in its judgment or award, exceed the parties' applications and grant a party a remedy that it did not ask for (*"ne ultra petita"*) applies in arbitration. It had previously been held[17] that this principle does not apply in a strict sense, but that tribunals should seek an "economically sensible" resolution of the dispute before them. However, in a more recent decision,[18] the Court of Appeal Cologne held that the principle is part of German public policy, vacating an award in which a tribunal exceeded the parties' applications.

In a judgment of 5 June 2014,[19] the Court of Appeal Frankfurt followed suit. At first instance the two applicants—shareholders and members of the board of a German stock corporation—sold their shares to the defendant in several tranches. They also provided the defendant with a guarantee regarding the corporation's annual balance sheets. Subsequently, one balance sheet had to be changed substantially, to the detriment of the company. The defendant exercised its call option to acquire the next tranche of shares, but set off counterclaims under the guarantee instead of paying the purchase price. The applicants initiated arbitration proceedings, applying for an order that the defendant pay the purchase price for the call option. The defendant counterclaimed for a declaratory award that the applicants were obliged to pay damages in an amount exceeding the purchase price. The tribunal found that the applicants had breached the guarantee, dismissed the action for payment of the

---

[17] See for example, Imperial Court, RGZ 149, 45; Federal Supreme Court, NJW 1959, 1493; Court of Appeal Hamburg, MDR 1965, 54.

[18] Order of 28 June 2011, file no. 19 Sch 11/10, SchiedsVZ 2012, 161.

[19] File No. 26 Sch 1/14.

purchase price, declared that the defendant was entitled to damages exceeding the purchase price and ordered the applicants to surrender the shares in question to the defendant.

The applicants appealed, arguing that the tribunal had exceeded the defendant's applications in ordering them to surrender the shares. The Court of Appeal upheld the appeal, holding that the relevant rule of the ZPO[20] constituted a "fundamental principle" and a "minimum standard of procedural justice" and was thus part of procedural public policy (even though the relevant provision does not technically apply to arbitration proceedings as it is not a provision of German arbitration law). As a result, in the absence of an agreement between the parties as to the procedural rules, the tribunal is free to determine those rules at its sole discretion.[21] However, the court held that the principle had to apply regardless as it was so fundamental. The award was vacated and the matter referred back to a tribunal to be newly established by the parties.

B.5   Arbitrability to Be Determined by the Law of the Forum

In proceedings[22] concerning the admissibility of arbitration proceedings in Germany, the Court of Appeal Munich clarified that the arbitrability of a subject matter of arbitration proceedings in Germany is exclusively determined under German law. The parties were two companies, one German and one French. They concluded a software and licensing agreement that contained a choice of German law and a standard ICC clause that provided for "all disputes concerning or in connection with this contract" to be submitted to

---

[20]   Sec. 308 para. 1, ZPO: "The court has no authority to award anything to a party that has not been requested."

[21]   Sec. 1042 para. 4 ZPO.

[22]   File No. 34 SchH 18/13, SchiedsVZ 2014, 262.

arbitration in Munich. Three years into the project, the French company filed suit against the German company at the Tribunal de Commerce in Paris for damages, alleging that the German company had entrusted a third party with part of the work the French company was supposed to perform under the contract. The French company's claim (that it constituted a *"rupture brutale"* of the business relationship within the meaning of the French *Code de Commerce*) was in tort, not contract, so it argued that a French state court had jurisdiction over the claim rather than an arbitral tribunal in Germany. The German company subsequently sought a declaration of admissibility of arbitration with respect to the entire dispute, which the Court of Appeal Munich granted. It held that—in accordance with the wording of the arbitration agreement—arbitration was admissible for all claims that "relate" to the contract, with no limitation as to their legal nature. The validity of the arbitration agreement was subject to German law either by virtue of an implied choice or because the seat of the arbitration was to be in Germany. The court noted that it is standard practice to construe arbitration agreements broadly and that claims in tort are in any event subject to referral to arbitration if the underlying facts could also give rise to a claim for breach of contract. Under German law, all "pecuniary claims" are arbitrable; whether the claim in question was arbitrable under French law was held to be immaterial.

C. LOCAL ARBITRATION INSTITUTIONS

By far the most important German arbitration institution is the German Institution of Arbitration (*Deutsche Institution für Schiedsgerichtsbarkeit*, "the DIS").

C. 1 The DIS

Background

The DIS was founded on 1 January 1992 as a result of a merger of two former German arbitration organizations: the German Arbitration Committee (*Deutscher Ausschuss für Schiedsgerichtswesen e.V.*) and the German Arbitration Institute (*Deutsches Institut für Schiedsgerichtswesen*). The seat of the DIS is Berlin, the main secretariat is in Cologne, and further offices are located in Berlin and Munich.

Types of Disputes Handled

The DIS Arbitration Rules can be applied in respect of all types of domestic and international arbitration; they are not sector-specific and suitable for all branches of trade for the purposes of the settlement of disputes.

Besides the DIS Arbitration Rules, the DIS offers supplemental sets of rules, including the Supplementary Rules for Corporate Law Disputes ("the DIS-SRCoLD").[23] The DIS-SRCoLD are designed specifically for the determination of disputes relating to resolutions of limited liability companies. In addition, based on a joint initiative of the DIS and the German National Anti-Doping Agency, on January 1, 2008 the DIS launched the German Court of Arbitration for Sport. Sports arbitration tribunals handle cases relating to alleged doping violations, disputes in respect of sports events, licensing or sponsorship disputes etc. using the DIS-Sports Arbitration Rules, a modified version of the DIS Arbitration Rules. The tribunals also hear appeals against decisions of disciplinary bodies of sports federations. In doping

---

[23]   http://www.dis-arb.de/en/16/rules/dis-supplementary-rules-for-corporate-law-dis putes-09-srcold-id15.

cases, the awards are subject to appeal to CAS.[24] It remains to be seen what impact the Pechstein case[25] will have on this branch of the DIS's activities once that dispute is resolved.

Number of Disputes Handled

In 2013, a total of 132 new cases were filed at the DIS. The DIS Arbitration Rules applied in 107 (82%) of these cases, while the majority of the rest were split between the Arbitration Rules of various Chambers of Industry and Commerce and the DIS Arbitration Rules for Sport.

Provisions on Confidentiality of Arbitration

The parties to an arbitration, their representatives, the arbitrators and the DIS secretariat, are obliged to maintain confidentiality in respect of arbitral proceedings. This includes, but is not limited to, the parties involved, the witnesses, the experts and other evidentiary materials.

Availability of Expedited Procedures

The DIS Arbitration Rules state that the arbitral tribunal must conduct the proceedings expeditiously. However, another supplementary set of rules offered by the DIS is the Supplementary Rules for Expedited Proceedings ("the DIS-SREP")[26]. The DIS-SREP provide for: (a) dispute resolution by a sole arbitrator as a rule; (b) a limit on the number of briefs exchanged; and (c) proceedings to be concluded within six months.

---

24   Rule 38.2 of the DIS-Sports Arbitration Rules.
25   Reported above in section B.3.

Consolidation of Disputes between the Same Parties and Joinder of Third Parties

The DIS Rules of Arbitration do not contain any rules regarding the consolidation of disputes or joinder of third parties.

Time Limits for Rendering of the Award

The DIS Arbitration Rules provide that the arbitral tribunal must render its award within a resonable period of time.

Fee Structure

For amounts in dispute of up to EUR5,000, the fee for the chairman of the arbitral tribunal or for a sole arbitrator shall amount to EUR1,365 and for each co-arbitrator, EUR1,050. For amounts in dispute between EUR5,000 and EUR100 million, the fees are determined on the basis of the amount in dispute, as set out in a schedule to the DIS Arbitration Rules. Upon filing the statement of claim, the claimant is required to pay an administrative fee to the DIS, though the parties are jointly and severally liable for the fee. The schedule to the Arbitation Rules also sets out how this fee is calculated. The arbitrators are also entitled to reimbursement of expenses, as well as to value added tax levied on the fees or expenses.

Treatment of Costs of the Arbitration

Unless the parties agree otherwise, the arbitral tribunal will make a decision about costs. The general principle is that the unsuccessful party bears the costs of the arbitral proceedings. It is open to an arbitral tribunal to order each party to bear its own costs, or to apportion them between the parties.

C. Local Arbitration Institutions

Special or Unusual Features (If Any)

Among a number of other tasks, the DIS acts as the appointing authority in proceedings under the UNCITRAL Arbitration Rules and in domestic and international ad-hoc proceedings.

Recent Developments (If Any)

There are no recent developments.

C.2 Other Arbitration Institutions

There are a number of other arbitration institutions in Germany that administrate arbitral proceedings under their own rules. More than a dozen such institutions are located in Hamburg alone. Typically they deal with disputes from specific areas of trade. For instance, the "Waren-Verein der Hamburger Börse e.V.", an association that represents foreign and wholesale traders in various fruits and vegetables, has been offering arbitration services for over 100 years. Its tribunals are composed of traders who are legally advised by lawyers employed by the association. A particular feature of the Waren-Verein's Arbitration Rules[27] is that they provide for the possibility of an appeal against a first instance award to a "Higher Arbitral Tribunal", if the amount in dispute exceeds EUR50,000 or if all parties have agreed that the award may be challenged.

Also in Hamburg, the arbitration court of the Hamburg chamber of commerce ("Schiedsgericht der Handelskammer Hamburg") has been providing arbitration services unrelated to a particular trade since 1884. While most other local chambers of commerce and industry refer to the DIS Arbitration Rules, the Hamburg

---

[27] The English version is available at http://www.waren-verein.de/en/permanent-court-of-arbitration/conditions-of-business.

chamber has its own rules, known as the "Regulativ", and administrates proceedings itself.

For construction disputes, the Deutsche Beton- und Bautechnik-Verein e.v. ("the DBV") offers its own dispute resolution rules, known as the "Streitlösungsordnung für das Bauwesen", recently amended on 1 July 2013. The DBV provides rules for arbitration and other types of ADR. The arbitration rules include provisions on third party intervention, which in practice can give rise to problems if parties cannot agree on arbitrators. The DBV's role in the proceedings is limited to the default appointment of an adjudicator, arbitrator for the respondent or chairman.

HONG KONG

James Kwan[1] and Annabella Chu[2]

A. LEGISLATION, TRENDS AND TENDENCIES

A.1 Legislation

International arbitration in Hong Kong continues to be governed by the Arbitration Ordinance (Cap. 609) ("Ordinance"), to which no significant legislative amendment was made in 2014.

A.2 Trends and Tendencies

In the past 12 months, courts in Hong Kong have continued to show support for arbitration, particularly the enforcement of arbitration awards. Recent decisions confirm that the bar for successfully challenging or preventing the enforcement of an award in Hong Kong is high.

---

[1]   James Kwan is a Partner in the Dispute Resolution Group of Baker & McKenzie in Hong Kong, where he leads the arbitration practice. He specializes in international commercial arbitration, with a focus on M&A, technology, sale of goods, infrastructure, and energy disputes; and has a range of international experience, having represented clients in arbitrations in Hong Kong, Asia, the Middle East, U.S. and Europe under the major institutional rules. The authors would like to thank Helen Liang for her assistance.

[2]   Annabella Chu is an Associate in the Dispute Resolution Group of Baker & McKenzie in Hong Kong. Her practice focuses on international arbitration and commercial litigation.

B. CASES

B.1 Court of First Instance Upholds Enforcement of Foreign Arbitral Awards

X Chartering v Y[3]

In this case, the Court of First Instance ("CFI") refused an application to set aside an order enforcing a foreign arbitral award made under section 86 of the Ordinance.

X Chartering and Y entered into a contract of affreightment ("Contract") on September 9, 2008. Under the contract, Y was obliged to make 15 shipments of coal from Indonesia to China during a period of two years commencing January 1, 2009. No shipments were ever made. X Chartering obtained a London arbitration award against Y for repudiation (the "Award"). Y unsuccessfully sought to appeal the Award in England on the ground that the tribunal had erred in its calculation of damages.

On July 2, 2013, X Chartering was granted leave to enforce the Award in Hong Kong by the CFI. Y applied to have the enforcement order set aside. Y contended that it was unable to present its case in the arbitration on a number of issues, including the arbitral tribunal's adoption of an erroneous measure of damages, and that it would be contrary to public policy to enforce the Award. The CFI rejected Y's arguments, finding that they amounted to an allegation that the tribunal had made an error of law, which has never been recognized as a ground for setting aside or refusing enforcement of an arbitral award in Hong Kong. The CFI confirmed that its only concern is with the process of the arbitral proceedings. It also found that both parties had made submissions, and witnesses on both sides were questioned during the arbitral proceedings.

---

[3]   [2014] HKCU 690.

Chan J of the CFI also took into account the fact that Y had previously sought to appeal the Award in England on different grounds. Y's failure to raise all grounds at once suggested "dilatory tactics", which was a consideration relevant to the exercise of the court's discretion to refuse to set aside the enforcement order.

Shanghai Fusheng Soya Food Co Ltd & Anor v Pulmuone Holdings Co Ltd[4]

The dispute between the parties arose from a joint venture ("JV") agreement entered into in September 2009. In May 2010, Pulmuone Holdings ("Respondent") commenced court proceedings against Shanghai Fusheng ("Applicant") on behalf of the JV Company in Shanghai ("Action"), seeking payment of RMB19.4 million to the JV Company. On July 6, 2010, the Respondent commenced arbitration against the Applicant ("Arbitration") for breach of the JV agreement seeking dissolution of the JV Company and contractual damages.

The arbitration hearing took place in June 2011. On May 15, 2012, the tribunal declared the arbitral proceedings closed. On the same day, the Shanghai court issued its decision in the Action (the "Judgment") ordering the Applicant to pay RMB1,892,807.90, a small fraction of the Respondent's claim. On June 14, 2012, the Applicant informed the arbitral tribunal of the Judgment. The tribunal did not admit the Judgment as the proceedings were closed and the Respondents did not consent to the admission. By an award dated August 11, 2012 (the "Award"), the tribunal found against the Applicant.

The Respondent sought enforcement of the Award in the CFI. The Applicant challenged enforcement arguing it was contrary to

---

[4]   [2014] HKCU 1201.

public policy to allow the Respondent to re-open issues during the arbitration that had already been decided in the Action. The CFI rejected the Applicant's argument and enforced the Award for two key reasons.

First, the Respondent had different capacities in the Action and the Arbitration: it was acting as the JV company's representative in the Action and a party to the JV agreement in the Arbitration. There was no substantial overlap of issue or remedy between the Judgment and Award.

Second, and more importantly, the Respondents participated and defended both the Action and the Arbitration. The Respondents had attempted to strike out issues which were purportedly duplicated in the Action during the Arbitration, but the applications were rejected by the tribunal. The Award was not contrary to public policy because there was "nothing shocking to the court's conscience, nothing offensive to notions of justice and morality, to permit the Respondent to enforce the Award".[5]

These two cases reflect the pro-arbitration attitude of the Hong Kong courts. They also demonstrate the strict approach the courts have adopted to the interpretation of their power to refuse enforcement of arbitral awards under s.86 of the Ordinance.

B.2 Challenge to the Tribunal's Jurisdiction and Challenge to Set Aside an Award

S Co v B Co[6]

S Co engaged B Co to be its consultant in relation to finalizing energy project bids to be submitted to the Nigerian government (the "Agreement"). Disputes arose. B Co accused S Co of hiring

---

[5]   At paragraph 37.

[6]   [2014] HKEC 825.

another consultant in breach of the Agreement and failing to pay B Co its full fees.

B Co commenced arbitration against S Co in Hong Kong on October 11, 2007. On April 9, 2010, S Co challenged the tribunal's jurisdiction. The tribunal dismissed the challenge in an interim award (the "Interim Award") dated April 5, 2013. The tribunal also made a costs award (the "Costs Award") directing S Co to pay 70% of B Co's arbitration costs.

S Co challenged the tribunal's jurisdiction in the CFI under s.34(3) of the Ordinance (Art. 16 of the UNCITRAL Model Law). It also sought to set aside the Interim Award and Costs Award under s.81 of the Ordinance (Art. 34 of the UNCITRAL Model Law) on the grounds, amongst others, that S Co was unable to present its case and the awards were contrary to public policy. The CFI rejected both of S Co's applications and ordered costs on an indemnity basis.

Regarding the jurisdictional challenge, after an extensive review of authorities, Chan J confirmed that once challenged by parties in accordance with s. 34 of the Ordinance, the jurisdiction of the arbitral tribunal will be reviewed *de novo*. In other words, the court is not bound by the tribunal's preliminary decision on its own jurisdiction. However, jurisdictional challenges "should not be a mere guise for challenging the tribunal's findings on the merits of the case."[7] The court takes into account the conduct of the parties during arbitration to determine whether the party has waived its right to object to any non-compliance with the Model Law. Failure by S Co to raise relevant grounds of jurisdictional challenge before the tribunal prevented S Co from relying on those grounds in its challenge before the court.

---

[7]   At paragraph 38.

Further, Chan J applied the test in *Grant Thornton International Limited v JBPB & Co (A Partnership)*[8] when interpreting the scope of the arbitration agreement. Since S Co's liability under separate letters of undertaking was necessary for the tribunal to decide B Co's claim under the Agreement, consultancy fees under the letters of understanding also fell within the tribunal's jurisdiction even though the letters of understanding did not contain any arbitration clause.

Regarding the application to set aside the Interim Award and Costs Award, the CFI rejected S Co's argument that it was unable to present its case, because S Co was not surprised or prejudiced by any new issue or claim made against it in the arbitration. The CFI confirmed the narrow scope of the public policy ground for setting aside an award and held that the Interim Award and Costs Award "comes nowhere near the standards required by the court for setting aside on the ground of public policy."[9] Neither the Interim Award nor the Cost Award were set aside under s.81 of the Ordinance.

B.3 Court Upholds Mainland Arbitration Award

Hong Kong Golden Source Ltd v New Elegant Investment Ltd & Anor[10]

Golden Source sought leave to enforce a mainland China arbitration award (the "Mainland Award") under section 84 of the Ordinance. New Elegant was ordered to deliver up some

---

[8] Unreported, HCCT 13/2002. This case was discussed in the 2013 International Arbitration Yearbook (Hong Kong). The test stated in this case was that only decisions which are clearly unrelated to or not reasonably required for the determination of the subject disputes, matters or issues submitted to arbitration should be held to fall outside the arbitration agreement.

[9] At paragraph 113.

[10] [2014] HKCU 2251.

shares (the "Shares") under the Mainland Award. The enforcement order was granted pursuant to s.92 of the Ordinance. The second respondent ("R2") sought to set the enforcement order aside, arguing that enforcement was against public policy. It was agreed that since the Mainland Award was granted in 2009, the present case should be governed by the pre-2010 Ordinance. However, as the parties accepted that the relevant principles under the old and the new Ordinances were similar, the application proceeded under the 2010 Ordinance.

R2 argued that he was the true owner of the Shares, and that the arbitration proceedings were a scheme calculated to deprive him of the Shares in breach of trust. Accordingly, the court should not help to complete such a scheme by enforcing the Mainland Award.

The CFI was not satisfied that this argument was sufficient to satisfy the public policy ground because (1) the allegations did not impinge upon the arbitral process or the substance of the award; and (2) the award seemed to be correct in principle. Even if the public policy ground were made out, the CFI would still refuse to exercise its discretion not to enforce the Mainland Award because: (1) R2 had since commenced high court proceedings in Hong Kong for ownership of the Shares, which was the most natural and appropriate forum to resolve the issue of ownership; (2) it was open for the parties to seek interim relief to preserve the assets in question from the high court; and (3) it was a "well established public policy that the court should lean towards the enforcement of foreign (including Mainland) arbitral awards".[11]

---

[11] At paragraph 42.

C. LOCAL ARBITRATION INSTITUTIONS

C.1 The Hong Kong International Arbitration Centre ("HKIAC")[12]

Background

The HKIAC was established in 1985 to meet the growing need for arbitral services in Asia. The HKIAC is fully self-financed and independent. Its location in Hong Kong's Central Business District provides comprehensive facilities, including over 20 separate meeting spaces capable of serving four to 180 individuals and multilingual support staff.

Types of Disputes Handled

Commercial disputes remain the key areas administered by the HKIAC (about 87%), followed by maritime (9%), construction, intellectual property, and private equity matters.

Number of Disputes Handled

In 2014, the HKIAC administered 107 arbitration proceedings, rising from 81 in 2013. The HKIAC handled 463 dispute resolution matters in 2013 (75% international; 25% domestic).

The HKIAC was used by parties from more than 30 jurisdictions in 2014. Chinese parties remain the most frequent users.

Provisions on Confidentiality of Arbitration

Art. 42.1 of the HKIAC Administered Arbitration Rules (2013) (the "Rules") provides that, unless otherwise agreed by the parties, no party may publish, disclose or communicate any information relating to (a) the arbitration under the arbitration

---

[12]   http://www.hkiac.org/en/

agreement(s) or (b) any awards. The prohibition is equally applicable to the arbitral tribunal, any emergency arbitrator, expert, witness, or secretary of the arbitral tribunal, and the HKIAC. The deliberations of the arbitral tribunal are also confidential (Art. 42.4).

Disclosure can be made by a party (a) to protect or pursue its legal rights or interests or to enforce or challenge the award in legal proceedings; (b) where required by law; or (c) to a professional or adviser (Art. 42.3).

HKIAC awards are not generally available. An award may only be published upon a request addressed to the HKIAC, in absence of objections from any party and after all references to the parties' names are deleted (Art. 42.5).

Availability of Expedited Procedures

Art. 41.1 provides for expedited procedures where (a) the aggregate amount in dispute does not exceed HKD25 million; (b) upon the parties' agreement; or (c) in cases of exceptional urgency. Normally, a sole arbitrator will be appointed, submissions are limited, the dispute will be decided on documents by default, and an award must be made within six months from the date the HKIAC provided the file to the tribunal (unless this time limit is extended).

Consolidation of Disputes between the Same Parties and Joinder of Third Parties

The tribunal has the power, at the request of a party and after consulting with the parties and any confirmed arbitrators, to consolidate two or more pending arbitrations under Art. 28 where (a) consolidation is agreed; or (b) all of the claims in the arbitrations are made under the same arbitration agreement; or (c) the claims are made under more than one arbitration agreement, but the HKIAC finds the arbitration agreements to be compatible and (i) the claims involve a common question of facts or law or (ii) rights to relief claimed are in respect of, or arise out of, the same transaction or series of transactions. The HKIAC will revoke the appointment of the existing arbitrators and appoint the tribunal in respect of the consolidated proceedings.

The tribunal is authorised to allow joinder of an additional party provided that the party is bound on its face by the arbitration agreement that gave rise to the arbitration. The joinder can be requested by an existing party to the arbitration or by the third party itself (Art. 27).

Time Limits for Rendering of the Award

The current Rules do not expressly stipulate a time limit for rendering the award, except for awards rendered under the expedited procedure (which must be made within six months). However, the arbitral tribunal and the parties are required to do everything necessary to ensure the efficiency of the arbitration under Art. 13.5.

Fee Structure

In general, three types of fees are payable for arbitrations administered by the HKIAC: (1) a registration fee of HKD8,000 payable by the claimant when submitting a Notice of Arbitration; (2) HKIAC's administrative fees (calculated by reference to a scale as a portion of the sum in dispute up to a maximum of HKD290,800 for a sum in dispute worth over HKD400 million); and (3) the arbitral tribunal's fees. The Rules expressly offer the parties a unique choice to remunerate the tribunal based on the amount in dispute or on an hourly basis. There is cap on an arbitrator's hourly rate, currently at HKD6,500.00 (unless both parties agree). If the parties consider that the dispute is a high-value, yet straightforward one, they can opt for an hourly arrangement to save costs. The parties may choose to determine the tribunal's fees based on the amount in dispute if the case is highly complex and would take the tribunal a considerable amount of time to decide.

A separate fee structure applies to emergency arbitrator procedures.

Treatment of Costs of the Arbitration

The HKIAC Secretariat will request deposits for costs on the constitution of the tribunal (Art. 40). The tribunal must determine the costs of the arbitration in its award, including (a) its fees; (b) its expenses; (c) the costs of expert advice and other assistance it required; (d) the expenses incurred by witnesses; (e) the legal costs of the parties; and (f) the registration and administrative fees payable to the HKIAC. Items (b) to (e) must be reasonable (Art. 33.1).

Special or Unusual Features (If Any)

In August 2014, the HKIAC added a provision stipulating the law of the arbitration agreement in its model clause: "The law of this arbitration clause shall be ... (Hong Kong law)." The HKIAC is the only arbitration institution that expressly encourages parties to clearly stipulate the governing law of the arbitration agreement. This distinguishes HKIAC from a number of arbitration institutions which adopt a set default position. For example, the draft 2015 ACICA Rules propose that the law of the seat should govern the law of the arbitration agreement unless the parties have agreed otherwise. The HKIAC's approach avoids a rigid test and makes it clear that the choice of law provision is optional, stating:

This provision should be included particularly where the law of the substantive contract and the law of the seat are different. The law of the arbitration clause potentially governs matters including the formation, existence, scope, validity, legality, interpretation, termination, effects and enforceability of the arbitration clause and identities of the parties to the arbitration clause. It does not replace the law governing the substantive contract.

Recent Developments (If Any)

See under *Special or Unusual Features* above.

HUNGARY

József Antal,[1] Zoltán Szür[2] and Bálint Varga[3]

A. LEGISLATION, TRENDS AND TENDENCIES

A.1 Legislation

International arbitration in Hungary continues to be governed by the Act LXXI of 1994 on Arbitration (the "Hungarian Arbitration Act"), to which no legislative amendment was made in 2014. However, it is noteworthy that the new Hungarian Civil Code (the "Civil Code"),[4] which entered into force on 15 March 2014, introduced a significant amendment relating to the approach to arbitration clauses in consumer contracts.

Pursuant to Section 6:104 (1) i) of the Civil Code, a contract between a consumer[5] and a business entity[6] containing terms and conditions that have not been individually negotiated is considered unfair if its object or effect is to exclude or hinder the consumer's right to take legal action or exercise any other legal remedy, particularly by requiring the consumer to take disputes

---

[1] Partner at Baker & McKenzie's Budapest office. Routinely assists clients in litigation, alternative dispute resolution and procurement matters, and has advised clients in numerous industry sectors from transportation to energy and financial services to telecommunications.

[2] Attorney at Baker & McKenzie's Budapest office. Works on civil and administrative lawsuits both domestic and international.

[3] Associate at Baker & McKenzie's Budapest office. Works on civil and administrative lawsuits both domestic and international.

[4] Act V of 2013 on the Civil Code of Hungary.

[5] Any natural person acting for purposes which are outside its trade, business or profession.

[6] Any person acting for purposes which are inside its trade, business or profession.

exclusively to arbitration. In other words, arbitration clauses in consumer contracts are to be considered unfair unless the parties to the consumer contract individually negotiated this term or it is expressly prescribed by law. We are not aware of any legislation which would prescribe arbitration relating to any kind of consumer contract. Therefore, if the arbitration clause is part of the general terms and conditions of the consumer contract or otherwise such term is not negotiated individually by the parties to the consumer contract, the arbitration clause is to be considered unfair. The unfair contract term will then be null and void.[7]

In light of the above, the business entity must individually negotiate the arbitration clause with the consumer, or else if any dispute arises relating to the consumer contract, the consumer has the right to avoid arbitration (that is, to challenge the arbitration clause).

The amendment was based on Uniformity Decision No. 3/2013 of the Curia[8] (the Decision"),[9] which provides more protection to consumers than the relevant EU Council Directive 93/13/EEC (the "Directive") requires.[10]

A.2 Trends and Tendencies

There was no significant change in the general attitude to arbitration over the last 12 months. A tendency to a regression in the use of arbitration may be resulting from (i) the economic recession; (ii) the amendment to the Hungarian Arbitration Act

---

[7] Dr. Wallacher, L. (2014). The unfairness of the arbitration clause in consumer contracts. *Európai Jog* vol. 3 pp. 10-16.

[8] Formerly known as the Supreme Court of Hungary.

[9] The Curia renders uniformity decisions in cases of principal importance in order to ensure the uniform application of law within the Hungarian judiciary.

[10] Point (q) of the Directive's annex considers the arbitration clause unfair only if the arbitration not covered by legal provisions.

B. Cases

in 2012 that excludes the possibility of arbitration as a means of resolving disputes relating to national assets located in Hungary;[11] and (iii) the amendment discussed at A.1, above. The statistics of the Permanent Arbitration Court attached to the Hungarian Chamber of Commerce and Industry ("HCCI Arbitration Court") confirm this trend.[12]

B. CASES

B.1 Arbitration Clauses Are Generally Unfair in Consumer Contracts

In the Decision (as discussed above), the Curia held the use of arbitration clauses to be unfair in consumer contracts if the arbitration clause in question is not negotiated individually by the parties to the consumer contract. The Curia examined three different court opinions relating to the lawfulness of the arbitration clause in the general terms and conditions of consumer contracts.

In one of these judgments, the Metropolitan Court of Appeal[13] had considered such arbitration clauses lawful on the basis of Section 7 (2) of the previous Hungarian Civil Code,[14] which granted a right to the parties to choose arbitration instead of litigation. Thus, these arbitration clauses were considered lawful because Section 209 (6) of the previous Civil Code declared that any contract terms defined by a legal provision cannot be deemed unfair.

---

[11] It seems likely that such, questionable exclusion will be terminated by the legislator in 2015. The related draft bill has been prepared for legislative debate before the Parliament.

[12] See also C.1, below ("Number of disputes handled").

[13] Metropolitan Court of Appeal's judgment No. ÍH 2012.67.

[14] Act IV of 1959 on the Civil Code of the Republic of Hungary.

In another opinion, the Court of Appeal of Szeged[15] did not exclude the possibility that such arbitration clause may be unfair under special circumstances; however, as a rule of thumb it also considered such arbitration clauses lawful on the basis of a government decree.[16] According to that decree, only clauses that exclude consumer's right to take legal action or exercise any other legal remedy covered by legal provisions must be deemed unfair.[17] As arbitration procedures are covered by the Hungarian Arbitration Act, an arbitration clause cannot be generally deemed unfair.

Finally, the Curia also examined the practice of the Metropolitan Court, which was contrary to the above legal positions. The Metropolitan Court, in a decision, had declared arbitration clauses to be unfair as, in the arbitration procedure, exemptions from costs and expenses cannot be granted to the consumer (in contrast to ordinary civil proceedings where reduction of charges may be granted in order to ensure the consumer's right to apply to the courts).

The Curia—despite the majority position—concluded that such arbitration clauses are unfair if, due to their exclusivity, they preclude ordinary court proceedings, thereby restricting the consumer's rights to enforce claims.

In the wake of the Decision, the new Civil Code accepted a more consumer protective approach relating to arbitration clauses as set out in point A.1 above; as a result, this change is likely to further discourage or prevent business entities from

---

[15] Court of Appeal of Szeged's judgment No. Pf.I.20.398/2012/2.

[16] Government Decree No. 18 of 1999 (II. 5.). This government decree implemented the Directive, and it expired on 15 March 2014, when the new Civil Code entered into force and incorporated also the Directive.

[17] Section 1 (1)i) of the Government Decree No. 18 of 1999 (II. 5.)

incorporating arbitration clauses in the general terms and conditions of their consumer contracts.

B.2 Arbitration Court's Liability for Damages

There were two court decisions[18] rendered in 2014 relating to this topic. In these decisions, the Curia declared that the arbitration courts' liability for damages can be established on the basis of the general non-contractual liability rules of civil law, notwithstanding any contractual exclusion or limitation clauses, e.g. in the arbitration court's rules of proceedings.

The following conditions must be met to establish an arbitration court's liability: (i) the general criteria of noncontractual liability; and (ii) the obviously unlawful judicature or interpretation of law affecting the merits of the arbitration court's award.

It was also declared that a previous invalidation proceeding (as a remedy being used against the allegedly unlawful award) is not a prerequisite of the establishment of the arbitration court's non-contractual liability because the invalidation proceeding is an extraordinary remedy (and its subject is different anyway).

C.   LOCAL ARBITRATION INSTITUTIONS

C.1   HCCI Arbitration Court and Other Permanent Arbitration Courts

Background

The HCCI Arbitration Court attached to the Hungarian Chamber of Commerce and Industry in Budapest[19] continues to be the most well-known and frequently used permanent arbitration

---

[18]   Curia's judgments no. Pfv.III.21.148/2013/4 and Pfv.IV.20.816/2014/11.

[19]   For further information, visit www.mkik.hu (also in English).

court in Hungary. The HCCI Arbitration Court is also considered to be the most prestigious one from the aspect of age, as in 2014 it celebrates the 65th anniversary of its foundation.

There are also other permanent arbitration courts operating in Hungary: (i) the Energy Arbitration Court; (ii) the Arbitration Court of Financial and Capital Markets, and (iii) the Arbitration Court attached to the Hungarian Chamber of Agriculture.

Types of Disputes Handled

The jurisdiction of the HCCI Arbitration Court encompasses the settlement of all disputes where: (i) at least one of the parties deals professionally with economic activity, and the legal dispute is in connection with this activity; (ii) the parties may freely dispose of the subject-matter of the proceedings; and (iii) the jurisdiction of the HCCI Arbitration Court was stipulated in an arbitration agreement or is required by an international convention.[20]

The Energy Arbitration Court, which is also seated in Budapest, started to operate in 2009. The Energy Arbitration Court is non-exclusively authorized to proceed in legal disputes on rights and obligations arising from the articles of acts on gas supply and electricity and from contracts concluded between license holders under the scope of these acts, provided that the parties referred to such matters to arbitration and that they are free to dispose of the subject-matter of the proceeding.[21] Targeted clients of the Energy Arbitration Court are traders, power stations and industrial costumers. The roll of arbitrators consists of industry experts and lawyers with considerable experience in the energy

---

[20]   Article 1 of the Rules of Proceedings of the HCCI Arbitration Court.

[21]   Article 1.2 of the Memorandum of the Energy Arbitration Court.

sector. The Rules of Proceedings[22] of the Energy Arbitration Court are similar to the Rules of Proceedings of the HCCI Arbitration Court. Still, it is worth pointing out that the Energy Arbitration Court endeavors to complete the proceedings within five months from the formation of the arbitral tribunal.[23]

The Arbitration Court of Financial and Capital Markets has exclusive jurisdiction to handle domestic and international arbitration cases arising in these industries.

The Arbitration Court attached to the Hungarian Chamber of Agriculture is designed to adjudicate arbitration cases of companies in the agricultural sector.

The HCCI Arbitration Court is the most significant arbitration institution in Hungary and generally proceeds in international arbitration cases.

Numbers of Disputes Handled

The statistics of the HCCI Arbitration Court are capable of showing the trends of international and domestic arbitration in Hungary, as the HCCI Arbitration Court is considered to be the most significant arbitration court.

According to these statistics, the number of domestic arbitration cases was reduced by more than 50% after the financial crisis of 2008. A one-third reduction can also be seen in the number of international arbitration cases. There were only 125 active cases (including 20 international cases[24]) before the HCCI Arbitration Court in 2014; nevertheless, in the last two decades, 6,493

---

[22]   *See* www.eavb.hu.

[23]   Article 6 of the Rules of Proceedings of the Energy Arbitration Court.

[24]   With some statutory exceptions, the HCCI Arbitration Court has exclusivity to proceed in international arbitration cases in Hungary.

arbitration cases were filed in total, containing 962 international cases, and 153 of them were conducted in foreign languages.

Provisions on Confidentiality of Arbitration

In the absence of an agreement between the parties to the contrary, arbitration proceedings are not public.[25] Arbitrators must keep confidential all information that they receive in the course of the proceedings[26] even after the proceedings have terminated. The HCCI Arbitration Court may not give any information on pending proceedings and on its decisions rendered, or on the contents thereof. The decision of the HCCI Arbitration Court may be published in legal journals or special publications only upon the permission of the President of the Arbitration Court and only in such a way that the interests of the parties do not suffer any harm (the parties will suffer no harm to any legitimate interest); furthermore, the names of the parties, their countries of residence, the nature and value of the services rendered, or any of these particulars can only be included in a publication with the express consent of both parties.[27]

Availability of Expedited Procedures

The sub-rules for expedited proceedings of the Rules of Proceedings of the HCCI Arbitration Court ("Rules of Proceedings") are applicable if the parties agreed this in an arbitration agreement. According to these rules, the parties have a shorter submission deadline. The dispute is settled by a sole arbitrator, unless the parties otherwise agree by requesting that the case be judged by an arbitral tribunal of three members. The sole arbitrator renders a decision without conducting an oral

---

[25] Section 29 of the Hungarian Arbitration Act.

[26] *Id.* at Section 11.

[27] Article 15 of the Rules of Proceedings of the HCCI Arbitration Court.

hearing, unless (i) either party requests such hearing in writing or (ii) the sole arbitrator considers this necessary.

Consolidation of Disputes between the Same Parties and Joinder of Third Parties

The Rules of Proceedings do not expressly regulate dispute consolidation options. However, Article 17 of the Rules of Proceedings provide that, in respect of issues not provided for by mandatory provisions of the Act on Arbitration[28] and by the provisions of the Rules of Proceedings, and failing an unanimous declaration by the parties, the arbitral tribunal proceeds at its own discretion, taking into consideration the general principles of proceedings appropriate for the domestic or international character of the legal relationship between the parties. Therefore, in our view, consolidation of disputes between the same parties may be possible during the arbitral proceedings based on Article 17.

As to the joinder of third parties, Article 30 of the Rules of Proceedings provides that any person having a legal interest in the outcome of the arbitral proceedings may submit an interpleader in order to assist the party having the same interest to win the case. A request concerning interpleading must be submitted to the Arbitration Court at least 15 days before the day of the first hearing. The admissibility of an interpleader will be decided by the arbitral tribunal. An interpleader may only be admitted if all parties give their consent and the third party's legal interest is certified before the arbitration court.

Time Limits for Rendering of the Award

Whenever possible, the HCCI Arbitration Court must complete the proceedings within six months, as from the formation of the

---

[28] Hungarian Arbitration Act.

arbitral tribunal,[29] while expedited proceedings are to be completed within a hundred days from the date of the filing of the statement of claim if possible.[30]

Fee Structure

The arbitration fee consists of the aggregate amount of the registration fee, the administrative expenses, the arbitrators' fee and applicable rates and taxes.[31] The registration fee is HUF25,000; in case of expedited proceedings with a sole arbitrator it is HUF10,000. The administrative expenses and the arbitrators' fee are determined as a percentage of the amount in controversy. For instance, if the amount in dispute is HUF10 million, the administrative expenses are HUF90,000 and one arbitrator's fee is HUF220,000.[32] The rates and taxes consist of a government fee and social insurance contribution. The government fee is 1% of the amount in controversy, but not less than HUF5,000 and no more than HUF250,000. The social insurance contribution is 27% of the arbitrator's fees, but is to be paid only by Hungarian citizens. In light of the above, if the amount in controversy is HUF10 million and an arbitral tribunal of three members hears the case, the aggregated amount to be paid is HUF 941,000; in case of Hungarian citizens it is HUF 1,137,020 as a result of the social insurance contribution.

---

[29] Article 10 of the Rules of Proceedings of the HCCI Arbitration Court.

[30] *Id.* at Article 45.

[31] The fee chart is attached to the Rules of Proceedings of the HCCI Arbitration Court as Annex No. 1 and 2.

[32] In case of an arbitral tribunal, the arbitrator's fee shall be multiplied by the number of the members of the arbitral tribunal, that is by three. The arbitrator's fee of the presiding arbitrator and of the sole arbitrator shall be increased by 30% of the arbitrator's fee.

C. Local Arbitration Institutions

Treatment of Costs of the Arbitration

The costs of the arbitration must be advanced by the claimant, but are borne at the end by the losing party in proportion to its fault established in the case.

Special or Unusual Features (If Any)

The parties may freely determine the language of the arbitral proceedings, if suitable conditions for proceedings in the given language can be provided.[33] However, it is noteworthy that if the proceedings are conducted in a language other than Hungarian, German or English, then the parties shall advance and bear the excess costs that may be incurred as a result of the use of such a foreign language in equal proportions.[34]

Recent Developments (If Any)

Not applicable.

---

[33] Article 9 of the Rules of Proceedings of the HCCI Arbitration Court.

[34] *See* Article 8 of the Regulation on the arbitration fees, costs and expenses of the parties.

INDIA

Zia Mody[1] and Aditya Vikram Bhat[2]

A. LEGISLATION, TRENDS AND TENDENCIES

A.1 Legislation

International arbitration in India continues to be governed by the Arbitration and Conciliation Act, 1996 ("Arbitration Act"), to which no legislative amendment was made in 2014.

A.2 Trends and Tendencies

The 246th report of the Law Commission of India published in August 2014 ("LCI Report") has recommended various amendments to the Arbitration Act. Acknowledging issues frequently arising in arbitration proceedings such as high costs and delays, the Law Commission has suggested amendments including: (i) the statutory recognition of institutional arbitration and emergency arbitrators appointed by institutions; (ii) the introduction of a model schedule of fees for arbitrators; (iii) provision for continuous hearings for evidence and argument, and restrictions on adjournment; (iv) introduction of time limits on courts to dispose applications to set aside awards and proceedings for enforcement of awards; (v) express clarification to the effect that allegations of fraud and

---

[1] Zia Mody is the Managing and Founding Partner of AZB & Partners and is one of India's foremost attorneys. She is a member of the London Court of International Arbitration. Zia has been nominated as one of the world's leading practitioners by The International Who's Who of Commercial Arbitration in 2013 and The International Who's Who of Business Lawyers 2013.

[2] Aditya Vikram Bhat is a Partner at AZB & Partners, Bangalore and is a member of the users council of LCIA India. His practice areas include litigation and arbitration.

complicated issues of fact are arbitrable; (vi) constituting dedicated benches of courts to hear cases related to arbitration; (vii) granting exclusive jurisdiction to the High Court for all issues arising out of international commercial arbitrations; (viii) removing the ability to appeal from decisions of the High Court on appointment of arbitrators; (ix) limiting grounds for challenges to awards; (x) enabling proceedings for enforcement to proceed even when a challenge is pending, in the absence of a court-granted stay; (xi) using the more recognized expression "seat of arbitration" instead of "place of arbitration" at appropriate places in the statute; (xii) ensuring independence of arbitrators; and (xiii) provisions for interest and costs to be imposed on the losing side.

While the above recommendations do not have the force of law until enacted by parliament and notified with the assent of the president of India, it is widely expected that these recommendations will be acted on by the Government of India.[3]

Meanwhile, there is a continuing trend to reduce judicial intervention in arbitrations (especially foreign-seated arbitrations) and challenges to arbitral awards based upon narrow grounds within the Supreme Court of India and the various High Courts. This is discussed in further detail in Section B.

---

[3] The authors understand from a press release dated December 29, 2014 by the Press Information Bureau of the Government of India that the Government of India has issued an ordinance amending the Act. This ordinance does not seem to have received the assent of the President of India nor has it been notified in the Gazette of India. As such, no amendments are in force as on January 19, 2015.

B. CASES

B.1 The Duty of Courts to Make Arbitration Clauses Work

The Supreme Court in *Enercon (India) Ltd. v. Enercon GMBH* [4] was faced with a complex joint venture dispute that had manifested itself in multiple litigations in India and England. Among other proceedings, the foreign joint venture partner (respondents before the Supreme Court of India) had initiated an arbitration proceeding in London, England ("London Arbitration") pursuant to an arbitration clause contained in an Intellectual Property License Agreement ("IPLA"). The London Arbitration was stayed by an Indian court (the "Anti-Arbitration Injunction") at the behest of the Indian joint venture partner on the basis that the IPLA was not a concluded contract and therefore there was no agreement to arbitrate between the parties. The Anti-Arbitration Injunction was initially vacated by an appellate court, but thereafter restored by the Bombay High Court exercising its supervisory jurisdiction. Separately, an arbitrator nominated by one of the parties described the arbitration clause in the IPLA as having defects and being "unworkable". The foreign joint venture partner nonetheless proceeded with its attempt to commence arbitration and obtained an anti-suit injunction ("Anti-Suit Injunction") in the English High Court to restrain the Indian partner from enforcing the Anti-Arbitration Injunction. The English High Court also granted an order freezing certain assets of the Indian partner. Subsequently, both these injunctions were vacated, and the parties proceeded before the Bombay High Court. The Bombay High Court found that there was a concluded contract governed by Indian law and referred the parties to arbitration.

---

[4]   (2014)5SCC1.

On appeal, the Supreme Court examined several issues including the existence and severability of the arbitration clause, governing law and seat of arbitration, and concurrent jurisdiction of the Indian and foreign courts. The Supreme Court held that when faced with an "unworkable" arbitration clause, it was the duty of the court to respect the intention of the parties to arbitrate and make the clause workable within the contours of the law. It was held that: (i) the intention of the parties was to treat India as the seat of arbitration since Indian law was made applicable to the curial aspects of the agreement, while London was merely the venue; and (ii) consequently, Indian courts would have exclusive jurisdiction over matters incidental to the arbitration and English courts would not have concurrent jurisdiction. The court referred the parties to arbitration and constituted the arbitral tribunal, while further granting an injunction restraining the proceedings in the English High Court.

While the case may not have substantially altered the law, the decision is significant due to the court's: (i) handling of a complex maze of proceedings and facts to eventually make an agreement to arbitrate workable; and (ii) constructive treatment of the issue of conflicting jurisdictions.

B.2 Fraud and Misrepresentation Are Not a Bar to Arbitrability

The dispute in the Supreme Court's judgment of *World Sport Group (Mauritius) Ltd. v. MSM Satellite (Singapore) Pte. Ltd.*[5] arose out of a facilitation agreement between the parties relating to the broadcast of an annual cricket tournament conducted by the Board for Control of Cricket in India ("BCCI"). Under the facilitation agreement, MSM, the respondent before the Supreme Court of India, was required to pay certain amounts to WSG, the appellant. The respondent had sought to rescind its obligations,

---

[5]   AIR2014SC968.

claiming that the contract was voidable due to fraudulent misrepresentation. The appellant initiated arbitration in Singapore. The respondent approached the Bombay High Court for an injunction restraining the arbitration. The court initially declined the injunction. An appellate bench granted the injunction and held, among other things, that since the facilitation agreement dealt with finances of the BCCI (which the court erroneously described as a public body), the facilitation agreement was "contrary to public policy". The court also held that since there were serious allegations of fraud involved, only a court could decide the dispute.

On appeal, the Supreme Court was called to examine whether the Bombay High Court: (a) had the jurisdiction to entertain the injunction proceedings, and (b) was right in granting the injunction. The Supreme Court found that although the Bombay High Court had jurisdiction to hear the injunction proceedings,[6] it was wrong in granting the injunction. The Supreme Court held that the Bombay High Court in these proceedings was only required to consider whether the arbitration clause was null, void, inoperative, or incapable of being performed. Further, it held that an arbitration agreement does not become inoperative or incapable of being performed merely because parties allege fraud and misrepresentation, and that courts cannot refuse to refer the parties to arbitration on this ground.

The issue of arbitrability of allegations of fraud was examined again in the case of *Swiss Timing Limited v Organizing*

---

[6] The facilitation deed was executed in 2009 and prior to the judgment of the Supreme Court in Bharat Aluminium in September 2012. After the decision of the Supreme Court in Bharat Aluminium, Indian courts may no longer entertain suits for injunctions in respect of arbitrations seated outside India, arising out of agreements to arbitrate entered into after the judgment in Bharat Aluminium.

Committee, Commonwealth Games.[7] Although the contract under consideration was being examined in separate criminal proceedings that had been initiated under the Indian Penal Code, 1860 and the Prevention of Corruption Act, 1988, an application was filed by Swiss Timing for the appointment of an arbitrator. The Supreme Court held that an objection to arbitration proceedings could not be raised on the grounds that criminal proceedings are ongoing and that such proceedings could continue simultaneously with the arbitration. Further, the court reiterated that the arbitral tribunal was competent to decide on its own jurisdiction, including the issue of whether the underlying contract is void.

B.3 Did the Court Regress on the Scope of Public Policy?

Conflict with "public policy" is a ground on which a domestic award may be challenged and the enforcement of foreign awards may be refused under the Arbitration Act. In the 2013 judgment in *Lal Mahal Ltd v Progetto Grano Spa*,[8] the Supreme Court had narrowed the interpretation of "public policy" in the context of a proceeding to enforce a foreign arbitral award. In *ONGC v Western Geco International Ltd.*,[9] the Supreme Court recently applied (albeit in the context of a challenge to a domestic award) a fairly expansive definition of the expression "public policy". The dispute in this case resulted in the arbitral tribunal passing an award imposing damages for a delay in the timelines stipulated under the contract concerned, which was challenged, among other things, on the grounds of a violation of public policy.

The Supreme Court chose not to be influenced by the jurisprudence of *Lal Mahal* and expanded on the 2003 judgment

---

[7]   2014(7)SCALE 515.

[8]   2013 (8) SCALE 489.

[9]   2014(9) SCC 263.

in *ONGC Ltd* v *Saw Pipes Limited*[10] to hold that the "fundamental policy of Indian law" constituted an aspect of "public policy" and that while it was not possible to arrive at a comprehensive definition of fundamental policy of Indian law, the phrase would include "...all such fundamental principles as providing a basis for administration of justice and enforcement of law...". The court further held that these principles would in turn include the requirement to adopt a "judicial approach" and to apply principles of "natural justice" and standards of "reasonableness" while adjudicating a challenge to an arbitral award.

C. LOCAL ARBITRATION INSTITUTIONS

Institutional arbitration is in its nascent stages in India. Users of arbitration (parties, their counsel, and even arbitrators) have just recently begun to understand the role that a robust domestic institution can play in the successful conduct of an arbitration. The LCI Report has emphasized the need to statutorily recognize and promote institutional arbitration. The report recognizes the work done by the Delhi High Court International Arbitration Centre and the Nani Palkhivala Arbitration Centre in Chennai. Apart from these, other high courts (Karnataka and Punjab & Haryana, for example) and chambers of commerce in some cities (Bombay and Madras, for example) have functional arbitration centers that administer arbitrations.

LCIA India is a notable emerging institution in India and was established in 2009 as a subsidiary of the LCIA.

Interestingly, SIAC has opened an offshore office in Mumbai to deal with the increasing number of arbitration proceedings arising from India, although this office does not directly administer any India-related arbitrations.

---

[10] (2003) 5 SCC 705.

C.1 LCIA India

Background

LCIA India was established in 2009 as a subsidiary of the LCIA, offering arbitration as well as mediation services. Its proceedings are conducted under the LCIA India Rules, 2010 ("LCIA India Rules"), which are framed specifically for arbitrations in India and are distinct from the LCIA Rules. LCIA India is based at the World Trade Tower in New Delhi and operates under a three-tier structure, comprising the Board of Directors (which deals with administrative matters), the Arbitration Court (which is the final authority for the proper application of the LCIA India Rules, appointing tribunals, determining challenges to arbitrators, and controlling costs) and the Secretariat (which is responsible for the day to day working of the institution).

Types of Disputes Handled

While no statistics are available on disputes being currently handled, arbitration clauses selecting LCIA India appear to be an emerging choice in a variety of commercial contracts as well as investment and shareholders agreements where arbitrations are seated in India. There are no restrictions under the LCIA India Rules as to the type of dispute or industry.

Numbers of Disputes Handled

There are no statistics available from LCIA India. The authors expect that the number of disputes currently handled is likely to be low due to LCIA India being relatively recent, while institutional arbitration itself is nascent in India. However, the authors understand from conversations with office bearers of LCIA India that the aggregate amounts involved in disputes being handled are nearly USD1.5 billion.

C. Local Arbitration Institutions

Provisions on Confidentiality of Arbitration

Pursuant to Article 30.1 of the LCIA India Rules, parties undertake to keep all awards, materials used in and created for the purpose of the arbitration, and all other documents that are not otherwise in the public domain confidential, unless the parties expressly agree in writing to the contrary. However, this duty to maintain confidentiality does not apply to disclosures that may be required of a party by legal duty, to protect or pursue a legal right or to enforce or challenge an award in *bona fide* legal proceedings before a court or other judicial authority.

Availability of Expedited Procedures

The LCIA India Rules permit an expedited timeline with respect to the formation of the arbitral tribunal. A party may apply in writing to the LCIA India Court for the expedited formation of the Arbitral Tribunal, at any time on or after the commencement of the arbitration. When such an application is made, the LCIA India Court may, in its discretion, curtail the time limits prescribed under the LCIA India Rules for the delivery of the response to the claims and of any matters or documents that are missing from the request for arbitration. The LCIA India Court is not permitted to curtail any other time limit.

Consolidation of Disputes between the Same Parties and Joinder of Third Parties

The LCIA India Rules do not provide for consolidation of proceedings. Joinder of third parties is permitted if the third party and the applicant party have consented to the joinder in writing.

Time Limits for Rendering of the Award

The LCIA India Rules do not prescribe a time limit within which the tribunal needs to pass the award.

Fee Structure

The costs of arbitration are determined by the LCIA India Court in accordance with a schedule of costs. The schedule of costs prescribes certain fixed payments to be made with respect to administrative charges and appointment of arbitrators, and a sum of 5% of the fees of the tribunal (excluding expenses) is also payable towards LCIA India's general overhead. In addition, the tribunal's fees, time spent by the Secretariat of the LCIA India in the administration of the arbitration and by the members of the LCIA India Court in deciding any challenge, are charged separately on an hourly basis.

Treatment of Costs of the Arbitration

Parties involved in the arbitration are jointly and severally liable to the arbitral tribunal and LCIA India for the costs of arbitration. The arbitral award will specify the total amount of costs involved in the arbitration and the proportion in which the parties will be required to bear such costs.

Special or Unusual Features

LCIA India is unique, as it is the only institution in India with an international reputation and pedigree that has a case management setup, and administers arbitrations under custom-drafted rules.

Recent Developments

The authors understand from conversations with office bearers of LCIA India that LCIA India is expected to publish new rules in early 2015. These rules are expected to include, among others, a provision for the appointment of emergency arbitrators.

INDONESIA

Andi Yusuf Kadir[1] and Putri Arnita Rahmaniar[2]

A. LEGISLATION, TRENDS AND TENDENCIES

International arbitration in Indonesia continues to be governed by Law No. 30 of 1999 on Arbitration and Alternative Dispute Resolutions ("Arbitration Law"), to which no legislative amendment was made in 2014. Indonesia has also ratified the New York Convention through Presidential Decree No. 34 of 1981.

B. CASES

B.1 Setting Aside Domestic Arbitration Awards

Under Article 70 of the Arbitration Law, a party can file an application to Indonesian courts to set aside a domestic arbitration award if there is a suspicion that one of the following conditions has occurred: (a) after the award was rendered, a letter or document submitted in the examination proceedings was admitted as forged or declared as a forgery; (b) after the award was rendered, documents which are dispositive were discovered,

---

[1] Andi Yusuf Kadir is a Partner of Hadiputranto, Hadinoto & Partners, a member firm of Baker & McKenzie International in Indonesia. He has extensively represented multinational corporations and local companies in domestic (BANI) and international arbitration (SIAC, ICC), complex litigation proceedings, court-sanctioned debt restructuring processes, and bankruptcy/insolvency litigation. He has acted for both creditors and debtors in restructuring and insolvency cases in Indonesian courts. He is also experienced in administrative law disputes with government departments and agencies, as well as employment litigation.

[2] Putri Arnita Rahmaniar is an Associate of Hadiputranto, Hadinoto & Partners, a member firm of Baker & McKenzie International in Indonesia.

having been concealed by the opposing party; or (c) the award was a result of fraud committed by one of the parties during the arbitration proceedings. The elucidation of Article 70 stipulates, "Reasons for setting aside mentioned in this article must be proven by a court decision. If the court decides that the reasons are proven or are not proven, this court decision can be used by the court as a basis to grant or reject an application. "

Some commentators have argued that Article 70 is inoperative. Under Article 71 of the Arbitration Law, an application to set aside a domestic arbitration award must be submitted within 30 days after the registration of the award at the relevant court. Article 59 (1) requires a domestic arbitration award to be registered at the relevant court within 30 days after the award is rendered. In other words, an applicant has 60 days at the most to obtain a court decision proving the reasons under Article 70 before submitting an application for setting aside the award, which is impracticable and inoperative. However, the Supreme Court has consistently advocated this position in *PT Padjadjaran Indah Prima v. PT Pembangunan Perumahan* [2008], *PT SMG Consultants v. Indonesian National Board of Arbitration (BANI)* [2012], *PT Binasentra Muliatata v. PT Bawana Margatama* [2012], *PT Nindya Karya v. PT Tranfocus* [2013] and *PT Bank Permata v. PT Nikko Securities Indonesia* [2013].

Furthermore, there is also no clarity on whether Article 70 is limitative. Thus, a question as to whether it is justifiable to introduce reasons other than the ones that have been stipulated under Article 70 remains unsolved. This confusion is largely due to inconsistent texts between Article 70 and the general elucidation of the Arbitration Law. While Article 70 appears to be exhaustive, the general elucidation of the Arbitration Law suggests otherwise. It stipulates "Chapter VII regulates the setting aside of an arbitration award. It is possible for several reasons, among others: [the reasons under article 70 are cited]."

B. Cases

The Supreme Court has also failed to provide consistent guidance here. In *PT Padjadjaran Indah Prima v. PT Pembangunan Rumah* [2008], the Supreme Court argued that Article 70 is limitative. This position was further upheld in *PT Cipta Kridatama v. Indonesian National Board of Arbitration (BANI)* [2011] and *PT Sumi Asih v. Vinmar Overseas Ltd* [2012]. However in *Comarindo Express Tama Tour & Travel v. Yemen Airways* [2005], the Supreme Court decided to set aside a BANI arbitration award on the basis that there was no valid arbitration agreement between the disputing parties. The same approach was also taken by the Supreme Court in *PT Royal Industries Indonesia v. PT Identrust Security International, et al* [2013].

On November 11, 2014, the Indonesian Constitutional Court issued Decision No. 15/PUU-XII/2014 to invalidate the elucidation of Article 70 of the Arbitration Law on the grounds that it is unconstitutional. The Constitutional Court argued that the elucidation of Article 70 has created legal uncertainty in respect of its application, particularly whether one needs to obtain a court decision proving one of the reasons under Article 70 has been fulfilled before commencing setting aside proceedings against an arbitration award. In addition, the Constitutional Court also held that the elucidation of Article 70 violates the Indonesian Constitution as it deprives Indonesian citizens of their rights to legal certainty and protection.

While the Constitutional Court decision provides clarity that one can commence setting aside proceedings without obtaining a court decision, it remains to be seen if the Indonesian courts will still allow an applicant to introduce reasons other than the ones that have been stipulated under Article 70 to set aside an arbitration award.

C. LOCAL ARBITRATION INSTITUTIONS

Background

Several arbitration institutions have been established in Indonesia, e.g. (i) *Badan Arbitrase Nasional Indonesia* (the Indonesian National Board of Arbitration or BANI): (ii) *Badan Arbitrase Syariah Indonesia* (the Indonesian Syariah Arbitration Agency or BASYARNAS), which specializes in commercial disputes governed by Shariah law; (iii) *Badan Arbitrase Pasar Modal Indonesia* (the Indonesia Capital Market Arbitration Board or BAPMI), which specializes in capital market disputes; and (iv) *Badan Arbitrase Perdagangan Berjangka Komoditi* (the Indonesian Commodities Arbitration Body or BAKTI).

Among those institutions, the most active one is BANI. It was established in 1977, on the initiative of the Indonesian Chamber of Commerce. BANI has offices in several major cities in Indonesia, including Jakarta, Surabaya, Denpasar, Bandung, Medan, Pontianak, Palembang and Batam. For this reason, this chapter focuses on BANI.

Types of Disputes Handled

BANI resolves disputes in various commercial, industry and finance sectors, which include corporate matters, telecommunication, mining, sea and air transportation, manufacturing, intellectual property rights, licensing, franchise, construction, shipping/maritime, environmental and others within the scope set by regulations and international practices. All disputes are resolved in accordance with BANI procedural rules (the "BANI Procedural Rules") or any other procedural rules as agreed by the parties. Additionally, it also provides study and research services as well as arbitration and alternative dispute resolutions training programs.

C. Local Arbitration Institutions

Numbers of Disputes Handled

There is no public information on the current statistics of disputes handled by BANI. Nonetheless, following the enactment of the Arbitration Law in 1999, there has been a growing number of disputes settled through BANI (over 30 cases on average per year since 2006; BANI only handled 7-10 cases per year prior to the enactment of the Arbitration Law).

Provisions on Confidentiality of Arbitration

The BANI Procedural Rules provide that all proceedings are closed to the public and all matters related to the appointment of the arbitrator, including documents, reports/minutes of hearings, statements of witnesses and awards, must be kept in strict confidentiality between the parties, arbitrators, and BANI, unless otherwise required by law or agreed by all parties to the dispute.

Availability of Expedited Procedures

Neither the Arbitration Law nor the BANI Procedural Rules provide any procedures for expediting arbitration proceedings. Nonetheless, both the Arbitration Law and the BANI Procedural Rules require proceedings to be completed within 180 days from the appointment of the arbitrators. This timeframe may be extended upon the consent of the parties if: (1) one of the parties submits an application for a certain special matter; (2) the extension is a consequence of a provisional decision or any other interlocutory decision; or (3) the extension is considered necessary by the arbitrators in order to allow them to properly examine the claim. Proceedings are deemed to be concluded once the arbitrators are satisfied that adequate testimony, other evidence and arguments have been submitted.

An arbitral award is final and binding, and is enforceable. It is not possible to appeal an award under the Arbitration Law. However, an award may be challenged to set it aside on limited grounds.

Consolidation of Disputes between the Same Parties and Joinder of Third Parties

The BANI Procedural Rules do not provide for the consolidation of disputes between the same parties. The Arbitration Law allows a third party to participate in arbitration proceedings if he or she has an interest in the dispute and his or her participation is agreed by the parties to the dispute and the arbitrator.

Time Limits for Rendering of the Award

In addition to the 180-day requirement for the settlement of dispute as set out above, the BANI Procedural Rules also require an award to be rendered within 30 days after the proceeding is concluded, unless the arbitrator considers that the time frame needs to be extended. In practice, the arbitration process may take from 160 days up to one year, depending on various factors. These factors may include the complexity of the case; whether the parties undertake a mediation process before the examination of the merits of the case; whether the examination process is conducted based solely on written submissions and documentary evidence submitted by the parties, or if an oral hearing is required for the examination process; and whether there is any other particular process that is undertaken by the parties before the conclusion of the examination process.

Fee Structure

There is no fixed arbitration fee under the Arbitration Law. As a general rule, the arbitration fee will be determined by the relevant arbitration institutions or the arbitrators (as the case may be). Under the BANI Procedural Rules, the arbitration fee will depend on the amount of the disputed claim and is calculated on a progressive basis ranging from 0.50% up to 10%.

The arbitration fee does not include: (1) the cost of summoning witnesses or experts and their transportation and fees, which should be borne by the party that requires the presence of the witness/expert, or borne by all parties if the presence of the witness or expert is required by the arbitrators; (2) the cost of transportation, accommodation and additional fees (whenever applicable) for arbitrators residing beyond a reasonable distance from where the arbitrators hold their hearing, which must be paid by the party that chooses that arbitrator; (3) expenses in relation to any venue for the tribunal sessions other than a venue provided by BANI, including the cost of the venue and transportation and accommodation (whenever applicable), which must be paid by the party who requested the different venue, or by all parties if the change of venue is required by the arbitrators; and (4) expenses for registering the arbitration award at the District Court having jurisdiction.

Treatment of Costs of the Arbitration

BANI will collect half of the aggregate estimated arbitration fees from each party and provide a time frame for each party to make the payment before the arbitration proceeding is commenced. If one of the parties fails to comply with its payment obligation, then the other party must make the payment in the same amount. The tribunal will then make an order in the award requiring the party who has not made the payment to do so.

The tribunal will determine in the award which party must pay the arbitration fees. In general, the losing party will have to pay the entire arbitration fees if the other party has been entirely successful. However, if a party has been only partly successful, then the arbitration fees will be divided between the parties. Under the BANI Procedural Rules, legal fees are generally borne by each party. However, in special circumstances, the arbitrator may order a party to pay the other party's legal fees, e.g. if that party deliberately and improperly prolonged the arbitration process.

Special or Unusual Features (If Any)

Not applicable.

Recent Developments (If Any)

Not applicable.

ITALY

Gianfranco Di Garbo[1]

A. LEGISLATION, TRENDS AND TENDENCIES

A.1 Legislation

Domestic and international arbitration in Italy continue to be governed by Articles 806-832 of the Code of Civil Procedure, and the enforcement of foreign awards continues to be governed by Articles 839 and 840 of the Code and by the New York Convention (in force in Italy since May 1969).

As a result of the Decree-Law of September 12, 2014 n. 132, during the course of any ordinary civil proceedings (except for employment and social security cases), including any appeal, the parties may decide to switch to arbitration: in such a case, after the appointment of the arbitrators, the process does not start from scratch, but continues as an arbitration, and the award has the same legal value as a judgment of the ordinary court.

A.2 Trends and Tendencies

Other reforms of the arbitration process are expected in the next months, because the government is keen to streamline litigious proceedings and has already expressed the view that arbitration is one of the means to achieve this purpose. The reform reported above may therefore be considered only as a first step.

---

[1] Gianfranco Di Garbo is a Partner of Baker & McKenzie in Milan and is the coordinator of the Italian Dispute Resolution Practice Group. He is also a member of the Firm's European and Global Dispute Resolution Practice Groups. His practice concentrates in litigation and arbitration in commercial, corporate and labor matters and since January 2013 he has been serving as an Honorary Judge of the Court of Lecco (Milan).

B. CASES

B.1 Recourse to *Arbitrato Rituale*

The Court of Reggio held that, when an arbitration clause exists, the will of the parties, absent a contrary express indication in the clause, must be interpreted as a recourse to formal arbitration (*arbitrato rituale*), which is regulated by the Code of Civil Procedure, rather than to informal arbitration (*arbitrato irrituale*), which is instead a form of dispute resolution whose purpose is to achieve an award having the value of a contractual determination.[2] In the past and especially before the last reform of the arbitration law,[3] this issue was highly debated in the jurisprudence on the matter, with different points of view.

The Court also held that the ordinary court is entitled to issue a preliminary order of payment (*decreto ingiuntivo*) based on a contract that includes an arbitration clause, but if the claim is opposed, the order of payment should be revoked and the competence of the arbitrators declared.

B.2. No Appeal before the Court of Appeals in Cases of Informal Arbitration

The Court of Appeals of Palermo has decided that an arbitration award cannot be appealed before the Court of Appeals if the arbitrators expressly qualified the arbitration as informal arbitration (*arbitrato irrituale*) (as defined at B.1, above).[4] If instead the arbitrators indicated that the arbitration has the nature of a formal arbitration (*arbitrato rituale*), the award must be appealed to the Court of Appeals.

---

[2]   Judgment of the Tribunal of Reggio Emilia of February 2, 2014 n. 3383.

[3]   Legislative Decree of February 2, 2006 n. 40.

[4]   Judgment of the Court of Appeals of Palermo of January 22, 2014 n. 5.3

B.3 Parties Bound by Arbitral Award

In a rather bizarre appeal to the Supreme Court, a party complained that an award should have been repealed, because it was not consistent with the expectation of both parties.[5] The Court of Cassation rejected the appeal, stating that the parties, by signing the arbitration clause, held themselves bound to the decision of the arbitrations as an expression of their own will, no matter whether their expectations were satisfied.

B.4 Binding Timetable for Delivering the Award in Informal Arbitration

The Court of Cassation has held that the deadline for delivering the arbitration award is binding on the arbitrators even in the case of an informal arbitration (*arbitrato irrituale*).[6] Therefore, if the award is not delivered within that term, the mandate to the arbitrators is considered as extinguished.

B.5 Shareholder Disputes Not Governed by Arbitration Clause

In an important judgment, the Court of Cassation held that a dispute concerning the purchase of shares among shareholders of a company whose by-laws contained an arbitration clause was not subject to arbitration, because the stock purchase agreement did not contain a reference to the arbitration clause of the by-laws.[7] The Court reasoned that the default regarding the obligation arising from the stock purchase agreement was not based on the articles of incorporation of the company and on the functioning of the corporation, but concerned the private relationship between shareholders, which did not depend on the contract by which the company was incorporated.

---

[5]   Judgment of the Court of Cassation of July 15, 2014 n. 16164.

[6]   Judgment of the Court of Cassation of June 11, 2014 n. 13212.

[7]   Judgment of the Court of Cassation of March 3, 2014.

C. LOCAL ARBITRATION INSTITUTIONS

In Italy, there are many local arbitration institutions. Article 832 of the Code of Civil Procedure states that, when the parties agree that the arbitration is governed by the regulations of an arbitral association or institution, the latter prevails over the general regulation of the Code.

The most important Italian arbitration institution is as follows:

C.1 The Chamber of Arbitration of Milan

Background

The Chamber of Arbitration of Milan (*Camera Arbitrale*, or "CAM") is a branch of the Chamber of Commerce of Milan and specializes in commercial dispute resolution.

The Chamber provides an array of alternative dispute resolution services and tools, which allow for a resolution of disputes within time limits and through methods that are different from judicial proceedings. The resolution of disputes is one of the regulatory market functions attributed by law to the Chambers of Commerce since 1993.[8]

By choosing an arbitration administered by the CAM, the parties entrust to the institution the administration and organization of the proceedings. Both arbitrators and parties must comply with its arbitral rules ("Rules"), so that the due process principle and the equal treatment of the parties are respected, although this does not prevent the parties from choosing other procedural rules: for instance, regarding the seat of the arbitration and the language of the proceedings.

---

[8]   Italian Law No. 580 of 1993.

C. Local Arbitration Institutions

If the CAM has to appoint the arbitrators, it will select them among major professionals expert in the field of the dispute, with renowned practical and theoretical expertise in the field of arbitration.

As a general principle, emphasized in the CAM's publications, all arbitrators, appointed by the parties or by the Arbitral Council of the CAM, are required to submit a statement of independence ("disclosure") to the parties and to their counsel on the subject matter of the dispute. When filing their disclosure, arbitrators must also consult the Guidelines drafted by the CAM for that purpose and are bound by a Code of Ethics, which is mandatory.

The Arbitral Council, together with the Secretariat of the CAM, monitors the activity of the arbitrators and the parties in order to guarantee a rapid solution of the dispute, although there are no strict time obligations in the Rules. The Secretariat of the CAM carries out a formal examination of the award, in order to reduce the possibilities of challenging the award to the minimum.

Types of Disputes Handled

The CAM handles commercial and civil disputes.

Numbers of Disputes Handled

It is estimated that there are about 200 procedures per year.

Provisions on Confidentiality of Arbitration

All subjects involved in the arbitral proceedings are required, according to the Rules, to comply with the confidentiality of the proceedings and the award, but the Chamber reserves the right to publish the award in a sanitized format, in accordance with the Rules and following guidelines drawn up by the Chamber in collaboration with LIUC – University of Castellanza.

Availability of Expedited Procedures

An expedited procedure is available, but under Italian law the enforcement of provisional reliefs issued by the arbitrators is questionable.

Consolidation of Disputes between the Same Parties and Joinder of Third Parties

The rules allow for disputes to be consolidated and third parties to be joined.

Time Limits for Rendering of the Award

The time limit for rendering the award is six months (subject to extension by CAM).

Fee Structure

CAM issues a tariff based on the value of the arbitration and the number of arbitrators.

Treatment of Costs of the Arbitration

According to a tariff issued by the CAM, costs are based on the value of the arbitration. The arbitrators may decide, in the award, that all the costs of the arbitration (and the attorney fees) are borne totally or partially by the losing party.

Special or Unusual Features (If Any)

Not applicable.

Recent Developments (If Any)

Not applicable.

C. Local Arbitration Institutions

C.2 Associazione Italiana per l'Arbitrato ("AIA")

Background

The AIA was founded in 1958, sponsored by the Italian section of the ICC and many industrial, financial and cultural institutions. The founder of AIA, Eugenio Minoli, was asked by the Government to attend the preparation of the New York Convention in 1958, and members of AIA also actively participated in the formation of the Geneva Convention of 1961 and the ICSID Convention of 1965.

Over the years, AIA has entered into cooperation agreements with many international arbitration institutions, including the AAA, the CAM, and the ICC; in particular, since 2011 the President and Secretary of AIA have been members of the Committee on Arbitration, which is responsible for the relationship with the Court of Arbitration.

In addition to its academic and promotional activity concerning arbitration, in particular through the important law magazine Rivista dell'Arbitrato, the AIA also administers arbitration proceedings under its own auspices.

Provisions on Confidentiality of Arbitration

The AIA's rules provide for confidential arbitrations.

Availability of Expedited Procedures

An expedited procedure is available, but under Italian law the enforcement of provisional reliefs issued by the arbitrators is questionable.

Consolidation of Disputes between the Same Parties and Joinder of Third Parties

The rules allow for disputes to be consolidated and third parties to be joined.

Time Limits for Rendering of the Award

The time limit for rendering the award is 240 days (unless it is extended by AIA).

Fee Structure

AIA issues a tariff based on the value of the arbitration.

Treatment of Costs of the Arbitration

According to a tariff issued by the AIA, costs are based on the value of the arbitration. The arbitrators may decide, in the award, that all the costs of the arbitration (and the attorney fees) are borne totally or partially by the losing party.

Special or Unusual Features (If Any)

Not applicable.

Recent Developments (If Any)

Not applicable.

JAPAN

Tetsuo Kurita,[1] Takeshi Yoshida,[2] Yuichiro Omori,[3] Hinako Sugiyama,[4] Michael Dunmore[5] and Rieko Yamauchi[6]

A. LEGISLATION, TRENDS AND TENDENCIES

A.1 Legislation

International arbitration in Japan is governed by the Japanese Arbitration Law that came into effect on March 1, 2004 (the "Arbitration Law"), to which no legislative amendments were made in 2014.

A.2 Trends and Tendencies

The Japan Commercial Arbitration Association ("JCAA") amended its Commercial Arbitration Rules, which came into effect on February 1, 2014. Please refer to section C below for details of the Rules.

---

[1] Tetsuo Kurita is a Counsel in the Litigation and Dispute Resolution Group at Baker & McKenzie, Tokyo office.

[2] Takeshi Yoshida is an Associate in the Litigation and Dispute Resolution Group at Baker & McKenzie, Tokyo office.

[3] Yuichiro Omori is an Associate in the Litigation and Dispute Resolution Group at Baker & McKenzie, Tokyo office.

[4] Hinako Sugiyama is an Associate in the Litigation and Dispute Resolution Group at Baker & McKenzie, Tokyo office.

[5] Michael Dunmore is an Associate in the Litigation and Dispute Resolution Group at Baker & McKenzie, Tokyo office.

[6] Rieko Yamauchi is a Paralegal in the Litigation and Dispute Resolution Group at Baker & McKenzie, Tokyo office.

B. CASES

There have been no significant court decisions in Japan in relation to arbitration in the last year.

C. LOCAL ARBITRATION INSTITUTIONS

C.1 Japan Commercial Arbitration Association ("JCAA")

Background

The originating body of the JCAA, "The International Commercial Arbitration Committee", was established in 1950 as part of the Japan Chamber of Commerce and Industry. In 1953, it became independent from the Chamber of Commence and Industry and was reorganized as the JCAA. In the first amendment since 2004, the new JCAA Commercial Arbitration Rules ("Rules"), which include modern provisions such as emergency arbitration, came into effect on February 1, 2014.

Types of Disputes Handled

The JCAA handles international commercial arbitrations, domestic commercial arbitrations, international commercial mediations and domestic commercial mediations.

Numbers of Disputes Handled

During the 2013 fiscal year (April 1, 2013 to March 31, 2014), the JCAA received 26 new requests for arbitration and continued to handle 29 ongoing arbitration cases filed in previous years. By the end of March 2014, among the 55 arbitrations handled, 21 arbitral awards were rendered, and five requests for arbitration were withdrawn.

C. Local Arbitration Institutions

Provisions on Confidentiality of Arbitration

Rule 38 provides that all proceedings are private and that facts learned through proceedings are not to be disclosed by the arbitrators, the JCAA (including its directors, officers, employees, and other staff), the parties, their counsel and assistants and other persons involved in the arbitral proceedings, except where disclosure is required by law or court proceedings.

Availability of Expedited Procedures

Rules 75-82 provide for expedited procedures. Expedited procedures are available for disputes where: (1) the parties agree to expedited procedures, or (2) the amount in dispute does not exceed JPY20 million and the dispute is to be settled by one arbitrator, unless the parties agree the expedited procedures are not to apply.

If a dispute is submitted under the expedited procedures, the time limit to render an arbitral award is three months from the date the arbitrator is appointed, which the arbitrator cannot extend.[7] The expedited procedures require, in principle that there shall only be a one day hearing. The expedited procedures do not permit amendments to claims, counterclaims or set-off defenses nor the joinder of third parties nor the consolidation of arbitrations.

Consolidation of Disputes between the Same Parties and Joinder of Third Parties

Rule 52 permits joinder where (1) all parties agree or (2) all claims come under the same agreement and consent of a third party is required to join the arbitration if the arbitral tribunal has

---

[7] However, the JCAA may extend the time limit by taking into consideration the complexity of the case or any other compelling reasons in the case under Rule 81.2.

been constituted. Joinder may be denied by the tribunal in some circumstances.

Rule 53 permits consolidation at the request of a party or when the tribunal finds it necessary to consolidate claims. For consolidation one of the following circumstances must be met: (1) all parties consent; (2) all claims arise under the same arbitration agreement; or (3) all claims arise between the same parties and: (a) the same or similar question of law or fact arises from the claims; and (b) the claims are capable of being conducted in a single proceeding.

Time Limits for Rendering of the Award

Rule 39.1 provides that the arbitral tribunal must use reasonable efforts to ensure that an award will be rendered within six months from the date the tribunal is constituted. This time limit may be subject to extension by the arbitral tribunal (Rule 39.3) However, it should be noted that under the expedited procedures, an award must be made within three months from the date the arbitrator is appointed. The timeline to render an award may not be extended under the expedited procedures, as mentioned above.

Fee Structure

The administrative fees of the JCAA are set out in a schedule of fees. The amount of the administrative fee is based on the amount of the dispute or the economic value of the claim. For example, if the amount in dispute is less than JPY5 million, then the administrative fee is JPY216,000. If the amount in dispute is more than JPY5 billion, the administrative fee is JPY15,120,000. If the amount of the dispute cannot be calculated or is extremely difficult to calculate, then the administrative fee is JPY1,080,000.

The amount of the tribunal's fees is also based on the amount in dispute or the economic value of the claim. If the tribunal consists of a sole arbitrator and the amount in dispute is not more than JPY20 million, then the sole arbitrator's fee is 10.8% of the amount in dispute. If the amount in dispute is JPY5 billion or over, then the sole arbitrator's fee is JPY17,280,000 plus 0.0864% of the excess over JPY5 billion. If the amount of the dispute cannot be calculated or is difficult to calculate, then the JCAA determines the amount of the sole arbitrator's fee.

If the tribunal consists of three arbitrators, then their fee is also determined in a similar manner. The maximum aggregate amount for multiple arbitrators is the maximum amount of remuneration of a sole arbitrator multiplied by the number of arbitrators (usually three) multiplied by 0.8.

Treatment of Costs of the Arbitration

Rule 83 allows the tribunal to allocate costs between parties based on the circumstances of each arbitration. Costs include administrative fees, arbitrator remuneration and expenses, other reasonable expenses incurred, and legal fees and expenses. According to the JCAA's official commentary on the Rules, when deciding on the allocations of costs, the arbitral tribunal may consider whether the party has been successful in the arbitration, the actions of a party during the arbitration, as well as noncompliance with the orders of the arbitral tribunal.

Rule 84 highlights that all parties are jointly and severally liable for payments made for arbitrator remuneration and expenses and other reasonable expenses incurred. Additionally, parties must be mindful of Rule 85.2, which provides that if either party does not make such payment, the suspension or termination of the arbitral proceedings shall be ordered by the arbitral tribunal upon request from the JCAA.

Special or Unusual Features (If Any)

Rules 54 and 55 permit parties to stay arbitration in favor of mediation. Rule 55.1 allows the parties to agree for the arbitrator to act as mediator. If the parties do so, they are expressly not permitted to challenge the arbitrator based on the grounds that the arbitrator acted as mediator.

Recent Developments (If Any)

The current Rules came into effect on February 1, 2014. Among the new features that have been introduced are emergency arbitrator provisions, which allow for a party to request that interim measures be decided by an emergency arbitrator before an arbitral tribunal is constituted (Rule 70.1). A sole emergency arbitrator will be appointed within two business days of the receipt of a legitimate application for relief (Rule 71.4). The Emergency Arbitrator is required to render a decision within two weeks from the date of appointment (Rule 72.4).

The Rules also include amendments related to interim measures by arbitral tribunals and expedited procedures. The Rules specify the types of orders and the requirements for interim measures by arbitral tribunals in accordance with the amendments adopted in 2006 to the UNCITRAL Model Law (Rule 66). Expedited procedures were formerly only available in cases involving requests for relief of up to JPY20 million. However, under the new Rules, a party can apply for expedited procedures as long as the parties agree in writing within two weeks from the date of receipt of the Request for Arbitration, regardless of the amount in dispute.

The new mediation rules are another noteworthy amendment. Originally there were no rules regarding mediation. Under Rule 54, "[t]he Parties, at any time during the course of the arbitral proceedings, may agree in writing to refer the dispute to

C. Local Arbitration Institutions

mediation proceedings under the International Commercial Mediation Rules of the JCAA." At the same time, the new Rules prohibit *ex parte* communication between the parties and the arbitral tribunal (Rule 50.3). The rules further prohibit the use of proposals, admissions, or other statements made by parties or arbitrators during a mediation procedure as evidence unless the parties agree that such evidence is permissible (Rule 54.3).

KAZAKHSTAN

Alexander Korobeinikov[1]

A. LEGISLATION, TRENDS AND TENDENCIES

International arbitration in Kazakhstan continues to be governed by the Law *On International Arbitration* (the "International Arbitration Law"), which was enacted on 28 December 2004. The law is based on the UNCITRAL Model Law.

Under amendments adopted in July 2014, the jurisdiction of international arbitration tribunals was extended to disputes arising out of concession agreements, even if these disputes are between local companies.

A.1 Trends and Tendencies

Whilst in 2004, the Kazakh Parliament adopted two separate laws which regulate international and domestic arbitration proceedings, 10 years' experience shows that there are a number of practical issues with the application of different laws. Therefore, in September 2014 a draft of a new Law on Commercial Arbitration was presented. This draft is also based on the UNCITRAL Model Law and will govern both international and domestic arbitration proceedings. One of the most significant amendments proposed in the draft is the unification of procedural rules for international and domestic arbitration proceedings and the setting forth of obligations for local arbitration institutions to adapt their rules of arbitration in line with the model rules adopted by the Supreme Court.

---

[1] Alexander Korobeinikov is a Senior Associate in Baker & McKenzie's Almaty office and a member of Baker & McKenzie International Arbitration Practice Group.

B. CASES

B.1 Investment Disputes

According to information published by the United Nations Conference on Trade and Development, most of the investment arbitration cases brought against Kazakhstan since 1996 have been determined fully or partially in favor of the investor. An example of a successful attempt by an investor to protect its interest can be found in the case *Anatolie Stati and others v. Kazakhstan*. After reviewing this case, the SCC Tribunal awarded the Moldovan investor more than USD500 million plus interest as compensation for the losses caused by the groundless cancelation of subsoil use licenses. This is the biggest award that has ever arisen from the ECT. The Republic of Kazakhstan is appealing the award to the Swedish court, but this appeal has not been reviewed yet.

B.2 Restrictions on Local Companies Settling Disputes in Foreign Institutions

Despite the recent amendments to domestic arbitration legislation, Kazakhstani court practice is still questionable and controversial. On the one hand, some courts are applying provisions of Kazakh law in line with recent international trends. On the other hand, the courts sometimes make decisions that contradict both legislation and previous court practice, as illustrated by the case described below.

In 2014, the Supreme Court of the Republic of Kazakhstan reviewed the claim of a Kazakh company relating to the validity of an arbitration clause contained in a contractual agreement with another local company, which referred to the LCIA Rules. The claim was based on the argument that under the International Arbitration Law disputes between local companies cannot be reviewed by foreign arbitration institutions. The Supreme Court agreed with this position and granted the claim.

This decision was highly criticized by local scholars and practitioners, because the International Arbitration Law clearly states that it covers only international arbitration proceedings handled in Kazakhstan and cannot be used for determining the competence of foreign arbitration institutions. This interpretation has been supported by the English courts in *AES Ust-Kamenogorsk Hydropower Plant Llp v Ust-Kamenogorsk Hydropower Plant JSC* [2011] EWCA Civ 647. However, after adoption of the new Law on Commercial Arbitration this problem most likely will be eliminated.

C. LOCAL ARBITRATION INSTITUTIONS

As of today, there are around 20 arbitration institutions in Kazakhstan. However, the most famous of these are the Kazakhstani International Arbitrage (the "KIA"), the International Arbitration Court (the "IUS") and the Center of Arbitration of the National Chamber of Entrepreneurs of the Republic of Kazakhstan (the "CA of NCE").

C.1 The Center of Arbitration of the NCE

Background

The CA of NCE was established in 2014 as a result of the reorganization of the International and Domestic Arbitration Courts at the Chamber of Commerce and Industry of the Republic of Kazakhstan. This reorganization took place as a result of amendments to Kazakhstani law relating to liquidation of the Chamber of Commerce and Industry and the establishment of the National Chamber of Entrepreneurs ("NCE").

Whilst the CA of NCE signed assignment agreements with the International and Domestic Arbitration Courts at the Chamber of Commerce and Industry of the Republic of Kazakhstan, technically, it is not a successor of these arbitration institutions. However, due to the fact that for most local companies membership of the NCE is mandatory and the CA of NCE will open branches in all Kazakhstani regions, this institution will be the biggest in Kazakhstan.

Types of Disputes Handled

The CA of NCE handles all types of commercial disputes between local and foreign companies, except disputes which are nonarbitrable under Kazakh law (such as disputes relating to the registration of rights over immovable property, challenges to decisions of state authorities, etc).

Numbers of Disputes Handled

As the CA of NCE was only established in 2014, this statistic is not available.

Provisions on Confidentiality of Arbitration

Under the International Arbitration Law and the Rules of Arbitration of the CA of NCE, confidentiality covers all documents and information disclosed by parties during arbitration proceedings and the arbitral award.

Availability of Expedited Procedures

Expedited procedures are not available under the Rules of Arbitration of the CA of NCE.

Consolidation of Disputes between the Same Parties and Joinder of Third Parties

The Rules of Arbitration of the CA of NCE set forth special rules for the joinder of third parties. In particular, under these Rules third parties can be joined to arbitration proceedings only if (i) all parties to the arbitration proceedings agree and (ii) the third party is a party to the relevant arbitration agreement. The application to join the third party must be filed before the filing of the statement of defense.

Time Limits for Rendering of the Award

Under the Rules of Arbitration of the CA of NCE, the general term for rendering the award is two months from the date of the constitution of the tribunal. However, this term may be extended by the Tribunal or the General Secretary of the CA.

Fee Structure

The fees for disputes handled by the CA of NCE consist of registration fees and arbitration fees. The registration fees amount to approximately USD330. The arbitration fees vary according to the amount of the claim, from 2% to 1.25 % of the amount of the claim.

Treatment of Costs of the Arbitration

Under the Rules of Arbitration of the CA of NCE, the tribunal orders that compensation for the costs of the arbitration be borne by a party to the arbitration proceedings in proportion to the amount of its claim granted by the tribunal, unless the parties agree otherwise.

Special or Unusual Features (If Any)

The CA of NCE has been designated to exercise the functions referred to in Article IV of the Geneva Convention.

Recent Developments (If Any)

There are no recent developments except those listed above.

C.2 International Arbitration Court

Background

The IUS was the first arbitration institution in Kazakhstan, established in 1993 shortly after declaration of the independence of the Republic of Kazakhstan. This institution was established by the famous local scholar Professor Petr Greshnikov. Since 2002, the IUS also has a branch in St Petersburg (Russia). This branch was established, amongst other reasons, for the purpose of avoiding the application of Kazakhstani law, which was unfavorable towards arbitration proceedings.

Types of Disputes Handled

The IUS handles all types of commercial disputes between local and foreign companies, except disputes which are nonarbitrable under Kazakh law (such as disputes relating to the registration of rights over immovable property, challenges to decisions of state authorities, etc).

Numbers of Disputes Handled

No statistics are available regarding how many disputes are handled by the IUS.

Provisions on Confidentiality of Arbitration

The Rules of Arbitration of the IUS, adopted in 2011, do not set forth special rules relating to confidentiality of arbitration proceedings.

Availability of Expedited Procedures

Expedited procedures are not available under the Rules of Arbitration of the IUS.

C. Local Arbitration Institutions

Consolidation of Disputes between the Same Parties and Joinder of Third Parties

The Rules of Arbitration of the IUS do not set forth any special rules on consolidation of disputes between the same parties or joinder of third parties.

Time limits for Rendering of the Award

Under the Rules of Arbitration of the IUS, the general term for rendering the award is 30 days from the date of the constitution of the tribunal.

Fee Structure

The fees for disputes handled by the IUS consist of registration fees and arbitration fees. The registration fees amount to EUR990. The arbitration fees vary according to the amount of the claim, from 2% to 0.07% of the amount of the claim.

Treatment of Costs of the Arbitration

Under the Rules of Arbitration of the IUS, usually the tribunal orders that compensation for the costs of the arbitration be borne by a party to the arbitration proceedings in proportion to the amount of its claim granted by the tribunal, unless the parties agree otherwise. However, the tribunal has a right to order equal compensation for the costs of the arbitration between the parties.

Special or Unusual Features (If Any)

Under the Rules of Arbitration of the IUS, in exceptional cases the Council of the IUS may dismiss an award issued under the Rules of Arbitration of the IUS. Also, under the Rules of Arbitration of the IUS parties are permitted to apply the UNCITRAL Arbitration Rules.

Recent Developments (If Any)

There are no recent developments except listed above.

C.3 Kazakhstani International Arbitrage

Background

The KIA was the first arbitration institution established after the adoption of the International Arbitration Law. This institution was established by the famous local scholar Professor Maidan Suleimenov.

Types of Disputes Handled

The KIA handles all types of commercial disputes between local and foreign companies, except disputes which are nonarbitrable under Kazakh law (such as disputes relating to the registration of rights over immovable property, challenges to decisions of state authorities, etc), acting as an international and domestic arbitration court.

Numbers of Disputes Handled

No statistics are available regarding how many disputes are handled by the KIA.

Provisions on Confidentiality of Arbitration

The Rules of Arbitration of the KIA (as amended in 2013) state that any information shared by parties during arbitration proceedings is confidential.

Availability of Expedited Procedures

Expedited procedures are not available under the Rules of Arbitration of the KIA.

C. Local Arbitration Institutions

Consolidation of Disputes between the Same Parties and Joinder of Third Parties

The Rules of Arbitration of the KIA set forth special rules for the joinder of third parties. In particular, under these Rules, third parties can be joined to arbitration proceedings only if (i) all parties to the arbitration proceedings agree and (ii) the third party is a party to the relevant arbitration agreement. The application to join the third party must be filed before the filing of the statement of defense.

Time Limits for Rendering of the Award

Under the Rules of Arbitration of the KIA, the general term for rendering the award is 60 days from the date of the constitution of the tribunal. However, this term can be extended by the Chairman of the KIA.

Fee Structure

The fees for disputes handled by the KIA consist of registration fees and arbitration fees. The registration fees amount to approximately USD385. The arbitration fees vary according to the amount of the claim, from 3% to 1.5% of the amount of the claim.

Treatment of Costs of the Arbitration

Under the Rules of Arbitration of the KIA, the tribunal orders that compensation for the costs of the arbitration be borne by a party to the arbitration proceedings in proportion to the amount of its claim granted by the tribunal.

Special or Unusual Features (If Any)

In addition to the Rules of Arbitration, the KIA has separate Rules of Settlement Proceedings and Rules of Administration of ad hoc proceedings.

Recent Developments (If Any)

There are no recent developments except listed above.

KOREA

June Yeum,[1] Andreea Micklis,[2] Saemee Kim[3] and Julie Kim[4]

A. LEGISLATION, TRENDS AND TENDENCIES

A.1 Legislation

International arbitration in Korea continues to be governed by the Korean Arbitration Act, last amended in 2010 (the "Arbitration Act"). The much-anticipated amendments have not yet been made.

A.2 Trends and Tendencies

In 2014, a special committee consisting of lawyers, academics and other arbitration professionals continued discussions of potential amendments to the Arbitration Act. Discussions centered on the extent to which Korea should adopt the UNCITRAL Model Law's 2006 amendments. By December 2014, the special committee had prepared a draft proposed amendment (the "Proposed Amendment"), soon to be submitted to Korea's lawmaking body for consideration. Below are the main features of the Proposed Amendment.

---

[1]   Junghye June Yeum is a Partner and co-head of the International Dispute Resolution Practice Group at Lee & Ko in Seoul, Korea. Prior to joining Lee & Ko, she was a Partner at Baker & McKenzie's New York office.

[2]   Andreea Micklis is an Associate in Lee & Ko's International Dispute Resolution Practice Group.

[3]   Saemee Kim is an Associate in Lee & Ko's International Dispute Resolution Practice Group.

[4]   Julie Kim is an Associate in Lee & Ko's International Dispute Resolution Practice Group.

Writing Requirement

The current version of the Arbitration Act largely tracks the pre-2006 UNCITRAL Model Law and requires that an arbitration agreement be in writing, contained in a signed document, letter, telegram, telex, or other means of telecommunication.[5] The Proposed Amendment adopts Option I of Article 7 of the UNCITRAL Model Law, which allows a valid arbitration agreement to be recorded in any form, whether or not it has been concluded orally, by conduct, or by other means. Under the Proposed Amendment, as under Option I, the writing requirement can also be satisfied by an electronic communication if the information contained therein is accessible so as to be usable for subsequent reference.

Judicial Review of Awards Denying Jurisdiction

While the Arbitration Act gives authority to the court to review an arbitral tribunal's ruling that it has jurisdiction,[6] it is silent on the court's authority to determine the propriety of an arbitral tribunal's denial of its jurisdiction. The Korean Supreme Court has held that the court has no authority to determine whether a denial by an arbitral tribunal of its jurisdiction is proper.[7] The Proposed Amendment would give express authority to the court to review a negative arbitral jurisdiction ruling as in other jurisdictions such as England and Singapore.

Interim Measures

Article 18 of the Arbitration Act provides that the arbitral tribunal may grant interim protective measures, unless otherwise

---

[5]   Article 8 of the Arbitration Act.

[6]   Article 17 of the Arbitration Act.

[7]   Supreme Court Judgment 2003Da70249, October 14, 2004.

agreed by the parties. In an effort to incorporate the 2006 version of the UNCITRAL Model Law, the Proposed Amendment has adopted certain sections of Chapter IV A of the UNCITRAL Model Law regarding interim measures. In particular, the Proposed Amendment includes provisions granting the arbitral tribunal power to order interim measures, including providing means to preserve assets or evidence that may be "relevant and material to the resolution of the dispute" (unless otherwise agreed by the parties).[8]

Presently, because only "arbitral awards" are enforceable under the Arbitration Act,[9] and it deems interim measures to be orders not awards,[10] the parties must apply to a competent court for enforcement of interim relief. The proposal to adopt Article 17 H(1) of the UNCITRAL Model Law would allow an arbitral tribunal's order granting interim measures to be enforceable in Korea. For now, however, the predominant view appears to be that only interim measures issued by an arbitral tribunal in an arbitration seated in Korea can be enforced.

The Arbitration Act does not list any grounds for refusing recognition or enforcement of interim measures. The Proposed Amendment provides that recognition or enforcement of interim measures may be refused, upon application from a party, in the limited circumstances set out.[11]

---

[8] Article 17(2) of the UNCITRAL Model Law.

[9] Article 37(1) of the Arbitration Act provides that "[r]ecognition or enforcement of arbitral awards shall be made by recognition or judgment by a court."

[10] Article 18 of the Arbitration Act.

[11] These circumstances are: 1) failure of a party to provide a security deposit; 2) termination or suspension of the interim measure by the arbitral tribunal or a court; or 3) where a court finds that it lacks the authority to enforce the interim measure issued by the arbitral tribunal. Compare this with Article 17 I of the UNCITRAL Model Law.

Court Assistance in Taking Evidence

The Arbitration Act currently authorizes Korean courts to assist arbitral tribunals in collecting evidence upon request by a party.[12] The Proposed Amendment clarifies that courts may collect evidence either directly, by calling witnesses and examining evidence, or indirectly, by providing assistance to the arbitral tribunal in doing the same. The parties and the arbitral tribunal may participate in both the direct and indirect collection of evidence. The Proposed Amendment further allows the court to order a witness to appear before the arbitral tribunal or produce documents in the arbitral proceeding.

Allocation of Arbitration Expenses

The Arbitration Act does not contain a provision on the allocation of arbitration expenses. The Proposed Amendment addresses this by granting the arbitral tribunal authority to allocate arbitration expenses between the parties, unless the parties agree otherwise.

Interest

The Arbitration Act in its current form does not contain any provisions regarding interest. The Proposed Amendment allows the arbitral tribunal to award interest in arrears as it deems appropriate, unless the parties agree otherwise.

Procedure for Enforcing Awards

The Arbitration Act applies where parties seek recognition or enforcement of (1) domestic awards[13] or (2) foreign arbitral

---

[12] Article 28 of the Arbitration Act.

[13] The term "domestic awards" is defined to mean awards rendered in an arbitration seated in Korea even where one of the parties is a non-Korean individual/entity.

awards not covered by the New York Convention.[14] As for international arbitration awards under the New York Convention, the Convention governs. In Korea, in order to enforce an award, an award creditor must commence a suit as a plaintiff would in full-blown litigation, which is conducted under the "judgment" procedure. The Proposed Amendment provides that an award creditor may bring an expedited proceeding under the "decision" procedure, which allows the court to dispose of discrete issues presented in a case without reviewing the merits of the entire case and does not require a trial or hearing, which is a mandatory step under the "judgment" procedure.

Additionally, similar to the UNCITRAL Model Law, the Proposed Amendment provides for the removal of the requirement that a "duly authenticated" or "duly certified" copy and/or translation of the award (if the award is not in Korean) be submitted to the enforcing court.

B. CASES

In 2014, Korean courts reviewed a total of seven international arbitration cases.

B.1. Enforcement of Awards That Lack Specificity

This case involved a dispute between a UK-based software provider and a Korean broadcaster. The software provider sought declaratory relief, asserting that the agreement between the parties had been terminated. The broadcaster argued that the agreement remained in force and claimed damages for deprivation of its right to use the software. The arbitral tribunal determined that the agreement had been terminated and ordered

---

[14]   *Id.* at Articles 37 to 39.

the broadcaster to perform its termination obligation under the agreement, giving no further details with respect to how this obligation was to be met.

The software provider sought enforcement in Korea. In January 2013, the Seoul Southern District Court refused enforcement, stating that the relief granted lacked sufficient clarity and specificity to be converted into a Korean judgment and carried out under Korean law. In January 2014, the Seoul High Court overturned the decision of the lower court, stating that even if the award lacked specificity, the prevailing party still had an interest in seeking enforcement as this not only empowered enforceability of the underlying award but also encouraged the parties to voluntarily comply with it. The High Court further stated that a conclusive enforcement judgment would also preclude the parties from seeking to set aside the award under the Arbitration Act.[15] The Korean broadcaster appealed. The case is currently pending before the Korean Supreme Court.

B.2 Use of "May" in an Arbitration Agreement Does Not Render It Optional

This case involved a dispute between a Korean investor and a Chinese entity over a shareholder's agreement to jointly develop an industrial complex. As part of the agreement, the parties incorporated a company to administer the project. Each retained the right to dissolve the company if the project failed to garner the requisite financing. The Chinese entity unilaterally exercised this option. The Korean investors sued, seeking damages for wrongful dissolution. The Chinese entity sought to dismiss the case based on the arbitration clause in the agreement.

In January 2013, the Suwon District Court found that there was a valid arbitration agreement between the parties and dismissed the

---

[15] Seoul High Court Judgment 2013Na13506, dated January 17, 2014.

case, rejecting the Korean investor's argument that the use of the permissive "may" in the arbitration agreement made arbitration optional. The Korean investor appealed and the Seoul High Court reversed the decision, reasoning that its permissive tone did make the arbitration clause optional. Further, the Seoul High Court held that despite the language referencing arbitration in the articles of incorporation, it could not be considered a valid arbitration agreement because the articles of incorporation could be amended. The Chinese entity appealed.

In April 2014, the Korean Supreme Court remanded the case to to the District Court with instructions to dismiss the case. The Supreme Court held that the dispute should be arbitrated on the ground that the wording "may be resolved by arbitration" was not deemed optional. Further, the Korean Supreme court determined that the parties' intention to arbitrate was derived from the arbitration clause stipulated in the articles of incorporation.[16]

B.3. Recovery of Arbitration Costs and Expenses

In 2014, Korean courts dealt with two enforcement cases seeking recovery of arbitration costs and expenses as part of the arbitral award. In one case, the Korean court awarded the winner full arbitration costs, while in the second, the court restricted interest awarded to the winning party to damages only, excluding interest on legal costs and the costs of arbitration.

In the first case,[17] a dispute arose out of a supply agreement between a Czech entity and a Korean company. The Korean company sought to suspend the supply of goods due to Korea's economic crisis, but the Czech company refused, initiating an ICC arbitration in England and claiming repudiatory breach. The

---

[16]   Supreme Court Judgment 2013Da71845, dated April 30, 2014.

[17]   Changwon District Court Judgment 2013GaHap31441, dated January 23, 2014.

arbitral tribunal rendered an award in favor of the Czech company and directed the Korean entity to bear all the arbitration costs and expenses.

The Czech company sought enforcement in Korea. The Korean company argued that requiring the losing party to pay all arbitral costs was in violation of Article V(2)(b) of the New York Convention. In January 2014, the Changwon District Court enforced the award, directing the Korean company to pay all of the arbitral costs. The court stated that since the public policy exception to the enforcement of arbitral awards was intended to protect the enforcing state's good morals and social order, it should be interpreted restrictively to promote certainty and stability in domestic rules and international commercial transactions. As such, the court enforced the award, concluding that it was rendered in accordance with the ICC Rules and furthermore, that it conformed with the Civil Procedure Act which also provides that litigation costs be borne by the losing party, even when it has not lost in whole.

In another case, the issue was whether a party seeking enforcement of an arbitral award was entitled to interest not only on the underlying damages award but also on the legal and arbitration costs incurred. The dispute arose from a license agreement between a Korean manufacturer and a Singaporean distributor. The manufacturer terminated the agreement and the distributor commenced arbitration, claiming damages for repudiatory breach. The tribunal awarded damages and interest.

The distributor sought enforcement in Korea. On April 30, 2014, the Seoul Central District Court held that since written documents are to be restrictively interpreted, the award should also be restrictively interpreted. Therefore, the court determined that the interest ordered in the award only applied to the damages and not to the legal and arbitration costs. The court also pointed out that interest was dealt with in a separate section of the award, and the claimant had not sought interest on the legal and arbitration costs throughout the arbitral process. No appeal was sought in either of these cases.

C. LOCAL ARBITRATION INSTITUTIONS

C.1 The Korean Commercial Arbitration Board ("KCAB")

Background

Founded in 1966 under the Arbitration Act, the KCAB is the only arbitral institution in Korea. It handles both domestic and international arbitrations. It has offices in Seoul and Busan and provides arbitration as well as mediation services.

Types of Disputes Handled

According to the KCAB's 2013 Annual Report, the top four types of international arbitration cases handled by it from 2010 to 2013 were "payment, product quality, delayed or cancelled shipment, and contract interpretation disputes".[18] During the same period, the main four industries encountered were international trade, construction, maritime, and intellectual property.[19]

Number of Disputes Handled

From its inception in 1966 to November 10, 2014, the KCAB has administered a total of 10,116 cases. International arbitrations[20] comprised approximately 13% of those cases.[21]

---

[18]   *KCAB 2013 Annual Report* at 12.

[19]   *Id.* at 10.

[20]   Under Article 2 of the KCAB International Arbitration Rules, "international arbitration" is defined as an arbitration where one of the parties is not Korean or the venue of the arbitration is designated outside Korea.

Provisions on Confidentiality of Arbitration

Under the KCAB's International Arbitration Rules,[22] the proceedings are not open to the public and information relating to the proceedings is not publicly available.[23]

Availability of Expedited Procedures

Chapter 6 of the KCAB's International Arbitration Rules governs expedited procedures. Expedited procedures are the default rule for any dispute where the amount does not exceed KRW200 million.[24] Parties may also contractually agree to expedited procedures for disputes above this amount.[25] Unless the parties agree otherwise, one arbitrator presides and is appointed by the KCAB Secretariat.[26]

Consolidation of Disputes between the Same Parties and Joinder of Third Parties

There are no specific provisions on consolidation of disputes between the same parties or the joinder of third parties under KCAB's International Arbitration Rules. Nevertheless, in practice parties may consolidate disputes or a third party may participate in arbitration with the consent of all parties and the arbitral tribunal.

---

[21]   *KCAB 2013 Annual Report* at 8.

[22]   KCAB's International Arbitration Rules, which came into effect on September 1, 2011, apply by default to all international arbitrations, as defined under Article 2 of the KCAB International Arbitration Rules, where the parties have agreed in writing to refer their arbitration under the KCAB International Arbitration Rules or before the KCAB (Article 3 of the KCAB International Arbitration Rules).

[23]   Article 52 of the KCAB International Arbitration Rules.

[24]   *Id.* at Article 38.

[25]   *Id.*

[26]   *Id.* at Article 40.

C. Local Arbitration Institutions

Time Limits for Rendering the Award

For cases resolved under the expedited procedure, the tribunal must render an award within three months from its constitution. [27] For all other cases, the arbitral tribunal must render an award within 45 days from the date on which final submissions are made or the hearings are closed, whichever comes later. [28]

Fee Structure

For international arbitrations, arbitration costs include the following: filing fees, administrative fees, and arbitrator costs. [29] Filing fees, paid by the claimant, are fixed at KRW1 million for any claim amount above KRW200 million and are waived below this amount. [30] Administrative fees are capped at KRW150 million and are calculated based on a sliding scale which corresponds to the amount in dispute. [31] Arbitrator fees are determined by the Secretariat and are also dependent on the claim amount. [32] Arbitrator fees and administrative fees can be calculated on KCAB's website. [33]

Treatment of Costs of the Arbitration

The parties are jointly and severally liable for arbitration costs. [34] The arbitration costs are generally borne by the losing party, but

---

[27]   *Id.* at Article 43.

[28]   *Id.* at Article 33.

[29]   *Id.* at Article 45.

[30]   *Id.* at Article 1 of Appendix 1; *Arbitration Costs*, http://www.kcab.or.kr/jsp/ kcab_eng/arbitration/arbi_35_ex.jsp.

[31]   *Id.* at Article 2 of Appendix 1.

[32]   *Id.* at Article 1 of Appendix 2.

[33]   *Arbitration Costs*, http://www.kcab.or.kr/jsp/kcab_eng/arbitration/arbi_35_ex.jsp.

[34]   Article 45(2) of the KCAB International Arbitration Rules.

the arbitral tribunal, at its discretion, can apportion these costs between the parties.[35]

Special or Unusual Features (If Any)

None.

Recent Developments (If Any)

The KCAB International Arbitration Rules of 2011 are currently under review.

---

[35] *Id.* at Article 47(1).

KYRGYZSTAN

Alexander Korobeinikov[1]

A. LEGISLATION, TRENDS AND TENDENCIES

A.1 Legislation

International arbitration in Kyrgyzstan continues to be governed by the Law *On Arbitration Courts* (the "Law"), enacted on 30 July 2002, to which no legislative amendment was made in 2014. The Law is based on the UNCITRAL Model Law.

A.2 Trends and Tendencies

Recently, a number of investors began arbitration proceedings against Kyrgyzstan. Most of these relate to the expropriation of foreign and domestic investments by the government of Kyrgyzstan that came to power as a result of the April 2010 Revolution.

As a result, the Kyrgyz Government decided to establish a special body, the Center of Representing the Government in Court Proceedings. This Center is responsible for handling any claims filed against the Kyrgyz Government or state authorities by foreign investors.

Due to these efforts, the Kyrgyz Government managed to obtain evidence to permit it to appeal awards on several of the most-discussed cases in front of the International Arbitration Court at the Moscow Chamber of Commerce. In these cases, the claimants stated that the Moscow Chamber of Commerce had the right to review investment claims against Kyrgyzstan based on

---

[1] Alexander Korobeinikov is a Senior Associate in Baker & McKenzie's Almaty office and a member of the International Arbitration Practice Group and the Firm's Global Dispute Resolution Practice Group.

the provisions of the 1997 CIS Moscow Convention for the Protection of Investor Rights (the "Convention"). Specifically, the claimants stated that the general dispute resolution provisions of the Convention, which establish the rights of foreign investors to seek resolution of investment disputes in international arbitration institutions, must be interpreted as the consent of the parties to the use of the Convention to resolve investment disputes in any international arbitration institution chosen by foreign investors. The Convention was ratified by most CIS countries, including Russia, Kazakhstan, Kyrgyzstan, and Belarus.

However, in September 2014, the CIS Economic Court (a court established by CIS countries for settling disputes between these countries and interpreting CIS treaties), based on an application by the Kyrgyz Government, issued a decision providing an official interpretation of the provisions of the Convention. In this decision, the CIS Economic Court supported the position of the Kyrgyz Government and stated that the provisions of the Convention cannot be treated as the consent of a state to refer disputes to international arbitration.

B. CASES

While recent court decisions relating to the enforcement or setting aside of arbitral awards are generally in line with international practice, it should be noted that the Kyrgyz courts do not have a wide range of experience with arbitration-related cases, and this lack of experience can lead to controversial decisions.

B. Cases

B.1 Narrow Interpretation of the Arbitration Clause

In 2014, the Kyrgyz state authorities continued their attempts to collect fines for alleged environmental violations from Kumtor Gold Company (the local subsidiary of the biggest foreign investor in Kyrgyzstan, Centerra Gold).

In particular, the local environmental protection inspection body filed a claim against Kumtor Gold Company, seeking a court order to collect environmental fines. Kumtor argued, amongst other things, that this dispute should be settled in line with the arbitration clause in the Revised Investment Agreement executed between Kumtor and the Government in 2009.[2] This argument was supported by the Court of Appeal, which dismissed the environmental authority's claim.

However, the Supreme Court held that the arbitration clause of the Revised Investment Agreement was not clear enough, and it had reasonable doubts that it could be enforced. In particular, it argued that the word "may" used in the arbitration clause did not fully exclude the jurisdiction of local courts.

This decision by the Supreme Court is very questionable and based on a very narrow interpretation of the wording of the arbitration clause. Therefore, we cannot discount the possibility that it was issued under the pressure of the Kyrgyz Government, which is likely to use this decision to push Kumtor Gold to reconsider the conditions of its agreements with the Kyrgyz Government.

---

[2] This arbitration clause states that the parties to the agreement may commence arbitration proceedings for settlement of disputes arising out of or in connection with this agreement under UNCITRAL Arbitration Rules or ICSID Arbitration Rules (if the Kyrgyz Republic becomes a party to the ICSID Convention).

C. LOCAL ARBITRATION INSTITUTIONS

Background

After adoption of the Law in 2002 and relevant sub-laws regulating the procedure for establishing and registering arbitration institutions, the local Chamber of Commerce and Industry decided to establish the International Arbitration Court ("IAC") for handling both domestic and international commercial disputes.

Types of Disputes Handled

The IAC handles all types of commercial disputes between local and foreign companies, except disputes which are nonarbitrable under Kyrgyz law (such as disputes relating to the registration of rights over immovable property, challenges of decisions of state authorities, etc).

Numbers of Disputes Handled

No statistics are available regarding how many disputes are handled by the IAC.

Provisions on Confidentiality of Arbitration

Under the Law and the Rules of Arbitration of the IAC, confidentiality covers all documents and information disclosed by parties during the arbitration proceedings.

Availability of Expedited Procedures

Expedited procedures are available under the IAC Rules of Expedited Arbitration if parties agree to use these Rules.

C. Local Arbitration Institutions

Consolidation of Disputes between the Same Parties and Joinder of Third Parties

The IAC Rules of Arbitration contain special rules on the joinder of third parties. Under these Rules, third parties can be joined to arbitration proceedings only if (i) all the parties to the arbitration proceedings agree and (ii) the third party is a party to the relevant arbitration agreement. The application to join the third party must be filed before the filing of the statement of defense.

Time Limits for Rendering of the Award

Under the IAC Rules of Arbitration the general term for rendering of the award is up to three months from the date of the constitution of the tribunal. However, this term may be extended by the IAC.

Fee Structure

The fees for disputes handled by the IAC consist of registration fees and arbitration fees. The registration fees amount to up to USD500, depending on the amount of the claim. The arbitration fees vary according to the amount of the claim, ranging from 4% to 0.5 % of the amount of the claim.

Treatment of Costs of the Arbitration

Under the IAC Rules of Arbitration, the tribunal orders that compensation for the costs of the arbitration be borne by a party to the arbitration proceedings in proportion to the amount of its claim granted by the tribunal, unless the parties agree otherwise.

Kyrgyzstan

Special or Unusual Features (If Any)

In addition to the Rules of Arbitration and the Rules of Expedited Arbitration, the IAC has separate Rules of Administration for ad hoc proceedings under the UNCITRAL Arbitration Rules.

Recent Developments (If Any)

There are no recent developments.

MALAYSIA

Elaine Yap[1] and Shiyamala Devi Manokaran[2]

A. LEGISLATION, TRENDS AND TENDENCIES

A.1 Legislation

International arbitration in Malaysia continues to be governed by the Arbitration Act 2005 (Act 646) ("Arbitration Act"). No legislative amendment was made in 2014.

A.2 Trends and Tendencies

The Legal Profession Act 1976 prohibits persons not licensed to practice law from doing any act which is customarily the function or responsibility of an advocate and solicitor in Malaysia. The statute was recently amended to expressly exclude the application of such provisions to foreign arbitrators, any person representing any party in arbitral proceedings, or any person giving advice, preparing documents and rendering any other assistance arising out of arbitral proceedings in Malaysia. The amendment, which came into force on June 3, 2014,[3] has paved the way for foreign arbitration practitioners to establish a physical presence in Malaysia, adding a further positive dimension to the arbitration landscape in Malaysia.

---

[1] Elaine Yap is a Partner in the Dispute Resolution Practice Group in Baker & McKenzie's Kuala Lumpur office.

[2] Shiyamala Devi Manokaran is an Associate in the Dispute Resolution Practice Group in Baker & McKenzie's Kuala Lumpur office.

[3] The amendment to the Legal Profession Act 1976 was reported in the International Arbitration Yearbook 2013-2014, which was published before the amendment came into operation.

B. CASES

B.1 Arbitration Award Not Enforceable without Registration

In *Christopher Martin Boyd v Deb Brata Das Gupta*,[4] the Federal Court heard an appeal on the applicable limitation period for the enforcement of an arbitration award. According to s.6(1)(c) of the Limitation Act 1953 ("Limitation Act"), "actions to enforce an award" cannot be brought after the expiration of six years from the date on which the cause of action accrued. S.6(3) of the Limitation Act, on the other hand, provides that an "action upon any judgment" cannot be brought after the expiration of 12 years from the date on which the judgment became enforceable.

This case concerned the validity of a bankruptcy notice issued on April 4, 2012, more than 12 years from the date of the arbitration award dated January 4, 2000. The Court of Appeal had found that the appellant's bankruptcy proceedings were time-barred.

In allowing the appeal, the Court of Appeal took the view that the registration or transformation of the award into a judgment was nothing more than a mere procedure to enforce an award. In support of this view, the Court of Appeal relied on the English Court of Appeal decision in *National Ability SA v. Tinna Oils and Chemicals Ltd, The Amazon Reefer*,[5] where it was held:

> There was a clear distinction between an arbitral award and a judgment. An arbitration agreement was in essence enforceable because of the implied contractual promise to pay an arbitral award contained in the arbitration agreement; all measures of enforcement essentially rested upon the contract. The provisions of s. 26 of the 1950

---

4   [2014] 9 CLJ 887.

5   [2010] 2 All ER (Comm) 257.

Act had to be seen in that context. They were simply procedural provisions enabling the award made in consensual arbitral proceedings to be enforced.

Based on the *Amazon Reefer* case, the Court of Appeal construed the words "to enforce the award" to mean the execution of the judgment.

Upon further appeal, the Federal Court disagreed and stated that there is a clear distinction between registration of an arbitration award and enforcement of a judgment. In principle, unlike an order or judgment of the court, an arbitration award does not immediately entitle a successful party to levy execution against the assets of the unsuccessful party. The arbitration award must first be converted into a judgment or order of the court before the successful party can levy execution. The arbitration award will be considered a judgment or order of the court only upon completion of that step.

The court found that the application to register the arbitration award was made well within the six-year period stipulated in s. 6(1)(c) of the Limitation Act. Once it took effect as a judgment, the bankruptcy proceedings that followed were filed within the 12 years prescribed under s. 6(3) of the Limitation Act.

B.2 Discretion of Court to Bridge the Limitation Period

In another recent case which considered the Limitation Act in connection with arbitration proceedings, the High Court in *DCEIL Imex Sdn Bhd v Pembinaan Punca Cergas Sdn Bhd* [6] applied section 30(5) of the Limitation Act on the suspension of time for the reckoning of limitation periods where arbitration proceedings are inconclusive. Section 30(5) accords the High Court the discretion to exclude time in the following instances,

---

[6]   [2014] 7 CLJ 552.

namely where the court either orders (a) that an award be set aside, or (b) after the commencement of an arbitration, that the arbitration shall cease to have effect with respect to the dispute referred.

In this case, the parties had commenced arbitration on April 6, 2006, but the appellant was wound up a year later on February 7, 2007. As a result, the arbitration proceedings were stayed. The assignee of the appellant under the same sub-contract then commenced a civil suit against the respondent, whereupon the respondent sought to plead a counterclaim.

The court determined that the counterclaim should be dealt with in the arbitration proceedings. The respondent was granted leave to proceed with its counterclaim in the arbitration. The appellant raised a preliminary objection to the arbitrator's jurisdiction to deal with the respondents' counterclaim against it on grounds that the assignee of the sub-contract had not consented to the arbitration proceedings. The arbitrator assumed jurisdiction, but the appellant successfully appealed the decision under section 18(8) of the Arbitration Act. Consequently, the arbitration was declared to be null and void.

When the respondent tried to plead the counterclaim in the civil suit, the limitation period had expired, and the assignee applied to strike out the counterclaim. The central issue for determination of the application was whether s.30(5) of the Limitation Act could be invoked in the circumstances.

The High Court decided that the relief under the second limb of s.30(5) of the Limitation Act covers a variety of situations where the court orders that the "arbitration ceases to have effect", including where the court makes a ruling under s.18(8) of the Arbitration Act that the tribunal has no jurisdiction to deal with a dispute in question. The court also agreed with the observation that a provision such as s. 30(5) of the Limitation Act does not operate automatically, but merely gives the court discretion. As the grant of the relief under this section only arises in situations where an award is set aside or where an arbitration ceases to exist, a claimant must remember to ask for an order to prolong time should this be necessary.

In the exercise of its discretion, the High Court allowed the counterclaim to be pleaded on a consideration of the peculiar factual matrix of this case and granted the orders sought. The court granted an order, consequential to the order declaring the arbitration null and void, that the time elapsed be excluded from the reckoning of time according to the policy of s.30(5) of the Limitation Act.

C.   LOCAL ARBITRATION INSTITUTIONS

C.1   Kuala Lumpur Regional Arbitration Centre ("KLRCA")

Background

The KLRCA was established in 1978 under the auspices of the Asian-African Legal Consultative Organization (AALCO). KLRCA was established to provide institutional support for the conduct of domestic and international arbitration proceedings in Asia. It is a nonprofit, nongovernmental and independent international body. Today, the KLRCA is the default appointing authority under the Arbitration Act and also the adjudication authority under the Construction Industry Payment and Adjudication Act 2012, which came into operation on April 15, 2014.[7]

---

[7]   The KLRCA is responsible for the setting of competency standards of an adjudicator, standard terms of appointment and fees of an adjudicator and providing administrative support for the conduct of adjudication according to the KLRCA Adjudication Rules and Procedure.

Types of Disputes Handled

The KLRCA Rules of Arbitration incorporate the entire UNCITRAL Rules in Part II, with additional rules designed by the KLRCA appearing in Part I and Schedules in Part III. It was last revised in 2013, when the KLRCA also introduced the KLRCA Fast Track Arbitration Rules and the Shariah-compliant KLRCA i-Arbitration Rules. As an administering institution applying these rules, the KLRCA handles a wide variety of commercial and noncommercial disputes,[8] including specialized disputes arising from commercial transactions premised on Islamic principles and domain name disputes.[9]

Numbers of Disputes Handled

The KLRCA handled a total of 273 cases in the year 2014 as at November 30, 2014, of which 216 were domestic and 57 international. This represents a tenfold increase since 2010.

Provisions on Confidentiality of Arbitration

The KLRCA Arbitration Rules require the arbitral tribunal, the parties, all experts, all witnesses and the KLRCA to keep confidential all matters relating to the arbitral proceedings, including the award made by the tribunal, unless its disclosure is necessary for purposes of implementation and enforcement. Matters relating to arbitral proceedings are broadly defined to

---

[8]   The disputes handled include agency, aviation and airports, banking and financial instruments, company, concession agreement, defamation, employment, energy, mining, oil and gas, family or probate matters, healthcare, information technology and telecommunications, infrastructure, construction and engineering disputes, insurance, intellectual property, investment, maritime, real estate, supply of goods and services, sports and entertainment, tenancy, tort, and trust.

[9]   The Asian Domain Name Dispute Resolution Centre (Kuala Lumpur Office) has been operated and managed by the KLRCA since October 2009.

mean everything from the existence of the proceedings to all documents produced in the proceedings.[10]

Availability of Expedited Procedures

Expedited procedures are available under the KLRCA Fast Track Arbitration Rules, which stipulate that the arbitration must be completed within a maximum of 160 days. These procedures provide, as a default, for documents-only arbitration for claims under USD75,000 (or RM150,000 in domestic arbitrations). Parties who wish to adopt these rules must specifically provide in their arbitration agreements that the KLRCA Fast Track Arbitration Rules shall apply.

Consolidation of Disputes between the Same Parties and Joinder of Third Parties

Arbitration proceedings may be consolidated or held concurrently under the KLRCA Arbitration Rules, provided the parties have agreed to confer such power on the arbitral tribunal.[11] The arbitral tribunal may also allow one or more third persons to be joined in the arbitration at the request of any party, provided, however, that they are a party to the arbitration agreement and that after hearing all parties, the arbitral tribunal finds that no prejudice will be occasioned to any of those parties.[12]

Time Limits for Rendering of the Award

The arbitral tribunal is obliged to render its final award within three months from the date of closing oral or written

---

[10] Rule 15 KLRCA Arbitration Rules.

[11] Rule 8 KLRCA Arbitration Rules.

[12] Article 17(5) Part II KLRCA Arbitration Rules.

submissions.[13] However, this time limit may be extended by the tribunal either with the consent of both parties,[14] or at the discretion of the Director of the KLRCA in the absence of such consent.[15]

Fee Structure

The fee of the arbitral tribunal and the administrative costs of the KLRCA are charged based on the amount of the dispute or as determined by the Director of the KLRCA.[16] As a general rule, the Schedules in Part III of the KLRCA Rules of Arbitration contain scales which will apply to an arbitration administered by the KLRCA, unless otherwise agreed by the parties or subject to any other agreement between the parties and the arbitral tribunal on the fee of the arbitral tribunal. The Director of the KLRCA has the discretion to adjust the fees payable in any unusual or unforeseen circumstances.[17]

Treatment of Costs of the Arbitration

Subsequent to the commencement of arbitration, the Director of KLRCA will fix a provisional advance deposit which must be paid by parties in equal proportion within 21 days of written notification, and the arbitration cannot proceed until the advance deposit is paid in full.[18] The Director of the KLRCA may determine the proportion of costs to be borne by the parties[19] or

---

[13] Rule 11(1) KLRCA Arbitration Rules.

[14] Rule 11(2) KLRCA Arbitration Rules.

[15] Rule 11(3) KLRCA Arbitration Rules.

[16] Rule 12 KLRCA Rules of Arbitration.

[17] Rule 12(6), KLRCA Rules of Arbitration.

[18] Rule 13 KLRCA Rules of Arbitration.

[19] Rule 12(9) KLRCA Rules of Arbitration.

fix separate deposits on costs for the claims and counterclaims.[20] The costs of the arbitration are in principle to be borne by the unsuccessful party or parties, although the arbitral tribunal may apportion such costs as it deems reasonable, taking into account the circumstances of the case.[21]

Special or Unusual Features (If Any)

The KLRCA i-Arbitration Rules incorporate a reference procedure to a Shariah Advisory Council or Shariah expert whenever the arbitral tribunal has to form an opinion on a point related to Shariah principles.[22] Both the KLRCA Arbitration Rules and the i-Arbitration Rules also contain provisions for the appointment of emergency arbitrators concurrent to or after the Notice of Arbitration is filed, but before the proper constitution of the arbitral tribunal, in the event a claimant seeks emergency interim relief. In such circumstances, the KLRCA is obliged to appoint an emergency arbitrator within two business days.

Recent Developments (If Any)

The KLRCA commenced operations in new and state-of-the-art facilities in Kuala Lumpur in October 2014, where space has been allocated for the Permanent Court of Arbitration to have its alternative venue in the Asian Region. The KLRCA has also signed an agreement with the Switzerland-based International Council of Arbitration for Sport to serve as the official host of an alternative hearing center for the Court of Arbitration for Sport and a memorandum of understanding with the Asian Domain Name Dispute Resolution Centre and Hong Kong International Arbitration Centre to administer domain name disputes.

---

[20]   Rule 13(5) KLRCA Rules of Arbitration.

[21]   Article 42(1) Part II KLRCA Rules of Arbitration.

[22]   Rule 11, KLRCA i-Arbitration Rules.

MEXICO

Salvador Fonseca González[1] and Juan Carlos Zamora Müller[2]

A. Legislation, Trends and Tendencies

A.1 Legislation

Arbitration regulation in Mexico has not changed since 2011, when there was significant reform. During this relatively short period of time, the legal framework has remained stable.

A.2 Trends and Tendencies

As discussed in the 2014 Arbitration Yearbook, reforms to the Amparo Law[3] that took place during 2013 made it possible to bring constitutional challenges against private entities or individuals that perform activities equivalent to those performed by government authorities. This new feature of the amended

---

[1]   Salvador Fonseca González is a Partner in Baker & McKenzie's Mexico City office. He has more than 18 years of experience representing corporate and individual clients in complex international and domestic arbitration and litigation. Mr. Fonseca has participated in cases under the rules of the major arbitral institutions and is familiar with dispute boards and other methods of solving disputes. He has served as sole arbitrator and chairman of arbitral tribunals in several international and local cases. He has lectured on International Commercial Arbitration at the most prestigious universities in Mexico.

[2]   Juan Carlos Zamora Müller is an Associate in Baker & McKenzie's Mexico City office. His practice focuses on dispute resolution, commercial litigation and arbitration. He has meaningful experience representing clients before Mexican courts and arbitral tribunals in ad hoc and ICC proceedings. He has served as associate professor in Procedural Law and Arbitration at the School of Law of the *Centro de Investigación y Docencia Economicas* in Mexico City.

[3]   Amparo refers to an extraordinary judicial remedy intended to allow a person to question whether or not a certain action or law conforms with the rights protected under the Mexican Constitution.

Amparo Law has been used to sue arbitrators and to challenge awards on the basis that the award violated the fundamental or human rights of the losing party.

Last year we expressed our hope that judges hearing such Amparo challenges would understand the nature of arbitration and deny this avenue of challenge. Whilst a high number of such challenges were brought, many of the decided cases confirm that arbitral awards cannot be challenged through Amparo proceedings.

This serves to underscore the trend that judges and practitioners in Mexico are becoming accustomed to arbitration, understand its value, and are committed to preserve it as a true alternative dispute resolution mechanism for commercial matters.

B. CASES

While there have been no relevant cases to report regarding arbitration in Mexico during 2014, the positive trend and the confirmation of previous precedents continue to show that Mexico is an arbitration-friendly jurisdiction.

C. LOCAL ARBITRATION INSTITUTIONS

C.1 Centro de Arbitraje de Mexico ("CAM")

Background

CAM was founded in 1997 with the purpose of fostering and promoting arbitration and to provide private entities and companies with access to a professional arbitration institution.

C. Local Arbitration Institutions

Types of Disputes Handled

CAM handles commercial disputes.

Numbers of Disputes Handled

No statistics are available.

Provisions on Confidentiality of Arbitration

All proceedings are confidential.

Availability of Expedited Procedures

There are no specific rules for expedited procedures.

Consolidation of Disputes between the Same Parties and Joinder of Third Parties

Consolidation is possible; however, there are no rules for joinder of third parties.

Time Limit for Rendering of the Award

There is no formal time limit for rendering the award; the average time taken is 14 months.

Fee structure

The General Council of CAM fixes the arbitrators' fees and the administrative expenses based on a "Scale of Arbitration Expenses" that provides for a progressive increase based on the amount in dispute.

Treatment of Costs of the Arbitration

The arbitral tribunal may decide which of the parties shall bear the costs and in what proportion.

Special or Unusual Features (If Any)

Up to 2012, no award rendered under the CAM rules had been set aside by the Mexican courts.

The CAM rules have provisions for the appointment of an emergency arbitrator.

Recent Developments (If Any)

Not applicable.

C.2 Centro de Mediación y Arbitraje de la Cámara Nacional de Comercio

Background

The *Centro de Mediación y Arbitraje de la Cámara Nacional de Comercio* ("CANACO"), was founded in 2000 as part of a restructuring of the Mexican Chamber of Commerce.

Types of Disputes Handled

CANACO handles commercial disputes through mediation and arbitration.

Numbers of Disputes Handled

No statistics are available.

Provisions on Confidentiality of Arbitration

All proceedings are confidential.

Availability of Expedited Procedures

CANACO has provision for expedited procedures where the parties so agree or where the dispute is under MXN611,814.

Arbitrations under the expedited procedures end with an unreasoned award.

Consolidation of Disputes between the Same Parties and Joinder of Third Parties

The CANACO rules do not provide for joinder of third parties or consolidation.

Time Limits for Rendering of the Award

No statistics are available.

Fee Structure

CANACO's Commission fixes the arbitrators' fees and the administrative expenses based on a "Scale of Arbitration Expenses" that provides for a progressive increase based on the amount in dispute.

Treatment of Costs of the Arbitration

The arbitral tribunal may decide which of the parties shall bear the costs and in what proportion.

Special or Unusual Features (If Any)

The CANACO rules have provisions for the appointment of an emergency arbitrator.

Recent Developments (If Any)

Not applicable.

MYANMAR

Leng Sun Chan[1] and Jo Delaney[2]

A. LEGISLATION, TRENDS AND TENDENCIES

A.1 Legislation

Arbitration in Myanmar is governed by the Arbitration Act 1944 ("Arbitration Act"), although this is about to be updated in 2015 as discussed below. The Arbitration Act is based on the English Arbitration Act 1934 and is closely aligned with the Indian Arbitration Act 1940. It applies to arbitrations that take place in Myanmar whether they are between two domestic parties, or a domestic party and a foreign party. The Arbitration Act sets out the essential provisions required for an arbitration to proceed, such as the definition of an arbitration agreement, the appointment of arbitrators in the event that the parties fail to agree on such appointment, and the process for challenging an arbitrator. The Arbitration Act sets out the form of an arbitral award and the manner in which an award is made, and states that an award is final and binding on the parties.

The Arbitration Act allows the Myanmar courts to support and supervise arbitration. The relevant provisions include the discretion to grant a stay of legal proceedings in favor of arbitration, and the power to grant interim orders or issue subpoenas for documents or witnesses. However, the courts'

---

[1]   Leng Sun Chan SC is the Head of Disputes in Baker & McKenzie.Wong & Leow, Singapore and is Baker & McKenzie's Asia-Pacific Head of International Arbitration.

[2]   Jo Delaney is a Special Counsel in Baker & McKenzie's Sydney office. Jo has 15 years experience in commercial, construction and investment arbitrations across a broad range of industries.

intervention in the arbitral process is limited to certain circumstances, and there are limited grounds on which an award may be set aside.

The Arbitration Act provides for the enforcement of an award in the Myanmar courts. It includes limited grounds on which enforcement may be challenged. The Arbitration Act does not expressly provide for enforcement under the New York Convention. Myanmar has acceded to the New York Convention, but the law giving effect to this has not yet been passed. Myanmar currently has the Arbitration (Protocol and Convention) Act, which applies to awards from Geneva Convention countries. However, Article VII of the New York Convention provides that the Geneva Protocol on Arbitration Clauses of 1923 and the Geneva Convention on the Execution of Foreign Arbitral Awards of 1927 shall cease to have effect when a State becomes party to the New York Convention. There will be significant changes to the enforcement of awards in Myanmar and of Myanmar awards abroad when the new legislation comes in.

Currently, it may be necessary under Myanmar law or regulation (or it may be requested by a Myanmar party) that the contract be governed by Myanmar law and that disputes be referred to arbitration or the courts in Myanmar. Such contracts may include contracts for the sale of goods, contracts relating to land or government contracts. There have been exceptions where the Myanmar government has agreed to the application of foreign law and international arbitration outside Myanmar (such as Singapore) under, for example, the ICC Rules or the UNCITRAL Arbitration Rules.

Unless such a requirement applies, the parties may agree to international arbitration outside Myanmar to resolve disputes. A neutral forum such as Singapore, Hong Kong, London or Sydney is preferable.

A. Legislation, Trends and Tendencies

There are certain provisions in the Arbitration Act that the parties may wish to exclude. For example, the parties may wish to exclude s.13(b), which provides that a question of law may be referred to the court.

Schedule 1 of the Arbitration Act sets out certain requirements that apply to the arbitration unless the parties have agreed otherwise. For example, Schedule 1 requires the tribunal to issue an award within four months of the tribunal being appointed. It may be difficult for the tribunal to comply with such a tight timeframe. The parties need to consent to the exclusion of these time limits or the arbitration clause may be rendered invalid under s.28(2) of the Arbitration Act. Schedule 1 also requires a sole arbitrator to be appointed unless the parties have agreed otherwise.

The extent to which the Myanmar courts may intervene in the arbitral process is unclear and uncertain. There are some provisions in the Arbitration Act which indicate that such intervention is limited. For example, s.32 of the Arbitration Act provides that:

> Notwithstanding any law for the time being in force, no suit shall lie on any ground whatsoever for a decision upon the existence, effect or validity of an arbitration agreement or award, nor shall any arbitration agreement or award be set aside, amended, modified, or in any way affected otherwise than as provided in the Act.

The grounds for the court to set aside an award are set out in s.30 of the Arbitration Act. These grounds include circumstances where the arbitrator has misconducted himself or the proceedings; the award is made after the issue of an order by the court superseding the arbitration or after arbitration proceedings have become invalid under s.35; and an award has been improperly procured or is otherwise invalid.

However, as indicated by s.30, there are circumstances in which arbitration proceedings may be rendered invalid. For example, s.35 provides that:

> No reference or award shall be rendered invalid by reason only of the commencement of legal proceedings upon the subject-matter of the reference, but when legal proceedings upon the whole of the subject-matter of the reference have been commenced between all the parties to the reference and a notice thereof has been given to the arbitrators or umpire, all further proceedings in a pending reference shall, unless a stay of proceedings is granted under s. 34, be invalid.

This means that if court proceedings have been commenced, then any arbitration proceedings will be invalid unless the court grants a stay of the court proceedings under s.34. This provides that the court will grant a stay if "there is no sufficient reason why the matter should not be referred to arbitration and the applicant was, at the time when the proceedings were commenced, and still remains, ready and willing to do all things necessary to the proper conduct of the arbitration."

The Arbitration Act recognizes three types of arbitration: (1) arbitration without intervention of a court; (2) arbitration with intervention of a court where there are no court proceedings pending; and (3) arbitration where there are pending court proceedings. If there is an arbitration agreement, the parties may refer a dispute to arbitration without any intervention of the courts. There are certain circumstances in which the courts may intervene, for example, by appointing arbitrators or granting interim measures as indicated above.

Alternatively, where there is an arbitration agreement, the parties may apply to a court having jurisdiction in the matter seeking an order that the arbitration agreement be filed in court under s. 20

of the Arbitration Act. The court will require the other parties to show cause as to why the agreement should not be filed in court. If no cause is shown then the court will order that the agreement be filed and may appoint an arbitrator if the parties cannot agree. The arbitration may proceed in accordance with the applicable provisions of the Arbitration Act.

Under s. 21, the parties may request the court to refer a dispute being heard by the courts to arbitration. Chapter IV (s.s 21 - 25) will then apply to the arbitration. The court will appoint an arbitrator.

The existence of these provisions in the Arbitration Act may indicate that the Myanmar courts may intervene in circumstances where the national courts would not normally be permitted to do so under the UNCITRAL Model Law.

Many of the provisions discussed in this section are likely to be changed when the new law is passed, as it is anticipated to be based largely on the UNCITRAL Model Law.

A.2 Trends and Tendencies

In July 2013, Myanmar formally acceded to the New York Convention. Myanmar has not yet enacted implementing legislation; however, there are proposals to amend the Arbitration Act, and a draft Arbitration Law ("Draft Law") has been circulated for consultation. The Draft Law is discussed in A.3 below. There is also a proposal to establish the Myanmar Arbitration Centre, which is considered in C below.

A.3 Draft Law

Subject to a few modifications, most of the Draft Law provisions are the same as the UNCITRAL Model Law. The discussion below focuses on the differences between them.

Place of Arbitration

S. 1(c) applies when the place of arbitration is in Myanmar. Unlike Article 1(2) of the Model Law,[3] s. 1(c) does not specify the articles that may apply if the place of arbitration is outside Myanmar.

International Commercial Arbitration

S. 2 provides for the definition of "international commercial arbitration" to apply to certain arbitrations, such as that arising out of contractual relationships that are considered as "commercial" under Myanmar law. This definition is relevant to later s.s in the Draft Law such as s.28(a), which provides that Myanmar law is to apply to arbitrations that are not "international commercial arbitrations", whereas parties to an international commercial arbitration can choose the substantive law to be applied. It is unclear what relationships would be considered as "commercial" under Myanmar law.

Administrative Assistance

S.6 provides: "In order to facilitate the conduct of arbitral proceedings, the parties, or the arbitral tribunal with the consent of the parties, may arrange for administrative assistance by a suitable institution or Court." The scope or intention of this clause is unclear. If the parties have agreed to refer the dispute to

---

[3]   Article 1(2) of the Model Law provides that Articles 8, 9, 17H, 17I, 17K, 35 and 36 may apply if the place of arbitration is outside that State. These articles relate to matters or circumstances in which the courts may assist an arbitration that is seated outside the State. For example, Article 8 empowers the court to stay court proceedings pending the outcome of arbitration proceedings even if the seat of the arbitration is outside Myanmar. Articles 35 and 36 relate to the recognition and enforcement of foreign arbitral awards. Some of these provisions are essential for the efficient and effective operation of international arbitration.

institutional arbitration, then the institution will provide administrative assistance in any event. Also, it is not clear in what circumstances the parties would require administrative assistance from the courts, and the extent to which the courts would be empowered to grant such assistance. There is a risk that s. 6 will be given a broad interpretation by the courts, resulting in a more interventionist approach.

Power to Stay Court Proceedings and Interim Measures

S.8 is similar to Article 8 of the Model Law, but does not include the qualification in Article 8 that allows the court not to grant a stay if it finds that the arbitration agreement is "null, void, inoperative or incapable of being performed". Article 8 also empowers the courts to stay court proceedings pending the outcome of an arbitration.

S.9 is similar to Article 9 of the Model Law, but appears to be more restrictive. It does not apply to all interim measures and provides examples of specific interim measures. The reference in s. 9(a)(vii) to "other interim procedures the Court can fairly and easily handle" is unclear. Further, it provides that the court will only have the power to make orders "if the arbitral tribunal lacks power to issue arbitral awards or effectively handle the case".

Tribunal's Powers

S.17 is similar to Article 17 of the Model Law and provides that the tribunal has the power to grant interim measures, such as the preservation of evidence. S. 17 provides for specific interim measures that may be granted by the tribunal, although they are not described as broadly as in Article 17, nor does s.17 include the general provision that the "tribunal may, at the request of a party, grant interim measures". Further, the 2006 amendments to Article 17 of the Model Law (Articles 17A to 17J) have not been included in the Draft Law.

Hearings

S. 24 is similar to Article 24 of the Model Law regarding hearings and proceedings, while s. 27 is similar to Article 27 of the Model Law regarding the court's assistance in taking evidence. However, s. 27 provides further detail on how such assistance is to be requested and executed. These additions clarify the process.

The Award

S. 31 is similar to Article 31 of the Model Law relating to the form and contents of an award. S. 31(f) has been added and provides that the costs of the arbitration shall be fixed by the tribunal and that the tribunal shall specify the party entitled to costs, the party who shall pay the costs, the amount of costs or method of determining the amount and the manner in which the costs are to be paid.

S. 34 is similar to Article 34 of the Model Law, which sets out the grounds on which an award may be set aside or annulled. S. 34(b)(i)(aa) expands the scope of Article 34(2)(a)(i) of the Model Law to include circumstances where "the arbitration award is not valid under the arbitration law which the parties are bound to comply with or there is no such law or if not legal under an existing law for the time being in force in the Union of Myanmar." In contrast, the corresponding ground for challenging the enforcement of an award in s. 50(a)(i) is drafted in the same language as Article 34(2)(a)(i) and Article 36(1)(a)(i) of the Model Law. Further, s. 34(b)(ii)(bb) provides some scope and content to the meaning of "public policy". It states: "an award is in conflict with the public policy of the Union of Myanmar if making the award was induced or affected by fraud or corruption or was in violation of natural justice".

S. 35 provides that an award is final and binding, similar to Article 35 of the Model Law. S. 36 provides for the enforcement of awards that have been made in Myanmar, which takes place under the Code of Civil Procedure 1908.

Appeals

S. 37 provides the types of appeals that may be brought under the Draft Law. The appeals relate to the circumstances in which the courts may support or supervise arbitration by, for example, granting interim measures under s. 9 or setting aside an award under s. 34. S. 37 does not provide any basis upon which an award may be appealed to the courts. Any award may be challenged under s. 34. The court's decision relating to that challenge may be appealed under s. 37(a)(ii).

Enforcement of Foreign Awards

Chapter XII (s.s 46 to 52) provides for the enforcement of foreign awards. S. 46 provides for the enforcement of foreign awards in accordance with the conventions attached in schedules to the Draft Law. We have not seen these schedules, but it is presumed that these schedules refer to the Geneva Convention, New York Convention and ICSID Convention.

S. 46 also seems to provide that the courts will only enforce an award made in a State that has been notified in the Gazette on the basis of reciprocity. It is not clear whether this applies to the New York Convention. According to the UNCITRAL website, Myanmar did not include any reservations or declarations (including in relation to reciprocity) in its ratification of the New York Convention.

S. 49(a)(iii) appears to add an additional requirement for the enforcement of an award. The New York Convention requires a party seeking to enforce an award to provide a copy of the arbitration agreement and the arbitral award (s. 49(a)(i) and (ii)). S. 49(a)(iii) also requires the party to provide "such evidence as may be necessary to prove that the award is a foreign award". It is not clear what evidence would be sufficient to satisfy this requirement.

S. 53 appears to address the issue of reciprocal enforcement of awards between India and Myanmar and provides:

> Nothing in this Chapter shall prejudice any rights which any person would have had of enforcing in India of any award or of availing himself in India of any award or of availing himself in the Republic of the Union of Myanmar, of any award if this Chapter had not been enacted.

India has adopted the reservation that it will only enforce awards made in a State that has been notified as such by the Indian government. Burma was notified as such a State with respect to the Geneva Convention (under s. 2 of the Indian Arbitration (Protocol and Convention) Act 1937). However, Burma/Myanmar has not been listed as one of the States notified by the Indian government for enforcement under the New York Convention.

Supplementary Provisions

Chapter XI (s.s 38 to 45) sets out the supplementary provisions. S. 38(a) refers to the confirmation of "arbitral awards among signatory member countries relating to a contractual agreement". It is not clear whether this is a reference to "signatory member countries" of the New York Convention. S. 39 refers to the court awarding interest on an award. S. 40 appears to address insurance premiums relating to claims referred to arbitration. S. 41 provides that the tribunal shall have a lien on the award for any unpaid costs of the arbitration. S. 42 addresses the circumstances resulting from the death of a party. S. 43 addresses the circumstances resulting from a party becoming insolvent. S. 45 provides for the application of the Limitation Act.

B. CASES

There were no significant cases related to arbitration in Myanmar in 2014.

C. LOCAL ARBITRATION INSTITUTIONS

The Union of Myanmar Federation of Chamber of Commerce and Industry has set up a committee to look into the formation of a Myanmar arbitration center. No target date has been announced, although it is hoped that the center will be established in 2015.

THE NETHERLANDS

Frank Kroes[1] and Esther Croonen[2,3]

A. LEGISLATION, TRENDS AND TENDENCIES

A.1 Legislation

On January 1, 2015, the revised Dutch Arbitration Act ("the New Act"), entered into force. The New Act is incorporated into book four of the Dutch Code of Civil Procedure ("DCCP") and into books three, six and ten of the Dutch Civil Code ("DCC"). It applies to arbitrations with a seat in The Netherlands initiated on or after January 1, 2015. The New Act aims at making arbitration more attractive by modernizing the process, codifying arbitration practice, and reducing costs. It is also aimed at improving the competitive position of The Netherlands by offering high-quality dispute resolution, both in state courts as well as in arbitration proceedings conducted in The Netherlands. The most important changes in the New Act are described below.

Efficiency and Effectiveness

The New Act creates the possibility for Dutch arbitration proceedings to be conducted entirely by electronic means. Even an arbitral award can be made electronically by containing an

---

[1]   Frank Kroes is a Partner in the Amsterdam office of Baker & McKenzie. His practice focus is on litigation and arbitration for financial institutions and other complex commercial disputes.

[2]   Esther Croonen is an Associate in the Amsterdam office of Baker & McKenzie. Her practice focus is on cross-border commercial litigation, corporate litigation and arbitration.

[3]   The authors would like to thank Renée Musters, an Associate in the Amsterdam office of Baker & McKenzie, for her contribution to this chapter.

electronic signature,[4] and the obligation to file an arbitral award at the court registry has been abolished.

Party Autonomy

Parties are offered maximized party autonomy under the New Act, as they enjoy broad freedom in determining the procedure to be followed by the arbitral tribunal in conducting proceedings. Parties may, for example, exclude the possibility of oral hearings, agree to the use of certain rules of evidence, or limit the powers of the arbitral tribunals.[5]

Challenge to an Arbitrator

On the basis of the New Act, parties can appoint a third party, for example an arbitration institute, to decide on a challenge to an arbitrator.[6] Previously, the court had to decide on such requests.

Setting Aside Proceedings

The New Act reduces the length of annulment proceedings before the Dutch courts. The Court of Appeal, and no longer the District Court, is competent in such proceedings. This reduces proceedings to two instances (i.e. the Court of Appeal and Dutch Supreme Court).[7] In addition, parties now have the option to agree to exclude the possibility of lodging an appeal to the Dutch Supreme Court, save for in the case of consumers.[8]

---

[4]   Article III (Section KKK) of the New Act, incorporated in Article 1072b DCCP.

[5]   For example Article III (Sections U-FF) New Act, incorporated in Articles 1038 - 1045 DCCP.

[6]   Article III (Sections O, P, Q) New Act, incorporated in Articles 1033, 1034 and 1035 DCCP.

[7]   Article III (Section BBB) New Act, incorporated in Article 1064a DCCP.

[8]   Article III (Section BBB) New Act, incorporated in Article 1064a (Section 5) DCCP.

A. Legislation, Trends and Tendencies

Validity of the Arbitration Agreement

The New Act provides that an arbitration agreement will be valid, if it is considered as such by the law which the parties have agreed upon; the law of the place of arbitration; or if the parties made no choice of law, the law applicable to the legal relationship governed by the arbitration agreement.[9]

Provisional Measures

The New Act enables parties to request interim measures pending arbitral proceedings.[10] Conservatory measures, such as pre-judgment attachments, are excluded.[11] The New Act prescribes that interim measures should relate to the claim or counterclaim in the pending arbitral proceedings. Unless the arbitral tribunal determines otherwise, the decision of the arbitral tribunal on the request for interim measures is considered to be an arbitral award and will be enforceable as such.

Arbitration outside the Netherlands

Under the New Act, parties who have agreed to arbitration outside The Netherlands will be able to request a Dutch court to grant interim measures of protection or a decision in summary proceedings of the President of the District Court.[12]

Consumer Protection

Finally, the New Act strengthens the position of consumers. It assumes that arbitration clauses contained in the general terms

---

[9] Article II New Act, incorporated in Article 166 of Book 10 DCC.

[10] Article III (Section DD) New Act, incorporated in Article 1043b DCCP.

[11] As described in the fourth title of the third Book DCCP.

[12] Article III (Section MMM) New Act, incorporated in Article 1074a DCCP.

and conditions of consumer contracts are "unreasonably onerous". Consumers can opt for dispute resolution by the court within one month from the date on which the user invokes the arbitration clause.[13]

B.   CASES

B.1   Arbitral Award under a BIT

On September 26, 2014, the Dutch Supreme Court decided for the first time on whether to overturn an arbitral award rendered under a BIT between the Republic of Ecuador ("Ecuador") and the United States of America ("US").[14] The proceedings concerned a dispute between Ecuador and a subsidiary of the American company Chevron Corporation ("Chevron"), Texaco Petroleum Company ("Texpet"), in connection with a concession agreement. Between 1991 and 1993, Texpet filed seven cases before the Ecuadorean court, claiming compensation due to alleged breaches of the concession agreement by Ecuador. The Ecuadorean court failed to rule on Texpet's claim for nearly 10 years. In 1997, Ecuador and the US entered into a BIT containing provisions for the reciprocal protection of investments by legal entities in each other's countries. In December 2006, based on the arbitration clause included in the BIT, Chevron commenced arbitral proceedings against Ecuador, claiming that Ecuador violated the provisions of the BIT by refusing to hear Texpet's claims and that these violations should be considered as investments within the meaning of the BIT. The arbitral award ordered Ecuador to pay Chevron an amount of

---

13   Article Ia New Act, incorporated in Article 236 sub n of Book 6 DCC.

14   Dutch Supreme Court, September 26, 2014, *ECLI:NL:HR:2014:2837 (Chevron Corporation and Texaco Petroleum Company / Republic of Ecuador).*

approximately USD96 million (to be increased with post-award interest). Ecuador applied to the Dutch courts to have the award overturned on the basis that Chevron's claims were not investments within the meaning of the BIT and the arbitrators were incompetent to rule on the dispute. The Court of Appeal of The Hague upheld the District Court's dismissal of Ecuador's claims.

The Dutch Supreme Court upheld both these dismissals and ruled that although the arbitration may, to a certain extent, have impinged on Ecuador's national sovereignty, this was a consequence of the BIT's wide definition of investments, upon which the parties had agreed and which deviated from the term's common usage. The Dutch Supreme Court held that the Court of Appeal was free to decide that the legal claims filed by Texpet/Chevron—which were pending when the BIT entered into force—should be regarded as investments even though this term is not usually taken to encompass such claims.

B.2 Arbitral Agreement Unreasonably Onerous

A remarkable decision was rendered by the Court of Appeal of Amsterdam on June 3, 2014 regarding the enforceability of an arbitration agreement contained in the general terms and conditions of a franchise agreement.[15]

A franchise agreement between a Dutch citizen and a Dutch subsidiary of Subway provided for arbitration to be held in accordance with the UNCITRAL Arbitration Rules, to be conducted in the English language in New York and governed by the law of Liechtenstein. The franchisee commenced court proceedings against Subway before the District Court of Amsterdam and argued that the arbitration agreement should be

---

[15] Court of Appeal of Amsterdam, June 3, 2014, *ECLI:NL:GHAMS:2014:2270 (Franchisee / Subway International B.V.)*.

considered invalid. Based on the franchise agreement and Liechtenstein law, the court declared the arbitration agreement valid and ruled that it had no jurisdiction. The franchisee lodged an appeal before the Court of Appeal of Amsterdam.

The Court of Appeal ruled that the question of the arbitration agreement's validity should be examined in accordance with Liechtenstein law. In its assessment, the Court of Appeal took into account that: i) the franchisee, a natural person, should be considered as the economically weaker party in relation to a multi-national corporation; ii) based on the arbitration agreement, the franchisee would be forced to travel to New York for a hearing, which imposes a great burden on the franchisee; iii) both the franchisee and the subsidiary of Subway are located in The Netherlands, while only the parent company of Subway resides in the US; and iv) given the prescribed language, the franchisee would need to engage an interpreter, which would increase costs. The Court of Appeal therefore held that the arbitration agreement should be considered unreasonably onerous and therefore void and unenforceable. The case was referred back to the District Court of Amsterdam, which will decide on the dispute between the franchisee and Subway.

B.3   Arbitration Agreement Not Applicable

The Court of Appeal of The Hague recently decided on the applicability of an arbitration agreement contained in an agreement for the delivery of goods entered into between two German entities (the buyers) and a Dutch company (the seller) and to which the parties agreed that the Vienna Convention on the International Sale of Goods ("CISG") applied. [16] In all prior confirmations and invoices relating to previous similar

---

[16]   Court of Appeal of The Hague, April 22, 2014, *ECLI:NL:GHDHA: 2014:1341(Otten / Rhumveld)*.

agreements between the parties, the Dutch seller referred to the conditions of The Netherlands Association for the Trade in Dried Fruit, Spices and Allied Products ("NZV"), which include an arbitration agreement.

The German buyers initiated court proceedings before the District Court of Rotterdam, claiming damages for the seller's delivery of nonconforming goods. The seller contested the jurisdiction of the District Court, referring to the arbitration agreement within the NZV conditions. The District Court declared itself incompetent on this basis. The buyers appealed to the Court of Appeal of The Hague on the basis that the NZV conditions did not apply because the seller had not given the buyers a reasonable opportunity to take notice of their contents, which was necessary for these conditions to apply.

The Court of Appeal considered that standard terms will become part of the agreement if, at the time the contract was formed, the parties expressly or implicitly agreed to the incorporation of those standard terms into the agreement and the other party is given a reasonable opportunity to take notice of these standard terms.[17] A party may be considered to have had a reasonable opportunity to take notice of the standard terms where: i) the terms are attached to a document used in connection with the formation of the contract or printed on the reverse side of that document; ii) the terms are available to the parties in the presence of each other at the time of negotiating the contract; iii) in electronic communications, the terms are made available to, and retrievable electronically by, that party and are accessible at the time of negotiating the contract; or iv) there are prior agreements between the parties subject to the same standard

---

[17] Reference is made to the decision of the German Bundesgerichtshof, October 31, 2011, *VIII ZR 60/01*.

terms.[18] The Court of Appeal ruled that the NZV conditions and the arbitration agreement included in it were not applicable and that the District Court had wrongly declared itself incompetent. This was because the buyers could only have been aware of the standard terms by searching for them on the internet because they were never sent the NZV conditions by the seller. Any reference to the NZV conditions in prior agreements was insufficient to incorporate them into the current agreement.

C. LOCAL ARBITRATION INSTITUTIONS

C.1 The Netherlands Arbitration Institute ("NAI")

Background

Although there are many specialized arbitration institutes within The Netherlands,[19] the NAI is the primary commercial arbitration institute. The NAI was established as a nonprofit foundation in 1949 and is based in Rotterdam. Its purpose is to promote ADR by offering rules for arbitration proceedings, binding advice (*bindend advies*) and mediation.

Types of Disputes Handled

The NAI handles both national and international (commercial) arbitration. There is no specific restriction as to the subject

---

[18] Reference is made to *CISG-AC Opinion No. 13, Inclusion of Standard Terms under the CISG, Rapporteur*: Professor Sieg Eiselen, College of Law, University of South Africa, Pretoria, South Africa. Adopted by the CISG Advisory Council following its 17th meeting, in Villanova, Pennsylvania, USA, on January 20, 2013, *see:* http://www.cisgac.com/ default.php?ipkCat=128&ifkCat=222&sid=222.

[19] For example: Counsel for Arbitration in the Construction Industry, P.R.I.M.E. Finance Foundation, Maritime Arbitration Rotterdam-Amsterdam Association and Arbitral Tribunal for the Graphic Industry Foundation and Transport.

matter of the arbitration. The NAI Arbitration Rules form the basis of the organization of the arbitral process by the NAI. Recently, the NAI presented revised Rules, taking into account the New Act as entered into force on January 1, 2015, which also became effective on January 1, 2015.

Numbers of Disputes Handled

In 2013 the NAI registered a total of 114 arbitrations, of which 49 were international, and in 2012 it registered a total of 109 disputes, of which 32 were international. In both these years, the number of summary proceedings was 11. The number of arbitrations that involved an amount of over EUR1 million increased from 30 in 2012 to 34 in 2013. The final statistics for 2014 are not currently available.

Provisions on Confidentiality of Arbitration

It is generally accepted that arbitration is confidential and that the parties and arbitrators involved in the arbitration proceedings are bound to secrecy. Although the New Act does not contain a specific provision on confidentiality, such provision is made in the NAI Rules.

Pursuant to the NAI Rules, arbitration is confidential, and all individuals involved either directly or indirectly are bound to secrecy, save and insofar as disclosure ensues from the law or the agreement of the parties.[20] Also, the NAI is authorized to have the award published anonymously unless a party objects within one month after receipt of the award.[21]

---

[20] Article 6 of the NAI Rules 2015 (article 55 sub 1 NAI Rules 2010).

[21] Article 51 of the NAI Rules 2015 (article 55 sub 2 NAI Rules 2010).

Summary Proceedings

The New Act stipulates that an arbitration agreement shall not preclude a party from requesting the court to order a conservatory interim measure or from applying to the President of the District Court for a decision in summary proceedings.[22] The NAI Rules also provide the possibility of summary arbitral proceedings.[23] This will not lead to a definitive ruling (as in the case of expedited proceedings), but a preliminary order, which will remain in force until a definitive award is made. Although a summary award can be executed in the same way as an ordinary arbitral award, the tribunal at the substantive hearing is not bound by the findings of the summary award.

Consolidation of Disputes between the Same Parties and Joinder of Third Parties

Pursuant to the New Act, a party may request a third party or the President of the District Court in Amsterdam to order consolidation of arbitral proceedings pending in The Netherlands with other arbitral proceedings pending in or outside The Netherlands, unless otherwise agreed by the parties.[24] Consolidation should not cause unreasonable delay to the pending arbitral proceedings. Also, there should be a close connection between the subject matters of the two arbitrations. A similar provision is adopted in the NAI Rules.[25]

The New Act states that, unless otherwise agreed by the parties, the arbitral tribunal may, upon written request of a third party who has an interest in the arbitral proceedings, permit such party

---

[22] Article III (Section D) New Act, incorporated in Article 1022a DCCP.

[23] Articles 36 and 35 sub 2 NAI Rules 2015.

[24] Article III (Section HH) New Act, incorporated in Article 1046 DCCP.

[25] Article 39 NAI Rules 2015.

to join or to intervene in the proceedings. For this to be possible, the same arbitration agreement must apply between the parties and the third party as that which applies between the original parties. The NAI Rules contain a similar provision.[26]

Time Limits for Rendering of the Award

Pursuant to the NAI Rules, the arbitral tribunal must inform the parties at the end of the hearing, or, if the parties have waived a hearing, after submission of the last written statement, of the period of time within which it will render its award.[27] There is no specific time limit provided in the NAI Rules. However, the arbitral tribunal must decide within a reasonable period of time. According to the NAI, the average duration of NAI arbitral proceedings is nine months.

Fee Structure

The fees of the arbitrator(s) are to be determined by the Administrator after consultation with the arbitrator(s).[28] The agreed hourly rate is set by reference to guidelines drawn up by the NAI's Governing Board. In determining the fees, the guidelines take into account the time spent on the case by the arbitrator(s), the amount in dispute, and the complexity of the case.

Treatment of Costs of the Arbitration

According to the NAI Rules, the losing party is to be ordered to bear the costs of the arbitration, except in special cases at the

---

26 Article 37 NAI Rules 2015.

27 Article 40 NAI Rules 2015.

28 Article 54 NAI Rules 2015.

discretion of the arbitral tribunal.[29] The arbitral tribunal may also award against the losing party the costs of any legal assistance incurred by the party in whose favor the award is rendered, if and to the extent that these costs are deemed necessary by the arbitral tribunal.[30]

---

[29]   Article 57 NAI Rules 2015.

[30]   Article 56 NAI Rules 2015.

PERU

Ana María Arrarte[1] and Sebastián Basombrio[2]

A. LEGISLATION, TRENDS AND TENDENCIES

A.1 Legislation

International arbitration in Peru continues to be governed by the Arbitration Act of 2008 (Decreto Legislativo 1071), to which no legislative amendment was made in 2014.

B. CASES

There have been no significant court decisions in Peru in relation to arbitration in the last year.

---

[1] Ana Maria Arrarte is a Partner in Baker & McKenzie's Lima office. Ms. Arrarte advises clients in civil and commercial procedural law matters, including arbitration, negotiation and conciliation. She is a member of the arbitrators' lists at the Center for Arbitration of the Lima Chamber of Commerce, the American Chamber of Commerce, the Center of Arbitration at the Professional Association of Engineers of Peru and the Center of Arbitration at the Pontificia Universidad Católica del Peru. In addition to her practice, for the past 18 years, Ms. Arrarte has been a Professor at Peru's most prestigious universities (Pontificia Universidad Catolica del Peru, Universidad de Lima, Universidad del Pacifico, among others). She has authored several articles on arbitration and litigation in both national and international law reviews, and has co-authored several books on litigation and arbitration.

[2] Sebastián Basombrío is a Senior Associate in Baker & McKenzie's Lima office, with experience in commercial and regulatory arbitrations. He has worked and currently works in arbitrations related to the construction, energy and mining sectors. He has taught law courses in Peru's most prestigious universities (Pontificia Universidad Catolica del Peru, Universidad del Pacifico, UPC).

C. LOCAL ARBITRATION INSTITUTIONS

C.1 Arbitration Center of the Lima Chamber of Commerce ("ACLCC")

Background

The ACLCC was founded in 1993[3] and is one of the most important arbitration institutions in Peru.

Types of Disputes Handled

The ACLCC handles domestic and international arbitrations.

Numbers of Disputes Handled

Since its creation, the ACLCC has handled more than 3000 cases.[4]

Provisions on Confidentiality of Arbitration

The ACLCC has very strict rules regarding confidentiality. Its procedural rules state that all arbitration proceedings are confidential unless both parties have agreed otherwise, or when there is a legal mandate to inform.

Availability of Expedited Procedures

The ACLCC's rules do not provide different procedures for different types of arbitration. However, both parties are free to modify the rules set forth by the ACLCC regarding the procedure as long as they both agree.

---

[3]   http://www.camaralima.org.pe/principal/categoria/presentacion/100/c-100.

[4]   *Id.*

C. Local Arbitration Institutions

Consolidation of Disputes between the Same Parties and Joinder of Third Parties

It is possible to consolidate disputes between the same parties, as well as to join third parties to the arbitration. However, there are no special provisions in the ACLCC's rules regarding these issues.

Time Limits for Rendering of the Award

The ACLCC's rules state that the Arbitration Panel has 30 working days to render the award from the date the arbitration proceedings end. However, the deadline is extendable for an additional 15 working days.

Fee Structure

The fee structure depends on the monetary value of the claim. Details are available on the ACLCC website:[5]

The fee for the expenses of the arbitration center ranges from PEN561.89 plus legal taxes for claims up to USD 2,500 to a minimum of PEN66,696.84 plus legal taxes for claims exceeding USD5 million.

Similarly, the fee for the arbitration court ranges from PEN2,005.92 plus legal taxes for claims up to USD2,500 to a minimum of PEN172,107.94 plus legal taxes for claims exceeding USD5 million. Fees for a single arbitrator range from PEN668.64 plus legal taxes for claims up to USD2,500 to a minimum of PEN57,396.31 plus legal taxes for claims exceeding USD5 million.

---

[5]   http://www.camaralima.org.pe/principal/categoria/tarifas/530/c-530.

Treatment of Costs of the Arbitration

The tribunal should consider any agreement by the parties when allocating the costs of arbitration. If there is no agreement, the costs will be paid by the losing party. However, the court may allocate costs between the parties if it considers that it is reasonable in the circumstances.

Special or Unusual Features (If Any)

The ACLCC also provides services as a nomination institution, and decides on recusals of arbitrators, in arbitrations not administered by it.

Recent Developments (If Any)

Not applicable.

C.2   Center of Analysis and Conflict Resolution of the PUCP

Background

The Center of Analysis and Conflict Resolution (the "CACR") of the Pontifical Catholic University of Peru (*Pontifica Universidad Católica del Perú* or PUCP) was founded in 2001,[6] and is another of the important arbitration institutions in Peru.

Types of Disputes Handled

The CACR handles domestic and international arbitrations.

Numbers of Disputes Handled

Since its creation, the CACR has handled more than 2000 cases.[7]

---

[6]   http://consensos.pucp.edu.pe/el-centro/historia/.

[7]   http://consensos.pucp.edu.pe/arbitraje/presentacion-2/.

C. Local Arbitration Institutions

Provisions on Confidentiality of Arbitration

The CACR has very strict rules regarding confidentiality. The procedural rules of the Arbitration Center state that all arbitration proceedings are confidential unless both parties have agreed otherwise, when there is a legal mandate to inform, or when one of the parties requests the annulment of the arbitration award.

Availability of Expedited Procedures

The CACR's rules do not provide different procedures for different types of arbitration. However, the parties are free to modify the rules set by the CACR for the procedure, provided that both agree.

Consolidation of Disputes between the Same Parties and Joinder of Third Parties

The CACR's rules allow the consolidation of arbitrations, provided that the consolidation is requested before the evidentiary phase of the arbitration. It is possible for third parties to participate in the arbitration, although there are no special provisions regulating this.

Time Limits for Rendering of the Award

The Arbitration Center's regulations state that the Arbitration Panel has 30 working days to render the award after the arbitration proceedings ended. However, the deadline is extendable for an additional 30 working days.

Fee Structure

The fee structure depends on the monetary value of the claim. Details are available on the CACR website. [8]

---

[8]   http://consensos.pucp.edu.pe/wp-content/uploads/2012/09/Tarifario.pdf.

The CACR's administrative fee ranges from a minimum of PEN4,500 for claims up to PEN145,000 to a maximum of PEN41,180 plus 0.1% of the amount exceeding PEN14.5 million. The fee for submission of the arbitration request ranges from PEN1,350 for claims up to PEN145,000 to 30% of the administrative fee for claims over PEN14,500. These figures are exclusive of legal taxes.

Similarly, the fee for the arbitration court ranges from PEN12,395 for claims up to PEN145,000 to PEN149,942 plus 0.7% of the amount exceeding PEN14.5 million for claims exceeding USD5 million. Fees for a single arbitrator range from PEN4,115 for claims up to PEN145,000 to PEN149,942 plus 0.7% of the amount exceeding PEN14.5 million for claims exceeding USD5 million. These figures are also exclusive of legal taxes.

Treatment of Costs of the Arbitration

The tribunal should consider any agreement by the parties when allocating the costs of arbitration. If there is no agreement, the costs will be paid by the losing party. However, the court may allocate costs between the parties if it considers that it is reasonable in the circumstances.

Special or Unusual Features (If Any)

The Arbitration Center also provides services as a nomination institution and as a secretary in ad hoc arbitrations.

Recent Developments (If Any)

Not applicable

PHILIPPINES

Donemark J.L. Calimon[1] and Grace Ann C. Lazaro[2]

A. Legislation, Trends and Tendencies

A.1 Legislation

The Department of Justice ("DOJ') recently issued Circular No. 038 prescribing the fees to be charged by the Office for Alternative Dispute Resolution ("OADR") in accrediting private ADR organizations, ADR practitioners and public ADR programs in the Philippines. The OADR, an attached agency of the DOJ, was created to promote, develop and expand the use of ADR in the Philippines.[3]

DOJ Circular No. 038 took effect on October 31, 2014. It was issued pursuant to DOJ Circular No. 49[4] setting out the guidelines to be adopted by the OADR for the mandatory

---

[1] Donemark J.L. Calimon is a Partner in Quisumbing Torres Law Offices, a member firm of Baker & McKenzie International in Manila, and currently heads its Dispute Resolution Practice Group. He specializes in commercial arbitration, both domestic and international. He is a member and officer of the Board of Trustees, and an accredited arbitrator, of the Philippine Dispute Resolution Center, Inc. (PDRCI), an accredited arbitrator of the Philippine Intellectual Office, a member of the Chartered Institute of Arbitrators, East Asia Branch (Philippine Chapter), and a director / officer of the Philippine Institute of Arbitrators.

[2] Grace Ann C. Lazaro is an Associate of in Quisumbing Torres Law Offices, a member firm of Baker & McKenzie International in Manila. Her practice covers commercial arbitration, both domestic and international, as well as general litigation.

[3] Republic Act No. 9285, Section 49.

[4] Otherwise known as the *Accreditation Guidelines for Alternative Dispute Resolution Provider Organizations and Training Standards for Alternative Dispute Resolution Practitioners*; see 2012-2013 International Arbitration Yearbook, pp. 340-341.

accreditation of private ADR providers offering their services to or in partnership with government agencies, and for voluntary accreditation of all other ADR providers in the Philippines.

Save for the above developments, international arbitration in the Philippines continues to be governed by the Republic Act No. 9285, or the Alternative Dispute Resolution Act ("ADR Act"), to which no legislative amendment has been made since its enactment in 2004.

A.2 Trends and Tendencies

Recent developments in international arbitration has prompted the OADR to recognize the need to update and improve the ADR Act. During its celebration of the ADR week from December 16 to 19, 2014 entitled "R.A. 9285: 10 Years After, Reflecting on the Past, Building for the Future", the OADR facilitated a discussion on the limitations of and possible amendments to the ADR Act.

Possible amendments to the ADR Act were raised. These included the adoption of the 2006 amendments to the 1985 UNCITRAL Model Law,[5] clarification of the rules on recognition and enforcement of relief granted by an emergency arbitrator,[6] and the elimination of the distinction between domestic and international arbitration, particularly with respect to the rules governing the recognition and enforcement of arbitral awards.

---

[5] The ADR Act adopted the 1985 Model Law to govern international commercial arbitration in the Philippines.

[6] For instance, the Hong Kong Arbitration Ordinance 2013, which came into force on 19 July 2013, now recognizes enforceability of emergency relief granted prior to the commencement of arbitration.

B. CASES

B.1 Can Non-Signatories Invoke Arbitration Clauses?

In the case of *Gilat Satellite Networks, Ltd. v. United Coconut Planters Bank General Insurance Co., Inc.* ("Gilat"),[7] the Supreme Court held that "the existence of a suretyship agreement does not give the surety the right to intervene in the principal contract, nor can an arbitration clause between the buyer and the seller be invoked by a non-party such as the surety".

In *Gilat*, One Virtual and Gilat entered into a Purchase Agreement for Gilat to supply various telecommunication equipment and accessories to One Virtual. To ensure prompt payment of the purchase price, One Virtual obtained a surety bond from United Coconut Planters Bank General Insurance Co., Inc ("UCPB") in favor of Gilat. As a result of One Virtual's failure to pay the amounts due to Gilat, the latter filed a complaint in court against UCPB to recover the amounts supposedly covered by the surety bond, plus interests and expenses. The lower court held UCPB to be liable. On appeal, the decision was vacated by the Court of Appeals on the basis of the arbitration clause contained in the Purchase Agreement. The court considered that One Virtual and Gilat should proceed to arbitration, the outcome of which would bind UCPB. Gilat appealed to the Supreme Court.

The Supreme Court reversed the decision of the Court of Appeals. It held that UCPB, a stranger to the Purchase Agreement, cannot invoke the arbitration clause. The court explained that an arbitration agreement, being contractual in nature, is binding only on the parties, as well as their assigns and heirs. Further, the court ruled that under the ADR Act, a referral to arbitration may take place if at least one party so requests, but

---

[7]   G.R. No. 189563, 7 April 2014.

in this case, there is no evidence to show that either party submitted their claims to arbitration. Finally, the Court held that the responsibility of a surety places him or her on the same level as that of the principal debtor. Thus, the creditor is given the right to proceed directly against the surety. To require the creditor to proceed to arbitration would render the very essence of suretyship nugatory and diminish its value in commerce.

By treating an arbitration clause as binding only on the signatory parties, *Gilat* veers away from the 2010 case of *Prudential Guarantee and Assurance, Inc. v. Anscor Land, Inc.* ("Prudential")[8] where the Court extended the enforceability of an arbitration clause to non-signatories such as a surety. In *Prudential*, the Court ruled that a surety had been properly impleaded in the arbitration proceeding between its principal and the obligee notwithstanding the absence of an arbitration clause in the surety contract. *Gilat* appears to modify the ruling in *Prudential* with respect to the binding effect of an arbitration clause upon non-signatories. It is difficult, nevertheless, to predict how the courts will apply the *Gilat* ruling considering that *Gilat* did not expressly overturn *Prudential*. The factual circumstances in the two cases are also different—*Prudential* had been impleaded in the arbitration proceeding, while in *Gilat*, a lawsuit was brought against UCPB, which it sought to avoid by seeking to refer the parties to arbitration.

B.2   Corporate Representatives of a Corporate Party Required to Submit to Arbitration

In the recent case of *Gerardo Lanuza, Jr. et. al. v. BF Corporation, et. al.* ("Lanuza"),[9] the Supreme Court held that

---

8   G.R. No. 177240, 8 September 2010; see 2013-2014 International Arbitration Yearbook, pp. 248.

9   G.R. No. 174938, 1 October 2014.

B. Cases

"corporate representatives may be compelled to submit to arbitration proceedings pursuant to a contract entered into by the corporation they represent if there are allegations of bad faith or malice in their acts representing the corporation."

BF Corporation agreed to construct a mall and a multilevel parking structure. The agreement contained an arbitration clause. After completion of the construction of the buildings, the project owner defaulted on payment. BF Corporation initiated arbitration proceedings against the project owner and members of its board of directors, some of whom (the petitioners in this case) sought to be excluded from the proceedings as they were non-parties to the relevant purchase agreement. The petitioners claimed that parties who are strangers to an agreement cannot be compelled to arbitrate.

The Supreme Court ruled that the petitioners could be compelled to submit to the arbitration proceedings between the project owner and BF Corporation "in order to determine if the distinction between [the project owner's] personality and [the directors'] personalities should be disregarded". The court explained that, as a general rule, a corporation's representative who did not personally bind himself or herself to an arbitration agreement cannot be forced to participate in arbitration proceedings pursuant to an agreement entered into by the corporation. He or she is generally not considered a party to that agreement. However, there are instances when the distinction between the personalities of directors, officers, and representatives and that of the corporation is disregarded, such as when those individuals are guilty of malice or bad faith in directing the affairs of the corporation. In those cases, the corporate representatives are treated as the corporation itself and are held liable for corporate acts. Due to the possibility that the personalities of the corporate representatives and the corporation could later be found to be indistinct, the Court ruled that the petitioners could be compelled to submit to arbitration. The court said that this ruling was consistent with the policy against multiplicity of suits and unnecessary delay.

Implications of Gilat and Lanuza Rulings

The cases of *Gilat* and *Lanuza* uphold the basic arbitration principle that only parties to an arbitration agreement may be compelled to submit to arbitration. However, *Lanuza* has clarified that the well-established corporate law doctrine of "piercing the corporate veil" may be applied for purposes of including corporate officers and directors in an arbitration involving a corporation if there are grounds to treat them as the "real" parties to the arbitration agreement between the corporation and a third party.

C. LOCAL ARBITRATION INSTITUTIONS

C.1 Philippine Dispute Resolution Center ("PDRCI")

Background[10]

The Philippine Dispute Resolution Center, Inc. ("PDRCI") is the main arbitration institution in the Philippines. It is a non-stock, non-profit organization that was incorporated in 1996 out of the Arbitration Committee of the Philippine Chamber of Commerce and Industry. The PDRCI's purpose is the promotion of the use of arbitration as an alternative mode of settling commercial disputes and providing dispute resolution services to the business community. Its membership is composed of prominent lawyers, members of the judiciary, academics, arbitrators, bankers, and businessmen. Its services include the administration of

---

[10] http://www.intracen.org/Philippine-Dispute-Resolution-Center-Inc-of-the-Philippine-Chamber-of-Commerce-and-Industry; last accessed on 9 December 2014.

commercial arbitrations, accreditation and appointment of arbitrators, and organization of seminars and training.

The PDRCI recently revised its rules of arbitration ("Rules") to include substantial modifications to the manner in which fees are assessed by the PDRCI to avoid delays in arbitration proceedings, modernization of various parts of the rules to allow for more efficient and effective administration of arbitrations, and new provisions on consolidation of arbitrations, multi-party and multi-contract arbitrations, expedited procedure and emergency relief. The new rules are expected to become effective during the first quarter of 2015.

Types of Disputes Handled

The PDRCI administers arbitrations involving commercial disputes, including maritime, banking, insurance, securities, capital markets and intellectual property issues.

Numbers of Disputes Handled

Based on information obtained from the PDRCI secretariat, the PDRCI handled a total of 12 arbitration cases in 2011 (nine domestic, three international), five arbitration cases in 2012 (all domestic) and nine arbitration cases in 2013 (seven domestic, two international).

Provisions on Confidentiality of Arbitration

Generally, the Rules prohibit disclosure of any information relating to the subject of arbitration, if the information was expressly intended by the source not to be disclosed or was obtained under circumstances that would create such a reasonable expectation on behalf of its source that it will not be disclosed.

Availability of Expedited Procedures

The Rules provide for an expedited procedure where the amount in dispute does not exceed the specified threshold, or if the parties agree or in cases of exceptional urgency. The expedited procedure involves adoption of simplified procedures and shortening of time limits, including the time for rendering the award.

Provisions on Consolidation of Disputes between the Same Parties and Joinder of Third Parties

Under the Rules, the PDRCI, or the arbitral tribunal if it has already been constituted, shall have the power to allow an additional party to be joined to the arbitration, upon a *prima facie* determination that an arbitration agreement under the Rules exists and that it binds all the parties and the additional party.

The Rules also empower the PDRCI, at the request of a party, after consulting with them and any confirmed arbitrators, to consolidate two or more arbitrations under the Rules, where: (a) the parties agree to consolidate; or (b) all the claims in the arbitrations are made under the same arbitration agreement; or (c) where the claims are made under more than one arbitration agreement, a common question of law or fact arises in both or all of the arbitrations, the rights to relief claimed are in respect of, or arise out of, the same transaction or series of transactions, and the PDRCI finds the arbitration agreements to be compatible. Where the PDRCI decides to consolidate two or more arbitrations, taking into account the circumstances of the case including, but not limited to, whether one or more arbitrators have been appointed and confirmed, the arbitrations will be consolidated into the arbitration that commenced first, unless all parties agree or PDRCI decides otherwise.

C. Local Arbitration Institutions

Time Limits for Rendering of the Award

The Rules do not provide a time limit for rendering an award, except if the arbitration is conducted in an expedited procedure, in which case the award must be made within six months from the date the PDRCI transmits the file to the arbitral tribunal. However, the PDRCI may extend this time limit in exceptional circumstances.

Fee Structure

By agreeing to arbitrate under the Rules, the parties are deemed to have accepted the PDRCI Guidelines on Fees ("Guidelines"). Under the Guidelines, the arbitrator's fees consist of a base amount to which an amount is added depending on the complexity of the case, number of parties and number of arbitrators. The administrative fees, on the other hand, are separately calculated for the claimant and the respondent on the basis of their respective claim or counterclaim.

Treatment of Costs of the Arbitration

Under the Rules, the cost of arbitration is fixed by the arbitral tribunal in its award. The cost may include the (a) arbitrators' fees, filing fees, administrative fees and expenses set by PDRCI; (b) travel and other expenses incurred by the arbitrators; (c) cost of expert advice and of other assistance required by the arbitral tribunal; (d) travel and other expenses of witnesses; and (e) cost of legal representation and assistance reasonably incurred by the successful party in connection with the arbitration. The cost of arbitration is in principle to be borne by the unsuccessful party. However, the arbitral tribunal may apportion the cost between the parties if it determines that apportionment is appropriate, taking into account the circumstances of the case.

Special or Unusual Features

As stated above, under the Guidelines, administrative fees are separately calculated for the claimant and the respondent on the basis of their respective claim or counterclaim. The separate assessment of fees is intended to avoid delays in arbitration proceedings, especially when a party fails or refuses to pay its share of the global advances on costs.

Recent Developments

To reflect recent trends in international commercial arbitration and in order to keep pace with other arbitral institutions, the PDRCI has included rules for the appointment of an emergency arbitrator through which a party may apply for an interim measure prior to the constitution of the arbitral tribunal. The emergency arbitrator appointed may conduct the proceedings in such a manner as he considers appropriate, taking into account the urgent nature of the proceedings. Unless extended by agreement of the parties or by the PDRCI, any decision, order or award of the emergency arbitrator must be made within 20 days from the date on which PDRCI transmitted the file to the emergency arbitrator.

POLAND

Marcin Aslanowicz[1] and Sylwia Piotrowska[2]

A. LEGISLATION, TRENDS AND TENDENCIES

A.1 Legislation

International arbitration in Poland continues to be governed by the Civil Procedure Code ("CPC"), to which no legislative amendment was made in 2014.

A.2 Trends and Tendencies

In October 2014, the main arbitration court in Poland, the Court of Arbitration at the Polish Chamber of Commerce in Warsaw ("SAKiG"), adopted new rules, which become effective and replace the current rules on January 1, 2015 (the "New Rules"). The New Rules are discussed in Section C below.

B. CASES

During 2014, the Supreme Court in Poland has issued several rulings which may have an impact on practice.

B.1 Grounds for Setting Aside an Arbitral Award

The Polish Civil Procedure Code provides an exhaustive list of the specific grounds for setting aside an arbitral award.[3]

---

[1]   Marcin Aslanowicz is a Partner at Baker & McKenzie's Warsaw office and heads the Firm's Litigation and Dispute Resolution Practice Group in Warsaw. Mr. Aslanowicz represents multinational and domestic clients in civil and commercial disputes before common courts and arbitral tribunals.

[2]   Sylwia Piotrowska is a Senior Associate at Baker & McKenzie's Warsaw office and a member of the Firm's Global Dispute Resolution Practice Group.

[3]   Article 1206.

According to the CPC, the court may only set aside an award where it finds that the relevant dispute is not capable of settlement by a court of arbitration or that an arbitral award is in conflict with the fundamental principles of the legal order of the Republic of Poland. This is known as the public order clause.

In its ruling of March 27, 2013,[4] the Supreme Court held that the court adjudicating on any petition to set aside an arbitral award cannot accept grounds for setting aside an arbitral award which are not either contained in the original petition to set aside or otherwise asserted prior to the deadline for filing the petition to set aside.

In this respect, the Supreme Court upheld and strengthened the view, as accepted and consolidated in previous rulings, that it is unacceptable both to cite new grounds for the complaint to set aside an arbitral award after the deadline for filing them has passed, and for the court to take a decision to set aside an award of its own motion.

B.2 Arbitration Provisions and the Scope of the Court's Powers to Examine Them

In its order of November 7, 2013, the Supreme Court[5] ruled on two important issues. The first is the extent to which an arbitration clause must clearly identify the subject matter and legal relationship covered by the clause. The second is the scope of the court's powers to examine whether there is a valid and relevant arbitration clause.

The case concerned a subrogated claim brought by an insurance company. The defendant sought to have the action dismissed on the basis that there was an arbitration agreement in the relevant contract. The court of first instance decided that the insurer only

---

4   Ruling of the Polish Supreme Court of 27 March 2013, case V CSK 222/12.

5   Ruling of the Polish Supreme Court of 7 November 2013, case V CSK 545/12.

inherited substantive rights and obligations from the insured, and so it was not bound by the arbitration agreement (which was a procedural issue). The Court of Appeal decided that, under insurance subrogation, the insurer steps into the shoes of the insured in relation to all aspects of the claim, including any arbitration agreement agreed between the insured and the defendant. It therefore dismissed the claim.

The Supreme Court took the view that an arbitration clause is an agreement which constitutes an independent legal transaction of the parties and is of an autonomous nature, even if it was included in the main agreement. Any legal relationship, as the subject matter of the arbitration provision, should be appropriately specific and individualized. In formulating an arbitration agreement, the parties decide on its subjective scope and, therefore, the limits of the jurisdiction of the court of arbitration. The will of the parties to subject disputes to settlement by the court is the most important and primary source related to that agreement. This means that the determination of what the will of the parties was when preparing the provision requires appropriate interpretation, taking into account the parties' objective and sense which best reflects their intentions. The Supreme Court emphasized that, because arbitration agreements have the primary purpose of excluding the court's jurisdiction, in case of any doubt, an interpretation that is restrictive of the court's jurisdiction should be adopted.

As regards the scope the court of law's powers to examine whether there is a valid and relevant arbitration clause, the Supreme Court took the stance that this scope not only includes the right to establish the existence of an agreement subjecting the settlement of the dispute to arbitration, but also the right to establish whether the claimant's claim, expressed in the plea and the facts cited in justification of it, falls within the subjective and objective scope of the arbitration agreement. Where, as in this case, an interlocutory hearing is held to ascertain whether the court has jurisdiction, this does not prevent the court from considering substantive legal issues. Therefore, where the court needs to establish whether the claim filed in the statement of claim lies within the scope of the arbitration provision, and this requires an examination of the content of the agreement and the intention of the parties which entered into it, the court cannot avoid establishing and resolving these issues. This applies to both the subjective and objective aspects of the provision.

C. LOCAL ARBITRATION INSTITUTIONS

C.1 SAKiG

Background

The Court of Arbitration at the Polish Chamber of Commerce was established on January 1, 1950. Initially it operated under the name of the Council of Arbitrators at the Polish Chamber of Foreign Trade as a separate, independent unit created to settle international trade disputes. Since 1990, the Court of Arbitration has continued its operations at the Polish Chamber of Commerce in Warsaw. Over years it has become the most renowned and popular permanent Polish arbitration court.

In the analysis below, we draw on the new rules that came into effect on January 1, 2015.

Types of Disputes Handled

SAKiG handles both domestic and international cases, with the latter accounting for approximately 20% of its caseload. It is especially popular as a forum for arbitrating disputes in Eastern Europe. It handles ad hoc arbitration proceedings on the basis of the UNCITRAL Rules as well under its own rules. It also conducts mediation proceedings and promotes arbitration in academic and commercial circles.

C. Local Arbitration Institutions

Number of Disputes Handled

No recent figures are available, but as of 2005, nearly 2,500 disputes had been submitted to SAKiG.

Provisions on Confidentiality of Arbitration

Unless otherwise provided by the parties, the arbitrators and staff and the members of SAKiG are required to maintain the confidentiality of all information concerning the proceedings.

Availability of Expedited Procedures

There are no specific provisions for expedited procedures under the SAKiG rules.

Consolidation of Disputes between the Same Parties and Joinder of Third Parties

Consolidation of proceedings is possible where the identity of the parties and arbitral tribunal in each of the proceedings is the same and either (i) the parties' claims in each of the proceedings are based on the same arbitration agreement, or (ii) the parties' claims in each of the proceedings are related, even if based on different arbitration agreements. Proceedings in which the parties are not identical may also be consolidated if the composition of the Arbitral Tribunal in each of the proceedings is the same, one of the conditions set out above is met, and the parties to all of the proceedings consent.

After consulting both parties, the Arbitral Panel may also, at the request of a third party, admit it to participate in the pending proceedings as an intervening third party on the claimant's or respondent's side, if the applicant can demonstrate a legitimate interest in such a joinder, and the party which the third party is to join agrees. The intervening third party will need to pay an arbitration fee, at the amount specified in the tariff of fees in force on the date on which the statement of claim is filed. If the third party fails to pay this fee, it will not be admitted to the proceedings. The intervening third party will not be entitled to choose an arbitrator and will not be able to take actions and make statements which are in conflict with the actions and statements of the party it joined in the proceedings.

Time Limits for Rendering the Award

The award must be issued within nine months after commencement of the proceeding and no later than 30 days after closing of the hearing. At the Secretary General's own initiative or upon application of the presiding arbitrator, the Secretary General may extend either of these periods if justified by the complexity of the issues in the dispute or other important considerations.

Fee Structure

A registration fee of PLN2,000 is payable by the claimant for disputes with a value of over PLN10,000 (or PLN500 for a value of PLN10,000 or less). In addition, an arbitration fee is payable, based upon a phased *ad valorem* rate.[6]

Treatment of Costs of the Arbitration

Any award issued by the tribunal must contain a decision on costs, including the costs of the proceedings and legal fees (up to the maximum amount of half of the arbitration fee or PLN100,000, whichever is less).

Special or Unusual Features (If Any)

Not applicable.

Recent Developments (If Any)

Not applicable.

---

[6]   See http://sakig.pl/uploads/upfiles/pdf/taryfa-en.pdf.

RUSSIAN FEDERATION

Vladimir Khvalei[1] and Irina Varyushina[2]

A. LEGISLATION, TRENDS AND TENDENCIES

A.1 Legislation

International arbitration in Russia continues to be governed by the 1993 Law "On International Commercial Arbitration" ("the 1993 Law"),[3] to which no legislative amendments were made in 2014.

A.2 Trends and Tendencies

As we reported last year,[4] draft amendments to Russian arbitration laws were introduced in January 2014 and discussed at length during the months that followed. At the end of July 2014, the draft laws were vetoed by the President's administration, which found that they overregulated the activities of arbitration courts. A new draft is expected at the beginning of 2015.

---

[1] Vladimir Khvalei is a Partner in Baker & McKenzie's Moscow office and heads its CIS Dispute Resolution Practice Group. He is also a steering committee member of the Firm's International Arbitration Practice Group and serves as a Vice President of the ICC International Court of Arbitration, a Member of the LCIA Court and as Chairman of the Board of the Russian Arbitration Association.

[2] Irina Varyushina is a Professional Support Lawyer in Baker & McKenzie's Moscow office.

[3] Russian Federation Law N 5338-1 of 07 July 1993.

[4] *See* Section A1 in the 2013-2014 edition of Baker & McKenzie International Arbitration Yearbook, p. 263.

B. CASES

B.1 Public Procurement Contract Disputes Are Not Arbitrable

In *Production-Technical Association for Capital Repairs and Development under the Health Department of Moscow v. ArbatStroy LLC,*[5] a dispute arose out of a contract entered into upon the results of an open electronic auction in accordance with Russian Public Procurement Law. The contract contained an arbitration clause referring any disputes out of or in connection with it to the Peresvet Arbitration Court.[6] This arbitration clause was included in the contract by the customer when placing the order.

The Supreme Arbitrazh Court reversed the lower courts' decisions and refused to issue the writ of execution of the award granted by the Peresvet Arbitration Court in favor of the customer. The Court found that disputes arising out of public procurement contracts are nonarbitrable, and therefore the award violated fundamental principles of Russian law.[7]

The Court identified several peculiarities of public procurement disputes that, in the Court's view, make them nonarbitrable. These peculiarities include (i) the legal relations concerned are of a public law nature; (ii) the Public Procurement Law predominantly imposes imperative regulation on the participants of the procurement process as opposed to the civil law principles of freedom of contract; (iii) incompatibility of the statutory principles of arbitration proceedings and those of order

---

[5] Case file at: http://kad.arbitr.ru/Card/e940b0c1-bbe0-403e-afd1-6864647297c8.

[6] The full name of the arbitration court is "Arbitration Court of investment and construction organizations of the Central Federal Circuit at LLC Peresvet Law Firm."

[7] *See* Resolution of the Supreme Arbitrazh Court № 11535/13 of 28 January 2014.

placement; and (iv) the Public Procurement Law contains a specific mechanism for resolving disputes in the course of placement orders.

In addition, the Court took note of the fact that no opportunity exists for the contractor to challenge a dispute resolution clause, which is not part of either tender/auction notification or documentation. Therefore, the winning party cannot disagree with the provision and accepts it by adhesion to the contract, which is in breach of the provisions of the Federal Law, Domestic Arbitration Courts in the Russian Federation (the "Domestic Arbitration Law"), which validates such arbitration clauses only when entered into after the dispute has arisen. The Court also noted that the formation of the Peresvet Arbitration Court was notified to the state Arbitrazh Courts[8] only two months before being included into the contract, but within a short time it had managed to register 122 cases, mostly filed by two customers. This contributed to the Court's finding of the violation of fundamental Russian law principles.

B.2   Wide Construction of Waiver of the Right to Object to State Court Jurisdiction

The case of *Demesne Investments Limited v. Metropolis CJSC*[9] concerned the interpretation of the CAP provision[10] enabling parties to object to the resolution of a case by a Arbitrazh Court by invoking the existence of a valid and binding arbitration agreement.

---

[8]   There is a statutory requirement of notifying the competent state court at the arbitration court's location of the commencement of the arbitration courts' activities, stipulated in Art.3(4) of the Domestic Arbitration Law .

[9]   Case file at: http://kad.arbitr.ru/Card/c111a7e4-b9d0-4988-82e4-19cfb4fb6588

[10]   Art. 148(5) of the Russian Federation Code of Arbitrazh Procedure.

The respondent objected to the jurisdiction of the Russian court at the third hearing, having attended a preliminary hearing and a subsequent hearing that was postponed by the court. By the time of the objections, the court had joined a third party and granted the claimant's motion to produce certain evidence. The claimant argued that by waiting that long before objecting to the court's jurisdiction, the respondent effectively waived its right to invoke the arbitration agreement and by its conduct impliedly accepted the state courts jurisdiction.

This reasoning found no support with the lower courts. The Cassation Court, however, reversed the judgments and ordered that the case be tried on its merits.[11] Invoking the claimant's right to file a claim against the respondent at the respondent's location, the Cassation Court went on to confirm that acceptance of the Court's jurisdiction can be implied by conduct. The Court then dismissed the respondent's contention that it filed no statements on the merits, and considered that the respondent had acted in bad faith. The Court further added that passive procedural behavior such as failure to appear and submit a defense, if disregarded, leads to inequality of the parties where a party can object to the court's jurisdiction long after the court has taken the case up for consideration. Where a party wants to invoke an arbitration agreement timely and in good faith, it is to do this before the state court starts to consider the dispute on the merits.

B.3 Recovery of Contractual Penalties Not a Violation of Public Policy

In *Privatization Agency of the Republic of Serbia v. OJSC Avtodetal-Service*,[12] the Privatization Agency of the Republic

---

[11] Resolution of the Arbitrazh Court of Urals Circuit of 19 August 2014.

[12] Case file at: http://kad.arbitr.ru/Card/7c5f7c19-f6d3-4603-a8de-2a653c776cb5.

of Serbia ("Agency") obtained an arbitral award from the Foreign Arbitration Court at the Commercial Chamber of Serbia against OJSC Avtodetal-Service whereby OJSC was ordered to pay contractual penalties of EUR2.9 million for failure to discharge its obligations under the Contract of Sale and Purchase of shares in a Serbian JSC in relation to a social program and for breach of a prohibition against disposing of certain property of this Serbian legal entity. The Agency filed for enforcement of the award in Russia, which was refused at first instance. At a retrial ordered by the Cassation Court, the claims were dismissed again; however, the Cassation Court reversed the decision of the trial court and granted the enforcement.[13]

The Cassation Court disagreed with the findings of the trial court[14] that the enforcement of the award would contradict Russia's public policy by breaching principles of the equality of the parties and inviolability of property and resulting in confiscatory penalties for OJSC.

The Court also dismissed the arguments put forward in opposition of enforcement that the dispute was of a public law nature. The Court differentiated between the overall privatization transaction providing for the transfer of state property to private parties and the civil law final stage of the purchase of shares and ruled that the parties' relations were of a civil law nature and therefore arbitrable.

---

[13] Resolution of Arbitrazh Court of Povolzhsky Circuit of 23 December 2014.

[14] Ruling of the Arbitrazh Court of Ulyanovsk region of 06 October 2014.

B.4. Moscow Convention No Basis for International Arbitration Proceedings

In three cases, the Kyrgyz Republic filed to set aside awards[15] or jurisdiction decisions[16] of the Arbitration Court at the Moscow Chamber of Commerce and Industry ("Moscow Chamber") that ruled in favor of investors. The Moscow Chamber found it had jurisdiction based on Article 11 of the 1997 Moscow Convention for the Protection of Investors' Rights ("Moscow Convention"). As the Moscow Convention did not specify a particular arbitration court to resolve disputes, the investors successfully argued that this constituted an open offer to arbitrate in any international arbitration court that resolved international investment disputes. Relying on the Rules and Arbitration Regulations of the Moscow Chamber, the arbitrators upheld jurisdiction over investors' claims.

The trial court in the Stans Energy and John Lee Beck cases dismissed the requests to set aside the arbitral awards, whereas proceedings in the OKKV case were stayed pending the decision of the CIS Economic Court.

The Kyrgyz Republic applied to the CIS Economic Court asking to clarify whether (1) a dispute based on the Moscow Convention may be heard by any international court or

---

[15] Award of 21 November 2013 in *The Republic of Kyrgyzstan v. OcOO O. K.K.B et al* ("OKKV case"), available in Russian at: http://italaw.com/sites/default/files/case-documents/italaw3258.pdf; Case file at: http://kad.arbitr.ru/Card/5faa0c68-c627-4bda-803b-460d42b5fbcc. Award of 13 November 2013 in *The Republic of Kyrgyzstan v. Lee John Beck and Central Asian Development Corporation* ("Lee John Beck case"), available in Russian at: http://italaw.com/sites/default/files/case-documents/italaw3256.pdf; Case file at: http://kad.arbitr.ru/Card/d112dd3b-8cf2-4a3c-a3d9-e56e8827a84e.

[16] Decision on Jurisdiction of 31 March 2014 in *The Republic of Kyrgyzstan v. Stans Energy Corp., Kutisay Mining* ("Stans Energy case"). Case file at: http://kad.arbitr.ru/Card/b99ab17b-160f-41d9-921b-a252dbfd0dd6.

international arbitration court, not specified either in the relevant BIT, national law or contract, and (2) Article 11 of the Moscow Convention contains an open offer to arbitrate.

The CIS Economic Court in its decision[17] disagreed with the interpretation of the investors and the Moscow Chamber. The Court stated that the reference in Article 11 of the Moscow Convention to international arbitration cannot form a sufficient basis for jurisdiction of an international arbitration tribunal.

Immediately after this decision, the judgments of the trial court in the Stans Energy and John Lee Beck cases were reversed by the Cassation Court and sent for retrial, taking into consideration the decision of the CIS Economic Court.[18] The hearings in these cases are scheduled for the end of January 2015. Proceedings in the OKKV case were resumed, and the claims of the Kyrgyz Republic to set aside the arbitral award were granted.[19]

C.   LOCAL ARBITRATION INSTITUTIONS

C.1   ICAC (Moscow)

Background

The International Commercial Arbitration Court at the Chamber of Commerce and Industry of the Russian Federation ("ICAC (Moscow)") is the successor of the Foreign Trade Arbitration Commission, created legislatively in 1932 and later renamed the Arbitration Court at the USSR Chamber of Commerce and Industry.

---

[17]   Decision of CIS Economic Court of 24 September 2014, available at: http://sudsng.org/download_files/rh/2014/rh-01-1_14_23092014.pdf .

[18]   Resolutions of the Arbitrazh Court of Moscow Circuit of 26 September 2014.

[19]   Decision of the Arbitrazh Court of Moscow of 19 November 2014.

Types of Disputes Handled

According to the 2012 statistics,[20] the following types of disputes were resolved by the ICAC (Moscow): services and works agreements; construction works contracts; credit agreements; lease agreements, and IP disputes as well as a small number of other foreign trade contracts.

Numbers of Disputes Handled

In 2013, the ICAC registered 274 claims from companies representing 47 countries of the world.[21]

Provisions on Confidentiality of Arbitration

Under §25 of the Rules of the ICAC (Moscow) ("the ICAC Rules"), arbitrators, reporters, experts appointed by the arbitral tribunal, the ICAC and its staff, and the CCI and its staff must refrain from disclosing information about disputes settled by the ICAC which they become aware of and which may impair the legitimate interests of the parties. Under §32 of the ICAC Rules, the hearing is to be held in camera. The arbitral tribunal may, with the consent of the parties, allow nonparticipating persons to appear at the hearing.

Availability of Expedited Procedures

There is no such availability.

Consolidation of Disputes between the Same Parties and Joinder of Third Parties

Under §28 of the ICAC Rules, a party is entitled to request that a third party be invited to join the arbitral proceedings. The request

---

[20] http://mkas.tpprf.ru/ru/Stat/stat2012.php.

[21] http://mkas.tpprf.ru/ru/Stat/.

for joinder is to be made before the end of the period for a statement of defense to be submitted. The joinder requires the consent of the parties to the dispute as well as the written consent of the third party.

Time Limits for Rendering of the Award

Under §24 of the ICAC Rules, the ICAC (Moscow) must take measures to secure completion of the arbitral proceedings in a case within 180 days from the date of composition of the arbitral tribunal. If necessary, the ICAC Presidium may, at the request of the arbitral tribunal or in its discretion, extend this period.

Fee Structure

Arbitration costs consist of an arbitrator's fee and an administration fee. Under §14 of the ICAC Rules, arbitration costs are paid in advance by the claimant. The ICAC may require a party to deposit an advance for the additional costs of the arbitral proceedings, which include expenses of examination by experts, oral and written translations, and reimbursement of the arbitrators' and witnesses' expenses. If a party wishes to elect an arbitrator who does not reside at the place where ICAC meetings are held, this party is to pay an advance on such arbitrator's expenses.

Treatment of Costs of the Arbitration

Under §6 of the ICAC Rules unless the parties have agreed otherwise, the arbitration fee shall be charged to the party against which the award is made in proportion to the amount of granted claims.

Special or Unusual Features (If Any)

Under §7 of the ICAC Rules there is a reporter appointed for every case by the executive secretary of the ICAC. The reporter keeps minutes of hearings, attends all in camera meetings of the tribunal and fulfills assignments relating to arbitration proceedings.

Recent Developments (If Any)

No recent developments.

C.2 Russian Arbitration Association ("RAA")

Background

The RAA was founded in April 2013 in Moscow by more than 50 international and Russian law firms. In line with the overall goal of promoting arbitration, the RAA is active in the following areas: administering disputes under the UNCITRAL arbitration rules; drafting proposals for improvement of arbitration laws in the Russian Federation; developing recommended standards for arbitration institutions; offering training programs for arbitrators; creating an online information resource on arbitration; developing programs for the support of young professionals in arbitration (RAA 40) and students (RAA-25); and launching online arbitration.

Types of Disputes Handled

According to the RAA Regulations on Arbitration Proceedings,[22] the RAA administers both international commercial and domestic arbitration disputes.

Numbers of Disputes Handled

As the Rules for administering arbitration disputes were approved only as from July 1, 2014, there are no registered cases yet.

---

[22] http://www.arbitrations.ru/upload/medialibrary/dd3/ar_en_web.pdf.

C. Local Arbitration Institutions

Provisions on Confidentiality of Arbitration

As the RAA administers disputes under the UNCITRAL Arbitration Rules, the relevant provisions of the UNCITRAL Arbitration Rules are applicable in this respect.

Availability of Expedited Procedures

In March 2015, the launch of the RAA Online Arbitration Rules is planned, enabling resolution of a dispute by exchanging pleadings and evidence via an online case system, without a hearing (unless an arbitrator in a particular case decides otherwise). Thus, the proceedings will as a rule last two months.[23]

Consolidation of Disputes between the Same Parties and Joinder of Third Parties

As the RAA administers disputes under the UNCITRAL Arbitration Rules, the relevant provisions of the UNCITRAL Arbitration Rules are applicable in this respect.

Time Limits for Rendering of the Award

The final arbitral award is to be issued within two months after close of proceedings. Should this requirement not be met, the arbitrators' fees are to be reduced by 10%, and each subsequent month of delay results in a further reduction of 10%.

Fee Structure

The correlation of administrative fee and arbitrators' fees follows the pattern of those of the ICC and SCC.

---

[23]   Legal Insight, October 2014, Issue #8(34), p.19.

Treatment of Costs of the Arbitration

The relevant provisions of the UNCITRAL Arbitration Rules are applicable in this respect.

Special or Unusual Features (If Any)

The RAA Arbitrators' Nominating Committee ("ANC") is a body within the RAA that will nominate arbitrators upon the request of either party should any party or the arbitrators appointed by them fail to appoint one or more arbitrators within the terms prescribed by the UNCITRAL Rules.

Recent Developments (If Any)

In March 2015, the RAA is expected to launch the RAA Online Arbitration Rules.

SINGAPORE

Chan Leng Sun[1] and Jennifer Fong[2]

A. LEGISLATION, TRENDS AND TENDENCIES

A.1 Legislation

International arbitration in Singapore continues to be governed by the International Arbitration Act ("IAA"), the Arbitration Act ("AA") and the Arbitration (International Investment Disputes) Act, to which no legislative amendments were made in 2014.

A.2 Trends and Tendencies

The Singapore International Commercial Court (the "SICC"), which is anticipated to have a diverse panel of judges (including eminent international judges), has been set up in January 2015. The SICC will have jurisdiction to hear cases that are international and commercial in nature. Further, a new Singapore International Mediation Centre, which is anticipated to have an international panel of experienced mediators, has also been established. These new institutions are envisioned to complement the existing arbitration industry in Singapore with the aim of offering users in the region a selection of efficient and dependable dispute resolution platforms, being litigation, arbitration or mediation.

---

[1] Chan Leng Sun, SC, is Head of Dispute Resolution in Baker & McKenzie.Wong & Leow, Singapore and is the Baker & McKenzie Asia-Pacific Head of International Arbitration.

[2] Jennifer Fong is a Senior Associate in Baker & McKenzie.Wong & Leow in Singapore.

B. CASES

B.1 Minority Oppression Claims Are Generally Not Arbitrable

In *Silica Investors v Tomolugen Holdings Ltd*,[3] the Singapore High Court ruled that a stay of Singapore court proceedings under s. 6(2) of the IAA cannot be granted in the case of a nonarbitrable claim, and that most minority oppression claims are generally not arbitrable, except in exceptional cases where all shareholders are bound by the arbitration agreement and the remedy or relief sought would affect only the parties to the arbitration.

B. 2 Rejection of the "Group of Companies" Doctrine

In *Manuchar Steel Hong Kong v Star Pacific Line Pte Ltd*,[4] the Singapore High Court clarified that an arbitral award cannot impose obligations on nonparties to an arbitration agreement, even if those nonparties were part of the same group, rejecting the applicability of the "group of companies" doctrine[5] in Singapore. The Singapore High Court held that the corporate veil would only be pierced in exceptional circumstances where there was evidence of abuse of the separate legal entity of companies.

B. 3 Test Where There Are Competing Arbitration and Jurisdiction Clauses

In *Oei Hong Leong v Goldman Sachs International*,[6] the court held that in a situation where there were two potentially

---

3   [2014] 3 SLR 815.

4   [2014] SGHC 181.

5   The "group of companies" doctrine refers to non-parties to the arbitration agreement which were part of the same group of companies and closely associated with a party to an arbitration agreement being bound by the arbitration agreement.

6   [2014] 3 SLR 1217.

applicable arbitration or jurisdiction clauses in closely related contracts, such as the Account Agreement governing the plaintiff's entire banking relationship and the ISDA Agreement governing specific derivative transactions which were the subject of the dispute, the court will apply a "careful and commercially-minded construction" of the two clauses and assess which of the contracts (and which dispute resolution clause) is more closely related to the dispute. This approach is similar to the tests of "locating the centre of gravity of the dispute" or the "commercial centre of the transaction" referred to in English cases such as *UBS AG v HSH Nordbank AG*.[7] The court found that the arbitration clause in the Account Agreement applied, as the Account Agreement was more closely related to the bank-customer relationship and the alleged misrepresentations arising out of that relationship.

B.4   Permanent Anti-Suit Injunctions Available for Singapore-Seated Arbitrations

In *R1 International v Lonstroff AG*,[8] the Singapore High Court confirmed that it had the power to grant a permanent anti-suit injunction for arbitrations seated in Singapore under the court's general jurisdiction to grant injunctions under s.4(10) of the Civil Law Act. It also clarified that the granting of permanent injunctions does not fall under the court's powers to grant interim measures under s.12A of the International Arbitration Act. However, the High Court did not grant the anti-suit injunction on the facts because it found that the parties had not agreed to arbitration. On appeal, the Court of Appeal found that

---

[7]   [2009] EWCA Civ 585.

[8]   [2014] SGHC 69.

the parties had agreed to arbitration and granted the permanent anti-suit injunction.[9]

B.5 Interaction between Principle of "Temporary Finality" and Right to Arbitrate

In *PT Perusahaan Gas Negara (Persero) TBK v CRW Joint Operation (Indonesia)*,[10] the Singapore High Court confirmed that a tribunal may issue a final award ordering an employer to make an interim payment (pending the resolution of the primary dispute) to a contractor, as parties are free to contractually agree that they should have substantive provisional rights (such as a right to interim payment), which are enforceable. The court stated that such an award will not be *res judicata* with respect to the underlying dispute and that the parties were still free to arbitrate the underlying dispute.

Further, the court in *HP Construction & Engineering Pte Ltd v Chin Ivan*[11] held that although an architect's certificates ordinarily enjoy "temporary finality", a stay of proceedings to recover sums based on such certifications in favor of arbitration would be granted if there was *prima facie* a *bona fide* dispute as to whether there was fraud, improper pressure or interference used to obtain such certificates. The court granted a partial stay of the proceedings in favor of arbitration with respect to certain aspects of the architect's certificates in question, which had been allegedly obtained as a result of fraudulent misrepresentations made to the architect.

---

[9] *R1 International Pte Ltd v Lonstroff AG* [2014] SGCA 56.

[10] [2014] SGHC 146.

[11] [2014] 3 SLR 1327.

B.6 Clarification of the Test for the Removal of an Arbitrator

In *PT Central Investindo v Franciscus Wongso* & Ors,[12] in considering whether there were justifiable doubts as to the arbitrator's impartiality under Article 12 of the UNCITRAL Model Law,[13] the court applied the "reasonable suspicion" test normally used to determine whether there has been apparent bias in court proceedings. The court considered whether: (a) there were factual circumstances that had a bearing on the suggestion that the tribunal was or might be seen to be partial; and (b) whether a reasonable and fair-minded person sitting in court and knowing all the facts would have a reasonable suspicion that the circumstances might result in the proceedings being affected by apparent bias if the arbitrator was not removed.

If the court has issued an order to remove the arbitrator, but an award has already been issued, a party need only furnish proof of the court order for removal to support its application to set aside the award, and the court will most likely set aside the award in the absence of compelling evidence to the contrary.[14]

B.7 Refusal to Re-Open Proceedings to Admit Potentially Relevant Evidence Upheld

In *ADG v ADI*,[15] the Singapore High Court upheld the tribunal's decision not to re-open proceedings in order to admit potentially relevant evidence that had materialized after the proceedings had been declared closed, holding that parties had been given a reasonable opportunity to be heard and that there was no breach of natural justice.

---

[12] [2014] SGHC 190.

[13] First Schedule, IAA.

[14] *PT Central Investindo v Franciscus Wongso* & Ors [2014] SGHC 190.

[15] [2014] SGHC 73.

C. LOCAL ARBITRATION INSTITUTIONS

Arbitration institutions with a presence in Singapore include:

(a) SIAC;[16]
(b) the Singapore Chamber of Maritime Arbitration ("SCMA");[17]
(c) the World Intellectual Property Organization ("WIPO");[18]
(d) the International Centre for Dispute Resolution – Singapore ("ICDR");
(e) the Permanent Court of Arbitration – Singapore facility ("PCA"); and
(f) the Law Society Arbitration Scheme[19] ("LSAS").

In addition, Singapore is the most popular seat in Asia for ICC arbitrations.

This section focuses on SIAC and SCMA, two of Singapore's best-known and respected international arbitration institutions. The WIPO, ICDR and PCA are each connected with their respective arbitral institutions based outside Singapore. They each provide services for Singapore-seated arbitrations conducted under their respective rules. Whilst the LSAS is used in general commercial disputes, it is less often used in international arbitrations.

C.1 SIAC

Background

SIAC was established in 1991 as a not-for-profit organization.

---

[16] www.siac.org.sg.

[17] http://www.scma.org.sg.

[18] http://www.wipo.int/about-wipo/en/offices/singapore/.

[19] http://www.lawsociety.org.sg/lsas/Default.aspx.

C. Local Arbitration Institutions

Types of Disputes Handled

SIAC handles a wide range of commercial and corporate disputes.

Numbers of Disputes Handled

As of 2013, the SIAC received 259 new cases, a 10.2% increase in new filings compared to 2012. The active caseload as of 31 December 2013 was 619 cases.[20]

Provisions on Confidentiality of Arbitration

Rule 35 of the SIAC Rules 2013 (the "SIAC Rules") provide that all matters relating to the arbitration proceedings (including the existence of the proceedings) and the award should be treated as confidential and that disclosure to third parties is not permitted without the prior written consent of the parties. There are limited exceptions such as disclosure for the purposes of enforcement of or challenge to the award or pursuing any legal right; pursuant to the order of the tribunal or court; or otherwise in compliance with laws binding on the disclosing party or pursuant to the request or requirement of any regulatory body. The tribunal has the power to take appropriate measures, including issuing an order or award for sanctions or costs, if a party breaches its confidentiality obligation.

Availability of Expedited Procedures

Expedited procedures are available upon application to the Registrar of SIAC (Registrar)[21] where the aggregate amount in dispute does not exceed SGD5 million, in cases of exceptional urgency or by agreement of the parties. Expedited arbitrations

---

[20]   http://www.siac.org.sg/2014-11-03-13-33-43/facts-figures/statistics.

[21]   Rule 5 of the SIAC Rules.

are usually conducted by a sole arbitrator, and the award to be made within six months from the date when the tribunal is constituted unless, in exceptional circumstances, the Registrar extends the time.

Consolidation of Disputes between the Same Parties and Joinder of Third Parties

There is no express provision for the consolidation of disputes between the same parties. The tribunal has power to join other parties to the arbitration agreement to an existing arbitration, with the written consent of the party to be joined.[22]

Time Limits for Rendering of the Award

The tribunal must submit the draft award to the Registrar for approval within 45 days from the date on which the tribunal declares the proceedings closed.[23]

Fee Structure

The tribunal's and SIAC's fees are determined in accordance with SIAC's Schedule of Fees, which is a set of scale fees varying in accordance with the amount in dispute.

Treatment of Costs of the Arbitration

The tribunal must specify in the award the total amount of the costs of the arbitration and, unless parties have agreed otherwise, must apportion the costs of the arbitration between the parties.[24] Costs of the arbitration include the fees and expenses of the tribunal, SIAC and the costs of any expert advice and other

---

[22]   Rule 24(b) of the SIAC Rules.

[23]   Rule 28 of the SIAC Rules.

[24]   Rule 31 of the SIAC Rules.

assistance required by the tribunal.[25] The tribunal has the discretion to award a party's legal and other costs. For Singapore-seated arbitrations, the IAA[26] and AA[27] also provide that any costs directed by an award to be paid shall be taxable (i.e. assessable if not agreed) by the Registrar and the Registrar of the Supreme Court respectively.

Special or Unusual Features (If Any)

There are no special or unusual features of SIAC arbitration.

Recent Developments (If Any)

The SIAC has established a new SIAC-SIMC Arb-Med-Arb Protocol ("Protocol") together with the Singapore International Mediation Centre ("SIMC"). "Arb-Med-Arb" is a process where a dispute is referred to arbitration before mediation is attempted. If the parties are able to settle their dispute through mediation, their mediated settlement may be recorded as a consent award. If the parties are unable to settle their dispute through mediation, they may continue with the arbitration proceedings. Under the new Protocol, the arbitrator(s) and the mediator(s) will be separately and independently appointed by SIAC and SIMC, respectively, under the applicable arbitration rules and mediation rules of each Centre. Unless the parties otherwise agree, the arbitrator(s) and the mediator(s) will generally be different persons.

---

[25] In this article, the term "costs of the arbitration" refers to the fees of the tribunal, those of the arbitral institution and costs of experts and other assistance required by the tribunal.

[26] S. 21 of the IAA.

[27] S. 39 of the IAA.

C.2 Singapore Chamber of Maritime Arbitration ("SCMA")

Background

Originally part of SIAC, the SCMA was reconstituted as a company limited by guarantee separate from SIAC. The aim of the SCMA is to provide a framework for maritime arbitration that is responsive to the needs of the maritime community.

Types of Disputes Handled

The SCMA handles maritime arbitrations.

Numbers of Disputes Handled

No information available.

Provisions on Confidentiality of Arbitration

Rule 42 of SCMA Rules, 2nd Edition, 2009 (the "SCMA Rules") provides for confidentiality on similar terms to Rule 35 of the SIAC Rules. However, unlike the SIAC Rules, the tribunal has no general discretion to permit disclosure upon application of a party.[28]

Availability of Expedited Procedures

The SCMA Rules[29] provide for an expedited procedure for small claims where the aggregate amount of the claim and/or counterclaim in dispute is less than or is unlikely to exceed USD75,000 (excluding interest and costs), or if the parties otherwise agree. Expedited arbitrations will be heard by a sole arbitrator unless the parties otherwise agree. There is no oral hearing and no discovery unless the Tribunal requires, and the

---

[28]   Cf. SIAC Rules, Rule 35(e).

[29]   SCMA Rules, Rule 44.

award must be issued within 21 days. The SCMA also offers the SCMA Expedited Arbitral Determination of Collision Claims for claims arising out of a collision between two or more ships.

Consolidation of Disputes between the Same Parties and Joinder of Third Parties

If the parties agree, the tribunal has the power to join other parties to the arbitration.[30] Further, where two or more arbitrations appear to raise common issues of fact and law, the tribunal has the power to order that those arbitrations be heard concurrently and that evidence and documents be shared between the concurrently heard arbitrations.[31]

Time Limits for Rendering of the Award

The tribunal shall render its award in writing within three month from the date when proceedings are closed, unless all parties agree otherwise.[32]

Fee Structure

The SCMA does not have scale fees, and parties are free to agree fees with the arbitrator. However, in the absence of agreement, it provides for a fixed booking fee of SGD1,125 per day for each hearing day booked with the arbitrator. The SCMA charges fees for specific services, such as fund holding, appointment, authentication of awards, etc.

---

[30] Rule 32.2 of the SCMA Rules.

[31] SCMA Rules, Rules 32.3.

[32] SCMA Rules, Rule 35.

Treatment of Costs of the Arbitration

In general, Rule 40 of the SCMA Rules provide costs of the arbitration and parties' legal costs to be dealt with in a similar fashion as the SIAC Rules (see C.1 above)

Special or Unusual Features (If Any)

There are no special or unusual features.

Recent Developments (If Any)

There are no recent developments.

SOUTH AFRICA

Gerhard Rudolph[1] and Darryl Bernstein[2]

A. LEGISLATION, TRENDS AND TENDENCIES

A.1 Legislation

The law of arbitration in South Africa derives from common law, legislation and the Constitution of the Republic of South Africa 1996. It is primarily regulated by the Arbitration Act 42 of 1965 (the "Arbitration Act").

The Arbitration Act is extensively influenced by the English Arbitration Acts of 1889 and 1950, recognizes the binding effect of an agreement to arbitrate and the referral of a dispute for determination by way of arbitration. The Arbitration Act follows traditional English principles, essentially reflecting English law as it stood in 1965. While the English statutes have since been amended to accommodate the development of international commercial law, the Arbitration Act remains unamended.

The Arbitration Act applies to both international and domestic arbitration proceedings. Parties are essentially free to adopt procedures of their choice within the framework of the Arbitration Act; indeed the arbitration agreement may itself specify the rules of procedure to be followed, or the parties may

---

[1] Gerhard Rudolph is a Partner in Baker & McKenzie's Johannesburg office. His practice involves primarily commercial dispute resolution and arbitration for a broad range of areas of practice, including banking, insurance, construction and engineering, mining and resources, and general corporate and commercial issues.

[2] Darryl Bernstein is a Partner in Baker & McKenzie's Johannesburg office. He regularly represents clients in international litigation and arbitration proceedings, often in the spheres of banking, insurance, information technology, mining and resources, and insolvency.

leave it to the arbitrator to decide the procedure, subject essentially to the principles of natural justice and broad procedural framework envisaged by the Arbitration Act.

Domestic arbitrations are typically conducted in terms of comprehensive rules adopted by agreement between the parties, importing either the Uniform Rules of Court[3] or the rules published and administered by the Arbitration Foundation of Southern Africa ("AFSA") or the Association of Arbitrators ("ASA"), being the major private arbitral institutions within South Africa. International disputes are typically governed by the rules of the International Chamber of Commerce ("ICC") or the London Court of International Arbitration ("LCIA").

The enforcement of foreign arbitral awards is governed by the Recognition and Enforcement of Foreign Arbitral Awards Act 40 of 1977 (the "Enforcement Act") which incorporates and ratifies the Convention on the Recognition and Enforcement of Foreign Arbitral Awards of 1958 (the "New York Convention"). Although the Enforcement Act deals comprehensively with the enforcement of foreign awards, it fails to deal expressly with their recognition. In order for a foreign arbitral award to be enforced, the Enforcement Act requires that an application be made to court for its recognition and enforcement. The court may decline the application where the content of the dispute is such that arbitration would not be permitted in South African law, or where the enforcement of the award is contrary to public policy.[4]

---

[3] The Uniform Rules of Court are a set of rules regarding the conduct of proceedings of the several provincial and local divisions of the Supreme Court of South Africa.

[4] Sections 4(1)(a)(i) and (ii) of the Enforcement Act.

A. Legislation, Trends and Tendencies

A.2 Proposed Changes to the Arbitration Act

During 2001, in the face of almost universal adoption of the UNCITRAL Model Law by countries in the process of updating their arbitration legislation and the ongoing development of international commercial law, the South African Law Reform Commission (the "SALC") submitted a comprehensive report on the status of South African domestic arbitration[5] in which it was recommended, *inter alia*, that a new domestic arbitration statute be introduced, combining the best features of the UNCITRAL Model Law and the English Arbitration Act of 1996, while retaining otherwise effective provisions of the Arbitration Act.[6] To date, however, the legislature has taken no steps to implement the SALC's recommendations.

Recently, however, it appears that Government has developed a renewed appreciation of the broader commercial benefits of arbitration and the importance of international arbitration. As a result, there is renewed impetus to move forward with reform on both domestic and international arbitration legislation. A draft bill, which has been waiting in the wings since 1997, has for the first time in some 17 years been resurrected. Pundits indicate that this bill has been revised by the SALC, bringing it up to date. Reports also indicate that a leading academic expert in the field has done immensely valuable work in doing so, and the Justice Department indicates that the Bill will go to Cabinet and, hopefully, to Parliament. We remain hopeful that these steps will indeed take place in 2015.

---

5   Project 94: Domestic arbitration report dated May 2001, available at www.justice.gov.za/salrc/reports/r_prj94_dom2001.pdf.

6   P Ramsden, *The Law of Arbitration* 19.

A.3 Trends and Tendencies

Commercial arbitration is a long-established mechanism for dispute resolution in South Africa. It has become increasingly popular in the last decade due to the relative speed and certainty with which resolution of disputes may be obtained, particularly in comparison to the staffing and resource constraints in the court system, which has resulted in backlogged court trial rolls and increasingly unaffordable access to courts. Arbitration is viewed in South Africa as a particularly flexible procedure for resolving disputes—the parties are at liberty to modify the procedure in accordance with the nature and extent of the particular dispute as well as the amount at stake.[7]

Arguably the most significant development in recent years affecting cross-border commercial dispute resolution in South Africa was the October 2009 launch of Africa ADR, an initiative of the Southern African Development Community ("SADC"). Africa ADR is a regional dispute resolution forum for the determination of cross-border disputes within the SADC region, established in conformity with the resolutions of the General Assembly of the United Nations, which encourage the use of alternative and appropriate methods for the resolution of civil disputes.[8] It is hoped that this forum will result in substantial change in respect of the manner in which cross-border arbitration agreements are concluded between parties within South Africa. Africa ADR is ready to commence its business operations. It has drawn up and confirmed its rules and procedures for arbitrations, mediations and conciliations. It is in the process of establishing local organising committees in all the countries in which Africa ADR will operate.

---

[7]   Butler & Finsen, *Arbitration in South Africa: Law and Practice* 2.

[8]   Accessed via www.africaadr.com.

B. CASES

The most significant recent decisions rendered by South African courts in relation to arbitration proceedings are summarized below.

B.1 Clause Induced by Fraud Not Enforceable

In *North East Finance v Standard Bank*,[9] the Supreme Court of Appeal (the "SCA") had to consider whether, in the face of substantive reasons to believe that a contract had been induced by fraud, a clause in a contract requiring parties to refer their disputes to arbitration should be enforceable against the party alleging the fraud.

North East conducted business by financing the acquisition of goods through the conclusion of rental agreements with end-users. It in turn discounted debts owed to it by end-users with Standard Bank in terms of an agreement of cession. Disputes then arose about the collection of rentals and the debiting of North East's bank account. Following negotiations and meetings, the parties entered into a 'settlement agreement', the purpose of which was to phase out and then terminate North East's collection function. The arbitration clause in the settlement agreement provided:

> In the event of any dispute of whatsoever nature arising between the parties (including any question as to the enforceability of this contract but excluding the failure to pay any amount due unless the defaulting party has, prior to the due date for such payment, by notice in writing to the other party disputed liability for such payment), such dispute will be referred to arbitration in the manner set out below.

---

[9]   (492/2012) [2013] ZASCA 76 (20 May 2013).

After an investigation into North East's deliberate failures to make disclosure of certain irregularities, Standard Bank concluded that it had been induced to conclude the settlement agreement through fraudulent misrepresentations and non-disclosures by North East. Standard Bank elected to resile from the agreement and to regard it as void *ab initio*. North East contended that any dispute between the parties had to be submitted to arbitration, including one as to the enforceability of the contract.

North East launched an application in the high court for an order that a dispute existed as to whether the settlement agreement was void, that the dispute was arbitrable in terms of the arbitration clause and that a dispute between the parties regarding the quantum of a payment to be made under the settlement agreement was also arbitrable.

The high court found that the arbitration clause was part of the agreement and had no separate existence; that the allegations of fraud were "not wholly unfounded" on the bank's version; that the arbitration clause did not refer to fraudulent misrepresentations inducing the contract specifically, such that this was not an issue to be determined by arbitration; that the agreement to arbitrate was not severable from the rest of the settlement agreement; and that, accordingly, the court would not compel the bank to comply with the clause.

On appeal, the SCA narrowed the issues for determination to whether the particular arbitration clause should be construed so as to compel submission to arbitration on whether the bank was induced by North East's fraud to conclude the settlement agreement and, if so, whether the allegations of fraud do not appear to be "wholly unfounded".

The SCA held that, if a contract is void from the outset, then all of its clauses fall with it. In doing so, the SCA upheld the principle as enunciated in *North West Provincial Government &*

another v Tswaing Consulting & others[10] that an arbitration clause "embedded in a fraud-tainted agreement" could not stand.

The SCA then considered the interpretation of the contract. North East argued that the arbitration clause itself provided that a dispute as to the enforceability of the settlement agreement had to be determined by arbitration. It contended that the validity of the whole agreement must also be determined by a reference to arbitration. Standard Bank argued that it had not foreseen that there might have been fraudulent conduct on the part of North East at the time of concluding the agreement. There was thus no intention that the arbitrator would be expected to resolve issues relating to fraud. It had envisaged that the arbitrator's role would be to determine disputes in respect of accounting issues.

The SCA considered that, in the light of the purpose of the settlement agreement, and having regard to what the parties envisaged (because it was what they could foresee) at the time of concluding the agreement, it was not intended that the validity or enforceability of the contract induced by fraudulent misrepresentations and non-disclosure would be arbitrable. The SCA also found that the settlement agreement was probably induced by fraud and Standard Bank could thus not be compelled to refer the questions of fraud, and the bank's right to resile from the agreement, to arbitration.

B.2 Foreign Arbitration Clause Does Not Oust Jurisdiction

In *Foize Africa (Pty) Ltd v Foize Beheer BV & others*,[11] the SCA had to determine an appeal from the High Court regarding the refusal of an application for an interdict against Foize Beheer, as foreign defendants. The issues it had to decide were:

---

[10]   2007 (4) SA 452 (SCA) para. 13.

[11]   2013 (3) SA 92 (SCA).

(a) whether a provision in a licensing agreement to refer disputes to arbitration in the Netherlands under the rules of the International Chamber of Commerce, and the application of Dutch law to the dispute, effectively ousted the jurisdiction of South African courts; and

(b) whether the South African courts retained discretion to stay South African litigation by reason of the arbitration clause and the factors to be taken into account.

Foize Africa, a South African company and the appellant before the SCA, sought interdictory relief designed to protect its rights under the licensing agreement. Foize Beheer BV in the appeal contended that the appellant, by submitting to the foreign court, had waived its right to seek relief in the courts of South Africa in respect of any matter arising out of or in connection with the licensing agreement and that the appellant was bound to proceed to arbitration in the Netherlands in respect of any such matter. Both these points were upheld in the High Court and Fozie Africa's application was dismissed.

Foize Africa alleged that the agreement had been signed pursuant to a fraudulent misrepresentation. It therefore sought relief as appellant in the SCA on the basis that the respondents be bound by the agreement and applied to obtain an interdict restraining certain respondents from acting in breach of their contractual obligations. The appellant founded its claim for relief against those respondents who were not party to the licensing agreement on the basis of an allegation that such respondents were wrongfully interfering with the contractual obligations of the contractually bound first and third respondents arising from the licensing agreement.[12] Thus the claim to an interdict arose from

---

[12] *Atlas Organic Fertilizers (Pty Ltd v Pikkewyn Ghwano (Pty) Ltd* 1981 (2) SA 173 (T) and authorities cited therein.

conduct of a delictual (tortious) nature, brought against persons who were not parties to the licensing agreement.

The SCA addressed the effect of a foreign jurisdiction and arbitration clause upon the jurisdiction of a court which would otherwise be able to deal with a dispute. The High Court, in upholding the respondents' objection, had found that by reason of the jurisdiction clause "the only courts being possessed of jurisdiction are the courts in the country of Holland" and that under the arbitration clause the appellant was bound by its agreement to proceed to arbitration. The High Court found in fact it had no jurisdiction in respect of the parties' dispute.

The SCA disagreed with this reasoning. It held that it can now be regarded as well-settled law in South Africa that a foreign jurisdiction or arbitration clause does not exclude a South African court's jurisdiction. Parties to a contract cannot exclude the jurisdiction of a court by their own agreement, and where a party wishes to invoke the protection of a foreign jurisdiction or arbitration clause, it should do so by way of a special or dilatory plea seeking a stay of the proceedings. That having been done, the court will then be called on to exercise its discretion whether or not to enforce the clause in question.

The SCA held that the High Court should therefore have approached the objection on the basis that it enjoyed discretion whether or not to enforce the clause, taking into account all the relevant facts and circumstances. South African case law demonstrates that no hard and fast rule can be laid down as to the stage when a court should exercise its discretion to enforce a foreign jurisdiction or arbitration clause. The SCA held that in each given case, much will depend upon its own particular facts and circumstances as well as the stage at which and the manner in which the issue of enforcement of the clause in question is raised.

The SCA held that this was clearly a matter in which the High Court *a quo* ought not to have taken a final decision at the application for interdict stage on whether a South African court should exercise jurisdiction in respect of the appellant's proposed action and the matter should have stood over for a decision by a trial court. On the bare facts then available it was, in truth, impossible to do justice to either side in regard to the disputed questions flowing from the clauses in question. The appeal therefore succeeded and an interim interdict against affected respondents was granted.

B.3   Tribunal Committed No Irregularity

In Enviroserv *Waste Management (Pty) Ltd v Wasteman Group (Pty) Ltd and others*,[13] the SCA was seized with an appeal in respect of an application for the setting aside of an arbitration appeal award under Section 33(1)(b) of the South African Arbitration Act.

Wasteman had succeeded in persuading the High Court that the second respondent, an arbitration appeal tribunal, had decided the most important aspect of the appeal according to its own finding of a tacit agreement. Wasteman's complaint, with which the High Court agreed, was that this issue was neither raised in the pleadings nor in the grounds of appeal and as such Wasteman had been afforded no opportunity to address it by evidence or argument.

The High Court concluded *a quo* that this amounted to a gross irregularity and concluded that the appeal tribunal had exceeded its powers.

---

[13]   [2012] 3 All SA 386 (SCA).

However, the SCA found in an appeal before it that the appeal tribunal's finding of an unpleaded tacit agreement was a proper step in deciding the issues before it, and no misdirection was held to have taken place on its part.

The SCA's important conclusion was that "the structure of the appeal award is cardinal in deciding what the tribunal decided and why. A court faced with an application under s 33(1)(b) of the Act which requires it to construe an award must at least be sure that it fully grasps the logic employed by the tribunal before it can contemplate the setting aside of the award".

In summary the SCA held that the appeal tribunal did not, contrary to the finding of the court *a quo*, base its interpretation on an unpleaded tacit agreement, constructed by the tribunal itself, and of which Wasteman had been afforded no notice in the proceedings. The application and interpretation of the agreement by the appeal tribunal was an inference drawn from the parties' later conduct as led in evidence which was one of the factors which led the appeal tribunal to conclude as it had. In the circumstances, the SCA upheld the appeal and concluded that the High Court *a quo* should not have found that the tribunal committed any irregularity or acted beyond its jurisdiction.

B.4 Application for Declaratory Order Was Premature

In *Zhongji Development Construction Engineering Company Limited v Kamoto Copper Company Sarl*,[14] the SCA was asked to determine whether an arbitration agreement between the parties applied as regards certain invoices in dispute between them and whether the High Court was correct in dismissing an application for a declaratory order that a particular dispute was arbitrable.

---

[14] [2014] JOL 32421 (SCA).

Interestingly, neither party before the courts was South African. The appellant, a Chinese company known as Zhongji Development Construction Engineering Company Limited was invited by a South African company, Bateman Minerals & Metals (Pty) Limited (Bateman), acting on behalf of a Congolese company known as DRC Copper and Cobalt Project SARL (the DCP), to tender for the supply and construction of piling and civil works at the DCP's mining site near Kolwezi in the Democratic Republic of Congo.

Their main agreement contained an arbitration clause, such arbitration to be administered by the Association of Arbitrators (Southern Africa) ("the Arbitration Association") in accordance with the Arbitration Association's Rules.

The works then became fraught with delays and other complications, were ultimately suspended pending merger talks between the DCP and the respondent, Kamoto Copper Company Sarl ("Kamoto"), all the while the appellant (who had already incurred costs and commenced certain works) was instructed to continue to incur additional costs and expenses in relation to the works. Bateman naturally assured the appellant that all such costs, expenses and works performed would be reimbursed. An interim agreement was concluded to tide the appellant over, although this agreement, concluded under time pressure and on the simplest of terms, was silent on dispute resolution procedures.

The merger then transpired, with Kamoto assuming certain of the DCP's obligations under the various agreements. Kamoto refused to make certain payments allegedly due to the appellant. Kamoto also refused to submit to arbitration relying on the merger, the interim agreement's silence as to arbitration and the fact that neither party was South African and all aspects of the agreements and the works took place outside of South Africa.

C. Local Arbitration Institutions

The SCA, quoting with approval from the Constitutional Court's decision in *Lufuno Mphaphuli & Associates (Pty) Ltd v Andrews and another*[15] emphasised that the South African "law of arbitration is not only consistent with, but also in full harmony with, prevailing international best practice in the field". The SCA went on to note that, just as London constitutes a convenient neutral forum for the conduct of arbitrations, so too does South Africa and the courts in South Africa have a legal, a socio-economic and a political duty to encourage the selection of South Africa as a venue for international arbitrations.

The SCA went on to find that under the Rules of the Arbitration Association, an arbitrator is able to decide matters relating to his own jurisdiction, including the validity or existence of an arbitration agreement. In the result there was no reason why the dispute before it should not be decided by the arbitration tribunal prior to an approach to the courts. The SCA held that the process of arbitration must be respected and the appellant's application was accordingly premature, perhaps unnecessary even noting that it was in some respects ironic.

C. LOCAL ARBITRATION INSTITUTIONS

C. 1 Arbitration Foundation of Southern Africa ("AFSA")

Background

AFSA was founded in 1996 as a joint venture between organised business, the legal and accounting professions. AFSA is based in Sandton however it has a number of branches around South Africa. The AFSA Rules were prepared on the basis of an array of international precedents and seek to harmonise global best practice in a manner familiar to South African lawyers.

---

[15]   2009 (4) SA 529 (CC).

AFSA provides a full service arbitration and mediation administration facility, although it tends to administer commercial arbitrations for the most part, while also providing domestic mediation and skills training.

The AFSA Secretariat is the body appointed by AFSA to supervise and make decisions on any steps to be taken and any directions to be given in terms of the AFSA Rules and is appointed by the Alternative Dispute Resolution Association of South Africa, a wholly owned subsidiary of AFSA.

Confidentiality

The AFSA Rules confirm that any AFSA arbitration to be conducted in private, and the arbitrator is empowered to exclude the presence of persons not strictly necessary from any hearing. The Registrar is equally enjoined to maintain confidentiality in regard to any matter being dealt with by AFSA, save as is required by law.

Expedited Procedures

Expedited procedures are catered for in a number of respects in the AFSA Rules. Arbitrators are afforded "the widest discretion and powers allowed by law to ensure the just, expeditious, economical, and final determination of all the disputes raised in the proceedings, including the matter of costs."

In addition, article 23 of the AFSA Rules provides for arbitrations to be held urgently by the consent in writing of the parties. The parties are required to jointly apply to the Secretariat for such an arbitration to be conducted.

AFSA also offers a set of Expedited Rules for smaller, less intricate disputes.

C. Local Arbitration Institutions

The Consolidation of Disputes between Same Parties and Joinder of Third Parties

According to article 11 of the AFSA Rules, the arbitrator has the power to have (but only with their express written consent) other parties joined in the arbitration proceedings, and to make an award on all issues submitted by all parties, including parties so joined.

Time Limits for Rendering an Award

In accordance with article 12 of the AFSA Rules, the arbitrator should make a final award as soon as may be practicable and not later than 60 calendar days after completion of the hearing, unless the parties in writing agree to an extension of this period or, in exceptional circumstances, the Secretariat extends such period.

Fee Structure and Treatment of Costs of the Arbitration

The AFSA administration fee is calculated as a percentage of the quantum of any referred dispute on the following basis: R1000 per R100 000 for amounts up to R1.5 million; amounts exceeding R1.5 million attract an additional 0.1% fee for the amount in excess. A claim of R2 million would attract a referral fee of R15,500.00 (R15,000 + R500) plus Value Added Tax (VAT). This amount is non-refundable and is paid equally by both sides. The parties are also required to pay for any other facilities required, including the arbitrator's fee, venue, transcription and other costs.

The arbitrator is required to deal with costs of arbitration in his award and decide which parties shall bear the costs of arbitration or in what proportions the parties shall bear the costs. These costs include the fees payable to AFSA in respect of the administrative charges, the provision of a venue, the arbitrator's fees and expense incurred by the arbitrator for the person of his or her arbitral duties. However the parties may agree otherwise in writing.

C.2 Association of Arbitrators ("ASA")

Background

The ASA was formed in 1979 with its stated aim to promote arbitration as a means of resolving disputes; to provide a body of experienced arbitrators and alternative dispute resolution specialists; to help arbitrators and alternative dispute resolution specialists work efficiently; and to make arbitration and alternative dispute resolution more effective.

ASA administers all manner of arbitrations, adjudications and mediations and has in place cooperation agreements with a number of international arbitration institutes, including the American Arbitration Association, the London Court of International Arbitration, and a number of other intuitions in China, India, Europe, Asia and Africa.

ASA additionally administers a number of disputes within the South African construction industry, and ASA adjudication is conducted in accordance with the referral terms of the standard form JBCC Principal Building Agreement.

The ASA Standard Procedure Rules for the Conduct of Arbitrations ("ASA Rules") are closely based on the UNCITRAL Arbitration Rules (2010).

According to the ASA website, they have assisted in some 8,974 cases.

Confidentiality

According to Article 34(6) of the ASA Rules, the parties are required to keep confidential all awards in their arbitration, together with all materials in the proceedings created for the purpose of the arbitration and all other documents produced in the proceedings, unless otherwise expressly agreed, save of course where disclosure is required by legal duty, or to protect or pursue a legal right or to enforce or challenge an award.

C. Local Arbitration Institutions

Availability of Expedited Procedures

ASA does not make provision for expedited procedures and only affords arbitrators an opportunity to address the issue with an order for costs which can take into account whether a "party has conducted the arbitration in an expeditious and cost-effective manner".

Provisions on the Consolidation of Disputes between Same Parties and Joinder of Third Parties

In terms of Article 17(5), the arbitral tribunal may, at the request of any party, allow one or more third persons to be joined in the arbitration as a party provided such person is a party to the arbitration agreement, unless the arbitral tribunal finds that it could be prejudicial to any of the parties. The arbitral tribunal may make a single award or several awards in respect of all parties so involved in the arbitration.

Time Limits for Rendering an Award

Article 34(5) of the ASA Rules states that the arbitral tribunal should make its award as soon as practicable, usually within 60 days after the closure of the hearing, or the submission of the last document to the arbitral tribunal in the event that there is no hearing, provided that the parties, at the request of arbitral tribunal, can extend this period in writing signed by them. The Association may also, at the request of the arbitral tribunal, extend this period by means of a written notice to the parties and the arbitral tribunal.

Fee Structure and Treatment of Costs of the Arbitration

According to Article 41 of the ASA Rules, unless the parties otherwise agree, the award of costs is in the discretion of the arbitral tribunal. In exercising its discretion, the tribunal may take into account such circumstances as it considers relevant, including, as set out above, the manner of either parties' conduct. The fee structure is not available.

C.3 Africa ADR ("AADR")

Background

Africa ADR was established in order to give effect to the General Assembly of the United Nations resolutions encouraging the use of alternative methods of dispute resolution. In the result, Africa ADR is a neutral, independent, non-profit, dispute resolution administering authority. It is aimed at being a corporate partnership between participating African arbitral institutions, businesses and the legal profession that facilitates trade and commercial interaction between countries in the region and those who invest in African countries. Africa ADR advertises a modern, speedier, cost-effective and less abrasive way of resolving commercial disputes across borders. The founder members of Africa ADR are Mauritius, Mozambique, the Democratic Republic of Congo and South Africa.

AADR constitutes a relatively new forum and its success and efficacy will be monitored with some interest by the African legal community.

Confidentiality

Article 25 (7) of the Rules for the Conduct of Arbitrations ("AADR Arbitration Rules") states that while hearings will be held in private unless the parties agree otherwise. The Tribunal may limit third or joined parties to be present for the whole or part of the proceedings if it feels that such a determination might assist with the protection of proprietary or privileged information and confidentiality.

C. Local Arbitration Institutions

Availability of Expedited Procedures

In terms of the AADR Arbitration Rules, specifically article 10, on or after the commencement of the arbitration, any party may apply in writing for the expedited formation of the proceedings. The party is required to set out fully the grounds for the urgency, and the other parties to the matter should be copied on the application. The Tribunal of AADR has discretion to decide whether the proceedings will be run on an urgent basis or not.

Provisions on the Consolidation of Disputes between Same Parties and Joinder of Third Parties

There is a detailed provision in the Arbitration Rules on the consolidation of disputes between parties and the joinder of third parties. Briefly, in terms of article 8 of the AADR Arbitration Rules, where there are two or more claims that involve the same parties and have a question of law or fact in common, after consultation with the parties then they may be included under one Notice to Commence Arbitration in pending proceedings or the decision may be deferred to the Tribunal's discretion. The Tribunal may, after hearing the parties, allow one or more third parties to be joined as a party, provided such third person and the parties have consented and the award will be made in respect of all parties involved in the arbitration.

Time Limits for Rendering an Award

There is no specific period in which the award is required to be rendered. However, in terms of the AADR Arbitration Rules, parties can extend the time limit stipulated by any applicable law for the rendering of the award and will, if required to by the Tribunal, confirm such waiver in writing.

Fee Structure and Treatment of Costs of the Arbitration

Costs are dealt with comprehensively in both the AADR Rules and a separate appendix to them. The arbitrator (or tribunal) awards and fixes costs, and undue delay, as well as any failure to adhere to the directions and rulings of the arbitrator, may be taken into account in making an award as to costs.

C.4 Commission for Conciliation, Mediation and Arbitration ("CCMA")

Background

The CCMA is a dispute resolution body established in terms of the Labour Relations Act, 66 of 1995 ("LRA"). Its Governing Body is the supreme policy making body of the CCMA and consists of a chairperson, three state representatives; three representatives from organised labour and three representatives from organised business; all of whom are nominated by National Economic Development and Labour Council and the Director of the CCMA nominated by the Governing Body.

The CCMA is an independent body established by law to carry out a range of workplace dispute resolution and prevention functions. The CCMA mainly handles unfair dismissal disputes, unfair labour practices, collective bargaining issues and severance pay disputes.

Dispute resolution is one of the CCMA's primary functions. In its first ten years in existence the CCMA handled over a million cases, and on average 120 000 cases are referred to the CCMA annually.

The CCMA Process

In order to lodge a dispute, parties are subject to strict time periods, although condonation may be obtained for out of time referrals. Matters involving disputed labour issues must be referred within 30 days from the date of the dispute. Unfair labour practice disputes must be referred within 90 days. Disputes which related to alleged discrimination must be referred within six months.

The referring party is required to complete a CCMA case referral form. Once this form is completed, the party has to ensure a copy is delivered to the other party.

The CCMA dispute referral process combines conciliation and arbitration at the outset of the process in a mandatory attempt to curtail proceedings and encourage settlement of disputes. Section 191(5A) of the LRA makes provision for this Con-Arb process, which is a speedier one-stop process of conciliation and arbitration for individual unfair labour practices and unfair dismissals. In effect, this process will allow for conciliation and arbitration to take place as a continuous process on the same day, save where one party objects to the process. In the face of an objection the conciliation still proceeds, but if it fails and does not result in settlement, the arbitration is held separately. At the conciliation stage legal representation is not allowed and the process is private and confidential and conducted on a without prejudice basis.

Availability of Expedited Procedures

In terms of Rule 31 of CCMA Rules, an application may be brought urgently where appropriate and in circumstances where the applicable time frames prescribed in the CCMA Rules would frustrate relief. These need to be appropriately motivated on affidavit in order to dispense with the ordinary time periods and procedures provided for in the CCMA Rules.

Provisions on the Consolidation of Disputes between Same Parties and Joinder of Third Parties

In terms of rule 4(2) of the CCMA Rules, if proceedings are jointly instituted or opposed by more than one employee, documents may be signed by an employee who is mandated by the other employees to sign documents. A list in writing, of the employees who have mandated the employee to sign on their behalf must be attached to the referral document

Rule 26 of the CCMA Rules governs how persons may be joined or substituted in the proceedings. In terms of this rule, the Commission or a commissioner may join any number of persons as parties in proceedings if their right to relief depends on substantially the same question of law or fact. Furthermore a commissioner may make an order joining any person as a party in the proceedings if the party to be joined has a substantial interest in the subject matter of the proceedings.

Time Limits for Rendering an Award

Section 138 (7) of the LRA provides that an arbitration award must be issued within fourteen days of the conclusion of the proceedings. This period may be extended if good cause is shown or reasons for the award are to be served and filed.

Fee Structure and Treatment of Costs of the Arbitration

The CCMA operates akin to court in South Africa and does not generally charge fees for its dispute resolution work. It may do so in exceptional circumstances as outlined below. The following are the circumstances in which CCMA may charge fees:

1. When conducting, overseeing or scrutinising any election or ballot at the request of a registered trade union or employers'

organization, the fee is between R1 730,00 to R3 460,00 for each day or part thereof.

2. When asked by employees, employers, registered trade union, registered federation of trade unions, federations of employers organisations or councils to provide advice or training relating to—

- Establishing collective bargaining structures;
- Designing, establishing and electing workplace forums and creating deadlock-breaking mechanisms;
- The functioning of workplace forums;
- Preventing and resolving disputes and employees' grievances;
- Disciplinary procedures;
- Procedures in relation to dismissals;
- The process of restructuring the workplace;
- Affirmative action and equal opportunity programmes; and
- Sexual harassment in the workplace,

the fee is between R1 730,00 and R1 920,00 for each day or part thereof.

The CCMA may charge R1 730,00 for each day of the hearing if the commissioner in an arbitration finds that the dismissal is unfair only because the employer did not follow a proper procedure

CCMA commissioners may include an order of costs in the arbitration award if a person or representative conducted the case in a manner which lacked seriousness or proceeded with or defended the dispute in arbitration without sufficient grounds for action just to annoy the other party. No loss of professional earnings may be claimed from the CCMA, a witness fee may only be paid if that witness was called by CCMA.

SPAIN

José María Alonso,[1] Alfonso Gómez-Acebo,[2] José Ramón Casado,[3] Víctor Mercedes[4] and Fernando de la Mata[5]

A. LEGISLATION, TRENDS AND TENDENCIES

A.1 Legislation

International arbitration in Spain continues to be governed by Law 60/2003, of December 23, on Arbitration, as last amended in 2011, to which no legislative amendment was made in 2014. However, some recent amendments to other regulations do affect arbitration.

Arbitration of IP Disputes

The Spanish Intellectual Property Commission is founded with the approval of Law 21/2014, of November 4, which amends the Revised Text of the Intellectual Property Law, approved by Legislative Royal Decree 1/1996, of April 12, effective as from

---

[1]   Managing Partner and Head of the Litigation & Arbitration Department at the Baker & McKenzie Madrid office. Member of the Steering Committees of the Global Arbitration Practice Group and the International European Disputes Practice Group.

[2]   Partner at the Baker & McKenzie Madrid office. Practices in the area of international arbitration and co-heads the International Arbitration Group at Baker & McKenzie Madrid.

[3]   Partner at the Baker & McKenzie Madrid office. Practices in the areas of corporate, commercial and civil litigation and arbitration.

[4]   Partner at the Baker & McKenzie Barcelona office and co-head of the Litigation & Arbitration Department.

[5]   Partner at the Baker & McKenzie Barcelona office and co-head of the Litigation & Arbitration Department.

January 1, 2015. This collegiate body will be under the Spanish Ministry of Education, Culture and Sport and will conduct and administer mediation and arbitration proceedings for disputes on collective management of copyrights and related claims of compensation for damages. Copyright management entities, consumers associations, broadcasting entities and any especially significantly affected consumers are entitled to apply for arbitration before the Intellectual Property Commission. After the filing of a request for arbitration, the parties will be banned from resorting to the ordinary courts to settle the dispute.

Arbitration of Telecommunications Disputes

Law 9/2014, of May 9, on Telecommunications, effective as from May 11, 2014, replaces former legislation in an attempt to stimulate investment in the area of broadband connections and to promote a stable regulatory environment. From an arbitration perspective, it enables consumers and end-users to resort to arbitration proceedings before Consumer Arbitration Boards to settle their disputes. Under this new regulation, telecommunications operators may also resort to arbitration before the National Markets and Competition Commission, governed by Law 13/2013, of June 4.

Protection of Consumers against Imposed Arbitration in Business-to-Consumer Operations

The Spanish Parliament recently approved Law 3/2014, of May 27, which amends the Revised Text of the Consumers and End-Users General Protection Law, approved by Legislative Royal Decree 1/2007, of November 16, effective as from March 28, 2014. The changes introduced by this legislation are aimed at implementing the Directive 2011/83/EU of the European Parliament and of the Council of October 25, 2011 on consumer rights, and reinforce the protection given to consumers. Among other amendments, Law 3/2014, of May 27, sets forth that arbitration clauses in B2C operations signed before the dispute arises shall not be binding on consumers.

B. CASES

B.1 Recognition and Enforcement of Foreign Arbitral Awards

The Catalonia High Court of Justice issued a ruling dated May 15, 2014 (Ruling No. 67/2014[6]) granting exequatur to an ICC award rendered in Paris against two Spanish entities, as a result of an arbitration initiated by IKEA. The two defendants challenged the request for exequatur filed by IKEA, *inter alia*, on the basis of formal defects, as IKEA had only submitted with the request a non authentic copy of the award. Additionally, it was alleged that the award was not yet final as it was under annulment proceedings before the French courts and was against the Spanish rules of public policy.

With regard to the authenticity of the copy of the award that has to be submitted with the request of exequatur, the court stated that, although this is in fact a formal requirement set forth by Article IV of the New York Convention, it is not a reason to deny exequatur as it may be amended,[7] as happened in the case at hand.

The court also confirmed that annulment proceedings initiated against the award do not affect its enforceability and, therefore,

---

[6] ECLI:ES:TSJCAT:2014:184A. The European Case Law Identifier (ECLI) is an identifier for case law in Europe, implemented by the European Union Court of Justice, the European Patent Office and several EU Member States on the basis of the Council conclusions of April 29, 2011 inviting the introduction of ECLI.

[7] Reference is made to the ruling rendered by our Supreme Court dated March 4, 2003 declaring that the Spanish procedural rules expressly admit the amendment of authenticity requirements throughout proceedings.

the award shall be deemed to be final, unless the French tribunals expressly declare the stay of its enforcement, which did not happen in the case at hand. In any event, the court pointed out that the burden of proof of the non enforceability of the award is on the defendant.[8]

The final ground of opposition on public policy was also dismissed by the court. The Spanish entities alleged that public policy had been infringed when the arbitrator ruled on the allocation of costs without a rationally based decision, thus infringing Article 24 of the Spanish Constitution. The court confirmed that public policy must be identified with basic constitutional principles and is only infringed when a real breach in due process occurs, thus causing a lack of proper defense to any of the parties, circumstances which did not happen in this case and which may not be comparable to a defect, if any, in the application of the rules of costs, which did not cause real defenselessness—especially when this supposed infringement was also brought to the annulment proceedings in France.

B.2 Issues Related to Evidence

A recent judgment issued by the Valencia High Court of Justice on January 7, 2014 (Judgment No. 1/2014[9]) partially set aside an award for breach of the right to be heard. During the proceedings, an expert report was allowed, on the basis of invoices that had to be produced by the respondent. The respondent failed to produce documents, and the arbitrator stated that the failure to produce documents would be taken into consideration by means of adverse inferences. The award, however, applied a strict notion of burden of proof and dismissed the claim as unsubstantiated.

---

[8] Also stated by the Catalonian High Court of Justice in its previous ruling dated November 17, 2011.

[9] ECLI:ES:TSJCV:2014:96.

The court held that the claimant's right to be heard had been breached, as it had not been given the opportunity to present its case by dismissing the claim as unsubstantiated, despite the fact that the respondent did not file the requested documents and the claimant's insistence on their production.

The Catalonia High Court of Justice, in a judgment dated May 22, 2014 (Judgment No. 37/2014[10]) set aside an award in which the arbitral tribunal had appointed, as an expert, the respondent's own technical service. The court held that in rejecting the claim for lack of proof on the basis of evidence issued by a non-independent expert and not giving the claimant the possibility of filing its own expert report, the parties had not been treated equally, breaching the claimant's right to be heard. Another judgment, in this case issued by the Madrid High Court of Justice, dated May 22, 2014 (Judgment No. 30/2014[11]), denied the annulment of an award in which the arbitrators had refused to hear certain witnesses. The court held that the refusal to hear evidence can only constitute a breach of the right to be heard if (i) the party can demonstrate a relationship between the facts it intended to prove and the evidence denied; and (ii) the party shows that such evidence and facts would have had an influence in obtaining a favorable decision. Otherwise, the right to be heard is not held to be breached.

B.3 Decision on Issues Not Submitted to Arbitration

Several recent decisions have ruled on when an award should be annulled for deciding on issues that were not submitted to arbitration. Two recent rulings by the Madrid High Court of Justice dated July 1 (Judgment No. 43/2014[12]) and July 16, 2014

---

[10]   ECLI:ES:TSJCAT:2014:5533.

[11]   ECLI:ES:TSJM:2014:10332.

[12]   ECLI:ES:TSJM:2014:10353.

(Judgment No. 45/2014[13]) and one of the Catalonia High Court of Justice dated July 10, 2014 (Judgment No. 47/2014[14]) decided on the issue, all denying requests to set aside on these grounds. With regard to the reasoning of the award, all three judgments ruled that a strict symmetry does not have to exist between what is requested and what is granted. Instead, an award is within what has been submitted to arbitration when the ruling, albeit not literally coinciding with what was requested, is rationally in line with the parties' requests and the facts that support them. Furthermore, an award may be considered to be within what has been submitted to arbitration when it rules on issues intimately linked to the decision requested, without which the dispute would not be completely settled. For an award to be annulled on these grounds, a substantial modification of the object of the proceedings must exist, resulting in the parties being deprived from effectively presenting their case on the issue, thus losing their right of defense.

In a related issue, a decision by the Catalonia High Court of Justice dated 14 July 2014 (Judgment No. 49/2014[15]) held that an arbitrator may apply legal rules not invoked by the parties as long as the factual basis brought by the them is not altered, the variation from the rules invoked is not substantial and the parties' reasoning is not affected.

B.4 Reasoning of Awards

A recent ruling, dated 1 July 2014 (Judgment No. 31/2014[16]) by the Madrid High Court of Justice decided on the issue of the annulment of awards on the basis of insufficient reasoning. The court denied a request to set aside an award that had not taken

---

[13] ECLI:ES:TSJM:2014:10354.

[14] ECLI:ES:TSJCAT:2014:7772.

[15] ECLI:ES:TSJCAT:2014:7773.

[16] ECLI:ES:TSJM:2014:10333.

into consideration expert reports that were regarded as essential by the party requesting annulment. As stated by the court, the need for reasoning of the award does not require extensive reasoning or that a detailed, point-by-point analysis be carried out, treating all aspects and perspectives raised by the parties. The need for reasoning only requires that the decision be based on law and within the factual background submitted by the parties. Only non-existent, arbitrary or excessively formal reasoning would allow for the setting aside of an award.

B.5 Arbitration of Corporate Disputes and Extension of Arbitration Agreement

A recent decision by the Catalonia High Court of Justice dated 6 February 2014 (Judgment No. 9/2014[17]) upheld an award issued in a dispute arising from a shareholder's agreement, even though the arbitration clause was not inserted in the agreement but in the company's bylaws. The court held that the arbitration agreement contained in the company's bylaws, which provided for arbitration in all disputes between the company and its shareholders and between shareholders, was extendable to disputes arising from a shareholder's agreement that did not contain such provision. In the case at hand, the shareholder's agreement had been signed by all shareholders, and the court concluded that, in such a case, the agreement is directly related to and interdependent with the internal dealings of the company, which would allow for the extension of the arbitration clause to the shareholder's agreement.

B.6 *Res Judicata* of Arbitral Awards

A decision of the Almeria Court of Appeal dated 10 March 2014 (Judgment No. 54/2014[18]) followed the criteria maintained by

---

[17] ECLI:ES:TSJCAT:2014:1921.

[18] ECLI:ES:APAL:2014:170.

the Supreme Court,[19] according to which an arbitral award has the same effects as an ordinary judgment, including *res judicata*. This entails that no other arbitral tribunal or court may rule on any of the disputes affected by the rendered award. In the case at hand, a creditor filed a debt recovery claim before an arbitral panel, which was accepted. The claim had been guaranteed by the debtor by way of a promissory note, and the claimant, once the award was rendered, filed before the ordinary courts a special claim for the enforcement of the promissory note. The debtor answered to the claim, arguing on the merits. The Court of Appeal held that while the claimant could enforce the promissory note by way of separate special proceedings before the tribunals, as this was not in the scope of the arbitration, the defendant was not entitled to argue again on the merits of the underlying relationship, ruled on by the award and therefore affected by the *res judicata* effect.

C.   LOCAL ARBITRATION INSTITUTIONS

C.1   Court of Arbitration of Madrid ("CAM")

Background

The CAM was founded in 1989 and operates under the Madrid Chamber of Commerce.

Types of Disputes Handled

The CAM handles both domestic and international disputes, normally of a commercial nature. According to 2013 statistics,[20] the CAM mainly handles cases concerning the

---

[19]   For instance, see the Rulings of the Spanish Supreme Court dated 22 June 2009 and 23 June 2010.

[20]   Available, in Spanish, at http://arbitramadrid.com/web/corte/estadisticas-de-la-corte.

banking sector (33%), construction (20%), corporate disputes (15%) and retail (13%).

Numbers of Disputes Handled

In 2013, the CAM handled over 200 cases, with an aggregate value exceeding EUR1.2 billion.

Provisions on Confidentiality of Arbitration

Pursuant to art. 48.1 of the CAM Rules, the CAM Court and the arbitrators have a duty to maintain the confidentiality of the arbitration and the award. Arbitrators have the power to take confidentiality measures. Awards may be published if (i) publication is requested or the CAM Court considers that publication is of interest; (ii) all reference to parties and identifying information is redacted; and (iii) none of the parties object.

Availability of Expedited Procedures

Art. 50 of the CAM Rules provide for an expedited procedure, applicable in cases involving an amount below EUR100,000, unless the CAM Court understands that reasons exist to justify ordinary proceedings.

Provisions on Consolidation of Disputes between the Same Parties and Joinder of Third Parties

Art. 9 provides for the consolidation of disputes and joinder of third parties. Pursuant to art. 9.1, the CAM Court may decide, after hearing the parties, to consolidate proceedings between the same parties taking into consideration issues such as the nature of the claims, their relationship and the stage of proceedings. Art. 9.2 allows for arbitral tribunals, after hearing the parties, to permit third parties to participate, as parties to the proceedings.

Time Limits for Rendering of the Award

Under art. 38.1 of the CAM Rules, in the absence of an agreement between the parties, an award must be rendered within six months of the statement of defense or, as the case may be, the answer to the counterclaim. This time limit can be extended by the parties' agreement. By reasoned decision, the arbitrators may extend the time limit by up to two months. Exceptionally, by reasoned request from the arbitrators, the CAM Court may further extend the time limit for an additional two months.

Fee Structure

Fees are determined on an *ad valorem* basis under a cost schedule. [21]

Treatment of Costs of the Arbitration

Pursuant to art. 39.6 of the CAM Rules, the arbitrators may impose costs on a "costs follow merits" approach, unless they deem this principle to be inapplicable on the basis of special circumstances.

Special or Unusual Features (If Any)

Not applicable.

Recent Developments (If Any)

On April 2014, Mr. Antonio Sánchez-Pedreño was appointed as the new Chairman of the CAM for a 4-year term, replacing Mr. Miguel Ángel Fernández-Ballesteros.

---

[21] A cost calculator is available at http://arbitramadrid.com/web/corte/costes. The cost schedule is available at http://arbitramadrid.com/web/corte/costes-arbitraje.

C.2 Barcelona Arbitration Court ("TAB")

Background

The TAB of the Catalan Arbitration Association was founded on January 15, 1989 by the Barcelona Bar Association, the Chamber of Commerce of Barcelona, the Notaries' Association of Catalonia and the Board of Law Societies of Catalonia.

Types of Disputes Handled

All kinds of civil and commercial arbitration disputes, either domestic or international, whether decided in equity or in law, are handled and administered by the TAB. If the parties so desire, the institution may also administer conciliation proceedings. The TAB mostly conducts and administers arbitration proceedings relating to corporate, banking, construction and distribution disputes.

Numbers of Disputes Handled

According to the institution's most recent statistics,[22] in 2012 the TAB handled 71 disputes.

Provisions on Confidentiality of Arbitration

Arbitration proceedings are confidential unless otherwise agreed by the parties.

Availability of Expedited Procedures

The TAB administers fast-track arbitration proceedings for disputes which are less complex or entail claims not higher than EUR30,000. Any disputes involving higher amounts may use fast-track proceedings if so agreed between the parties and the

---

[22] Available at the webpage of the Arbitration Court of Barcelona http://www.tab.es.

complexity of the issue so justifies. In the same way, parties in disputes involving small claims may continue to use ordinary arbitration proceedings to resolve their differences, if they so desire.

Provisions on Consolidation of Disputes between the Same Parties and Joinder of Third Parties

In cases where a variety of related agreements contain arbitration provisions contemplating submissions to the TAB drafted in essentially similar terms, the parties to any such agreement which may have failed to sign one or some of the other related agreements shall have standing to act as claimant or respondent to initiate and/or take part in arbitration proceedings arising from such agreements when such arbitration affects them because of the subject matter of all the related agreements.

Time Limits for Rendering the Award

Subject to any agreement on the contrary by the parties, the arbitrator shall issue the award within six months from the statement of defense. The period for rendering the award may be extended only by the TAB, if the arbitrators so request, and for a maximum of two months, except in cases where the institution exceptionally decides otherwise.

Fee Structure

Fees are determined on an *ad valorem* basis under a cost schedule. [23]

---

[23] A cost calculator is available at http://www.tab.es/index.php?option=com_content&view=article&id=253&Itemid=153&lang=es.

Treatment of Costs of the Arbitration

The costs of the arbitration proceedings have tobe imposed on the party that has had its pleas rejected. If the pleas are partially upheld or dismissed, the arbitrator may reduce the imposition of costs on such party proportionally, unless there are reasons to consider that it acted recklessly.

Special or Unusual Features

On September 1, 2014 new Rules for the appointment of an Emergency Arbitrator, approved by the Governing Body of the TAB, came into effect. Urgent interim relief may now be granted before the formation of a tribunal through the appointment of a temporary sole arbitrator. The emergency arbitrator may decide on the request without a hearing. Once a tribunal is formed, it may vary, execute, or revoke any award made by the temporary arbitrator.

Recent Developments

An overall amendment of the Rules of the institution (of July 2004) is currently under way.

C.3 Civil and Mercantile Court of Arbitration ("CIMA")

Background

The CIMA was created in July 1989. The CIMA is a private association offering arbitration services for the resolution of civil and commercial disputes.

Types of Disputes Handled

The CIMA handles both international and domestic disputes, normally of a civil and commercial nature. According to 2013 statistics,[24] the CIMA handles more domestic (80%) than international (20%) proceedings.

Numbers of Disputes Handled

In 2013, the CIMA handled over 40 cases, with an aggregate value in excess of EUR180 million.

Provisions on Confidentiality of Arbitration

Pursuant to art. 62 of the CIMA Rules, the Court or the arbitral tribunal, at the request of either party, may take measures to protect the confidentiality of the arbitration. Awards may only be made public with the consent of all parties, when a party has a legal duty to disclose it, to protect or enforce a right or as a consequence of legal proceedings.

Availability of Expedited Procedures

There are no rules for expedited procedures.

Provisions on Consolidation of Disputes between the Same Parties and Joinder of Third Parties.

Art. 13 and 14 provide for the joinder of third parties and the consolidation of disputes. Pursuant to art. 14.1, the CIMA Court may, at the request of either party and after consulting all parties and arbitrators, join the request for arbitration to the pending proceedings between the same parties, taking into consideration issues such as the nature of the claims, their relationship and the stage of the proceedings. Art. 13 allows for the Court, at the request of any party and after hearing all of them, to permit one or more third parties as parties to the arbitration, as long as they are a party to the arbitration agreement.

---

[24] Available in Spanish at CIMA's annual report of 2013.

C. Local Arbitration Institutions

Time Limits for Rendering of the Award

Under art. 45 of the CIMA Rules, in the absence of an agreement between the parties, the Arbitral Tribunal should rule on the dispute six months after the filing of the statement of defense, or after the expiry of said time limit. Unless otherwise agreed by the parties, this period of time may be extended by the arbitral tribunal for a maximum period of two months, by means of a reasoned decision.

Fee Structure

Fees are determined on an *ad valorem* basis under a costs schedule.[25]

Treatment of costs of the arbitration

Art. 46 of the CIMA Rules sets the criteria that the arbitrator or arbitral tribunal must follow to determine the costs of the proceedings.

Special or Unusual Features (If Any)

The CIMA Rules provide for an emergency arbitration procedure (Annex I) as well as an internal appeal mechanism which the parties must opt into in their arbitration agreement (Section VIII of the Rules, arts. 52-61).

Recent Developments (If Any)

Recently, a new set of rules have been approved, entering into force on 1 January 2015.

---

[25] A cost calculator and fee schedule are available at http://cimaarbitraje.com/?page_id=66&lang=en.

C.4 Spanish Court of Arbitration ("CEA")

Background

The CEA was founded in 1981 and operates under the aegis of the High Council of the Chambers of Commerce, Industry and Navigation.

Types of Disputes Handled

The CEA handles both domestic and international disputes, mostly of a commercial nature.

Numbers of Disputes Handled

No statistics are available.

Provisions on Confidentiality of Arbitration

Under art. 10.1 of the CEA Rules, the CEA Court, the arbitrators and the parties, unless otherwise agreed, have a duty to maintain the confidentiality of the arbitration, issues discussed therein and the award and its contents. Publication of awards is possible if both parties expressly agree.

Availability of Expedited Procedures

Arts. 35 and 36 of the CEA Rules provide for an expedited procedure, applicable to cases involving an amount under EUR300,000, unless the CEA Court understands that reasons exist to justify ordinary proceedings.

Provisions on Consolidation of Disputes between the Same Parties and Joinder of Third Parties

Art. 19 of the CEA Rules provides for the joinder and intervention of third parties in the proceedings. Art. 19.1 allows the CEA Court to decide, after hearing the parties, to consolidate proceedings between the same parties, taking into consideration issues such as the nature of the claims, their relationship and the stage of proceedings. Consolidation of proceedings may be agreed when a connection exists that could lead to contradictory or mutually exclusive awards. Art. 19.2 allows for arbitral tribunals, after hearing the parties, to permit third parties to participate, as parties to the proceedings, provided the third party proves a legitimate and direct interest in the proceedings and consents in writing.

Time Limits for Rendering of the Award

Pursuant to art. 28.1 of the CEA Rules, in the absence of an agreement between the parties, an award must be rendered within five months of the statement of defense or, as the case may be, the answer to the counterclaim. This time limit can be extended by the parties' agreement. The time limit for rendering the award may be exceptionally extended by the CEA Court for one month.

Fee Structure

Fees are determined on an *ad valorem* basis under a costs schedule. [26]

Treatment of Costs of the Arbitration

Pursuant to art. 38.1 of the CEA Rules, the arbitrators may impose costs on a "costs follow merits" approach, unless they deem the principle to be inapplicable on the basis of special circumstances. Decisions on costs must be reasoned.

---

[26] A cost calculator and fee schedule are available at http://corteespanolaarbitraje.es/?page_id=4577&lang=en.

Special or Unusual Features (If Any)

The CEA Rules provide for an arbitration appeal mechanism to which the parties must expressly adhere. This mechanism is regulated in art. 39 of the CEA Rules.

Recent Developments (If Any)

Not applicable.

SWEDEN

Jonas Benedictsson,[1] Stefan Bessman[2] and Anina Liebkind[3]

A. LEGISLATION, TRENDS AND TENDENCIES

A.1 Legislation

No significant legislative changes in relation to arbitration have occurred in Sweden during 2014. International arbitration in Sweden continues to be governed by the Swedish Arbitration Act, which entered into force in 1999.

A.2 Trends and Tendencies

In February 2014, a parliamentary committee was appointed by the Swedish Government to review and modernize the Swedish Arbitration Act. The committee has been instructed to submit its report, including proposals for revisions of the Swedish Arbitration Act, by August 15, 2015.

The issues to be addressed by the committee include: the need for specific provisions in the Arbitration Act for multi-party disputes; measures to further enhance efficient court procedures in challenge proceedings; possible measures by which challenge proceedings before Swedish courts in cases involving

---

[1] Jonas Benedictsson is a Partner in Baker & McKenzie's Stockholm office. His practice includes various aspects of arbitration, litigation, alternative dispute resolution and insolvency. He leads Baker & McKenzie's Dispute Resolution Practice Group in Stockholm.

[2] Stefan Bessman is a Partner in Baker & McKenzie's Stockholm office. He focuses in particular on dispute resolution in the fields of banking, finance, insurance and reinsurance.

[3] Anina Liebkind is an Associate in Baker & McKenzie's Stockholm office and a member of Stockholm's Arbitration & Litigation Practice Group.

international parties may be held in English; and potential new provisions of the Swedish Arbitration Act to determine the applicable law for the dispute.

B.   CASES

B.1   Violation of Public Policy

A party sought annulment of an SCC award, alleging that the award violated fundamental principles of Swedish law on the protection of property and freedom of contract because it had deviated from the conditions agreed by the parties for the transfer of ownership. The court concluded that this case was not so exceptional as to constitute an application of the law leading to unreasonable results, and therefore the award did not violate public policy.[4]

Swiss law applied to the contract, which provided that the buyer would become the owner of the property (an amusement ride) upon signing an acceptance report and paying the full purchase price. The buyer failed to sign the acceptance report. The tribunal regarded the provision as a reservation of title clause, which under Swiss law must be registered to be valid. The tribunal considered that since the clause had not been registered, it had no effect, and therefore ownership of property had transferred to the buyer despite it not having signed the acceptance report.

The court explained that the *travaux preparatoires* of the Swedish Arbitration Act indicate that awards are annulled on public policy grounds only in very exceptional cases, such as when an award orders somebody to act illegally, or if it

---

[4]   Judgment of the Svea Court of Appeal, November 13, 2014, Case No T 1417-14.

disregards mandatory law meant to protect a third party or a general interest, and that in jurisprudence it has been discussed whether an award could violate public policy if it were considered to lead to an unreasonable result under Swedish law. The court considered that the requirement for registration of the clause under Swiss law could not be deemed to violate fundamental principles of Swedish law. The fact that the tribunal concluded that the buyer had become the owner of the amusement ride despite not signing the acceptance report did not qualify as public policy grounds for annulment.

B.2 Right to Claim Compensation for Costs After the Award Was Rendered

The tribunal rendered a negative award on jurisdiction. At the time of the award, the respondent had presented, but not specified, its claim for compensation of costs incurred in the arbitration. After the award was rendered, the respondent requested supplementation of the award so as to include its compensation for costs or, alternatively, that an additional award be made. The tribunal rejected the respondent's request. The respondent appealed the award and requested the court to amend the award to include its claim for compensation for costs. The court found the respondent to be entitled to compensation for costs and ordered an amendment of the award.[5]

The court explained that the tribunal's decision not to supplement the award or to render an additional award cannot be appealed. However, how a tribunal deals with a case procedurally can be appealed. The court referred to the commentary of the Swedish Arbitration Act, which indicates that errors in the conduct of arbitral proceedings ought to be

---

[5] Judgment of the Court of Appeal for Western Sweden, September 24, 2014, Case No. T 2290-13. The Court granted leave to appeal before the Supreme Court.

reviewed in accordance with the same principles applicable to procedural errors committed by public courts, and that the provisions contained in Section 28 Chapter 20 of the Swedish Code of Judicial Procedure ought to apply by analogy, implying that the court can rectify errors. In the opinion of the court, it must have been clear to the tribunal that the respondent did not understand that the proceedings would be closed through the tribunal's negative decision on jurisdiction. The tribunal's failure to communicate this to the respondent led to the respondent not being compensated for its costs.

B.3 Signature of Agreement; Existence of an Arbitration Clause

The Appeal Court found that the respondent (claimant in the arbitration) had failed to establish the existence of a binding arbitration clause and remanded the case to the District Court.[6] In its decision the Appeal Court reversed a decision of the District Court in which the District Court had found that the parties were bound by a valid arbitration clause.

The District Court had decided that the claimant (respondent in the arbitration) failed to prove that a document called an "Agreement for delivery (...)" was a mere certification and not an agreement, and ruled that irrespective of whether the agreement was signed by both parties or not, the parties had attested to discussing its entry into force, showing that the parties agreed on when the agreement should enter into force. Furthermore, the agreement provided that it replaced previous agreements between the parties, and through this wording the arbitration clause also covered disputes arising from prior dealings between the parties.

In a similar manner as the District Court, the Appeal Court deemed the certification document to be an agreement, as it dealt

---

6   Decision of the Göta Court of Appeal, September 8, 2014, Case No. Ö 775-14.

with issues other than just certification. However, the Appeal Court found that it had not entered into force because no copy of the agreement with both signatures had been presented, and the oral evidence did not establish that the document had been signed by both parties or that the parties would have applied the agreement in such a manner as to render it binding between the parties.

B.4 No Enforcement of Foreign Award against Company Not Named on Award

The court dismissed an application where a party sought enforcement in Sweden of an award rendered in Honduras.[7] Enforcement was sought against "NCC AB", which was not listed as a party in the award. The requesting party alleged that by mistake the award listed "NCC AS" as the party, but that the tribunal in reality meant "NCC AB" and that, in any case, "NCC AB" had assumed liability for the obligations of "NCC AS" under the award.

The court explained that s.57 of the Swedish Arbitration Act provides that an application for enforcement shall be denied when the opposing party has not been afforded an opportunity to comment on the application. The court's review of the application for enforcement is mainly formal, and the court does not review the merits of the issues decided in the award. The court reviews who the correct parties are based on what the award states. The award stated as respondent the "subsidiary in Costa Rica of the company NCC International A.S., a company incorporated in Sweden." The application for enforcement was against "NCC AB", and it was not obvious that this was a typo in such a manner that "NCC AB" was the company intended in the award. Also, the question of whether "NCC AB" had assumed

---

7   Decision of the Supreme Court of Sweden, March 18, 2014, Case No. Ö 2237-12.

liability for "NCC AS" obligations under the award could not be reviewed within the scope of an application for enforcement.

B.5 Guidance of the Proceedings

The court found that a sole arbitrator's failure to clarify a material issue relating to the right to terminate the contract did not constitute a failure to guide the proceedings, and rejected the challenge.[8]

In rejecting the challenge, the court explained that in its opinion the responsibility to clarify any ambiguity in the parties' cases must lie primarily with the parties and not with the arbitral tribunal. In this case, the arbitrator had presented several draft recitals on which the parties had commented, and the arbitrator subsequently adjusted the recitals. Thus, both parties had the opportunity to request clarifications from each other.

B.6 Enforcement of Foreign Award

A party sought enforcement in Sweden of an award rendered in China under the CIETAC Arbitration Rules.[9] The opposing party resisted enforcement, alleging that some of the costs awarded arose from agreements reached after the framework agreement, which was the agreement which gave rise to the dispute and which contained the arbitration clause. Therefore, those costs were not covered by the framework agreement and fell outside the scope of the arbitration clause. The court granted enforcement; it found that the arbitral award did not include a decision over an issue not connected with the framework agreement, and therefore the costs fell within the scope of the arbitration clause.

---

[8] Judgment of the Svea Court of Appeal, July 8, 2014, Case No. T 1459-13.

[9] Decision of the Svea Court of Appeal, June 27, 2014, Case No. Ö 3377-13.

The court explained that under s.54(3) of the Swedish Arbitration Act, enforcement will be denied when the award includes a decision on an issue falling outside the scope of the arbitration clause. The arbitration clause in the framework agreement submitted to arbitration "all disputes in connection with this contract (...)", and the requesting party had commenced arbitration to obtain compensation for costs incurred due to the opposing party's breach of the framework agreement. In the court's view, the opposing party failed to provide evidence to support its position that the costs awarded were insufficiently connected to the framework agreement.

C.   LOCAL ARBITRATION INSTITUTIONS

Although arbitrations are administered by some local Chambers of Commerce in other parts of Sweden, the Arbitration Institute of the Stockholm Chamber of Commerce is the only institution with any real impact and thus suited for an international comparison.

C.1   The Arbitration Institute of the Stockholm Chamber of Commerce ("SCC")

Background

The SCC is part of, but independent from, the Stockholm Chamber of Commerce and was established in 1917. The SCC was recognized in the 1970s by the US and the Soviet Union as a neutral center for the resolution of East-West trade disputes, and the SCC has since expanded its services in international commercial arbitration. In recent years, the number of cases filed with the SCC has increased considerably, and the SCC has emerged as one of the most important and frequently used arbitration institutions worldwide.

Types of Disputes Handled

The SCC caseload includes both domestic and international arbitration cases. About 50 per cent of the cases are international in the sense that they involve at least one non-Swedish party. The SCC remains a popular center for the resolution of East-West trade disputes, and also for investment treaty disputes.

Numbers of Disputes Handled

In 2013, 203 cases were registered with the SCC, which was a slight increase from the 177 cases registered in 2012. More recent statistics are not currently available.

Provisions on Confidentiality of Arbitration

According to the SCC Arbitration Rules, the SCC and the arbitral tribunal must maintain the confidentiality of the arbitration and the subsequent award unless otherwise agreed by the parties.[10] Counsel, who are members of the Swedish Bar Association, are also bound by the ethical rules of confidentiality laid down by the Bar rules.

Availability of Expedited Procedures

The SCC Expedited Rules were developed for minor disputes regarding less complex issues and involving less money. They offer a speedy and cost-efficient dispute resolution, a so-called "fast track arbitration". Today the SCC administers both domestic and international arbitration cases under the SCC Expedited Rules. The parties decide whether to use the SCC Expedited Rules or the SCC Arbitration Rules, either by specifying the applicable rules in the arbitration agreement or deciding once the dispute has emerged.

---

[10]   Article 46 of the SCC Arbitration Rules and Article 45 of the SCC Expedited Rules.

C. Local Arbitration Institutions

The SCC Expedited Rules include rules on the conduct of the proceedings in order to streamline the proceedings. For example, the statements of claim and defense specifically have a requirement of brevity and must be submitted within 10 working days of each other.

Consolidation of Disputes between the Same Parties and Joinder of Third Parties

The SCC Arbitration Rules include a rule on consolidation at Article 11. This provides that if arbitration is commenced concerning a legal relationship in respect of which another arbitration between the same parties is already pending under the rules, the SCC board of directors may, at the request of a party, decide to consolidate the new claims with the pending proceedings. The board can only make such a decision after consulting the parties and the arbitral tribunal.

Other than for consolidation, the SCC Arbitration Rules do not include any specific provisions to streamline proceedings in multi-party situations.[11] There are also no provisions in the Swedish Arbitration Act or precedent case law that address multi-party scenarios. As a result, it is unlikely that joinder or consolidation can take place without the consent of all parties. However, the review of the Arbitration Act, which is currently under way, will hopefully bring forth more detailed guidance for multi-party proceedings.

Time Limits for Rendering of the Award

Unless otherwise agreed by the parties, the SCC Arbitration Rules envisage the submittal of statements of claim and defense

---

[11] The SCC Arbitration Rules do however take into account multi-party arbitration in the procedure for appointment of arbitrators.

and potential additional written submissions, as well as an oral hearing if either party so requests or if this is deemed appropriate by the tribunal.[12] When the tribunal is satisfied that the parties have had a reasonable opportunity to present their case, it will declare the proceedings closed and proceed to render an award.[13]

According to Article 37 of the SCC Arbitration Rules, the final award must be made not later than six months from the date the arbitration was referred to the arbitral tribunal. The SCC board of directors may extend this time limit upon a reasoned request from the arbitral tribunal or if it is otherwise deemed necessary. Extensions are frequently sought and granted. The average time for proceedings in an international arbitration – from referral to the arbitrators until the final award – tends to range from 11-14 months.

Fee Structure

The costs of arbitration in SCC cases are defined in Article 43 of the SCC Arbitration Rules, under which the costs consist of: (i) the fees of the arbitral tribunal; (ii) the SCC administrative fee; and (iii) the expenses of the arbitral tribunal and the SCC. The SCC determines the costs of the arbitration and has a schedule of costs to which it adheres.[14] The SCC board determines an amount to be paid by the parties as an advance on costs corresponding to the estimated fees and expenses of the arbitral tribunal, the administrative fee and the expenses of the SCC.

Each party is expected to pay half of the advance, but if a party fails to make the required payment the other party will be afforded the opportunity to do so. If a party fails to pay its part of

---

[12] Articles 24 and 27 of the SCC Arbitration Rules.

[13] Articles 34 and 36 of the SCC Arbitration Rules.

[14] Article 43 and Schedule III of the SCC Arbitration Rules.

the advance, the tribunal can render an interim award ordering that party to compensate the party that paid its share of the advance. If the requested advance is not posted at all, then the board must dismiss the case.[15] Under the Swedish Arbitration Act, the arbitrators may also request security for their fees, and there are rules requiring a party to provide the entire security and termination of proceedings where security is not paid.

Treatment of Costs of the Arbitration

Unless otherwise agreed by the parties, the arbitral tribunal may upon request of a party, make an order as to the distribution of the costs of the arbitration.[16] In determining the final distribution of costs, the tribunal enjoys wide discretion and will generally allocate costs on the basis of the outcome of the case and the relative success of the parties on the principal issues. Other relevant factors such as the outcome of procedural issues dealt with by the tribunal, or any unnecessary, negligent or obstructive behavior by the parties that has caused increased costs may also be taken into account.

Costs will typically include reasonable costs for legal representation, expenses for witnesses and experts as well as the fees and expenses of the arbitral tribunal, and the SCC.[17] The SCC board of directors will determine the fees of the arbitral tribunal, the administrative fee and the expenses of the tribunal

---

[15] Article 45 of the SCC Arbitration Rules and Article 44 of the SCC Expedited Rules.

[16] Articles 43(5) and 44 of the SCC Arbitration Rules and Articles 42(4) and 43 of the SCC Expedited Rules.

[17] Article 43 of the SCC Arbitration Rules; see also Appendix III of the SCC Arbitration Rules that defines in further detail the heads of costs. Expenses that arbitrators may have reimbursed are subject to limits set in the SCC Arbitrator's Guidelines.

and the SCC.[18] There is some level of predictability in terms of the fees of the arbitral tribunal, since the fixed-fee schedule of the SCC includes minimum and maximum amounts for most disputes.[19]

Special or Unusual Features (If Any)

None.

Recent Developments (If Any)

None.

---

[18] Article 43(2) of the SCC Arbitration Rules.

[19] Appendix III of the SCC Arbitration Rules.

SWITZERLAND

Joachim Frick,[1] Anne-Catherine Hahn,[2] Urs Zenhäusern[3] and Luca Beffa[4]

A. LEGISLATION, TRENDS AND TENDENCIES

A.1 Guidelines for Arbitrators

The arbitration court of the Swiss Chambers Arbitration Institution (the "Court") recently issued the "Guidelines for Arbitrators" (the "Guidelines"), which became effective on August 1, 2014. The Court is the administering body for arbitrations conducted under the Swiss Rules of International Arbitration of the Swiss Chambers of Commerce (the "Swiss Rules"). The main goal of the Guidelines is to control and reduce the cost of arbitrations, and their key principles are as follows:

The arbitral tribunal may, after consulting with the parties, appoint an administrative secretary (Article 15(5) Swiss Rules).

---

[1]   Joachim Frick is a Partner in Baker & McKenzie's Zurich office. He regularly represents clients in arbitration proceedings as party counsel. He has written various publications on Swiss and international commercial arbitration proceedings and teaches arbitration as honorary professor at University of Zurich.

[2]   Anne-Catherine Hahn is a Partner in Baker & McKenzie's Zurich office. She practises mainly in the area of international commercial arbitration and litigation and also acts as a Lecturer at the University of Fribourg.

[3]   Urs Zenhäusern is a Partner in Baker & McKenzie's Zurich office. He regularly represents clients in arbitration proceedings as party-counsel and also acts as an arbitrator.

[4]   Luca Beffa is a Senior Associate in Baker & McKenzie's Geneva office. His practice focuses primarily on international arbitration and litigation, as well as sports law. He regularly acts in arbitration proceedings both as counsel and arbitrator..

When requesting a deposit (Article 41 of the Swiss Rules), the arbitral tribunal must ensure that any administrative costs are included. This should prevent surprises for the parties regarding supplemental administrative costs.

Principles relating to the reasonableness of arbitrators' expenses are set out as follows:

Travel expenses, rental of hearing rooms and equipment, expenses for an interpreter and/or court reporter, courier fees and expenses of any expert appointed by the tribunal are to be reimbursed against receipts. General office expenses and overheads are not to be claimed. Each arbitrator or secretary is entitled to a flat rate daily allowance to cover all personal living expenses for each day spent outside his or her usual place of business (CHF300 per day or, if hotel accommodation is needed, CHF800 per day). All other costs are at the arbitral tribunal's own expense.

To protect an emergency arbitrator from having to advance costs, he or she may request the applicant for emergency relief and/or the party requesting a specific expense to directly pay the provider of the requested service (airline, travel agent, hotel, etc.).

Each member of the tribunal is required to record time spent from the time the file is transmitted.

Advance payments to the arbitrators and/or secretary are only approved by the Court once significant steps in the arbitration have been achieved.

A.2 Statistical Data

Following up on last year's reporting on the growing popularity of emergency arbitrators, we note that there have been four proceedings with the appointment of an emergency arbitrator by the Court up to December 2014.

Overall, the Swiss Chambers' Institution handled 104 new cases in 2014—an increase of 53% compared to the previous year. About 30 % of the parties came from Switzerland and 70% from abroad. A sole arbitrator was appointed in 59%, a tribunal of three arbitrators in 32% of the proceedings (9% unknown).[5]

The number of challenges against arbitral awards now amounts to approximately 35 per year, mainly concerning challenges against sports arbitration awards rendered by the Court of Arbitration for Sport ("CAS") in Lausanne. The overall picture as to the success of appeals is unchanged: only about 7.5 % of all appeals are successful, with a lower number (6.88 %) in commercial arbitration cases, and a higher number (9.52 %) in sports arbitration cases.

The duration of the appeal proceedings before the Swiss Federal Tribunal roughly averages out at five months. Given that an award has to be challenged within 30 days after it has been rendered by the arbitral tribunal, a Swiss arbitral award is, on average, final and legally binding within six months of its issuance.

B. CASES

The Swiss Federal Tribunal rendered about 30 decisions in international arbitration matters in 2014. The following is a quick overview of the most interesting cases.

B.1 Lack of Jurisdiction *Ratione Temporis*

In a decision dated January 28, 2014,[6] a Swiss company initiated arbitration proceedings against a French company on the basis of an ad hoc arbitration clause contained in two agreements for the lease of aircraft. The clause provided for a sole arbitrator

---

[5]   The figures were provided by Rainer Füeg, Swiss Chambers' Arbitration Institution.

[6]   ATF 140 III 75 or decision 4A_490/2013.

appointed by the Geneva courts, with the seat of the tribunal in Geneva. The arbitrator was appointed; proceedings were commenced in June 2010 and were declared closed in May 2011.

The claimant complained on several occasions between June 2012 and June 2013 that the sole arbitrator had not yet rendered the final award. At the beginning of June 2013, the arbitrator informed the parties that he would resign, should the award not be rendered by the end of June 2013; however, no award was rendered, and he did not resign. In a letter to the arbitrator dated August 8, 2012, countersigned by the respondent's counsel, the claimant's counsel declared that the arbitrator's offer to resign would be "accepted on 30 August 2013, should no award be issued and received by then". This deadline was then extended by consent between the parties and the arbitrator to September 2, 2013. The arbitrator failed to meet the deadline, and the award was delivered to the respondent's and claimant's counsel on 3 and 4 September 2013, respectively. On October 4, 2013, the claimant moved to set aside the award before the Swiss Federal Tribunal arguing that the tribunal had been improperly constituted.[7] The Swiss Federal Tribunal upheld the challenge, holding that the arbitrator lacked jurisdiction to render the award after the expiry of the deadline.[8]

---

[7] According to Article 190(2)(a) PILA, an award can be set aside "where the sole arbitrator has been improperly appointed or where the arbitral tribunal has been improperly constituted".

[8] According to Article 190(2)(b) PILA, an award can be set aside "where the arbitral tribunal has wrongly accepted or denied jurisdiction". It is interesting to note in this respect that the Swiss Federal Tribunal admitted the challenge even if the Swiss company had not invoked the correct provision, i.e. Article 190(2)(b) PILA, but the "incorrect" one, i.e. Article 190(2)(a) PILA. The Swiss Federal Tribunal excused this failure by admitting that this issue was debated among scholars and that, thus, dismissing the challenge for such a formalistic reason would violate the due process rights of the Swiss company.

B. Cases

B.2 Severability of the Arbitration Agreement

In a decision dated February 27, 2014,[9] the Swiss Federal Tribunal confirmed that the invalidity, expiry or termination of a contract very rarely has an impact on the validity of an arbitration agreement contained therein. The dispute arose out of a patent license agreement containing an ICC arbitration agreement, as well as termination clauses providing that: "...expiration and termination of this Agreement shall not affect the ability of any Party to seek resolution of any matter arising prior to such expiration or termination pursuant to Article 11 herein...", and that "...all rights granted to and obligations undertaken by the Parties hereunder shall terminate immediately upon the expiration of the Term [...] or the termination of this Agreement [...] except for: [...] (d) The procedures set forth in Article 11 herein in respect of any matter arising prior to such expiration or termination...".

One of the parties to the agreement terminated it with respect to one patent. The other parties challenged the termination and initiated arbitration proceedings. The respondent unsuccessfully sought to challenge the tribunal's jurisdiction, arguing that, in accordance with the contractual clauses quoted above, the tribunal could not have jurisdiction over a dispute that had arisen after the termination of the agreement. The Swiss Federal Tribunal confirmed that the scope and validity of an arbitration agreement must be interpreted broad, and understood as reflecting the parties' intent to submit all potential claims in connection with the agreement to the jurisdiction of an arbitral tribunal, including termination. In accordance with the doctrine of severability, the arbitration agreement remains binding after the expiry or termination of the underlying contract, unless the parties have agreed otherwise. However, such agreement must be unequivocal, which was not the case in this instance.

---

[9]   ATF 140 III 134 or decision 4A_438/2013.

B.3 *Res Judicata*

In a decision dated May 27, 2014,[10] the Swiss Federal Tribunal provided detailed guidance on how the principle of *res judicata* is interpreted in Switzerland. It confirmed that *res judicata* is a procedural public policy principle in Switzerland and applies on an international level in respect of foreign courts, and its violation can lead to the annulment of an award. The Swiss Federal Tribunal confirmed that, unless provided otherwise by an international treaty, the question as to whether the *res judicata* requirements are met must be resolved in accordance with Swiss law.

The Swiss Federal Tribunal noted that in Switzerland, the question of *res judicata* arises where the matter in dispute is identical to the one which was decided upon by the foreign court, i.e. if the same parties submitted the same claim or claims based on the same facts. Regarding the identity of the parties, the Swiss Federal Tribunal confirmed that, in principle, the parties' role in the two proceedings, as well as the presence of third parties, are irrelevant. It admitted however that, in specific circumstances, a thorough analysis of the situation and the parties' and third parties' role in the first proceedings might be advisable, in particular in order to defeat maneuvers aiming a torpedoing the arbitration proceedings.

B.4 Lack of Jurisdiction *Ratione Personae*

In a decision of August 28, 2014,[11] the Swiss Federal Tribunal confirmed that an arbitral tribunal acting in appeal proceedings no longer has jurisdiction if the appeal is withdrawn. A dispute

---

[10] ATF 140 III 278 or decision 4A_508/2013.

[11] Decision 4A_6/2014.

arose between a football player and his new club as against his former club. FIFA found the player and his new club were liable to pay compensation to the former club for illegal termination of the contract. The player and his new club appealed against this decision before the CAS; however, the player failed to pay the advance on costs on time, and his appeal was considered withdrawn. Relying on this withdrawal, the former club challenged the CAS jurisdiction to hear the appeal. The CAS, however, upheld both its jurisdiction and the appeal of the new club, and sent the case back to FIFA. The former club moved to set aside the CAS award before the Swiss Federal Tribunal, arguing that the CAS lacked jurisdiction.

The Swiss Federal Tribunal held that the CAS award qualified as an interim award and not as a final award, because it did terminate the appeal proceedings but not the first instance proceedings before FIFA. Therefore, whilst the CAS was competent to decide on the appeal raised against the decision of FIFA by the player's new club, it lacked jurisdiction *ratione personae* to annul the decision by which FIFA ordered the player to compensate his former club.

B.5 Grounds for Setting Aside Interim Awards

In another decision of 28 August 2014,[12] the Swiss Federal Tribunal clarified the grounds for the setting aside of interim awards. A Luxembourg company and a Turkish individual entered into several share purchase agreements, providing for conflicting dispute resolution clauses. The Turkish individual initiated arbitration before the Basel Chamber of Commerce under the Swiss Rules on the basis of an arbitration clause contained in some of the agreements. The Luxembourg company challenged the jurisdiction of the Basel Chamber of Commerce,

---

[12]   Decision 4A_74/2014.

arguing that the parties had not agreed to arbitrate their dispute, since they had provided for dispute resolution clauses in favor of ordinary courts in the other agreements, and alternatively, that the arbitration clause on which the Turkish individual based its request provided for ad hoc arbitration.

The sole arbitrator appointed by the Basel Chamber of Commerce confirmed his jurisdiction in an interim award, which was challenged by the Luxembourg company on the basis that the arbitrator had wrongly accepted jurisdiction. The Swiss Federal Tribunal upheld the arbitrator's reasoning and, thus, dismissed the challenge. The Swiss Federal Tribunal clarified that, notwithstanding the wording of Article 190(3) PILA, which provides that an interim award can only be set aside for the grounds set forth in letters (a) and (b) of Article 190(2) (i.e. improper constitution of the arbitral tribunal and incorrect decision on jurisdiction), the grounds set forth in letters (c), (d) and (e) of the same provision (i.e. *ultra petita* decisions and denial of justice, violations of fundamental principles of procedure and incompatibility with public policy) can also be invoked to set aside an interim award provided that they are strictly limited to issues directly concerning the composition or jurisdiction of the tribunal.

C. LOCAL ARBITRATION INSTITUTIONS

Switzerland has a number of local arbitration institutions that offer dispute resolution services. The most important arbitration institution is the Swiss Chambers' Arbitration Institution. It is a Swiss association established in 2004 by the Chambers of Commerce and Industry of Basel, Berne, Geneva, Neuchatel, Ticino, Vaud and Zurich. The ICC also has a body in Switzerland, namely the ICC Switzerland, which has established the Swiss Commission of Arbitration. Another important arbitration institution is the Court of Arbitration for Sport in Lausanne, established in 1984 by the International Olympic Committee. Another institution is the WIPO Arbitration and Mediation Center, established in 1994, which handles disputes in relation to intellectual property between private parties.

C.1 The Swiss Chambers' Arbitration Institution (the "SCAI")

Background

The Swiss Chambers' Arbitration Institution was established in 2004. It is supported by the Court, a body composed of experienced arbitration practitioners. The Court decides on certain issues as provided for in the Swiss Rules, such as the appointment or revocation of arbitrators. The current version of the Swiss Rules entered into force on June 1, 2012. These Rules are available in 13 languages (with further languages to follow soon).

Types of Disputes Handled

The SCAI handles all types of disputes, provided that there is an agreement to arbitrate referring to the Swiss Rules or to the arbitration rules of the Chambers of Commerce and Industry that adheres to the Swiss Rules.

Numbers of Disputes Handled

Since 2004, more than 800 disputes have been referred to arbitration under the Swiss Rules. The number of new cases amounts to about 70 each year. About 25% of the parties come from Switzerland, some 50% from Western Europe, and the remaining 25% from Eastern Europe, America, Asia and Middle East.

Provisions on Confidentiality of Arbitration

Article 44 of the Swiss Rules contains a provision obliging the parties—but also the arbitral tribunal, tribunal-appointed experts, the secretary of the arbitral tribunal and the members and the staff of the SCAI and the Court—to keep confidential all awards and orders as well as all materials submitted by another party in the proceedings that are not already in the public domain. An exception allows disclosure to protect or pursue a legal right, or as regards enforcement or challenge of an award.

Availability of Expedited Procedures

The Swiss Rules provide for an expedited procedure if the parties agree or if the amount in dispute does not exceed CHF 1,000,000.[13] Since 2004, it has been used for about one third of all arbitration cases. Such cases are usually referred to a sole arbitrator, who is to render an award within six months.

Provisions on Consolidation of Disputes between the Same Parties and Joinder of Third Parties

Article 4(1) of the Swiss Rules provides for the consolidation of arbitral proceedings. The decision to consolidate is made by the Court upon receipt of the notice of arbitration in consultation with all parties and the arbitrators (if appointed). If the Court decides to consolidate two cases, it may revoke the appointment of arbitrators and appoint new ones. Article 4(2) of the Swiss Rules allows a party to pending arbitral proceedings to request that one or more third persons participate in the arbitration (joinder). The provision also permits one or more third persons to request to participate in proceedings already pending.

---

13   Article 42 of the Swiss Rules.

C. Local Arbitration Institutions

Time Limits for Rendering of the Award

The tribunal does not have to render its award within a specific period of time.[14]

Fee Structure

When filing a notice of arbitration, the claimant has to pay a registration fee of CHF4,500–CHF8,000, depending on the amount in dispute. The tribunal, once constituted, will request each party to deposit an equal amount as an advance for the fees and costs of the arbitrators and the administrative costs of the SCAI in accordance with the Schedule of Costs. The fees and expenses of the arbitral tribunal must be reasonable in amount, taking into account the amount in dispute, the complexity of the subject-matter of the arbitration, the time spent and any other relevant circumstances, including discontinuation in the case of settlement.

Treatment of Costs of the Arbitration

The costs of the arbitration are in principle borne by the unsuccessful party.[15] However, the arbitral tribunal may apportion any of the costs of the arbitration among the parties if it determines that such apportionment is reasonable.

Special or Unusual Features (If Any)

Article 43 of the Swiss Rules provide for emergency relief prior to the constitution of the tribunal. Applications for emergency

---

[14]   However, Article 15(7) of the Swiss Rules states that all participants in the arbitral proceedings shall act in good faith, and make every effort to contribute to the efficient conduct of the proceedings and to avoid unnecessary costs and delays.

[15]   Article 40(1) of the Swiss Rules.

relief are heard by a sole emergency arbitrator, who can also issue *ex parte* preliminary orders, who is required to decide within 15 days of receiving the file from the Secretariat. Where appropriate, the Court can refuse to appoint an emergency arbitrator, in which case the arbitral tribunal will decide on interim measures after its constitution.

Recent Developments (If Any)

As outlined above, new Guidelines for Arbitrators came into force on August 1, 2014.

TAIWAN

Tiffany Huang,[1] Anna Hwang[2] and Jonathan Ho[3]

A. LEGISLATION, TRENDS AND TENDENCIES

A.1 Legislation

International arbitration in Taiwan continues to be governed by the Arbitration Law of the Republic of China (ROC) ("Arbitration Law"), to which no legislative amendment was made in 2014.

A.2 Trends and Tendencies

Pursuant to the Cross-Strait Bilateral Investment Protection and Promotion Agreement between Taiwan and Mainland China, Taiwan appointed the Chinese Arbitration Association, Taipei (the "CAA") as its cross-strait disputes settlement institution on October 1, 2013. Meanwhile, the Chinese government has designated two institutions, namely, the China International Economic and Trade Arbitration Commission ("CIETAC") and the China Council for the Promotion of International Trade ("CCPIT"). The CAA, CIETAC and CCPIT provide mediation services for investors and host parties in relation to investment compensation disputes. Over the last 12 months in 2014, these institutions have handled dozens of cases.[4] Please note that the cross-strait disputes settlement body provides only mediation services. There have been no specific new trends for arbitration in Taiwan over the past year.

---

[1] Tiffany Huang is the Managing Partner and responsible partner of the Energy, Environment and Infrastructure Group in Baker & McKenzie's Taipei office.

[2] Anna Hwang is a Partner in Baker & McKenzie's Taipei office.

[3] Jonathan Ho is an Associate in Baker & McKenzie's Taipei office.

[4] http://ecfa.org.tw/ShowDetail.aspx?pid=6&cid=19&pageid=1.

B. CASES

B.1 Requirement to Provide the Parties with Opportunities to State Their Opinions

In a recent Supreme Court case,[5] the court held that the arbitral tribunal has discretion over whether to hold an oral argument hearing if the parties have been provided with sufficient opportunities during the entire procedure.

The arbitral tribunal in this case held eleven hearings throughout the arbitration procedure. At the last hearing, the parties agreed that they had no further statements or arguments to make. Consequently, the arbitral tribunal decided not to hold any further hearing when one party petitioned for a supplemental award on a business tax issue. The case was brought to the Supreme Court to decide whether the arbitral tribunal violated paragraph 1 of Article 40 of the Arbitration Law, which requires the tribunal to allow the parties to address their arguments before closing the case.

The Supreme Court held that there was no violation of the Arbitration Law. The court confirmed that the arbitral tribunal has discretion over whether to hold an oral argument hearing if the parties have been provided with sufficient opportunities during the entire procedure. In this case, eleven hearings were deemed as sufficient for the parties to raise any issues and to respond.

---

[5]   103-Tai-Shang-Tze No. 759 (April 17, 2014).

C. LOCAL ARBITRATION INSTITUTIONS

C.1 The CAA

Background

The CAA is the leading arbitral institution in Taiwan. Formerly known as the Commercial Arbitration Association of the ROC, the CAA has been administering cases efficiently and impartially since its establishment in 1955.

Types of Disputes Handled

The CAA handles arbitration or mediation proceedings for disputes relating to construction, maritime affairs, securities, insurance, international trade, intellectual property rights, real estate, and any other dispute that may be settled privately.

Numbers of Disputes Handled

The CAA handles about 200 domestic and international cases each year.

Provisions on Confidentiality of Arbitration

Article 6 of The Arbitration Rules of Chinese Arbitration Association, Taipei ("CAA Rules") provides: "Unless otherwise agreed on by the parties or required by the applicable law, the arbitrators and the administrators of the CAA shall keep all matters confidential."

Availability of Expedited Procedures

Article 36 of the Arbitration Law provides that the parties may opt to adopt expedited procedures where a claim is a small claim, or where the parties consent to expedited procedures for their relevant claim. In a small claim proceeding, the CAA must appoint a sole arbitrator within seven days from a day following the CAA's receipt of the claimant's Request for Arbitration. Generally, a small claim hearing is to be completed within one day in order to provide an expedited resolution to small claim disputes.[6]

The definition of a small claim is as provided in the Code of Civil Procedure, namely, actions with regard to proprietary rights where the price or value of the claim is not more than NTD500,000. A "small claim", irrespective of the price or value of the claim, can also include disputes or actions in relation to the following:

1. A fixed-term lease of a building or other object of work, or a fixed-term lender-borrower relationship;

2. An employment contract with a term of less than one year;

3. A claim against the owner of a hotel or a food and beverage store or a carrier, arising from food/accommodation, freight costs or the deposit of baggage or money or property;

4. The protection of possessions;

5. The fixing of boundaries or the demarcation of real property;

6. Claims in a negotiable instrument;

7. Claims in a cooperative association;

8. Claims in interest, bonus, rent, alimony, retirement/s everance payment, or other periodical payments;

9. A lease of personal property or a lender-borrower relationship with respect to the use of personal property;

10. A guarantee in respect of the claims provided in the first to the third subparagraphs inclusive, and the sixth to the ninth subparagraphs inclusive.

---

[6] Article 44 of the CAA Rules.

Consolidation of Disputes between the Same Parties and Joinder of Third Parties

The Arbitration Law is silent on these issues. Where the Arbitration Law is silent, the arbitral tribunal may adopt the Code of Civil Procedure *mutatis mutandis* or other rules of procedure which it deems proper.

According to Article 205 of the Code of Civil Procedure, "The court may order arguments to be held jointly where the claims in multiple actions are initiated separately but are related or could be asserted in a single action. Arguments of several actions that have been ordered to be held jointly may be decided jointly". Therefore, consolidation of disputes between the same parties in an arbitration case is possible.

As to the mechanism for a joinder of third parties, the Code of Civil Procedure provides that the "third party participation" system may be adopted in the arbitration proceedings, but is subject to further requirements such as consent from the tribunal, the parties, and the third parties.

Time Limits for Rendering of the Award

The award has to be rendered within six months from the establishment of the arbitral tribunal. However, the arbitral tribunal may extend this period for an additional three months if the circumstances so require. In practice, parties in complex cases tend to extend the period based on need.

Fee Structure

The arbitration fee must be paid by the party requesting the arbitration upon submission of the request. The calculation of the fee is based on the claim amount in a given ratio under the Rules on Arbitration Institution, Mediation Procedures and Fees. The claim amount is determined by the arbitral tribunal pursuant to the Code of Civil Procedure. For cases valued under NTD60,000, the fee will be NTD3,000. The ratio starts from 5% of the claim amount and decreases as the claim amount goes up. In Taiwan, the party requesting the arbitration only needs to pay the fee to the CAA. The fee for the arbitrators will be paid by the CAA from the fee it receives. 40% to 60% of the arbitration fee will be awarded to the arbitrators. Compared to court fees in Taiwan, the arbitration fee can be lower because the fee ratio dramatically decreases as the case amount goes up. For example, when the claim amount is NTD 1 billion, the arbitration fee will be approximately NTD5.1 million (0.51%) ,while the court fee is around NTD7.8 million (0.78%). However, please note that the arbitration fee is subject to an additional value-added tax plus documentation costs.

Treatment of Costs of the Arbitration

The allocation of the arbitration fee, settlement fee or mediation fee must be stated in the main text of the arbitral award, the settlement agreement or the mediated agreement respectively.[7] However, there is no formula for such allocation, and the arbitral tribunal has full discretion. This means the treatment of fees will vary from case to case, although usually the losing party will bear the fee. The parties must bear their own attorney fees unless there is an agreement that these fees will also be borne by the losing party.

Special or Unusual Features (If Any)

Not applicable.

Recent Developments (If Any)

Not applicable.

---

[7] Article 34 of the Rules on Arbitration Institution, Mediation Procedures and Fees.

THAILAND

Chirachai Okanurak,[1] Pisut Attakamol[2] and Timothy Breier[3]

A. LEGISLATION, TRENDS AND TENDENCIES

International arbitration in Thailand continues to be governed by the Thai Arbitration Act B.E. 2545 (2002) ("Arbitration Act"), to which no legislative amendment has been made since its enactment.

B. CASES

It is difficult to track the practical implementation of the Arbitration Act, as the vast majority of cases remain confidential and institutions administering arbitrations in Thailand do not publish case records. Nevertheless, cases do become a matter of public record when their enforcement is challenged in Thai courts.

---

[1]   Chirachai Okanurak, Co-Head of the Dispute Resolution Practice Group in Baker & McKenzie's Bangkok office, is a highly regarded practitioner in the field of arbitration and has accumulated vast experience working in the areas of civil claims, corporate compliance, insurance, construction disputes, bankruptcy and debt restructuring.

[2]   Pisut Attakamol is a Partner in the Dispute Resolution Practice Group in Baker & McKenzie's Bangkok office specializing in arbitration and has expertise in various types of complex commercial disputes, corporate litigation, telecommunications law and regulations, litigation in the Administrative Court, employment protection law and employment disputes.

[3]   Timothy Breier is a Partner in the Dispute Resolution Practice Group in Baker & McKenzie's Bangkok office and works closely on a variety of projects and cases for international clientele primarily involving international arbitration, compliance and anti-corruption, construction matters, bankruptcy, and contractual disputes.

B.1 Enforcement of Arbitral Award

Supreme Administrative Court Case No. Or. 487/2557 involved disputes arising from a public concession for wastewater treatment between a joint venture of six private entities ("the claimants") and the Pollution Control Department ("the respondent"). The claimants filed an arbitration case against the respondent on the grounds of breach of concession, as the respondent had failed to remit payment for the claimants' construction work. It was not revealed which arbitration rules applied or which institution administered the dispute. The tribunal rendered an award in favor of the claimants, requiring the respondent to pay outstanding fees, plus damages and interest, and to return the claimants' performance guarantee.

Upon receiving copies of the ruling, the claimants filed a motion pursuant to s.39 of the Arbitration Act, requesting that the tribunal correct typographical errors. The request was to correct a statement in the award from "the respondent shall pay the fee of Baht 6,000,000 to the claimants" to "the respondent shall pay the fee of Baht 6,000,000 *per annum* to the claimants". The tribunal made the corrections requested by the claimants.

The respondent refused to comply with the award. Subsequently, the claimants filed a motion to enforce the award with the Central Administrative Court, while the respondent filed a motion to set aside the award.

The respondent argued that the tribunal's corrections to the award were outside the scope of s.39 of the Arbitration Act, as they constituted a significant change that increased the respondent's burden. It further claimed that enforcement of the award would be contrary to Thai public policy, since the composition of the arbitral tribunal was not in accordance with the Arbitration Act, which provides that the parties' appointed arbitrator may be appointed by an order of the competent court.

The respondent claimed that during the formation of the three-arbitrator tribunal, the respondent had not appointed its arbitrator within the given timeframe. As a result, the claimants had obtained an order from the Civil Court appointing an arbitrator for the respondent. However, since these disputes had arisen from a concession agreement, they were regarded as administrative, and therefore subject to the jurisdiction of the Administrative Court, not the Civil Court.

In addition, the respondent claimed that the award did not clearly state why the respondent had to be liable to the claimants for each item of damage. Therefore, the award contravened s.37(2) of the Arbitration Act, which provides that the tribunal must clearly state the reasons for granting its award.

The Central Administrative Court ruled that there was no valid cause to set aside the award under s.40 of the Arbitration Act, and decided to enforce the award. The respondent appealed the ruling, but the decision was upheld by the Supreme Administrative Court. The Supreme Administrative Court reasoned that, in correcting the award, the tribunal had lawfully made minor corrections of insignificant errors, pursuant to s.39 of the Arbitration Act. The respondent was entitled to invoke s.10 of the Arbitration Act Governing Decisions of Power and Duty between the Courts B.E. 2542 to object to the Civil Court's jurisdiction in appointing an arbitrator for the respondent, but had chosen to waive that right. Therefore, the Civil Court's decision must be deemed lawful and final under s.18 of the Arbitration Act. Even though the claimants later filed for enforcement of the award with the Central Administrative Court, the Civil Court's appointment of the arbitrator was not affected, and therefore the tribunal was still empowered to consider and rule on the dispute. Hence, the Supreme Administrative Court took the view that enforcement of the award would not be contrary to public policy or good morals under s.40(2)(b) of the Arbitration Act.

With respect to the claim that the tribunal did not clearly mention the reasons for its decision, the Supreme Administrative Court ruled that the award had already set out that the respondent was obligated to pay the construction fee to the claimants as agreed, in the relevant installments, upon the claimants' completion of work. As such, it was sufficiently clear as to why the respondent had to be liable for such damages to the claimants. The court held that the award was made in full compliance with s.37(2)of the Arbitration Act.

B.2 Scope of Parties' Right to Seek Court's Assistance during Arbitration

In Supreme Court Case No. 7546/2550, the respondent submitted a defense and counterclaim after the claimant had made its submission of claim to arbitration. Both were rejected by the tribunal. The reason for such rejection was not made public. The respondent then filed a motion with the Central Intellectual Property and International Trade Court seeking an order to compel the tribunal to accept the respondent's defense and counterclaim and to stay the proceedings until such time.

The court considered that in refusing to accept the respondent's defense and counterclaim, the tribunal had exercised its power in accordance with s.25(2) of the Arbitration Act, which provides that the arbitral tribunal has the power to conduct any proceedings in any manner that it deems appropriate, including the power to determine the admissibility and weight of evidence. The respondent would only be able to petition the court to direct the tribunal to take action regarding the tribunal's decision not to admit its defense and counterclaim if so permitted under the law. However, in this case there was no law permitting the respondent to seek the court's order to overturn the decision of the arbitral tribunal. Therefore, the respondent had no right to request the court to compel the tribunal to accept its defense and counterclaim or to stay the proceedings.

B. Cases

B.3 Challenge to the Tribunal's Discretion in Order to Set Aside Arbitral Award

Supreme Court Case No. 10668/2553 involved a contractual dispute arising from a construction contract. The hirer, as the claimant, initiated arbitration proceedings against the contractor, as the respondent, on the grounds of breach of contract. A central issue in dispute was whether or not there was a *force majeure* event which had prevented the respondent from fulfilling its obligations to the claimant. An arbitral award was rendered in favor of the respondent such that the respondent was released from its contractual obligation as a result of *force majeure*.

The claimant then filed a motion with the court to set aside the award, asserting that in deciding that there was a *force majeure* event pursuant to the relevant provision of the contract, the tribunal had taken into account a piece of documentary evidence that had not been properly certified and legalized by the competent consul of state and was therefore inadmissible according to relevant procedural law. Since the award was made in reliance on such unlawfully admitted evidence, enforcing the award would be contrary to public policy and good morals under s.40(2)(b) of the Arbitration Act.

The court ruled that the claimant's objection to the tribunal's findings of evidence did not fall within the ambit of s.40(2)(b) of the Arbitration Act. Rather, the court found that the respondent's objection was a challenge to the tribunal's powers of discretion regarding the merits of this case, which the court was not permitted to reconsider. Furthermore, enforcement of the award would not be contrary to public policy and good morals because the *force majeure* issue was decided in accordance with the provisions of the construction contract, which had no connection with public policy or good morals under s.40(2)(b) of the Arbitration Act. Since there was no valid cause to set aside the award, the court dismissed the claimant's request.

B.4 Status of Judgment of the Court of First Instance in Arbitral Proceedings

In Supreme Court Case No. 10057/2555, the insurer, as the claimant, filed an arbitration case against the reinsurer, as the respondent, seeking compensation under a reinsurance contract. The underlying contract provided that any disputes were to be resolved by an arbitral tribunal in accordance with Thai law and the principle of *ex aequo et bono* and take into account all agreements between the parties.

During the presentation of evidence in the arbitration proceedings, the respondent made its claim based on a judgment of a court of first instance. The tribunal admitted that claim and rendered an award in favor of the respondent based, at least in part, on the legal principles applied by the court of first instance in its judgment. Subsequently, the respondent filed a motion for enforcement of the award, and the claimant filed a motion to challenge the award under s.40 (5) of the Arbitration Act, which provides that the court may refuse enforcement of an arbitral award if the person against whom the award will be enforced furnishes proof that the arbitral proceedings were not conducted in accordance with the agreement of the parties.

The court found that the reinsurance agreement did not clearly provide that the tribunal must decide disputes in accordance with relevant final court judgments. It also observed that s.146 of the Civil Procedure Code of Thailand provides that when deciding the same legal issue, the judgment of a higher court carries more weight than that of a lower court. Hence, considering that the decision of the court of first instance in this case could be overturned by a higher court in the future, the tribunal had no legal authority to rely on the court judgment. Therefore, the fact that the tribunal had based its ruling on the court judgment was contrary to the parties' agreement under s.40 (5) of the Arbitration Act. As a consequence, the court issued an order to refuse enforcement of the arbitral award.

C. LOCAL ARBITRATION INSTITUTIONS

There are two primary institutional arbitration options in Thailand, the Thai Commercial Arbitration Committee of the Board of Trade of Thailand and the Thai Arbitration Institute ("TAI"). The Thai Arbitration Committee has been one of the pioneers in the arbitration field in Thailand and is active in promoting arbitration in the business community, although it is infrequently utilized in practice. It revised its arbitration rules in 2003 to be congruent with the Arbitration Act. TAI is the more prominent and active institution.

Aside from the above, other organizations active in the field of arbitration in Thailand include the Security and Exchange Commission, which established arbitration proceedings in 2001 for claims arising under its own laws between securities companies and private clients, as well as the Department of Insurance which established the Office of Arbitration in 1998 to handle arbitral proceedings relating to claims under insurance policies. Shortly thereafter, the Department of Insurance issued a regulation requiring all insurance companies to include an arbitration clause in their policies that allows beneficiaries of insurance policies to choose to process their claims through arbitration or in the court, at their discretion. In the event the beneficiary decides to refer their claim to arbitration, insurance companies are required to participate in the arbitral proceedings. This regulation has led to the filing of a significant number of arbitration cases under the Department of Insurance.

C.1 TAI

Background

TAI was originally established in 1990 under the umbrella of the Ministry of Justice. TAI revised and reissued its arbitration rules ("TAI Arbitration Rules") in 2003 to be congruent with the

Arbitration Act. Moreover, TAI was repositioned under the Office of the Judiciary, a constitutionally separate secretariat, in order to ensure its neutrality in cases involving governmental agencies. The TAI Arbitration Rules apply to all arbitrations organized by TAI, except where the parties agree to use other rules with the consent of the Director of the Alternative Dispute Resolution office, a section within the Office of the Judiciary that administers TAI.

Similar to the UNCITRAL Rules, neither the Arbitration Act nor the TAI Arbitration Rules contain detailed procedural requirements, providing the tribunal with broad discretion in deciding how to proceed. In addition, neither the Arbitration Act nor the TAI Arbitration Rules empower a tribunal to order interim measures of protection, which must instead be sought from a Thai court of competent jurisdiction.

Types of Disputes Handled

Most types of commercial disputes involving a breach, termination or invalidity of the underlying contract can be handled by TAI.

Number of Disputes Handled

In 2014, TAI administered 102 new disputes, of which 90 were categorized by TAI as domestic disputes and 12 as international disputes. The majority of these cases involved construction contract disputes. 121 cases were finalized in TAI in 2014; 64 cases resulted in an award, 32 cases were withdrawn, 22 cases were settled, and three cases were dismissed.

Provisions on Confidentiality of Arbitrations

The TAI Arbitration Rules provide that the arbitral proceeding shall be held *in camera* and that the arbitrators, Director of TAI and TAI must not disclose the award to the public without the consent of the parties. However, there is no prohibition against the parties disclosing the award.

Availability of Expedited Procedures

There are no expedited procedures available under the TAI Arbitration Rules.

Consolidation of Disputes between the Same Parties and Joinder of Third Parties

There are no provisions for the consolidation of disputes between the same parties and joinder of third parties under the TAI Arbitration Rules.

Time Limits for Rendering an Award

The TAI Arbitration Rules provide that the award will be rendered within 180 days from the day on which the last arbitrator was appointed. In practice, however, tribunals do not adhere to this rule, and awards are typically rendered a few months after the submission of closing statements.

Treatment of Costs of the Arbitration

Pursuant to the TAI Arbitration Rules, costs and expenses in the arbitral proceedings as well as arbitrator's fees, but not including attorney's fees and expenses, must be specified by the arbitral tribunal in its award. The tribunal will apportion costs (e.g. administrative secretariat fees, fees to subpoena witnesses, photocopies, recorded transcripts, and food and beverage costs) and the arbitrator's fees between the parties, in the tribunal's sole discretion. Prior to commencement of arbitration proceedings, the Director of TAI may request security for costs, administrative fees and arbitrator's fees. If a party fails to provide such security, the Director may report this to the tribunal in order for it to consider suspension of the arbitration proceedings.

Fee Structure

Fees are charged based on the number of arbitrators (one or more than one) and the amount in dispute. Comparatively speaking, arbitrator fees are quite low. TAI charges minimal institutional fees for its services.

Special or Unusual Features (If Any)

Under Thai law, the right to recover actual lawyer's fees and expenses is generally not recognized. This custom is embedded in the Arbitration Act, which provides that unless otherwise agreed by the parties, the tribunal is not entitled to award attorney's fees and expenses. However, under the TAI Arbitration Rules, attorney's fees and expenses must not be specified in the arbitral award. Consequently, in a case under the TAI Arbitration Rules, it is arguable whether a tribunal is entitled to award attorney's fees and expenses, even with the agreement of the parties.

Recent Developments (If Any)

There have been no recent developments regarding the TAI Arbitration Rules; however, in October 2014, TAI introduced the Conciliation Rules B.E. 2557 (2014), which are modelled on the UNCITRAL Conciliation Rules. The TAI conciliation rules define when conciliation is deemed to have commenced and include procedural details relating to the appointment and role of conciliators, as well as the general conduct of proceedings. The TAI conciliation rules also address confidentiality, admissibility of evidence in other proceedings, and limits to the rights of parties to commence judicial or arbitral proceedings while conciliation is in progress.

TURKEY

Ismail G. Esin,[1] Ozgun Celebi[2] and Dogan Gultutan[3]

A. LEGISLATION, TRENDS AND TENDENCIES

A.1 Legislation

International arbitration in Turkey continues to be governed by the International Arbitration Law of 2001 ("IAL"),[4] to which no legislative amendment was made in 2014. However, there were two legislative changes in 2014 affecting arbitration.

The first amendment concerns the competent court with respect to arbitration. Prior to the amendment to Article 5 of the Law on the Formation, Duties and Powers of Civil Courts of First Instance and District Courts of 2004[5] in June 2014, uncertainty prevailed as to which court possessed competence over disputes falling within the ambit of the IAL, as well as over disputes regarding the recognition and enforcement of foreign arbitral awards under the New York Convention and/or the Turkish Private International Law of 2007 ("TPIL").[6] Article 3(1) of the

---

[1]   Ismail G. Esin is the Managing Partner of Baker & McKenzie's Istanbul office. Ismail is a member of the Istanbul Bar Association, the ICC Turkish National Committee, the LCIA, the IBA, the Swiss Arbitration Association, the German Arbitration Institute, the German-Turkish Chamber of Industry and Commerce, and the American Business Forum in Turkey.

[2]   Ozgun Celebi is an Associate in Baker & McKenzie's Istanbul office. She is also a member of the Istanbul Bar Association.

[3]   Dogan Gultutan is an Associate in Baker & McKenzie's Istanbul office. He is also a member of the Istanbul Bar Association and the Bar of England & Wales and a scholar of The Honourable Society of Lincoln's Inn.

[4]   Law No. 4686.

[5]   Law No. 5235.

[6]   Law No. 5718.

399

IAL provides that, where judicial intervention is permitted by the IAL, the competent court is the civil court of first instance (*asliye hukuk mahkemesi*). Article 60(2) of the TPIL identifies the court of first instance (*asliye mahkemesi*) as the competent court with respect to recognition and enforcement proceedings. It was unclear whether Article 5(1) of the Turkish Commercial Code of 2011 ("TCC"),[7] which provides that commercial courts possess competence with respect to all commercial disputes, prevailed over Article 3(1) of the IAL and Article 60(2) of the TPIL. Although court decisions suggested that it did prevail,[8] the uncertainty remained. This debate gained momentum after the amendment to Article 5(3) of the TCC on June 26, 2012, which provides that the relationship between the civil court of first instance and the commercial court of first instance is one of competence, a matter that requires *ex officio* consideration, and not one of division of workload.

The lack of uniformity appears to have been resolved by the June 2014 amendment. The provision now states that all arbitration-related disputes arising from the IAL and Chapter 11 of the Code of Civil Procedure of 2011,[9] as well as all requests regarding the recognition and enforcement of foreign arbitral awards, shall be heard and determined by the commercial court of first instance, sitting as a panel of three judges. Although this provision may be

---

[7]   Law No. 6102.

[8]   See, Court of Appeal (*Yargıtay*) 15th Civil Division, File No. 2014/3330, Decision No. 2014/4607; Court of Appeal (*Yargıtay*) 11th Civil Division, File No. 2012/18274, Decision No. 2013/16901; Court of Appeal (*Yargıtay*) 11th Civil Division, File No. 2012/16024, Decision No. 2013/14728; Court of Appeal (*Yargıtay*) 11th Civil Division, File No. 2000/3992, Decision No. 2000/4704; Court of Appeal (*Yargıtay*) Legal General Assembly, File No. 2011/13-568, Decision No. 2012/47; Court of Appeal (*Yargıtay*) 11th Civil Division, File No. 2012/2110, Decision No. 2012/3915.

[9]   Law No. 6100, applicable to domestic arbitrations.

A. Legislation, Trends and Tendencies

interpreted as stating that such disputes that fall within the competence of the commercial courts of first instance must be heard by a panel, and disputes that are not categorized as commercial under Turkish law therefore fall within the competence of the civil courts of first instance, this interpretation does not appear to be in line with the spirit of the provision and the former interpretation appears more plausible. This interpretation is also more in line with judicial practice.[10]

The second legislative amendment relates to the establishment of the Istanbul Arbitration Center ("IAC"). The necessity to establish an arbitration center in Istanbul, for the supervision of arbitral proceedings, between Turkey and/or Turkish parties in particular, and the provision of meeting and discussion forums for arbitration practitioners, had been the subject of discussion for many years.[11] On November 29, 2014, the Law on the Istanbul Arbitration Center ("LIAC")[12] was published, authorizing the establishment of the IAC. The institution is intended to act as a supervisor of arbitral proceedings for both international and domestic disputes. The LIAC entered into force on January 1, 2015. The law sets forth the organs of the center, including their functions and duties, but does not specify any procedural rules; the center has been entrusted with the task of drafting the rules. Consistent with the general principles of arbitration, the law imposes a confidentiality obligation on center employees. The LIAC also provides that, with the exception of members of the board of advisors, IAC organ members and

---

[10] See supra, note 8.

[11] See, e.g., Hakan Pekcanıtez, "*İstanbul Tahkim Merkezi Kanun Taslağı*" ("Draft Law on the Istanbul Arbitration Center"), Dokuz Eylül Üniversitesi Hukuk Fakültesi Dergisi (Dokuz Eylül University Law Faculty Journal) Cilt (Volume): 12, Özel S. (Special Edition), 2010, pp. 635-655 (Edition Year: 2012).

[12] Law No. 6570.

personnel cannot act as arbitrators or mediators in disputes before the IAC, unless expressly approved by the parties (Article 14).

The LIAC foresees the establishment of national and international courts of arbitration, each with three members, appointed by the board of directors, in addition to the chairman of the board of directors and the IAC general secretary (Article 12).

B. CASES

B.1 Contrasting Decisions on Hybrid Jurisdiction Clauses

15th Civil Division of the Court of Appeal

On an application for a declaration that an arbitration agreement was invalid, the 15th Civil Division of the Court of Appeal held that only the arbitral tribunal has jurisdiction to determine the validity of an arbitration agreement.[13]

The dispute arose under an agreement concerning the establishment of a hydroelectric power-plant. Article 32 of the agreement contained an arbitration clause. However, the same article provided that: "[I]n case of dispute, the Courts and Execution Offices of Bursa shall have jurisdiction". Upon being asked to rule upon the interplay between the two conflicting provisions, the lower court held the arbitration agreement valid. On appeal, the Court of Appeal upheld the decision and held that it was not competent to determine the validity of the arbitration agreement: its determination was within the arbitral tribunal's exclusive jurisdiction. However, in a powerful dissenting judgment, Judge Kurt stated that where a jurisdictional objection is raised by the defendant due to the existence of an arbitration

---

[13] Court of Appeal (*Yargıtay*) 15th Civil Division, File No. 2014/3330, Decision No. 2014/4607.

agreement, the court does have jurisdiction to determine the validity of the arbitration agreement. He also dismissed the lower court's reasoning that there was clear and express intent to arbitrate and that reference to the courts and execution offices of Bursa in the agreement was restricted to matters such as interim measures, since no such restriction could be found in the agreement.

The decision is significant in that the 15th Civil Division of the Court of Appeal appears to have struggled to keep the arbitration agreement alive. It is a perfect example of the Court of Appeal's positive attitude towards arbitration. Although on a literal reading the clear and express intent to arbitrate does not appear to exist, it seems that the parties did actually intend that disputes be resolved through arbitration; the agreement contained a detailed arbitration agreement. However, the 15th Civil Division of the Court of Appeal's ruling regarding jurisdiction to determine the validity of an arbitration agreement should be placed under tight constraints. A court must be able to determine the validity of an arbitration agreement in order to adjudicate upon jurisdictional objections raised.

11th Civil Division of the Court of Appeal

On an application for the appointment of arbitrators, the 11th Civil Division of the Court of Appeal held that, prior to making an appointment, the court must primarily determine whether the arbitration agreement is valid, bearing in mind the exceptional character of arbitration, and should only appoint an arbitrator if it is satisfied that a valid arbitration agreement exists.[14] Whether or not a clear and definitive party intent to arbitrate exists should be considered *ex officio* by the court.

---

[14] Court of Appeal (*Yargıtay*) 11th Civil Division, File No. 2012/18274, Decision No. 2013/16901.

Similar to the case before the 15th Civil Division of the Court of Appeal (see above), the agreement contained both an arbitration clause and a jurisdiction clause: "All disputes arising from the construction and implementation of this agreement shall be resolved by an arbitral tribunal deemed appropriate by both parties"; "In the event disputes cannot be resolved by arbitration, the Courts of Istanbul shall have jurisdiction". The defendants argued the invalidity of the arbitration agreement, alleging the absence of clear and definitive intent to arbitrate. The lower court disagreed and held the arbitration agreement valid. However, the 11th Civil Division of the Court of Appeal accepted the defendants' argument and concluded that the arbitration agreement was invalid, noting the exceptional character of arbitration and the requirement that parties' intent to arbitrate must be clear and definitive.

The decision is important, since it balances the effect of the 15th Civil Division of the Court of Appeal's decision whereby the courts' jurisdiction was almost eliminated with regards to assessing the validity of arbitration agreements. Further, the decision is a stark warning to those who draft arbitration agreements that an agreement containing both an arbitration agreement and a jurisdiction clause will not normally be effective under Turkish law.

B.2 Cost Award against Successful Party Not Contrary to Turkish Public Policy

On an application for the enforcement of a foreign arbitral award, the 11th Civil Division of the Court of Appeal ruled that the awarding of costs in favor of the unsuccessful party does not contravene Turkish public policy.[15]

---

[15] Court of Appeal (*Yargıtay*) 11th Civil Division, File No. 2012/16024, Decision No. 2013/14728.

In an arbitration commenced under the auspices of the Swiss Chambers of Commerce, the arbitral tribunal dismissed the claimants' claim on the merits, but ordered the defendants to pay the costs and value added tax. Upon the claimant's request to enforce the award in Turkey, the defendants resisted, arguing that the awarding of costs in favor of the unsuccessful party contravenes Turkish public policy. Overruling the lower court's decision, the 11th Civil Division of the Court of Appeal held that the issue did not fall within any of the grounds expressed in the TPIL for the setting aside of foreign arbitral awards and that the awarding of costs in favor of the unsuccessful party does not contravene Turkish public policy.

C. LOCAL ARBITRATION INSTITUTIONS

Local arbitral institutions are not abundant in Turkey. Consequently, arbitration clauses usually refer to arbitration under the auspices of the ICC or make use of ad hoc arbitration. This is one reason why the establishment of the IAC is considered a positive step for the development of arbitration in Turkey. Although rarely made use of, there are several local institutions under whose supervision arbitral proceedings can be conducted. The most well-known of these are the Istanbul Chamber of Commerce ("TICC") and the Turkish Union of Chambers and Commodity Exchanges ("TUCCE").

C.1 TICC Arbitration Center

Background

The TICC has provided services as an arbitration institution since 1979, with its Regulation on Arbitration, Mediation and Expert Arbitration ("Istanbul Rules"), recently revised on March 8, 2012 and in force since October 16, 2014. The rules are based on the UNCITRAL Rules and were also inspired, to some extent, by the ICC Rules, as well as other contemporary regulations on arbitration.

Types of Disputes Handled

The Istanbul Rules dictate that for an arbitration to be filed with the TICC, one of the parties to the dispute must be a member of the TICC. Therefore, only commercial disputes are handled by this institution. The institution handles both domestic and international disputes.

Numbers of Disputes Handled

Unofficial statistics obtained from the TICC show that 126 arbitrations were filed from 1979–2005 (an average of 4.6 per year). The average thereafter is 7.8 cases per year.

Provisions on Confidentiality of Arbitration

Article 46 of the Istanbul Rules imposes a confidentiality obligation on arbitrators, parties, secretariat personnel and all those involved, and entrusts arbitrators with the power to take necessary measures to protect business secrets and confidential information.

Availability of Expedited Procedures

Not applicable.

Consolidation of Disputes between the Same Parties and Joinder of Third Parties

Not applicable.

C. Local Arbitration Institutions

Time Limits for Rendering of the Award

The award must be rendered within one year from the date the sole arbitrator notifies acceptance of nomination to the Secretariat, or, where a tribunal is appointed, from the date the arbitral tribunal drafts its first meeting minutes where a tribunal is appointed (Article 36). The time limit can be extended by party agreement or by the Court of Arbitration on its own initiative, or upon the arbitral tribunal's reasoned written request.

Fee Structure

The Secretariat determines arbitrator fees pursuant to the Tariff on Arbitrators' Fees, in force at the time of commencement of proceedings. The Tariff provides different mechanisms of fee calculation for international and domestic arbitrations, although this may be varied by the Secretariat, if the circumstances so justify.

Treatment of Costs of the Arbitration

The final award must include a calculation of the costs and indicate in what proportion these are to be allocated between the parties (Article 43). Upon submission of the request for arbitration, the Secretariat calculates the advance on costs and requests both parties to pay in equal proportions within 15 days. Upon failure of one party to pay its proportion, the other party is entitled to pay the entire amount. If the advance on costs is not paid, proceedings will be suspended. If payment is not made within an additional 15 days, the arbitral tribunal will terminate the proceedings.

Special or Unusual Features (If Any)

Not applicable.

Recent Developments (If Any)

Not applicable.

C.2 Turkish Union of Chambers and Commodity Exchanges' Court of Arbitration ("TUCCE")

Background

The TUCCE, operative since the 1950s, has been equipped with the power and duty to take the necessary steps for the creation of dispute resolution mechanisms by a law in force since July 1, 2004. As a consequence, the TUCCE has served as an arbitration institution since 2004, based on its arbitration regulation ("Arbitration Regulation").

Types of Disputes Handled

Under the Arbitration Regulation, the TUCCE is entitled to deal with financial, commercial and industrial disputes arising between Turkish companies, between Turkish and foreign companies or between foreign companies.

Numbers of Disputes Handled

Unofficial statistics verbally obtained from the TUCCE show that 12 arbitrations were filed in 2014, rising from an average of four cases per year for the period between 2004 and 2013.

Provisions on Confidentiality of Arbitration

Unrelated third parties are not permitted to attend hearings, unless the parties agree or the arbitral tribunal decides otherwise (Article 33, Arbitration Regulation). The arbitral tribunal is obliged to take necessary measures to protect business secrets and confidential information.

C. Local Arbitration Institutions

Availability of Expedited Procedures

Not applicable

Consolidation of Disputes between the Same Parties and Joinder of Third Parties

Not applicable.

Time Limits for Rendering of the Award

The award must be rendered within one year, commencing as of the date the parties and arbitrators sign the terms of reference or the date it is approved by the Court of Arbitration (Article 36, Arbitration Regulation). The time limit can be extended by party agreement or by the Court of Arbitration on its own initiative or upon the arbitral tribunal's reasoned request.

Fee Structure

Administrative costs and arbitrator fees are determined pursuant to the Regulation on Arbitrators' Fees and Principles Relating to Costs ("Regulation on Fees and Costs"). The Regulation on Fees and Costs provides for the application of the International Arbitration Tariff Communique then in force. For disputes arising between Turkish companies, a 50% reduction is made. Where the amount in dispute is unascertainable, the Court of Arbitration determines the arbitrator fees.

Treatment of Costs of the Arbitration

Under the Regulation on Fees and Costs, both parties must pay a fixed advance on expenses (TRY3,000). The Court of Arbitration may decide for the payment of additional advance payments where previous payments prove insufficient. The arbitral award must determine how the costs of arbitration is to be allocated between the parties.

Special or Unusual Features (If Any)

Not applicable.

Recent Developments (If Any)

Not applicable.

UKRAINE

Igor Siusel,[1] Olga Shenk,[2] Kseniia Pogruzhalska[3] and Vladyslav
Kurylko[4]

A. LEGISLATION, TRENDS AND TENDENCIES

A.1 Legislation

The ICSID Convention, ratified in 2000, continues to take
priority over national legislation in Ukraine. The Decree On
Issues on Selection of Candidates for Appointment as
Representatives from Ukraine to be Included in the Conciliators'
List and the Arbitrators' List of ICSID, adopted on April 2,
2013, remains in force.

A.2 Trends and Tendencies

In general, Ukraine is becoming friendlier towards arbitration.
The arbitration community is working on legislative amendments
to reduce the number of cases before the courts considering
recognition and setting aside of arbitral awards, as well as
interim measures in support of arbitration.

---

[1] Igor Siusel is a Partner in the Kyiv office of Baker & McKenzie. He advises
and represents clients from various industries in domestic and international
arbitration and litigation, recognition and enforcement of arbitral awards,
enforcement of court judgments and bankruptcy proceedings. He is a member of
the Ukrainian Bar Association and the Ukrainian Arbitration Association.

[2] Olga Shenk is an Associate in the Kyiv office of Baker & McKenzie and a
member of the Firm's Global Dispute Resolution, Compliance and Employment
Practice Groups. She is a member of the Ukrainian Arbitration Association.

[3] Kseniia Pogruzhalska is an Associate in the Kyiv office of Baker & McKenzie
and a member of the Firm's Global Dispute Resolution and Energy, Mining and
Infrastructure Practice Groups. She is a member of the Ukrainian Arbitration
Association.

[4] Vladyslav Kurylko is an Associate in the Kyiv office of Baker & McKenzie and a
member of the Firm's Global Dispute Resolution Group.

B. CASES

B.1 Burden of Proving Grounds for Refusal of Recognition of Arbitral Award

In late 2012, a global technological company filed an application with the Ukrainian courts requesting the recognition and enforcement of an arbitral award rendered by the Vienna International Arbitral Centre ("VIAC") against a Ukrainian debtor. The courts of all three instances refused to satisfy the application on the ground that the Applicant had failed to prove that the Respondent had been properly notified of the arbitration proceedings. The courts noted that this was the obligation of the Applicant, by virtue of provisions of the Code of Civil Procedure of Ukraine. The Applicant appealed the case to the Supreme Court, which accepted the appeal and remanded the case for reconsideration to the Supreme Commercial Court. The Supreme Court noted that the lower courts had wrongly applied provisions of the Code of Civil Procedure to the proceedings, where in fact the New York Convention should have been applied due to the principle of supremacy of international treaties ratified by the Ukrainian parliament over domestic legislation. The Supreme Court noted that the New York Convention expressly shifts the burden of proof as to notice of arbitration proceedings from the party seeking recognition and enforcement of the award on to the party raising objections to such recognition and enforcement. This is a landmark decision of the Supreme Court, which finally resolves the long-standing controversy in Ukrainian litigation practice regarding which party must satisfy the burden of proof to establish grounds for refusal of recognition and enforcement of an arbitral award.

B.2 Arbitration Clause in Main Agreement Retains Its Binding Force for the Assignee

This case was brought to the commercial court by a Ukrainian company seeking recognition of title to company shares against two Ukrainian companies. The claimant had pledged its corporate share in one of the defendants as a security under a loan facility executed between this defendant and the European Bank of Reconstruction and Development ("EBRD"). The pledge agreement contained an arbitration clause which referred all disputes arising from the agreement to a sole arbitrator under the UNCITRAL rules, under administration of the LCIA. The rights under the pledge agreement along with the monetary claims of the first defendant were subsequently assigned by the EBRD to the second defendant. The second defendant challenged the jurisdiction of the Ukrainian courts over the dispute and filed a motion for termination of proceedings. The courts of all three instances, as well as the Supreme Commercial Court, granted the motion and decided that the Ukrainian courts lacked jurisdiction to consider the dispute in light of the valid arbitration agreement. The Supreme Commercial Court noted that the new creditor in the case, as well as acquiring rights under the pledge agreement, was also bound by the arbitration agreement.

This decision exemplifies the positive attitude that the Ukrainian courts will sometimes take in determining the binding force of an arbitration agreement for the assignee under the main contract. However, at the same time, it is worth noting that this issue remains controversial.

B.3 Ukrainian Debtor Seeks to Avoid Enforcement Based on Lack of Authority of Counsel

In 2011, one of the world's largest oil and natural gas service companies applied to a Ukrainian court for enforcement of an LCIA award against a Ukrainian debtor. In order to avoid the enforcement of the arbitral award in Ukraine, the Ukrainian debtor claimed that it had not authorized the legal counsel who represented it in the LCIA (who had been appointed under an assignment letter signed by its parent company) to act on its behalf in the arbitration. Moreover, the Ukrainian debtor claimed that it was not informed of the arbitration proceedings pending in the LCIA.

The applicant proved in the Ukrainian courts that all correspondence and documents in the arbitration proceedings were duly communicated by the LCIA to the respondent's legal counsel, whose powers were recognized by the LCIA. Moreover, the applicant provided the court with evidence that the request for arbitration and the arbitral award were duly sent by the LCIA to the Ukrainian debtor's legal address in Ukraine.

Ultimately, the Supreme Commercial Court of Ukraine allowed the application and held that the circumstances confirmed that the Ukrainian debtor was duly notified and represented during the arbitration proceedings.

C.   LOCAL ARBITRATION INSTITUTIONS

The International Commercial Arbitration Court at the Ukrainian Chamber of Commerce and Industry (the "ICAC" at the "UCCI") and the Maritime Arbitration Commission at the Ukrainian Chamber of Commerce and Industry (the "MAC" at the UCCI) are the two permanent Ukrainian international arbitration intuitions capable of handling arbitrations in Ukraine.

C. 1   The ICAC at the UCCI

The ICAC was founded in 1992. The Statute of the ICAC was adopted in 1994, along with the Law of Ukraine "On International Commercial Arbitration" ("ICAL"). The current edition of the Rules of Arbitration was adopted in 2007 and amended in 2012.

C. Local Arbitration Institutions

Types of Disputes Handled

The ICAC can decide any dispute that the parties refer to it, in accordance with the arbitrability rules prescribed by Ukrainian law. Typically, the ICAC handles a wide range of disputes, including international sale of goods, contract/service, carriage of goods, leases, insurance, joint ventures, financial arrangements, etc.

Numbers of Disputes Handled

The latest available statistics relate to the year of 2013, during which 428 arbitrations were instituted at the ICAC by parties located in 55 countries. Again during 2013 only, the ICAC issued awards in respect of 297 arbitrations.

Provisions on Confidentiality of Arbitration

Article 12 of the Rules of Arbitration imposes confidentiality obligations on the President of the ICAC, his or her deputies, arbitrators and secretariat staff.

Availability of Expedited Procedures

No rules on expedited procedure exist.

Consolidation of Disputes between the Same Parties and Joinder of Third Parties

Article 43 of the Rules of Arbitration provides that the essential element of joinder of third parties to the dispute is consent of all parties to the proceedings. Consent of the third party should be executed in writing. A motion for joinder of a third party can be filed only prior to the expiry of the deadline for filing the reply to the request for arbitration.

No rules governing the consolidation of disputes between the same parties exist.

Time Limits for Rendering of the Award

As provided in Article 13 of the Rules of Arbitration, the arbitral proceedings cannot continue for more than six months following the formation of the arbitration tribunal. This term can be extended, however, by the Presidium of the ICAC upon request of the arbitration tribunal or any of the parties.

Fee Structure

The Rules of the ICAC on Arbitration Fees and Costs govern the fee structure of arbitration proceedings. The fees levied by the ICAC from the parties are: (i) a registration fee (currently USD600), which must be paid upon the filing of the request for arbitration; and (ii) an arbitration fee, determined according to the value of the particular dispute (e.g., for disputes valued at USD500,001 – USD1 million, the fee is USD15,200 plus 1% of the claim's value).

Treatment of Costs of the Arbitration

The arbitration tribunal must deal with the distribution of arbitration costs and fees in the arbitral award. The arbitration fee will generally be compensated by the losing party, unless otherwise agreed by the parties. In case of partial satisfaction of the claims, the compensation will be proportionate to such satisfaction. Arbitration costs incurred by the parties may also be awarded against the losing party, to the extent that the tribunal deems reasonable.

Special or Unusual Features (If Any)

Not applicable.

Recent Developments (If Any)

Not applicable.

C. 2 The MAC at the UCCI

Background

The MAC at the UCCI was founded in 1994. It is governed by the Statute of the MAC, which was adopted in 1994, the ICAL, and the Rules of Arbitration (as amended in 2012).

Types of Disputes Handled

The MAC deals predominantly with commercial maritime disputes, including disputes arising from charter contracts, cargo shipping, maritime insurance, sale and pledge of sea vessels, etc.

Numbers of Disputes Handled

The latest available statistics relate to the year of 2012, during which the MAC administered 10 maritime arbitration proceedings.

Provisions on Confidentiality of Arbitration

Article 12 of the Rules of Arbitration applies as described at C.1 above.

Availability of Expedited Procedures

No expedited procedure is prescribed.

Consolidation of Disputes between the same Parties and Joinder of Third Parties

In relation to joinder of third parties, Article 43 of the Rules of Arbitration applies as described at C.1 above. No rules governing the consolidation of disputes between the same parties exist.

Time Limits for Rendering of the Award

Article 13 of the Rules of Arbitration applies as described at C.1 above.

Fee Structure

The Rules of the MAC on Arbitration Fees and Costs govern the fee structure of arbitration proceedings. The fees that are levied by the MAC from the parties are: (i) a registration fee (currently USD400), which must be paid along with filling of the request for arbitration, (ii) an arbitration fee, determined according to the value of particular dispute (e.g., for disputes valued at USD500,001 – USD1 million, the fee is USD14,600 plus 1% of the claim's value).

Treatment of Costs of the Arbitration

The arbitration tribunal must deal with the distribution of arbitration costs and fees in the arbitral award, in the same way as described at C.1 above.

Special or Unusual Features (If Any)

Not applicable.

Recent Developments (If Any)

Not applicable.

UNITED ARAB EMIRATES

Gordon Blanke[1] and Soraya Corm-Bakhos[2]

A. LEGISLATION, TRENDS AND TENDENCIES

A.1 Legislation

Arbitration in the UAE continues to be governed by specific provisions of the UAE Civil Procedures Code ("CPC").[3] A long-anticipated stand-alone federal arbitration law intended to remedy the current procedural defects of the CPC, and to bring legislation into line with prevailing international standards and best practice, is yet to be adopted.

A.2 Trends and Tendencies

In Dubai, the new Emirates Maritime Arbitration Centre ("EMAC") will contribute to, and broaden, the specialist maritime dispute resolution capabilities currently available in the

---

[1] Dr. Gordon Blanke, MCIArb, LLM., is sector leader of the International Arbitration Practice in Baker & McKenzie.Habib Al Mulla, Dubai and Abu Dhabi. He has wide-ranging experience in all types of international commercial arbitration, having acted as advising counsel under most leading institutional arbitration rules (including ICC, LCIA, DIAC, DIFC-LCIA, ADCCAC, GCC, SCC and JAMS Rules) and ad hoc arbitrations seated in the US, Europe and the Middle East in relation to a wide variety of industry sectors.

[2] Soraya Corm-Bakhos is a Senior Associate in Baker & McKenzie.Habib Al Mulla, Dubai. She specialises in both local and international commercial arbitration in a variety of industry sectors under major institutional arbitration rules (such as ICC, SCC, DIAC and ADCCAC) and ad hoc.

[3] Commonly referred to as the "UAE Arbitration Chapter". There have been no amendments to this legislation in 2014. For an article-by-article commentary on the UAE Arbitration Chapter, *see* G. Blanke, *Annotated Guide to Arbitration in the UAE - Volume I:The UAE Arbitration Chapter*, Thomson Reuters, 2014.

Emirate. It remains to be seen what institutional rules the EMAC rules of arbitration will be modelled on.[4]

An amendment[5] to the Law Concerning the Dubai International Financial Centre ("DIFC")[6] establishes a Dispute Resolution Authority comprised of the DIFC courts and an arbitration institute. It is not yet clear to what extent the arbitration institute will itself dispense arbitration services or whether it will be confined to promoting the profession and practice of arbitration within the DIFC only.[7]

A draft practice direction, expected to be adopted in January 2015, is another bold initiative by the DIFC to promote its arbitration capabilities.[8] The practice direction would allow a DIFC court judgment to be converted into a DIFC-LCIA arbitration award, which could then be enforced overseas through international enforcement instruments, including the New York Convention. If adopted, the Practice Direction would offer a court judgment creditor an alternative, possibly more attractive, method of enforcement.[9]

---

[4] *See* G. Blanke, *Dubai announces plans to establish Emirates Maritime Arbitration Centre: Do they hold water?*, Kluwer Arbitration Blog, 2 October 2014, electronically available at http:// kluwerarbitrationblog.com/blog/2014/ 10/02/dubai-announces-plans-to-establish-emirates-maritime-arbitration-centre-do-they-hold-water/.

[5] Dubai Law No. 7 of 2014.

[6] Dubai Law No. 9 of 2004 (as previously amended by Dubai Law No. 14 of 2011).

[7] For further detail, *see* G. Blanke, *DIFC introduces Arbitration Institute,* electronically available at http://kluwerarbitrationblog.com/blog/2014/06/04/difc-introduces-arbitration-institute/.

[8] No. X of 2014.

[9] *See* G. Blanke, *DIFC Court Practice Direction on the conversion of DIFC Court judgments into DIFC-LCIA awards goes full steam ahead!*, electronically available at http://kluwerarbitrationblog.com/blog/2014/07/20/the-difc-and-arbitration-raising-the-stakes-2/.

B. CASES

B.1 Extensions of Time in DIAC Arbitrations

In early 2014, the Dubai Court of Appeal confirmed the time extension provisions for rendering final awards under the Dubai International Arbitration Court (DIAC) Rules.[10] It held that arbitration proceedings may be extended for subsequent periods of six months at a time under Article 36.4 of the DIAC Rules. Although not discharged from general obligations of procedural expediency, arbitrators will have reassurance that in complex disputes extensions of time may be obtained in good measure.[11]

B.2 Recognition and Enforcement of Domestic and Foreign Awards

Two recent cases confirm the DIFC's status as host jurisdiction for the recognition of domestic and foreign arbitration awards.

In November 2014, an award creditor incorporated in Singapore sought from the DIFC courts an order for recognition and enforcement of a DIAC award that it had obtained against a UAE-based debtor.[12] The DIFC Court of Appeal found that the DIFC courts were not subject to any requirements for *in personam* or subject-matter jurisdiction, and it confirmed that the courts do have competence to hear

---

[10] *See* Dubai Court of Appeal, Case No. 249 of 2013, judgment of 15 January 2014 in *Middle East Foundations LLC v. Meydan Group LLC (formerly Meydan LLC)*.

[11] *See* G. Blanke, *Dubai Court of Appeal confirms time extension provisions under the DIAC Rules and other pro-arbitration dicta*, electronically available at http://kluwerarbitrationblog.com/blog/2014/04/28/dubai-court-of-appeal-confirms-time-extension-provisions-under-the-diac-rules-and-other-pro-arbitration-dicta/.

[12] *See* DIFC Court of Appeal, Case CA-005-2-14, ruling of 3rd November 2014, in *Meydan Group LLC v. Banyan Tree*.

actions for the ratification of domestic Dubai awards. This is so even if there is no apparent nexus with the DIFC and even if (as was the case here) it is not certain that the debtor has any assets there.

In another case, the DIFC Court of First Instance made a similar finding in relation to the ratification and enforcement of foreign awards rendered outside the UAE.[13]

There is some concern, however, that when the Dubai Courts are faced with a follow-on action for enforcement of such judgments in Dubai, they may seek to rely upon a public policy argument to the effect that any recognition and enforcement of an award obtained in Dubai or elsewhere properly rests with them and not the DIFC courts in cases where the award debtor's assets are located in mainland Dubai.[14]

C.   LOCAL ARBITRATION INSTITUTIONS

C.1   Dubai International Arbitration Centre ("DIAC")

Background

First created in 1994 as the Centre for Commercial Conciliation and Arbitration, DIAC is an autonomous, permanent nonprofit organization that has become the leader among arbitration centers in the UAE and wider Middle East and North Africa

---

[13]   *See* DIFC Court of First Instance, Case No. ARB 002/203, undated, 2014. No appeal of this decision was mounted by the award debtor within the prescribed time period.

[14]   *See* G. Blanke, *DIFC Court of Appeal confirms the DIFC's status as host jurisdiction for recognition of domestic awards*, electronically available at http://kluwerarbitrationblog.com/blog/2014/11/11/difc-court-of-appeal-confirms-the-difcs-status-as-host-jurisdiction-for-recognition-of-domestic-awards/.

region. It administers cases under the DIAC Arbitration Rules (DIAC Rules), which came into effect in May 1997.[15]

Types of Disputes Handled

Cases involve the widest range of contractual disputes in a variety of industry sectors including, in particular, real estate and construction.

Numbers of Disputes handled

DIAC administered 310 references in 2013 and 165 references up to December 8, 2014.

Provisions on Confidentiality of Arbitration

By agreeing to the DIAC Rules, unless they expressly agree otherwise in writing, the parties undertake to keep confidential all awards, materials and otherwise nonpublic documents, save for the usual exception where disclosure may be required "by legal duty, to protect or pursue a legal right or to enforce or challenge an award in bona fide legal proceedings before a state court or other judicial authority" (Article 41). The arbitral tribunal's deliberations are likewise confidential.

Availability of Expedited Procedures

A party can apply for the expedited formation of the tribunal where there is "exceptional urgency". The DIAC Executive Committee also has the discretion to adjust any time-limit imposed by the Rules (Article 12).

---

[15] Replacing the formerly applicable Rules of Commercial Conciliation and Arbitration of the Dubai Chamber and Industry No. 2 of 1994.

Provisions on Consolidation of Disputes between the Same Parties and Joinder of Third Parties

There are no provisions in the Rules relating to consolidation and joinder of third parties, but in practice, the DIAC has consolidated disputes.

Time Limits for Rendering of the Award

Under Article 36 of the DIAC Rules, the tribunal must render its award within six months from receipt of the file. This time limit may be extended by up to six months by the tribunal, and further extensions of up to six months at a time may be granted by the DIAC Executive Committee.

Fee Structure

Fees are determined by reference to the DIAC Table of Fees and Costs[16] and are based on a fixed percentage of the amounts in dispute. Each request to commence arbitration or to introduce a counterclaim must be accompanied by a non-refundable registration fee of AED5,000. The DIAC Executive Committee may depart from this general rule and fix the fees at a higher or lower figure than that which would result from a strict application of the DIAC Table of Fees and Costs (Article 3.3 of the DIAC Rules Appendix Costs of Arbitration).

Treatment of Costs of the Arbitration

The costs of the arbitration include the Centre's administrative fees and the tribunal's fees and expenses, including any experts appointed by it (Article 2.1). Under Article 4.1 of the DIAC Rules, the tribunal has the power to make decisions on costs at any time during the proceedings and Article 4.2 confirms that the "final award shall fix the costs of the arbitration and decide which

---

[16]   Contained in the DIAC Rules of Appendix Costs of Arbitration.

of the parties shall bear them or in what proportion they shall be borne by the parties". As reported in the 2013 Yearbook,[17] the Dubai Court of Cassation has confirmed that counsel fees in arbitrations are not recoverable under the DIAC Rules unless the tribunal has been granted a specific power to award such costs.

Special or Unusual Features (If Any)

Under Article 22 of the DIAC Rules, the tribunal must notify the parties of the date of a preliminary meeting within thirty days from the date of transmission of the file to the tribunal.[18] According to UAE case law, arbitrators should notify the parties of the date and venue of the first hearing within thirty days from accepting the arbitration.

Recent Developments (If Any)

There have been recent changes to the DIAC Board of Trustees, and Dr. Habib Al Mulla has been appointed as Chairman and is the first Emirati to hold that position. A new Director is expected to be appointed in early 2015, following the departure of the former Director, Mr. Nassib Ziade.

C.2 DIFC-LCIA Arbitration Centre

Background

The DIFC-LCIA Arbitration Centre launched on February 17, 2008 as a joint venture between the DIFC and LCIA. The DIFC-LCIA Rules are closely modelled on the LCIA Rules.

---

[17] See Gordon Blanke and Soraya Corm-Bakhos, "United Arab Emirates" in *Baker & McKenzie International Arbitration Yearbook 2013-2014*, Juris 2014, pp 345-357, at pp. 350-351.

[18] This complies with the arbitrators' obligation to hold a "first session" within the meaning of Article 208(1) of the CPC.

Types of Disputes Handled

Any contracting party, foreign or domestic, and whether or not connected to the DIFC, may arbitrate under the auspices of the DIFC-LCIA Arbitration Centre.[19] The Centre administers cases arising from the widest range of disputes in a variety of industry sectors.

Numbers of Disputes Handled

No statistics are available. However, only very few references have been made to date.

Provisions on Confidentiality of Arbitration

Article 30 of the DIFC-LCIA Rules expressly provides for the proceedings to be confidential. Unless the parties agree otherwise in writing, they undertake as a general principle to keep confidential all awards, materials and otherwise nonpublic documents. The deliberations of the tribunal are likewise confidential (Article 31).

Availability of Expedited Procedures

Article 9 of the DIFC-LCIA Rules allows a party to apply to the LCIA Court for the expedited formation of the tribunal if there is "exceptional urgency". The same Article also gives the LCIA Court the discretion to shorten any time-limit provided by the Rules.

Provisions on Consolidation of Disputes between the same Parties and Joinder of Third Parties

The tribunal has the power to allow one or more third persons to be joined in the arbitration (Article 22).

---

[19]   DIFC Arbitration Law No. 1 of 2008.

C. Local Arbitration Institutions

Time Limits for Rendering of the Award

There is no specified time limit for rendering the award.

Fee Structure

The DIFC-LCIA Arbitration Centre Schedule of Arbitration Costs provides for a registration fee of AED9,750.[20] Administrative charges are determined by the LCIA Court on a time-spent basis and at an hourly rate of AED1,300 for Registrar/Deputy Registrar/Counsel and AED650 for other secretarial personnel. Tribunal fees are also charged on a time-spent basis at rates appropriate to the particular circumstances of the case. The fee rates for arbitrators range between AED1,085 and AED2,525 per hour.

Treatment of Costs of the Arbitration

Unless the parties agree otherwise, the tribunal will determine each party's costs (including legal and other costs) depending on the Parties' relative success and failure in the award or arbitration, unless specific circumstances dictate otherwise (Article 28).

Special or Unusual Features (If Any)

None.

Recent Developments (If Any)

It is expected that the DIFC-LCIA Rules will be amended to take account of the new LCIA Arbitration Rules,[21] in particular to enable the appointment of an emergency arbitrator.

---

[20] Payable in advance on filing the Request for Arbitration.

[21] Which came into force on October 1, 2014.

C.3 The Abu Dhabi Commercial Conciliation & Arbitration Centre ("ADCCAC")

Background

The ADCCAC was established on February 19, 1993 by the Abu Dhabi Chamber of Commerce and Industry ("ADCCI"). On October 20, 2013 the ADCCAC introduced new Procedural Regulations of Arbitration (the "New Rules").

Types of Disputes Handled

The ADCCAC administers the widest range of commercial disputes and is the preferred arbitration centre for disputes involving the Abu Dhabi government and related entities.

Numbers of Disputes Handled

No statistics are available.

Provisions on Confidentiality of Arbitration

Article 33 of the New Rules expressly provides that awards, all materials, documents, expert reports, witness statements, records and all procedures are confidential unless the parties agree otherwise in writing and unless otherwise required by law.

Availability of Expedited Procedures

No expedited procedures are available under the New Rules.

Provisions on Consolidation of Disputes between the Same Parties and Joinder of Third Parties

The New Rules contain no provisions on the consolidation of disputes between the same parties and joinder of third parties.

C. Local Arbitration Institutions

Time Limits for Rendering of the Award

The tribunal must render its award within six months from receipt of the file (Article 27). This time limit may be extended by the tribunal by up to three months, and further extensions may be granted by the ADCCAC Committee upon request.

Fee Structure

Tribunal fees are based on a fixed percentage of the amounts in dispute. There is a minimum fee of AED125,000 for a three-member tribunal and of AED50,000 for a sole arbitrator for disputes up to AED1 million. There is also a non-refundable registration fee of AED1,000, and the ADCCAC will charge an administrative fee of 15% of the tribunal's fees.

Treatment of Costs of the Arbitration

The New Rules give the tribunal the power to award arbitration "costs" and "expenses". However, Article 28 provides no further explanation of what specific types of costs are included.[22]

Special or Unusual Features (If Any)

Article 24 of the New Rules continues the practice of "open sessions" (the main mode of conducting proceedings before UAE courts). It is hoped that practitioners will interpret this to mean that hearings should be conducted as in any other international arbitration.

Recent Developments (If Any)

None.

---

22 Given the Dubai Court of Cassation's ruling that counsel fees are not recoverable under the DIAC Rules unless the tribunal is given a specific power to award them, it is unfortunate that the new Rules do not widen the definition of the "costs" and "expenses" of arbitration to include legal fees.

UNITED KINGDOM (ENGLAND AND WALES)

Ed Poulton, Ekaterina Finkel and Louise Oakley[1]

A. LEGISLATION, TRENDS AND TENDENCIES

International arbitration in England and Wales[2] continues to be governed by the Arbitration Act 1996 (the "Arbitration Act"), to which no legislative amendment was made in 2014.[3] The Arbitration and Mediation Services (Equality) Bill, however, currently proposes amendments regarding the application of equality legislation to arbitration and mediation services.

---

[1] Edward Poulton is a Partner in Baker & McKenzie's London office. He is a member of the Firm's International Arbitration Practice Group. Ekaterina Finkel and Louise Oakley are Associates in Baker & McKenzie's London office. Both Ekaterina and Louise act on a broad range of matters including both international arbitration and commercial litigation. The authors gratefully acknowledge the assistance of Matthew Totman, Emily Tilden-Smith, Matthew Foster and Jemma Purslow.

[2] England and Wales are two of the four countries that make up the United Kingdom. They have a common legal system, whereas the other two countries in the United Kingdom (Scotland and Northern Ireland) have separate systems. For the purposes of the current publication we intend only to refer to the laws of England and Wales. Any reference to "England" or "English" in this section should also be taken to include "Wales" or "Welsh".

[3] *See also*, the Civil Procedure Rules and Practice Direction, Part 62; the Arbitration Act 1996 (Commencement No. 1) Order 1996 SI 1006/3146; the High Court and County Courts (Allocation of Arbitration Proceedings) Order 1996 SI 1996/3 125; The Unfair Arbitration Agreements (Specified Amount) Order 1996 SI 1996/3211; Arbitration Act 1950, Part II Enforcement of Certain Foreign Awards.

B. CASES

B.1. Friendly Discussion as a Condition Precedent to Commencing Arbitration

The High Court recently upheld a contractual agreement to seek to resolve a dispute by friendly discussion prior to commencing arbitration.[4] An agreement for the sale and purchase of iron ore provided for arbitration in London under the ICC rules and that in case of any dispute, the parties "should first seek to resolve the dispute or claim by friendly discussion. If no solution can be arrived at between the Parties for a continuous period of 4 (four) weeks then the non-defaulting party can invoke the arbitration clause and refer the disputes to arbitration."

One of the parties referred the claim to arbitration, and the other challenged the jurisdiction of the arbitral tribunal under s.67 of the Arbitration Act. The court noted that English law does not generally recognize an agreement to negotiate, holding such agreements unenforceable due to a lack of certainty.[5] However, distinguishing previous English authority and referencing the recent approach of the courts of Australia[6] and Singapore[7] and some ICSID tribunals,[8] the court held that the agreement in the underlying contract was enforceable, as the agreement was not

---

[4] *Emirates Trading Agency Llc v Prime Mineral Exports Private Limited* [2014] EWHC 2104 (Comm).

[5] *Ibid.* at para. 39 .

[6] *Ibid.* at para. 42 citing *United Group Rail Services v Rail Corporation New South Wales* (2009) 127 Con LR 202.

[7] *Ibid.* at para 54 citing *International Research Corp. PLC v Lufthansa Systems Asia Pacific Pte Ltd.* [2012] SGHC 226 and *HSBC Institutional Trust Service v Toshin Development Singapore Pte Ltd.* [2012] 4 SLR 378.

[8] *Ibid.* at para 57 citing *Tulip Real Estate Investment and development Netherlands BV v Republic of Turkey* (ICSID Case No. ARB/11/28) at paras. 56-72.

incomplete or uncertain; an obligation to seek to resolve a dispute by friendly discussions in good faith has an identifiable standard, namely, fair, honest and genuine discussions aimed at resolving a dispute.[9] The fact that there was a time limit to the agreement to hold friendly discussions was an important factor in the court's decision.[10] The court also held that enforcement of such an agreement was in the public interest.[11] On the facts of the case, the court held that the condition precedent to arbitration had been satisfied.

B.2. Pathological Arbitration Clause Held to Be Invalid

In this case,[12] three individuals were parties to three agreements that contained identical governing law and jurisdiction clauses. The clauses stated that in the event of a dispute "the parties will endeavour to first resolve the matter through Swiss arbitration. Should a resolution not be forthcoming the courts of England shall have non-exclusive jurisdiction". One individual commenced proceedings in the English courts against the other parties, who applied for a stay of proceedings pursuant to s.9 of the Arbitration Act.

The court held that the sole question it had to consider was whether the clause constituted an "arbitration agreement" within the meaning of s.6(1) of that Act.[13] The judge held that the clause imposed no binding obligation on the parties to refer the dispute to arbitration, but merely envisaged that the parties "endeavour" to agree a form of arbitration between them in Switzerland.[14]

---

9   *Ibid.* at para. 64.

10 *Ibid.* at para. 63.

11 *Ibid.* at para. 64.

12 *Kruppa v Benedetti & Anpr* [2014] EWHC 1887 (Comm).

13 *Ibid.* at para. 1.

14 *Ibid.* at para. 12.

It was not possible to have an effective multi-tier clause consisting of one binding tier (i.e. arbitration) followed by another binding tier (i.e. litigation).[15] The court noted that the clause did not provide for the seat of the arbitration, the identity, number or qualification of arbitrators, or a designated court that could appoint an arbitrator in the absence of agreement between the parties.[16] It was these issues that the parties were to endeavor to agree, failing which the English court would have non-exclusive jurisdiction.

B.3   A High Threshold in Defining the Parties to an Arbitration Agreement

In this case,[17] two individuals argued that they and a third individual were bound by an arbitration agreement between two companies, which provided that "any dispute, controversy or claim arising between the Parties ... shall be finally settled by arbitration".[18] The court noted that it would only grant the anti-suit injunction if there was a high degree of probability that the individuals were bound by the arbitration agreement. The court found that the individuals were not "Parties" as defined in the main agreement and therefore were not bound by the arbitration clause; accordingly, it refused to grant the injunction. Interestingly, the court noted that, had the words "arising between the Parties" not been included, it might have been easier to conclude that the arbitration clause was intended to apply to affiliates of the companies, including the individuals.[19]

---

[15]   *Ibid.*

[16]   *Ibid.* at para. 14.

[17]   *Rochester Resources Limited, Viktor Vekselberg and Leonard Blavatnik v Leonid Lebedev and Coral Petroleum Limited* [2014] EWHC 2926 (Comm).

[18]   *Ibid.* at para. 19.

[19]   *Ibid. per Jonathan Hirst QC* at para. 47.

B. Cases

B.4 Courts of the Seat Appropriate Courts to Grant a Worldwide Freezing Order

The claimant applied to continue a worldwide freezing order ("WFO") against the respondent, a Zambian mine owner, in support of an LCIA arbitration seated in London.[20] The court considered whether there was a risk of dissipation of assets and found that there was. The court then considered whether, nevertheless, it was just and convenient to continue the WFO. The court found that it was, notwithstanding the fact that (i) the respondent's assets were almost exclusively located in Zambia and so enforcement would not take place in England, but in Zambia; and (ii) Zambia has a legal system based on English law, its courts could grant a WFO, and there was no evidence to suggest that the legal remedies available were inadequate. The court upheld the principle that the courts of the seat are an appropriate place to seek a freezing order over assets irrespective of where those assets are located.

B.5 The Test of a "More Difficult" Enforcement

The court more recently refused to grant a freezing order, even where the respondent had assets in England.[21] The dispute arose out of a contract between an Indian company and a Nigerian special purpose vehicle, the respondent, which provided for LCIA arbitration in London. The Indian company obtained an *ex parte* freezing injunction over assets owned by the respondent pending the conclusion of the arbitration proceedings and award. The High Court refused to continue the freezing order, a decision that was upheld by the Court of Appeal.

---

[20] *U&M Mining Zambia Ltd v Konkola Copper Mines Plc* [2014] EWHC 3250 (Comm).

[21] *IOT Engineering Projects Ltd v Dangote Fertilizer Ltd and another* [2014] EWCA Civ 1348 (Bailii).

The Court of Appeal confirmed that the first test was whether enforcement would be rendered "more difficult" if the freezing injunction was lifted. The court held that 'more difficult' meant "more difficult than usual", noting that enforcement was rarely straightforward. The court was not persuaded that the assets would be used other than in the ordinary course of business, as the respondent provided a suitable parent guarantee. The court also rejected the argument that the alleged difficulty of enforcing an award in Nigeria in itself justified the freezing order. The court relied on the fact that Nigeria was a party to the New York Convention and had enacted domestic legislation similar to English law to conclude that there was not sufficient evidence that enforcement in Nigeria would be particularly difficult.

B.6. Exhausting Arbitral Remedies before Challenging an Award

The High Court has given guidance, for the first time, on what it means to "exhaust" any available arbitral process of appeal or review in the context of ss. 70 and 73 of the Arbitration Act.[22] An award was issued by a tribunal appointed by the International Cotton Association ("ICA"). The buyer appealed the award under the ICA's bylaws, but failed to pay the advance on costs within the specified deadline. The ICA refused to extend the time limit and dismissed the appeal. The buyer challenged the award under ss. 67 and 68 of the Arbitration Act. In response, the seller argued that ss. 70(2)(a) and/or 73(2) prevented the buyer from bringing a challenge, as it had not exhausted an available arbitral process of review.

The court rejected this argument and allowed the challenge to proceed, holding that "section 70(2) is primarily about the order in which a party can turn to an arbitral process and court proceedings". The policy behind sections 70(2) and 73(2) was to

---

[22]   *A Ltd v B Ltd* [2014] EWHC 1870 (QB).

give the arbitral mechanism the opportunity to first correct itself, but not to exclude the court's review.

B.7 Issue Estoppel to Bar Enforcement

The High Court refused enforcement of an award, finding that a previous Austrian judgment refusing enforcement created an issue estoppel, or alternatively, that the award was not binding under section 103(2)(f) of the Arbitration Act.[23] This appears to be the first English case in which issue estoppel has been applied to bar enforcement.

The claimant obtained an award against the Czech Republic. In their arbitration agreement the parties had included an additional review process to take place after the issuance of the award. A dispute arose as to whether this review process had been validly commenced. The claimant attempted to enforce the award in Austria, but the Austrian Supreme Court refused enforcement, finding that an award could not be enforced or rejected by a national court if it could be challenged under an arbitral process of review. Additionally, the Austrian Supreme Court and, in earlier proceedings, the Municipal Court of Prague, ruled that issues regarding the review process should be determined by the review tribunal.

In proceedings to enforce the award in England, the court refused enforcement. It held that, where a foreign court decides that an award is not binding, there is no reason, providing the other conditions for issue estoppel are met, why that decision should not give rise to an issue estoppel between the parties.

B.8 Post-Award Interest Where Award Annulled at the Seat

More recently, the High Court found that it was not precluded from enforcing an award which had been set aside by a court at

---

[23] *Diag Human SE v Czech Republic* [2014] EWHC 1639 (Comm).

the seat and that post-award interest was, in principle, available, even though the awards in question did not provide for the payment of interest.[24]

The court considered in a preliminary hearing that four awards rendered by tribunals seated in Russia and subsequently annulled by the Russian courts could be enforced. It held that it should not recognize a court decision that potentially was, as argued by the claimant, contrary to natural justice and domestic concepts of public policy.[25] It also held that, although the arbitrators had not made a decision on whether to award interest, awarding interest would not have the effect of altering the arbitrators' decision. The court found that the claim to enforce the awards in England was a claim to enforce a debt and, although the circumstances in which the arbitrators declined to award interest may be relevant to the exercise of the court's discretion to award interest, there was no absolute bar to such an award.

C.   LOCAL ARBITRATION INSTITUTIONS

C.1   London Court of International Arbitration (the "LCIA")

Background

The heritage of the LCIA dates back to the late 19th century, when the Court of Common Council of the City of London set up a committee to draw up proposals for the establishment of a tribunal for the arbitration of both domestic and international commercial disputes. Today, the LCIA is one of the world's leading international institutions for commercial dispute resolution. It comprises the Company (concerned with the

---

[24]   *Yukos Capital SARL v OJSC Rosneft Oil Company* [2014] EWHC 1288 (Comm).

[25]   *Ibid. per Simon J* at para 20.

operation and development of the LCIA's business), the LCIA Court (whose functions include the appointing of tribunals, controlling costs and acting as final authority for the application of the LCIA Rules) and the Secretariat (headed by the Registrar, who is responsible for the day-to-day administration of disputes referred to the LCIA).

Types of Disputes Handled

As its name suggests, the LCIA typically deals with international disputes. An average of 80% of parties in pending LCIA cases are not of English nationality. The content of these disputes is varied and includes agreements relating to mining, labor services, offshore oil and gas, the sale and purchase of business assets and shares or commodities, joint ventures, construction and engineering, telecommunications, and professional services. The three areas that have traditionally given rise to the most LCIA referrals are commodity transactions, financial agreements, and joint ventures and shareholders' agreements. The most significant industry sector is the oil and gas industry, along with the broader energy and resources sector.

Numbers of Disputes Handled

2013 saw the LCIA's casework reach a record high of 290 arbitration referrals and 11 requests for mediation or other ADR.

Provisions on Confidentiality of Arbitration

Unless agreed otherwise by all parties in writing, hearings are held in private. As a general principle, all materials in the arbitration which are created or produced for the purpose of the arbitration are to be kept confidential. The deliberations of the tribunal are confidential to its members, unless required otherwise by any applicable law. The LCIA will not publish any award, in whole or part, without the prior written consent of all the parties and the tribunal.

Availability of Expedited Procedures

Prior to the constitution of the tribunal, it is permissible to apply for the expedited formation of a tribunal, for example to deal with any requirement for interim measures. There is also provision for the appointment of an emergency arbitrator. On a successful application to the LCIA Court in cases of "exceptional urgency" under Rule 9B, such an arbitrator would be appointed within three days. However, this Rule only applies to arbitration agreements concluded on or after October 1, 2014, unless parties to an earlier agreement have specifically agreed in writing to opt into it. It is also possible for parties to opt out of this provision.

Consolidation of Disputes between the Same Parties and Joinder of Third Parties

Where there are multiple ongoing arbitrations, these may be consolidated where all the parties agree in writing. In addition, the tribunal has the power to consolidate multiple arbitrations provided they have been commenced under the same arbitration agreement or under any compatible arbitration agreement(s) between the same disputing parties. If no tribunal has yet been formed, the LCIA Court may determine, after giving the parties a reasonable opportunity to state their views, that two or more arbitrations commenced under the same arbitration agreement, between the same parties and under the Rules can be consolidated. Third parties can be joined where an existing party applies for the joinder and the third party expressly consents. There is no need for other parties to also consent.

C. Local Arbitration Institutions

Time Limits for Rendering of the Award

Under the Rules, a final award is to be made "as soon as reasonably possible"[26] following the last submission from the parties. In practice, the length of time it takes for an award to be rendered varies considerably, depending on the nature of the case and the efficiency of the individual tribunal.

Fee Structure

The costs of an LCIA arbitration are determined in accordance with the Schedule of Costs.[27] A nonrefundable registration fee of £1,750 is payable with the Request for Arbitration. The administration fees of the Secretariat are determined by reference to the hourly rates of the Registrar, counsel or administrative staff. A sum equivalent to 5% of the fees of the tribunal (excluding expenses) is payable towards the LCIA's general overhead. The tribunal's fees will be calculated by reference to work done by the arbitrator(s), the complexity and factual matrix of the case, and the experience and qualifications of the arbitrator(s). The tribunal must agree the fee rates (not to exceed £450 per hour) in writing prior to its appointment.

Treatment of Costs of the Arbitration

The usual outcome in English arbitration is that the successful party recovers the majority (but usually not all) of its costs from the unsuccessful party. Accordingly, the unsuccessful party can expect to be liable for all of its own costs, the fees and expenses of the LCIA and the tribunal, and most of the costs of the other side.

---

[26] 2014 Rules, Article 15.10.

[27] Schedule available here: http://www.lcia.org/Dispute_Resolution_Services/schedule- of-costs.aspx.

Special or Unusual Features (If Any)

The Rules contain an Annex of General Guidelines (the "LCIA Guidelines") intended to "promote the good and equal conduct of the parties' legal representatives".[28] The provisions of the LCIA Guidelines largely mirror the optional International Bar Association Guidelines, but the LCIA Guidelines are novel in that they are mandatory. In the draft version, it was proposed to provide the tribunal with the power to remove a party's counsel, but it was suggested during consultation that this would lead to challenges under the Arbitration Act 1996 (particularly s.68). In the published version, sanctions are limited to a written reprimand or caution or "any other measure necessary to fulfil within the arbitration the general duties required of the Arbitral Tribunal under Articles 14.4(i) and (ii)".[29] It remains to be seen what impact the LCIA Guidelines will have and whether the sanctions will ensure compliance.

Recent Developments (If Any)

The LCIA Rules were amended in October 2014, replacing the previous Rules from 1998.

---

[28]   Annex, para. 1.

[29]   2014 Rules, Article 18.6.

UNITED STATES

Matthew G. Allison,[1] Justin Marlles[2] and Kyle Richard Olson[3]

A. LEGISLATION, TRENDS AND TENDENCIES

A.1 Legislation

The Federal Arbitration Act ("FAA"), implemented in 1925, continues as the controlling and well-established foundation for a strong national policy in favor of arbitration. In the last year, there has been no legislation that has advanced in any significant way to amend or alter the FAA or the broad acceptance of arbitration as a viable and well-accepted vehicle for resolution of both domestic and international disputes. State laws further encourage and promote arbitration as an acceptable mechanism for dispute resolution.

A.2 Trends and Tendencies

Many arbitral institutions have made rule changes in an attempt to better streamline arbitration, thereby making a more striking

---

[1] Matthew G. Allison is a Partner in Baker & McKenzie's Chicago office. Mr. Allison concentrates his practice on complex international and multi-jurisdictional arbitration and litigation. He has represented many foreign and multi-national corporations in arbitrations under the rules of the ICC, ICDR, HKIAC and other institutions.

[2] Justin Marlles is a Senior Associate in Baker & McKenzie's Houston office. His practice involves international litigation and arbitration, with a focus on clients in the energy industry. Justin previously served as in-house litigation counsel for BHP Billiton and Petrohawk Energy Corporation.

[3] Kyle Richard Olson is an Associate in Baker & McKenzie's Chicago office. Mr. Olson focuses his practice on international commercial arbitration and complex business litigation. He has represented multi-national companies in numerous international arbitrations that have gone to hearing, including disputes before the ICC and ICDR.

comparison to the costs and time delays experienced in litigation of disputes in US courts. The AAA unveiled an amended set of arbitral rules effective June 1, 2014. The express purpose of those rules was to make AAA and ICDR arbitration more efficient. Notably, the AAA's amended rules now expressly tailor discovery to a standard more akin to the International Bar Association ("IBA"). The International Institute for Conflict Prevention and Resolution ("CPR") and JAMS (formerly Judicial Arbitration and Mediation Services) also issued amended rules in 2014 with the express purpose of streamlining and economizing arbitral proceedings. These amendments are discussed later in this chapter.

B. CASES

B.1 Local Litigation Requirement in UK-Argentina BIT is Procedural

In *BG Group PLC v. Republic of Argentina*, 134 S. Ct. 1198 (2014), the Supreme Court reversed a decision by the United States Court of Appeals for the District of Columbia Circuit that had vacated a USD185 million ICSID award rendered under the UK-Argentina BIT due to the plaintiff's failure to comply with the BIT's local litigation requirement.

The award stemmed from Argentina's actions in 2000 and 2001, when it changed the currency to which foreign companies' in-country natural gas sales were pegged from US dollars to Argentine pesos. As a result, British gas company BG Group PLC filed an investor-state proceeding at ICSID against Argentina for breach of the UK-Argentina BIT's guarantee of fair and equitable treatment for foreign investors. Article 8 of the BIT required that foreign investors first submit any dispute with the Argentine government to the courts of Argentina for a period of eighteen months before commencing international arbitration. However, the arbitral tribunal waived this requirement on the grounds that Argentina had passed laws hindering foreigners' access to the Argentine courts. BG group eventually obtained a USD185 million award from the Washington, DC-seated arbitral tribunal. Argentina subsequently moved to vacate the award on the grounds that the tribunal lacked jurisdiction due to BG Group's failure to comply with the local litigation requirement.

Key to the Supreme Court's analysis was whether the dispute over Article 8 was one of arbitrability going to the core of Argentina's consent to arbitrate, in which case the decision of the ICSID tribunal was not binding on the US courts. Alternatively, if Article 8's local litigation clause was merely procedural in nature, the tribunal's decision to set aside the local litigation requirement would be entitled to extreme deference. The Supreme Court held that the BIT's local litigation requirement was procedural in nature, rejecting the notion that it was part of a standing offer to arbitrate by Argentina. The Court wrote that the local litigation requirement was merely procedural because it determines "when the contractual duty to arbitrate arises, not whether there is a contractual duty to arbitrate at all." As a result, the tribunal was the correct decision-maker, and its ruling was entitled to deference.

The Supreme Court's decision is one of the few occasions on which the highest court in the United States has dealt with interpretation of a BIT. It has also proven somewhat controversial because the Supreme Court reached its decision by applying pure domestic US contract law to interpreting the treaty's provisions, rather than the Vienna Convention on the Law of Treaties or other sources of international law.

B.2 Incorporation of Clause by Reference; No Waiver by Co-Defendants' Conduct

In the case of *Al Rushaid v. National Oilwell Varco, Inc.*, 2014 US App. LEXIS 12569, Case No. 13-20159 (5th Cir. July 2, 2014), the United States Fifth Circuit Court of Appeals ruled that an arbitration clause may be incorporated into a contract when that contract states it is "based on" a separate agreement containing the arbitration clause. The Fifth Circuit also found that a defendant could not be held to have waived its right to compel arbitration simply because it benefited from the actions of co-defendants who participated in litigation of that case at the trial court level.

Al Rushaid, part of a Saudi Arabian engineering and construction conglomerate, sued oilfield services company National Oilwell Varco, Inc. ("NOV") and its affiliates for breach of contract in the Texas courts. The contracts at issue were based on price quotes for work issued by NOV and its affiliates. These quotes were then accepted by Al Rushaid in the form of a purchase order. The price quote issued by NOV's Norwegian affiliate contained a provision stating that its terms and conditions were "based on" those set forth in another document that contained an ICC arbitration clause. NOV's Norwegian affiliate sought to compel arbitration based on this clause, even while the other NOV companies engaged in extensive discovery and other pre-trial activities.

By comparing the relatively brief terms and conditions of NOV Norway's price quote with the extensive set contained in the separate document with the arbitration clause, the appellate court concluded that use of the phrase "based on" was intended to mean that the two documents were actually part of the same contract. The Fifth Circuit determined that although the other NOV companies had engaged in extensive pre-trial activities including obtaining over 130,000 pages of documents from Al Rushaid, these activities could not be attributed to NOV Norway merely because it was an affiliated entity that would benefit from the actions of its co-defendants. The Fifth Circuit indicated that it would only be appropriate to attribute the pre-trial activities of the other NOV companies to NOV's Norwegian affiliate if they were alter egos of one another or if the corporate veil could be pierced, thereby setting a high bar for grouping related companies together when assessing whether the right to arbitrate a dispute has been waived.

B.3 Second Circuit Raises Threshold Required to Show Personal Jurisdiction

The United States Second Circuit Court of Appeals refused to enforce an arbitral award against a Turkish company on the grounds that it was not subject to personal jurisdiction in New York, in the case of *Sonera Holding B.V. v. Çukurova Holding A.Ş.*, 750 F.3d 221 (2d Cir. 2014). In reaching its decision, the Second Circuit applied the elevated standard for general personal jurisdiction requiring a defendant's contacts with the forum state for the litigation to be so substantial that the defendant is essentially "at home" there.

Sonera brought an ICC arbitration against Çukurova, successfully obtaining a USD932 million award from a Swiss-seated arbitral tribunal. Although Çukurova is based in Istanbul, Turkey and conducts no operations in New York, Sonera filed for recognition of the award in the United States District Court for the Southern District of New York as part of a global enforcement effort. Çukurova resisted enforcement of the award on the grounds that it was not subject to general personal jurisdiction in New York (no claim of specific personal jurisdiction appears to have been raised by Sonera). This defense was rejected by the lower court, which ruled that continuous and systemic contacts sufficient for a finding of general personal jurisdiction existed, including: Çukurova's negotiations with two New York private equity funds regarding the sale of an unrelated business; Çukurova's sale of American Depositary Shares to a London company, which subsequently offered them on the New York Stock Exchange; a contract between a US Company and an affiliate of Çukurova; a New York office location used by affiliates of Çukurova; and a claim by an affiliate of Çukurova that it was Çukurova's "gateway to the Americas."

The Second Circuit's inquiry focused on whether asserting personal jurisdiction over Çukurova would comply with due process. The Second Circuit concluded that it would not, relying on *Daimler AG v. Bauman*, 134 S. Ct. 746 (2014), in which the United States Supreme Court ruled that general jurisdiction only extends beyond an entity's state of incorporation and principal place of business when the entity's contacts with another state are so substantial as to make it "at home" there. The appellate court explained that Çukurova's limited contacts with New York did not make it "at home" there, holding that even a company's engagement in a substantial, continuous, and systemic course of business does not, by itself, make it "at home" in the forum state.

B.4 NY Convention Time Bar Does Not Apply to English Judgment Based on Award

The United States Court of Appeals for the District of Columbia Circuit, in *Commissions Import Export S.A. v. Republic of the Congo*, 757 F.3d 321 (DC Cir. 2014), examined the interplay between the New York Convention as implemented under US federal law, and the separate US state laws dealing with the recognition of judgments from non-US courts. In doing so, the DC Circuit ruled that the three-year limitations period for obtaining recognition of an international arbitration award in the federal statute implementing the New York Convention does not supersede the limitations periods of US state laws governing the recognition of foreign country judgments, even when that judgment is based on an arbitration award.

The roots of this case lie in an ICC award obtained in 2000 by Commissions Import Export S.A. against the Congolese government and Caisse Congolaise d'Amortissement, its financing bank, arising from the Republic of Congo's failure to pay for public works and supply materials. In 2009, Commissions Import Export S.A. obtained an English High Court judgment recognizing the award, and it filed suit two years later in the US in an effort to enforce the English High Court judgment. The Republic of Congo and its co-defendant argued that the federal law implementing provisions of the New York Convention should prevail.

The DC Circuit examined the purpose of the federal statute as intended by Congress, as well as whether the District of Columbia statute interfered with that purpose. The appellate court distinguished between recognition of an arbitral award itself and foreign court judgments based on that award, finding that the federal law could not be interpreted to extend beyond arbitral awards to foreign court judgments. Further, in reviewing the legislative history of the implementing provisions, the court emphasized remarks by the US State Department that the New York Convention and its implementing provisions were not intended to spread federal jurisdiction beyond areas where it did not already exist. The DC Circuit's decision is important because it offers award-holders a useful 'work-around' to avoid the relatively short three-year limitations period for commencing award recognition proceedings in US Courts.

B.5 Availability of Class Arbitration Must Generally Be Determined by Courts

In *Opalinski v. Robert Half International Inc.*, 761 F.3d 326 (3d Cir. 2014), the United States Third Circuit Court of Appeals considered the question of whether courts or arbitrators should decide if an arbitration agreement allows for class arbitration, a form of arbitration comparable to a class action with named claimants litigating on behalf of themselves and other unnamed but similarly situated individuals. The Third Circuit held there was a presumption that the gateway question of arbitrability of class claims should be answered by trial courts unless the arbitration agreement itself contains explicit language providing otherwise.

Opalinski and McCabe sued their former employer Robert Half in a class action on behalf of themselves and other similarly situated employees for failing to pay for overtime work as required by federal law. The defendant sought to compel arbitration of only Opalinski and McCabe's claims, with the plaintiffs arguing in response that the arbitrator was entitled to hear the full range of class claims brought on behalf of the named plaintiffs and numerous other unnamed employees. The US District Court for the District of New Jersey opined that the determination of whether a class arbitration could take place belonged to the arbitrator.

The Third Circuit reversed. First, the appellate court asked whether the issue at hand involved a "question of arbitrability." It answered this in the affirmative, explaining that courts should be "wary" of requiring parties to submit to class arbitration, and describing class arbitration as so radically different from other forms of arbitration that there can be no assumption it is allowed merely because the parties signed onto a standard arbitration clause. Second, the Third Circuit asked if the parties had clearly and unmistakably provided for the arbitrator to decide questions of arbitrability. Because the clause in question did not contain explicit language delegating questions of arbitrability to the arbitrator, the Third Circuit opined that this issue did not belong to the arbitrator. The Third Circuit decision is important because it is only the second time that a federal court of appeals has addressed the issue of who decides if a class arbitration can proceed.

C. LOCAL ARBITRATION INSTITUTIONS

The United States is home to several international arbitration institutions. Chief among them are the International Center for Dispute Resolution ("ICDR"), JAMS, and the International Institute for Conflict Prevention and Resolution ("CPR"). These institutions enjoy strong reputations among US and international businesses for administering, and resolving, international arbitral disputes.

C.1   ICDR

Background

The ICDR was established in 1996 as the international arm of the AAA. Headquartered in New York City, it provides arbitration and mediation services in more than 80 countries and employs a staff fluent in 14 languages. The ICDR is comprised of a worldwide panel of more than 600 independent arbitrators and provides a party-centered process over a broad range of industries and legal issues.

Types of Disputes Handled

Under the umbrella of the AAA, the ICDR handles a full range of types of international commercial disputes.

Numbers of Disputes Handled

In 2013, the ICDR received 1,165 arbitral demands. This represents a 17% increase from 2012.

Provisions on Confidentiality of Arbitration

The ICDR rules generally place confidentiality obligations on the arbitrators and ICDR administrators, but do not do so for the parties themselves (ICDR International Arbitration Rule 34.)

Availability of Expedited Procedures

The most recent version of the ICDR international arbitration rules, which became effective June 1, 2014, provides for expedited procedures. The expedited procedure provides for the appointment of a sole arbitrator and requires that arbitrator to issue a procedural order within 14 days of his or her appointment. The parties then have 60 days to make written submissions unless the arbitrator deems there to be a need for additional time. In cases with claims or counterclaims exceeding USD100,000, an oral hearing may also be held. The hearing must take place within 60 days from the procedural order's issuance and must not last more than one day absent permission by the arbitrator for more time. Upon the close of hearing (if one is held), or upon the date of the final written submissions, the arbitrator must issue an award within 30 days unless a different time frame is agreed to by the parties.

Consolidation of Disputes between the Same Parties and Joinder of Third Parties

Rule 8 allows a party to request appointment of a "consolidation arbitrator" who may consolidate multiple pending AAA (and ICDR) arbitrations into one proceeding. The ICDR has the discretion to consolidate if at least one of the following has happened: the parties have agreed to consolidate; all of the claims were made under the same arbitration agreement; or, in the event that claims are made under different arbitration agreements, the claims involve the same parties, the disputes arise in connection with the same legal relationship, and the tribunal concludes that the arbitration agreements are compatible.

Rule 7 entitles a party to join a third party to the arbitration. The joinder request must occur prior to the appointment of the tribunal. If it does not, the parties, including the third party subject to the joinder request, must agree to the joinder.

Time Limits for Rendering of the Award

Unless otherwise agreed by the parties, specified by law or determined by the ICDR, the tribunal must issue a final award within 60 days of the close of the hearing (Rule 30).

Fee Structure

The ICDR has two administrative fee options for a claimant or counterclaimant: the Standard Fee Schedule and the Flexible Fee Schedule. The Standard Fee Schedule has a two-payment schedule, whereas the Flexible Fee Schedule has a three-payment schedule that offers lower initial filing fees but possibly higher total administrative fees. The ICDR's administrative fees are based on the amount of the claim or counter-claim, and do not include arbitrator compensation.

Treatment of Costs of the Arbitration

Absent agreement to the contrary, parties arbitrating before the ICDR generally must bear their own costs. However, Rule 20 gives the tribunal the discretion to impose costs on a party where it fails to make "every effort to avoid unnecessary delay and expense in the arbitration."

Special or Unusual Features

The ICDR now permits parties to agree to allow each other to appeal the arbitral award to an ICDR appeal tribunal.

Recent Developments

The June 1, 2014 Rules included an amended Rule 22. which expressly limits discovery to documents "relevant and material to the outcome of the disputed issues", consistent with the standard embraced by the IBA Rules. In addition, the ICDR (and AAA more broadly) now offer Optional Appellate Arbitration Rules that permit appellate review of arbitration awards by a special appeal tribunal.

C.2   JAMS

Background

Formerly known as Judicial Arbitration and Mediation Services, Inc., JAMS was founded in the US in 1979 and is the largest private provider of mediation and arbitration services worldwide. JAMS is a for-profit organization headquartered in Irvine, California, with 28 offices in total, including large centers within its international affiliate, JAMS International, in Toronto and London. JAMS employs nearly 300 full-time neutrals, including retired judges, along with 195 associates.

Types of Disputes Handled

JAMS handles multi-party, complex cases in virtually all areas of the law.

Numbers of Disputes Handled

On average, JAMS handles 12,000 cases—including both arbitration and mediation—annually in locations around the world.

C. Local Arbitration Institutions

Provisions on Confidentiality of Arbitration

The JAMS International Rules address confidentiality of an arbitration, specifically stating that the Tribunal and the administrator "will maintain the confidentiality of the arbitration" (JAMS International Rules, Article 16.1.) Article 16.2 of JAMS' International Rules also provides that the arbitration award, unless otherwise required by law, "will remain confidential unless all the parties consent to its publication." However, the JAMS rules do not specifically require the parties to maintain confidentiality of the arbitration.

Availability of Expedited Procedures

JAMS provides an Optional Expedited Arbitration Procedure in which parties can choose a process that limits discovery. The parties may include a request for such procedure in their arbitration agreement (JAMS Rule 16.1(a).) The parties can also opt into the expedited procedures by "indicating the election in the Demand for Arbitration" (JAMS Rule 16.1(b).) If one party elects the expedited procedures and "any other party" does not agree to them, "each Party shall have a client or client representative present at the First Preliminary Conference" (JAMS Rule 16.1(c).) Although the JAMS rules do not explicitly say so, it appears that JAMS then has the discretion to determine at the First Preliminary Conference whether to proceed with the expedited procedures.

The Arbitrator "shall set a discovery cutoff" not to exceed 75 calendar days after the Preliminary Conference for fact discovery, and 105 calendar days for any expert discovery (JAMS Rule 16.2(g).) The expedited Hearing must occur within 60 calendar days after the fact discovery cutoff date and, if more than one day, must be handled in consecutive days (JAMS Rule 16.2(i).)

Consolidation of Disputes between the Same Parties and Joinder of Third Parties

JAMS' International Arbitration Rules provide for consolidation of disputes and joinder of third parties. Article 6.1 provides the JAMS International administrator with the discretion to decide, "after consulting with the parties to all proceedings and with the arbitrators, that the new case will be referred to the Tribunal already constituted for the existing proceedings" (JAMS International Rules Article 6.1.) The Article requires JAMS to "take into account all circumstances, including the links between the two cases and the progress already made in the existing proceedings."

Additionally, Article 6.2 of the JAMS International Rules provides for joinder of third parties in two circumstances. First, if a third party that "seeks to participate in an arbitration already pending" requests to join, the Tribunal must "decide on such request, after consulting with all the parties, taking into account all circumstances it deems relevant and applicable" (JAMS International Rules Article 6.2.) Second, if a party to an already pending arbitration "intends to cause a third party to participate in the arbitration" and requests accordingly, the Tribunal must likewise decide on the joinder using the same guidance criteria.

Time Limits for Rendering of the Award

JAMS International Arbitration Rules states that "the final award should be rendered within three months" after the dispute is heard by the Tribunal and submitted for decision.

Fee Structure

In JAMS International proceedings, the claimant bears a non-refundable USD1000 filing fee per party at the commencement of the case, with 10% professional and administrative fees billed in advance periodically as the case progresses. The professional fees include time spent for hearings, pre- and post- hearing reading and research, and award preparation. The administrative fees include access to an international panel of judges, attorneys and other ADR experts, administration through the duration of the case, and use of JAMS conference facilities (JAMS International Arbitration Rules, Article 33.)

Treatment of Costs of the Arbitration

Article 34 defines arbitration "costs" as consisting of, among other things, the Tribunal's fees as well as the "reasonable costs for legal representation of a successful party". The Tribunal's fees are calculated "by reference to work done by its members in connection with the arbitration" and "will be charged at rates appropriate to the particular circumstances of the cases including its complexity and the special qualifications of the arbitrators" (JAMS International Rules Article 34.2.) Under Article 34.4, the Tribunal is required to "fix the arbitration costs in its award." Importantly, under that same Article, the Tribunal "may" apportion costs "among the parties" if the Tribunal "determines that such apportionment is reasonable, taking into account the circumstances of the case."

Special or Unusual Features

Consistent with JAMS' high resolution rate in mediating complex business disputes to resolution, JAMS applies a unique "mediator in reserve policy" for international arbitrations.

Recent Developments

On July 1, 2014, JAMS made effective its latest version of the Comprehensive Arbitration Rules and Procedures. The JAMS rules now permit the arbitral hearing to be conducted by videoconference and/or by telephone. Further, parties can agree to use the JAMS Optional Arbitration Appeal Procedure at any time, which differs from the previous requirement that parties had to agree to the Optional Appeal Procedures prior to the final award (JAMS Rule 34.) Finally, JAMS' Expedited Procedures were amended to clarify that any party may request the procedure's application (JAMS Rule 16.1-2.)

C.3   CPR

Background

CPR is a nonprofit alternative dispute resolution institute that was founded in 1979 with the aim of lowering the cost of litigation for businesses. It now provides arbitration and mediation services across a range of commercial disputes, and offers a dual set of rules that govern both nonadministered (*ad hoc*) and administered disputes. CPR offers a diverse panel of more than 600 "distinguished neutrals", hailing from more than 20 countries, to preside over business disputes in more than 20 specialized practice areas. These neutrals include former judges, prominent attorneys and academics.

Types of Disputes Handled

CPR handles the full range of international commercial disputes.

Numbers of Disputes Handled

No statistics are readily available.

Provisions on Confidentiality of Arbitration

Rule 20 of the CPR Rules for Administered Arbitration of International Disputes ("CPR Rules") expressly provides for confidentiality in arbitration. Unlike the counterpart rules from the ICDR and JAMS above, however, Rule 20 of the CPR Rules requires the parties, as well as the arbitrators and CPR administrators, to "treat the proceedings, any related disclosure and the decisions of the Tribunal, as confidential" except when used in ancillary judicial proceedings. The rule takes comparatively greater care in ensuring the confidentiality of the entire proceeding and further provides that "to the extent possible, any specific issues of confidentiality should be raised with and resolved by the Tribunal" (CPR Rule 20.)

Availability of Expedited Procedures

The CPR Rules do not specifically provide for expedited procedures. CPR Rule 9.2 merely states that the "Tribunal is empowered to impose reasonable time limits on each phase of the proceeding, including without limitation, the time allotted to each party for presentation of its case and for rebuttal." The Rule continues: "In setting time limits, the Tribunal should bear in mind its obligation to manage the proceeding efficiently in order to complete proceedings as economically and expeditiously as possible" (CPR Rule 9.2.) In addition, the CPR must approve any extensions beyond one year from the constitution of the Tribunal (CPR Rule 15.8(b).)

Consolidation of Disputes between the Same Parties and Joinder of Third Parties

The CPR Rules contain provisions that address consolidation of disputes and joinder of third parties. CPR Rule 3.13 empowers the CPR with the discretion to consolidate "two or more arbitrations pending under these Rules into a single arbitration" at the "request of a party and following consultation with the parties." To be sure, such discretion to consolidate is not triggered unless at least one of the following is present: the parties agreed to consolidate; all of the claims in the arbitrations are made under the same arbitration agreement; or the claims in the arbitration arise "in connection with the same legal relationship" and the "CPR finds the arbitration agreements to be compatible" (CPR Rule 3.13(a)(1)-(3).) Moreover, in exercising its discretion to consolidate, the CPR "may" consider "any circumstances it considers to be relevant", including the "existence of common issues of law or fact creates the possibility of conflicting decisions in the separate arbitration proceedings," and the "risk of undue delay or prejudice to the rights of or hardship to the parties opposing consolidation" outweighing the "prejudice resulting from failure to consolidate" (CPR Rule 3.13(b).)

With respect to joinder, the CPR has the discretion to permit one or more third parties to be joined to the arbitration where a (current) party makes a joinder request prior to the appointment of "any arbitrator" (CPR Rule 3.12(a).) A third party sought to be joined "after the appointment of any arbitrator" can only be joined where all parties, including the third party, so agree (CPR Rule 3.12(a).)

Time Limits for Rendering of the Award

The CPR Rules provide that the "final award should in most circumstances be rendered within 12 months of the constitution of the Tribunal" (CPR Rule 15.8(a).)

Fee Structure

The CPR provides for a flat fee structure based on the amount in dispute, with a USD1,750 filing fee applying in all cases. Arbitrators are compensated on a "reasonable basis determined at the time of appointment", and the parties are jointly and severally responsible for such fees (CPR Rule 17.1.) The Tribunal "shall determine the necessary advances on the arbitrator(s) fees and expenses and advise CPR which, unless otherwise agreed by the parties, shall invoice the parties in equal shares" (CPR Rule 17.2.) Moreover, administrative expenses are capped at USD34,000 absent special circumstances; and the Tribunal "shall invoice the parties in equal shares" for the administrative expenses unless the parties agree otherwise (CPR Rule 18.2.)

Treatment of Costs of the Arbitration

The CPR Rules require the Tribunal to "fix the costs of arbitration in its award" (CPR Rule 19.1.) The CPR Rules permit the Tribunal to "apportion the costs of arbitration between or among the parties in such manner as it deems reasonable" absent an agreement otherwise by the parties (CPR Rule 19.2.)

Special or Unusual Features

The CPR provides "expert panels"—experienced neutrals on CPR's global and industry-specific panels—while still allowing parties to designate for appointment any arbitrators of their choosing. In addition, the CPR offers a "screened" arbitrator selection process to address concerns about the party appointment process. Under this "screened" process, parties may agree that the arbitrators can be appointed without knowing which party selected them.

Recent Developments

On December 1, 2014, CPR issued a new set of Rules entitled "Administered Arbitration of International Disputes" to further its status as a leader in global dispute resolution. Drawing from UNCITRAL, as well as best arbitration practices generally, CPR implemented these rules with a view to offering a comparatively expeditious and cost-efficient arbitration process.

UZBEKISTAN

Alexander Korobeinikov[1]

A. LEGISLATION, TRENDS AND TENDENCIES

A.1 Legislation

Arbitration proceedings involving at least one Uzbek party are regulated in Uzbekistan by the Law on Arbitration Courts (the "Law"), which was adopted in 2006.

The main provisions of the Law are based on UNCITRAL Model Law principles, but there are some significant differences. For example, an arbitral tribunal may only apply Uzbekistan legislation, and violation of this rule is a ground for setting aside an award. In addition to the Law, arbitration is regulated by the relevant provisions of the Civil Procedural Code and the Commercial Procedural Code.

In May 2014, provisions of the Law, the Civil Procedure Code and the Commercial Procedural Code that set forth rules for issuance of interim measures orders for security of claims in the framework of arbitration proceedings were amended. The effect of these amendments was that such interim measures orders can only be issued by the state courts in the place of the location of the defendant, or at the place of location of its assets.

A.2 Trends and Tendencies

There is no specific legislation that sets forth rules for international arbitration proceedings in Uzbekistan. Therefore, Uzbek authorities are currently considering adopting a specific

---

[1] Alexander Korobeinikov is a Senior Associate in Baker & McKenzie's Almaty office and a member of Baker & McKenzie's International Arbitration practice group.

law regulating international arbitration and the enforcement of foreign awards.

Additionally, the Uzbek Parliament is considering amendments to Article 10 of the Law on Guarantees and Measures for the Protection of the Rights of Foreign Investors (the "Law on Guarantees and Measures"). The current wording of Article 10 allows foreign investors to interpret it as the Uzbek Government's consent to settle foreign investors' claims under the ICSID Convention. While the Uzbek Constitutional Court issued a decision in 2006 which stated that the provisions of the Law on Guarantees and Measures could not be interpreted in this way, the Uzbek Parliament is going to amend the wording of this Article to avoid any misinterpretation.

B.   CASES

B.1   Investment Arbitration Cases

In 2014, one of the biggest investment arbitration claims ever filed against Uzbekistan was settled amicably. The Russian telecommunication company, Mobile TeleSystem, and the Uzbek Government executed a settlement agreement whereby they agreed to establish a joint venture company which would be allowed to provide telecommunication services in Uzbekistan.

Aside from this, there have been no significant investment arbitration decisions involving Uzbekistan in the last year. However, we are awaiting the decision in the investment arbitration case of *Oxus Gold PLC v Republic of Uzbekistan*, which was heard in early 2014. This case concerns a claim by UK company Oxus Gold PLC, under the UNCITRAL Rules of Arbitration for compensation for loss of its investment in: (i) the Amantaytau Goldfields project in the Kyzylkum desert; and (ii) the Khandiza base metals project in the Surkhandarya region.

C. Local Arbitration Institutions

Four other investment arbitration cases are currently pending before ICSID against Uzbekistan, including *Vladislav Kim & others* v *Republic of Uzbekistan.*[2] The claimants in this case are seeking compensation for expropriation of their cement production business, located in Uzbekistan. The tribunal will address Uzbekistan's objections to jurisdiction as a preliminary question, and therefore the proceedings on the merits were suspended in September 2014.

B.2 Uzbek Court Practice Relating to Arbitration

Since the legal basis for arbitration in Uzbekistan was formed relatively recently, Uzbek courts do not have significant experience applying these laws, meaning that their practice is disputable and inconsistent. In addition, Uzbek court decisions are not usually publicly disclosed in Uzbekistan. Therefore, we are not aware of any significant Uzbek court decisions in relation to arbitration in the last year.

C. LOCAL ARBITRATION INSTITUTIONS

After adoption of the Law in 2006 and relevant sub-laws regulating the procedure of establishing and registering arbitration institutions, the number of arbitration institutions registered in Uzbekistan significantly increased, and currently there are around 50 arbitration institutions. However, as in most other CIS countries, the most popular of them are two arbitration institutions established by the local Chamber of Commerce and Industry: the Domestic Arbitration Court ("the DAC") and the International Commercial Arbitration Court ("the IAC").

---

[2] (ICSID Case No. ARB/13/6), the others are: Federal Elektrik Yatırım ve Ticaret A.Ş. and others v. Republic of Uzbekistan (ICSID Case No. ARB/13/9); Spentex Netherlands, B.V. v. Republic of Uzbekistan (ICSID Case No. ARB/13/26); and Güneş Tekstil Konfeksiyon Sanayi ve Ticaret Limited Şirketi and others v. Republic of Uzbekistan (ICSID Case No. ARB/13/19).

C.1 The DAC and the IAC

Background

The DAC was established in 2007 shortly after adoption of the Law, to arbitrate domestic disputes. In 2011, the Uzbek Chamber of Commerce and Industry decided to establish the IAC to review disputes in which at least one of parties is a foreign company.

Types of Disputes Handled

The DAC and the IAC handle all types of commercial disputes between local and foreign companies, except disputes which are non-arbitrable under Uzbek law (e.g., disputes relating to registration of rights over immovable property, challenge of decisions of state authorities, etc.).

Numbers of Disputes Handled

Between 2007 and 2014, the DAC and the IAC (along with their regional branches) handled around 5,000 cases.

Provisions on Confidentiality of Arbitration

Under the Law and the Rules of Arbitration of the DAC and the IAC, confidentiality applies to all documents and information disclosed by parties during the arbitration proceedings, as well as the arbitral award. Additionally, arbitrators cannot provide witness statements regarding information received during the arbitration proceedings.

Availability of Expedited Procedures

Expedited procedures are not available under the Rules of Arbitration of either the DAC or the IAC.

C. Local Arbitration Institutions

Consolidation of Disputes between the Same Parties and Joinder of Third Parties

The DAC and the IAC Rules of Arbitration do not contain any special rules relating to consolidation of disputes and joinders of third parties.

Time Limits for Rendering of the Award

Under the IAC Rules of Arbitration, the general period for rendering an award is 120 days from the date of the constitution of the tribunal. However, this term may be extended by the Presidium of the IAC. The DAC Rules of Arbitration do not provide any time limits for rendering the award, stating only that the award is to be issued as soon as possible after the constitution of the tribunal.

Fee Structure

The arbitration fees for disputes handled by the DAC are 1% of the amount of the claim. For disputes handled by the IAC, depending on the amount of the claim, the rate varies from 1% to 3% of the amount of the claim. For members of the Uzbek Chamber of Commerce and Industry, these rates are reduced by 25%.

Treatment of Costs of the Arbitration

Under the DAC and the IAC Rules of Arbitration, the tribunal orders the costs of the arbitration to be borne by the claimant in the arbitration proceedings in proportion to the amount of its claim granted by the tribunal. For example, if the claimant is awarded 60% of the amount claimed, it is responsible for 40% of the costs. If a claimant is wholly successful, the respondent is responsible for the entirety of the parties' costs.

Special or Unusual Features (If Any)

There are no special or unusual features of either the DAC or IAC, except as described above.

Recent Developments (If Any)

There are no recent developments.

VENEZUELA

Henry Torrealba[1] and Edmundo Martínez[2]

A. LEGISLATION, TRENDS AND TENDENCIES

A.1 Legislation

Commercial arbitration in Venezuela continues to be governed by the Law on Commercial Arbitration ("LCA") (April 7, 1998; Official Gazette No. 36.530) based on the UNCITRAL Model Law. The LCA governs domestic and international arbitration.

Foreign arbitral awards continue to be enforceable in Venezuela without need for an exequatur. Enforcement may only be denied for the reasons provided for in Article 49 of the LCA.

Venezuela is a party to the following treaties relating to arbitration: the New York Convention; the Inter-American Convention on Extraterritorial Validity of Foreign Judgments and Arbitral Awards and the Panama Convention.

Venezuela became a member of Mercosur in August 12, 2012. On July 30, 2012, the National Assembly passed the Law Approving the Amendment of the Los Olivos Protocol for the Settlement of Disputes signed in Brasilia on January 19, 2007. According to the provisions of the Protocol in force, the State of

---

[1] Henry Torrealba L. is a Principal in Baker & McKenzie's Caracas office. He heads the Civil, Commercial and Criminal Litigation Department of the office. He has acted as president of arbitral tribunals and sole or co-arbitrator in several arbitrations before the Arbitration Center of the Caracas Chamber.

[2] Edmundo Martinez is a local Partner in Baker & McKenzie's Caracas office. He is a member of the Civil, Commercial and Criminal Litigation Department of the office. He is also a member of the Firm's Trademark Practice Group, International Arbitration Practice Group and also the Global Dispute Resolution Practice Group.

Venezuela and its individuals, through the procedures established, can access this mechanism for the settlement of disputes arising in the interpretation and application of the Mercosur rules.

In relation to investment arbitration, Venezuela withdrew from ICSID on July 24, 2012. However, ICSID arbitration is still applicable for: (a) those contracts in which the parties expressly agreed to that remedy; and (b) cases concerning BITs that specify the ICSID for the resolution of investment disputes.

A.2 Trends and Tendencies

Domestic arbitration has become a very common mechanism to resolve commercial disputes in Venezuela. Several rulings from the Constitutional Chamber of the Supreme Court have supported arbitration and remarked that, according to the Constitution, the law will promote arbitration. There is a trend from the government, however, to exclude disputes related to real estate lease agreements from arbitration.

A draft for a Civil Procedural Code, recently filed for discussions by the Civil Chamber of the Supreme Court to the National Assembly, derogates from the arbitration rules contained in the current Code that give competence to ordinary trial courts. Therefore, if the draft is approved as it is, the only applicable rules for arbitration will be those contained in the LCA.

In relation to foreign investment arbitration, the government continues to avoid international arbitration for resolving foreign investment disputes with the State. Indeed, the Law of Foreign Investments, published in Official Gazette No. 6.152, Extraordinary of November 18, 2014, enacted by the President in the execution of the Enabling law of November 19, 2013, included a provision (Article 5) that the foreign investment will be subject to the jurisdiction of the courts of the country.

That provision also establishes that "...The Bolivarian Republic of Venezuela may participate and use other mechanisms to resolve disputes within the frame of the integration of Latin America and the Caribbean." Since domestic arbitration is included in the justice system, it is possible to argue that this provision does not restrict foreign investment disputes from being resolved by local arbitral tribunals.

B. CASES

Last year, there were no relevant court decisions in Venezuela in relation to arbitration.

C. LOCAL ARBITRATION INSTITUTIONS

The most important arbitral institutions in the country are the Arbitration Center of the Caracas Chamber (the "CACC") and the Business Center for Conciliation and Arbitration (the "CEDCA").

C.1 Arbitration Center of the Caracas Chamber ("CACC")

Background

The Arbitration Center was created on June 7, 1989, as an entity of the Caracas Chamber of Commerce. It was the first arbitration center in the country. This center and the CEDCA (which is discussed below) are the most important institutional arbitration centers in the country.

Types of Disputes Handled

The CACC handles domestic and international arbitration in all kinds of civil and commercial disputes, including banking, insurance, telecoms, etc.

471

Numbers of Disputes Handled

CACC has a caseload of more than 150 disputes.

Provisions on Confidentiality of Arbitration

Mediation and arbitration are confidential. Only the parties involved and their attorneys-in-fact have access to the file. If a competent authority requests the file, only a copy will be delivered.

Availability of Expedited Procedures

There is an expedited procedure for lower amount cases.

Consolidation of Disputes between the Same Parties and Joinder of Third Parties

According to the Rules of the CACC, the consolidation of disputes is possible before the execution of the Reference Terms Minutes. If there is a previous procedure being heard and a new procedure must be consolidated, the parties may request that the Executive Committee joins both procedures in one. For this purpose, both procedures must be handled pursuant to the Rules of the CACC, and both must be related to the same juridical relationship. There are no provisions which govern the joinder of third parties.

Time Limits for Rendering of the Award

The award should be rendered within 6 months from the date of the Reference Terms Minutes. In exceptional cases, the Arbitral Tribunal may request an extension before the Executive Direction of the CACC.

Fee Structure

The administrative costs of the arbitration, as well as the fees of the arbitrators, are determined on the basis of progressive cumulative percentages linked to the amount involved in the case. For this purpose, the amount is converted into Tax Units, which are updated from time to time by tax authorities in the country according to inflation.

Special or Unusual Features (If Any)

The CACC is the representative in Venezuela for entities such as the ICC and the Inter-American Commercial Arbitration Commission. The list of arbitrators is open—the parties may appoint arbitrators who do not belong to the list of the CACC. However, for the selection of the sole arbitrator or the third arbitrator in cases of disagreement by the parties or the arbitrators, the selection is made by the Executive Committee from the list of arbitrators of the CACC. It is usual for parties to provide in the arbitration clause that that the arbitrators must be selected from the list of arbitrators of the CACC.

Recent Developments (If Any)

The Rules of the CACC were updated in November 2012 and include rules for granting preliminary injunctions.

C.2 Business Center for Conciliation and Arbitration ("CEDCA")

Background

The CEDCA is an independent Arbitration Center, created in 1999. It was promoted in its creation by the Venezuelan American Chamber of Commerce and Industry.

Types of Disputes Handled

The CEDCA handles commercial disputes, in general derived from the breach of contractual obligations. From its foundation through to 2013, the types of cases handled by CEDCA included: Services 30%; Leasing 21%; Banking and Financial

Intermediation 21%; Other 10%; Works and Construction 10%; Capital Markets 4%; Oil and Gas 2%; Civil 1%; and Telecommunications 1%.

Numbers of Disputes Handled

The CADCA has a caseload of 110 disputes.

Provisions on Confidentiality of Arbitration

Except if there is an agreement to the contrary, or the applicable rules require otherwise, all matters relating to the arbitration and the award itself will be confidential. Any interested person may request a copy of the award, except if the parties have expressly agreed on its confidentiality.

Availability of Expedited Procedures

The Rules of the CEDCA provide for an expedited procedure for those disputes not exceeding VEF1 million and which do not contain more than one party as plaintiff or defendant. This procedure is much faster (approximate duration 40 days) and is also more cost-effective. It is tried and decided by a sole arbitrator chosen by the parties. In the CEDCA, 34% of cases have been tried through the expedited procedure.

Consolidation of Disputes between the Same Parties and Joinder of Third Parties

The Rules of the CEDCA do not contain provisions on these issues.

Time Limits for Rendering of the Award

In the CEDCA, arbitrators must complete the procedures in the least possible time. 70% of the arbitrations have a maximum duration of 12 months. The Arbitral Tribunal must issue the award within a term not exceeding 60 business days from the date of the approval of the Reference Terms Minutes, which is signed by the parties in the first hearing. This term might be extended by virtue of a supported petition of the Arbitral Tribunal or ex-officio if it is deemed necessary.

Fee Structure

The fees of the arbitrators as well as the administrative costs of the CEDCA are determined by taking into consideration the amount of the complaint and the number of arbitrators.

Treatment of Costs of the Arbitration

Each party is required to deposit half of the costs and fees in advance. If one party deposits its share and the other does not, the party which deposited its share may deposit the other party's share, or the proceedings will be suspended or terminated. The final award will establish the costs of the arbitration, which includes the administrative rate, fees of the arbitrators, and fees of the experts appointed by the parties, and will dictate the proportion in which such costs should be divided between the parties. If one of the parties has not deposited its advance for costs and fees, the Arbitral Tribunal is fully empowered to order that the reluctant party pay an indemnification in favor of the party which has paid such costs.

Special or Unusual Features (If Any)

The CEDCA emphasizes conciliation and has succeeded in resolving 35% of the disputes referred to it in the conciliation phase of the arbitration proceedings. Of these cases, 66% have been resolved within a term of one to three months.

The Rules of the CEDCA also provide for precautionary injunctions.

The mechanism for appointing arbitrators is based on the reduced list system. Each party has the right to remove 40% of the names appearing in the list, and those names that do not appear in the reduced list cannot then be selected.

Before its publication, the award must be submitted to the parties and the Executive Director for consideration, and they can make observations within five business days. After the expiration of that term, the final award will be published containing the clarifications that the arbitrators deem convenient.

Recent Developments (If Any)

The Rules of CEDCA were updated in 2013.

VIETNAM

Frederick Burke[1] and Tran Chi Anh[2]

A. LEGISLATION, TRENDS AND TENDENCIES

A.1 Legislation

In Vietnam, both domestic and international arbitration proceedings are governed by the Law on Commercial Arbitration ("LCA").[3] The recognition and enforcement of foreign arbitral awards remains subject to the relevant provisions of the Civil Procedure Code ("CPC").[4]

On March 20, 2014, the Supreme People's Court provided guidance for the implementation of several articles of the LCA in its Resolution No. 01/2014/NQ-HDTP (the "Resolution"). In particular, the Resolution specifies: (i) under what circumstances jurisdiction over a dispute lies with a court rather than an arbitration tribunal; (ii) when the terms of an arbitration agreement render it invalid or incapable of being performed under Vietnamese law; and (iii) under what circumstances a waiver of the right to challenge a breach of an arbitration agreement or Vietnamese arbitration laws will be enforceable. The Resolution clarifies that an arbitration agreement is

---

[1] Frederick Burke is Manager Partner in Baker & McKenzie (Vietnam) Ltd. He leads the Vietnam Dispute Resolution Practice and is an active arbitrator at the Vietnam International Arbitration Center.

[2] Tran Chi Anh is an Associate in Baker & McKenzie's Ho Chi Minh City office. Tran has advised and represented major clients in arbitration cases and arbitral award enforcement procedures in Vietnam.

[3] Law on Commercial Arbitration No. 54/2010/QH12 of the National Assembly adopted on 17 June 2010.

[4] Law on Civil Procedures No. 24/20004/QH11 of the National Assembly adopted on15 June 2004, as amended in 2011.

"incapable of being performed" if, among other reasons, it: (i) stipulates the use of arbitration rules from a different center than the one that will hear the arbitration; and (ii) the charter of the center hearing the arbitration does not permit using the arbitration rules of other arbitration centers; and (iii) the parties to the dispute do not agree to use the arbitration rules of the center hearing their dispute.[5] Under the Resolution, the Supreme People's Court seems to have given for the first time some limited guidance on what constitute fundamental principles of Vietnamese law. Specifically, the Resolution provides that an arbitral award is deemed contrary to fundamental principles of Vietnamese law where it breaches a fundamental principle of conduct that applies broadly to the drafting and implementing of Vietnamese law.[6] The Resolution also refers to certain principles contained in the Civil Code, the Commercial Law and the LCA, such as the principles of freedom of contract and arbitrator impartiality, as examples of fundamental principles of Vietnamese law.

A.2   Trends and Tendencies

Even though the number of disputes resolved by arbitration is increasing every year, it constitutes a small number in comparison to litigation. According to a recent report of the Ministry of Justice of Vietnam ("MOJ"), 432 disputes were resolved by arbitration from 2011 to 2013 (an average of 144 cases per year). In contrast, 14,767 commercial cases were resolved in first instance courts in 2013 alone. Thus, it appears that slightly less than 1% of commercial disputes were resolved by arbitration. Furthermore, according to the MOJ report, arbitration in Vietnam faces some limitations, including: the grounds for setting aside arbitral awards are too broad in

---

[5]   Resolution, Article 4.4.

[6]   Resolution, Article 14.2(dd).

comparison with law and practice in international arbitration; there is a lack of positive support from the courts; and restrictions on the qualifications of arbitrators.

As arbitral proceedings are normally confidential, the little that is known about such proceedings comes from the very few available decisions of Vietnamese courts on applications to set aside an arbitral award. The MOJ reported at a conference it organized in October 2013 that about 12% of awards of the Vietnam International Arbitration Centre ("VIAC") issued between 2003 and 2013 were challenged in the court by an application to set aside the award. About 34% of the domestic arbitral awards that were challenged in court were eventually set aside by Vietnamese courts. This was considered a high percentage, which has led to criticisms that the courts have been unreasonably strict in reviewing the procedural issues that may result in an award being set aside.

The Resolution is regarded as a significant development in arbitration law in Vietnam. The Resolution has clearly established the supportive role of the courts in arbitration proceedings and therefore confirmed a positive attitude of Vietnamese courts to dispute resolution through arbitration. Furthermore, with the specific clarification on grounds to set aside an arbitral award in the Resolution, it is hoped that the number of awards being set aside will significantly decrease.

B. CASES

B.1. VIAC's Arbitral Award Upheld against a State-Owned Shipping Company

Among the most significant court cases relating to arbitration in the last year was the case between Vietnam National Shipping Lines ("Vinalines") and a consortium consisting of SK E&C, a

South Korean company, and the Vietnam Waterway Construction Corporation ("Vinawaco"). Vinalines is Vietnam's largest shipping corporation and a national, wholly state-owned corporation.

In 2009, Vinalines and Vinawco signed a contract for the construction of a pier at Van Phong international transshipment port. After extended delays and serious breaches by Vinalines, Vinawco terminated the contract. In September 2012, the Government issued an official announcement suspending the project. A South Korean contractor, SK E&C, claimed heavy losses due to Vinalines' breach of the contract and filed a legal action. The case was then referred to VIAC.

In January 2014, the arbitral tribunal issued an award in which it ordered Vinalines to pay VND47.9 billion in compensation to SK E&C. On February 26, 2014, the arbitral tribunal corrected some figures in the arbitral award and issued a second decision ordering Vinalines to pay over VND65 billion in compensation, plus interest.

Vinalines made an application to the People's Court of Hanoi City to set aside the tribunal's arbitral award in accordance with the LCA. Vinalines raised some procedural issues and claimed that the arbitral award was contrary to the fundamental principles of Vietnamese law. In July 2014, Prime Minister Nguyen Tan Dung requested the Supreme People's Court to review the petition after Vinalines wrote to the Government requesting that the arbitral award be set aside.

Under Vietnamese law, the court should only set aside an arbitral award if there are serious procedural flaws during the arbitration proceedings or if the award is deemed contrary to fundamental principles of Vietnamese law. The People's Court of Hanoi City rejected Vinaline's arguments, finding that they did not provide any supporting evidence and that there was no basis for setting aside the award. The court concluded that the arbitral tribunal and the parties were in compliance with arbitration procedures provided in the LCA and Vietnamese law. Accordingly, Vinalines was ordered to comply with the tribunal's award and pay over VND 65 billion to SK E&C. The court decision took effect on October 3, 2014.

Vinalines is not the only Vietnamese enterprise that has requested the court to abrogate arbitral awards. Many similar cases have reportedly occurred in the past. As arbitral awards are not respected, businesses are hesitating to bring cases to Vietnamese arbitration tribunals.

C. LOCAL ARBITRATION INSTITUTIONS

There are seven arbitration centers operating in Vietnam as of December 2014. The most well-known is ("VCCI"), a nongovernmental arbitration center established by the Vietnam Chamber of Commerce and Industry.

C.1 Vietnam International Arbitration Center

Background

On April 28, 1993, the Prime Minister issued Decision No. 204/TTg, creating VIAC by merging the Foreign Trade Arbitration Committee and the Maritime Arbitration Committee, founded in 1963 and 1964 respectively, which had been under the management of the Ministries of Foreign Trade and Transportation rather than the VCCI.

Types of Disputes Handled

VIAC has jurisdiction to resolve disputes arising out of commercial activities and other activities as provided by law.

According to statistics published by VIAC, 70% of disputes resolved in VIAC arise from sales contracts, 5% from outsourcing, 3% from services, 5% from construction, 1% from distribution or agency agreements, 4% from investments or business corporation agreements, 3% from banking and finance, and 9% from other fields.[7]

Numbers of Disputes Handled

Currently, arbitration is not widely understood, or used, by commercial entities in Vietnam. In general, the number of arbitrations handled by VIAC and other arbitration centers in Vietnam remains low when compared to the number of disputes handled by Vietnamese courts. However, in recent years the number of arbitrations heard in Vietnam has grown quickly; particularly those heard by VIAC, from fewer than 10 in 1993 to approximately 100 in 2013:[8]

Provisions on Confidentiality of Arbitration

VIAC's Arbitration Rules (the "VIAC Rules") do not specifically address the issue of arbitration confidentiality. However, under the LCA, arbitrators "must keep confidential the content of disputes that they handle, unless they have to provide such information to the competent state agencies as required law."[9]

Availability of Expedited Procedures

The VIAC Rules do not provide for expedited procedures.

---

[7] *See* http://eng.viac.vn/statistical/types-of-disputes-a277.html.

[8] *See* http://eng.viac.vn/statistical/numbers-of-disputes-in-viac-over-17-year-period-from-1993-to-2013-a274.html.

[9] The LCA, Article 21.5.

C. Local Arbitration Institutions

Consolidation of Disputes between the Same Parties and Joinder of Third Parties

The VIAC Rules do not specifically address the issues of the consolidation of disputes or the joinder of third parties. However, the Resolution provides a legal basis for the consolidation of disputes in arbitration by establishing the general principle that arbitral tribunals may consolidate multiple disputed "legal relations" (cases) into one single case. Specifically, the Resolution provides that tribunals may consolidate such disputes if (i) the parties so agree; or (ii) the arbitration rules so allow.[10]

Time Limits for Rendering of the Award

Neither the LCA or the VIAC Rules set a time limit for the rendering of an arbitral award. While, in practice, the time required will largely depend on the complexity of the dispute in question, it generally takes six months to a year for an arbitral award to be rendered after the VIAC has accepted the matter.

Fee Structure

The VIAC Rules set the fees for disputes heard by panels of three arbitrators, based on the amount in controversy, ranging from VND15 million for disputed amounts up to VND100 million to VND3,063 million plus 0.1% of the amount in dispute over VND500 billion.[11] For disputes resolved by a sole arbitrator, the applicable arbitration fees will be 70% of the fees for disputes heard by a panel.

Where a request for arbitration or counterclaim does not specify the amount in dispute, the President of the VIAC is entitled to fix the arbitration fees by taking into consideration the nature of the

---

[10] The LCA, Article 7.4.

[11] *See* http://eng.viac.vn/bieu-phi.

dispute, the time that may be required to resolve it, and the number of arbitrators hearing the case.

Treatment of Costs of the Arbitration

Under the VIAC Rules, the arbitral tribunal hearing a case is entitled to allocate arbitration costs to either or both parties at its sole discretion, unless otherwise agreed by the parties.[12]

Special or Unusual Features (If Any)

There are no special or unusual features to report.

Recent Developments (If Any)

There are no recent developments to report.

---

[12]   VIAC Arbitration Rules, Article 34.2